FOURTEENTH EDITION

THE COMPLETE SERIES 6 STUDY BOOK

Dennis M. Doyle, CLU, CFP, CPCU, ChFC

EDUCATIONAL TRAINING SYSTEMS, INC.

ABOUT THE AUTHOR

DENNIS M. DOYLE, CLU, CFP, CPCU, ChFC, has been President of Educational Training Systems, Inc. of Southborough, Massachusetts, since it was founded in 1969. He is a graduate of the University of Maine and has studied and contributed to numerous university and industry programs. Mr. Doyle has spoken before industry groups in 46 states, in Europe and Canada. His company is a research and teaching organization for the insurance, securities, and financial services industries.

Educational Training Systems, Inc.
"the university in the sky"
116 Middle Road
P.O. Box 410
Southborough, MA 01772-0410

CONTENTS

LIST OF TERMS DEFINED

INTRODUCTION

This self-study text is intended to prepare you for the *NASD Series 6 Registration Exam*. Assuming conscientious study, it is all that you should need to prepare yourself for the exam. The self-study approach used in this book may differ from the training you have had in the past. It has been designed specifically to allow you to learn at your own pace —— to learn the material *you* need to learn and to ensure mastery learning. You will *participate* in the instruction by *reading, studying, writing answers* in the book, and by following these steps:

1. Take the chapter *pretest* to identify the material in each chapter you need to learn so that you won't spend time studying material you already know.
2. Read the *tutorial* information presented on the concepts with which you are unfamiliar.
3. Answer the *quick quiz questions* to check your understanding of newly acquired concepts. Be sure to write the answer to each question *before* checking your answer.
4. Apply your understanding of chapter material by completing the *real life situation*.
5. Recheck your familiarity with chapter concepts by completing the *check your understanding* section.
6. Review your final preparation for the exam by completing *sample NASD exams* at the end of the book. Do not review your answers in the *rationale* before completing the exam.

This may sound like a larger commitment than you had in mind but, remember, it is an *individualized, self-study text* so you are the one who decides how much effort you will have to put forth to ensure passing the exam. In order to be fully prepared for the exam, we recommend that you plan to spend two to two-and-one-half hours per chapter. This material is concentrated and will require careful study. You must master *all* the terms and concepts so that you will be assured of passing the examination.

To summarize, read the material presented on concepts with which you are unfamiliar, digest it, answer the questions, and turn the page to check your answers. Then proceed to review. Apply the chapter information by completing the "real life situation." Review by taking the "check your understanding" test and/or retaking the pretest.

Keep in mind that this program of study is *not* a test. It is a method designed to teach you what you need to know to pass the *NASD Series 6 Registration Exam.*

As the financial services industry changes the examinations which are used to qualify individuals for registration must change. New products and new regulations have resulted in modifications to the NASD Investment Company/Variable Contracts Products Limited Representative's Examination. The current *weighing percentage* of questions is as follows:

Section		Number of Questions
1.0	Securities and Markets; Investment Risks and Policies	23
2.0	Investment Companies, Taxation and Customer Accounts	36
3.0	Variable Contracts and Retirement Plans	16
4.0	Securities Industry Regulations	25
		100

The Series 6 examination is a two and one-quarter hour test consisting of 100 questions of which you must answer 70% correct to receive a passing grade. Scratch paper and calculators will be provided at the test center.

ACKNOWLEDGMENTS

The author is appreciative of the assistance of many in the preparation of this updated edition of *The Complete Series 6 Study Book*.

For this book to be useful to the practioner as well as being a preparatory book for an examination, Dr. Benjamin Branch, Business Professor at the University of Massachusetts, and other industry professionals provided reviews of chapters within their areas of expertise.

Special thanks to Bruce Avedon, Neal Duggan, Carl Kaliszewski and Timothy McMaster, all highly regarded industry experts.

Notwithstanding the helpful contributions of the above individuals and others, the author alone assumes responsibility for the accuracy of the contents herein.

Dennis M. Doyle, *CLU, CFP, CPCU, ChFC*

*The Value of Education: "The educated differ from the
uneducated as much as the living from the dead."*
Aristotle

1

INVESTMENT
SECURITIES

PRETEST
(Circle one)

1. The main categories of investment securities are: Reference:
    a.   Corporate securities   Page 1-5
    b.   U.S. government securities
    c.   State and municipal bonds
    d.   Money market instruments
    e.   All of the above

2. All corporations must issue: Reference:
    a.   Preferred stock   Page 1-7
    b.   Common stock
    c.   Bond debt
    d.   Participating preferred stock
    e.   All of the above

3. A key advantage of preferred stock is that it: Reference:
    a.   Comes before common stock in the event of corporation   Page 1-8
         liquidation
    b.   Usually preferred dividends must be paid before common
         dividends
    c.   Can carry with it a call provision
    d.   Stipulates a specific dividend to be paid annually
    e.   All of the above

4.   Which of the following could a typical money market fund hold as   Reference:
       investments?   Page 1-17
       I.   Bankers acceptances
       II.   U.S. Treasury bills
       III.   Blue chip common stock
       IV.   Certificates of deposit
              a.   I and II only
              b.   II and III only
              c.   I, II, and IV only
              d.   III only
              e.   All of the above

5.   _____ bonds have a corporate building or other form of security   Reference:
       pledged as collateral for the debt.   Page 1-9
              a.   Mortgage
              b.   Unsecured
              c.   Debenture
              d.   Secured
              e.   None of the above

6.   The most common form of bond is a: Reference:
              a.   Debenture bond   Page 1-10
              b.   Mortgage bond
              c.   Refunding bond
              d.   Convertible bond
              e.   None of the above

7.   Direct short-term promissory notes of this country's biggest   Reference:
       corporations with good credit ratings would most likely be in   Page 1-18
       the form of:
              a.   Wire transfers
              b.   Commercial paper
              c.   Bankers acceptances
              d.   Money market shares
              e.   Tax anticipation notes

8.   Purchasing existing bonds and issuing new bonds at a lower rate is   Reference:
       an example of: Page 1-10
              a.   Amortization
              b.   Conversion feature
              c.   Redemption bonds
              d.   Collateral trust bonds
              e.   Refunding (possibly using the call provision)

9. Stock rights are issued to:
    a. Preferred stockholders
    b. Convertible preferred stockholders
    c. Common stockholders
    d. Warrant holders
    e. Put and call holders

    Reference:
    Page 1-12

10. The capital structure of a corporation could consist of:
    I.   Common stock
    II.   Preferred stock
    III. Bonds
    IV.   Puts and calls
        a. I only
        b. I and II only
        c. I, II, and III only
        d. I and III only
        e. All of the above

    Reference:
    Page 1-7

11. The two major differences between stock rights and stock warrants
    are warrants are not _____ and they are for a _____
    period of time.
    a. Preemptive/shorter
    b. Preemptive/longer
    c. Nonmarketable/shorter
    d. Nonmarketable/longer
    e. None of the above

    Reference:
    Page 1-12

12. Leverage in a corporate capital structure would generally mean
    the presence of:
    a. Equity
    b. Debt
    c. Engagement in a speculative business
    d. Restricted securities
    e. Nonmarketable issues

    Reference:
    Page 1-10

13. Preferred stock can be:
    I.   Convertible preferred
    II.   Cumulative preferred
    III. Participating preferred
    IV.   Straight preferred
        a. I and II only
        b. IV only
        c. I and IV only
        d. II and IV only
        e. All of the above

    Reference:
    Page 1-8

14. Federal income taxes on interest accruing to Series EE bonds are taxed to a taxpayer under which of these methods?

Reference:
Page 1-14

    I. Current method
    II. Deferred method
    III. Series EE bonds do not accrue interest
    IV. Federal obligations are tax exempt

        a. I only
        b. III only
        c. IV only
        d. I and II only
        e. III and IV only

15. Treasury bills are sold on a(n) _____ basis and _____ carry a specified rate of interest.

Reference:
Page 1-15

    a. Auction/do
    b. Negotiated/do not
    c. Discount/do
    d. Discount/do not
    e. None of the above

16. Treasury bills generally mature from _____ to _____.

Reference:
Page 1-15

    a. Ninety-one days to fifty-two weeks
    b. One year to two years
    c. One year to five years
    d. Five years to twenty years
    e. All of the above

17. Municipal bonds may be categorized as:

Reference:
Page 1-16

    I. General obligation bonds
    II. Limited obligation bonds
    III. Mortgage bonds
    IV. Industrial revenue bonds

        a. I only
        b. II only
        c. I and III only
        d. II and III only
        e. I, II and IV only

18. All of the following are considered inherent rights of common stockholders *except*:

Reference:
Page 1-7

    a. Rights to dividends when declared by the Board of Directors
    b. Preemptive rights
    c. Right to vote for officers of the corporation
    d. Rights to purchase more shares of common stock before they are offered to anyone else
    e. Right to elect the Board of Directors

19.   The extinguishing of a debt over the period of indebtedness would   Reference:
      be referred to as: Page 1-10
         a.   Refunding
         b.   Conversion
         c.   Depreciation
         d.   Amortization
         e.   Redemption

20.   What would be the value of a right prior to the ex-rights date when   Reference:
      the market price of the stock is $44, the subscription price for each Page 1-12
      share is $30 and it takes twenty (20) rights to buy one new share?
         a.   67 cents
         b.   70 cents
         c. $1.40
         d. $14.00
         e.   None of the above

ANSWERS: 1-e; 2-b; 3-d; 4-c; 5-d; 6-a; 7-b; 8-e; 9-c; 10-c; 11-b; 12-b; 13-e; 14-d; 15-d;
16-a; 17-e; 18-c; 19-d; 20-a

OVERVIEW

Investment securities for study in chapter 1 include four major categories: *corporate securities, U.S. government securities, state and municipals bonds,* and *money market instruments*. Please note that the term *securities* is used here to represent a broad category of investment *assets* – each of which is represented by an evidence of ownership, such as a stock certificate.

It is essential to understand the differences among these four types of investment securities. The most important difference to consider is whether or not any *guarantee* is present to the investor and, if so, who is doing the guaranteeing. That is, is the security guaranteed by the federal government or a corporation or other form of business – or is no guarantee at all provided (e.g., as with common stock)? Even U.S. government agency bonds carry a certain risk that the specific government agency responsible will be unable to pay them off.

Let's begin our study with the largest single segment of securities as far as total dollar volume is concerned – corporate securities.

Author's Note to Candidates

Chapter 1 forms the foundation for all learning in later chapters. The general concepts involved here must be understood by each Series 6 examination candidate. Even if you are familiar with much of this material, please do not take it too lightly – for any gaps in your knowledge will work to your disadvantage later in the book.

I. CORPORATE SECURITIES

Corporate securities come in two flavors: *debt* and *equity*.

EQUITY   DEBT

In the following pages we will discuss the major characteristics of each form of corporate securities: that is, the characteristics of debt securities and the characteristics of equity securities.

The Corporation as a Form of Business

There are generally considered to be three forms of business organizations in the United States: *sole proprietorships, partnerships,* and *corporations.*

SOLE PROPRIETOR   PARTNERSHIP   CORPORATIONS

The *corporate form* of business partnerships is the most important for study here since it is the form used by most major businesses in the United States (and indeed, even most medium-sized businesses). The primary reason for the popularity of this form of organization is the wealth of built-in advantages it gives to the owners of the business – both personally and as a forum in which to conduct their business activities. This chapter will begin to make clear the rationale for incorporating a business.

Capitalization All businesses that wish to incorporate under state law must issue, or start with, *equity capital*. Although equity capital is considered to be both *preferred* and *common stock*, all corporations *must issue* common stock. A corporation which issues a greater percentage of preferred stock and bonds in relation to its common stock is considered to be speculatively leveraged due to the increased liability to preferred stock and bondholders.

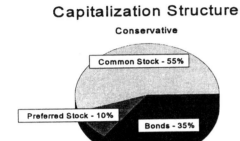

Capitalization Structure

Conservative

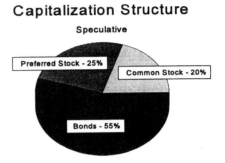

Capitalization Structure

Speculative

Common stock is the pure ownership interest in a business contributed at its inception and, possibly, throughout its lifetime. Many businesses will need to borrow money in addition to their equity capital to provide the larger base of funds needed in the business. This borrowed money is referred to as *debt* and most commonly takes the form of *bond debt*.

Equity Securities

Corporations raise money by the initial and subsequent sales of common stock to investors to generate equity capital. Once an investor "buys into" a business, certain rights accrue to this investor. Rights of common stockholders are:

- Right to dividends when declared by the Board of Directors.
- Preemptive rights to purchase additional stock before it is sold to anyone else (where granted by corporation).
- Voting rights to elect the Board of Directors that oversees the operation of the company.
- The right to transfer ownership.

Preferred stock can also be issued by a corporation. It usually stipulates a specific dividend to be paid annually. This assurance of a specified annual dividend is considered to be the major advantage of preferred stock. Another valuable feature is the fact that dividends to preferred stockholders must be paid before dividends to common stockholders. Thus, the fixed dividend payment plus possible appreciation are the two main attractions of preferred stock.

Preferred stock may carry with it unusual provisions. An example of one such provision that protects the corporation is the *call provision*, which allows the corporation – at stipulated times and in stipulated dollar amounts – to "call in" the preferred stock and retire it. Once this happens to a preferred stockholder, he or she has no choice but to return the stock to the corporation for the amount stipulated in advance in the preferred stock agreement.

In essence, this limits the appreciation potential of the preferred stock. Various types of preferred stock include:

- *Straight Preferred* – no unusual provisions other than the stipulated dividend.

- *Cumulative Preferred* – an important feature to the investor because if a preferred dividend is not paid during a year, it will *accumulate*; and all accumulated dividends must be paid in later years prior to common stockholders receiving their dividends.

- *Participating Preferred* – an unusual feature that is not very common in the United States, whereby preferred shareholders will participate in dividends paid to common stockholders if the corporation earnings exceed a certain level.

- *Convertible Preferred* – one of the most popular types of preferreds because it allows the shareholder to "swap," at a later time, his or her preferred stock for common stock in the corporation. If the company does well and its common stock is rising, convertible preferred will become more valuable because it can be converted to common (in a predetermined amount). Thus, convertible preferred has some upside (conversion) and some downside (dividend payments) protection to the shareholder.

Author's Note to Candidates

For your benefit, quick quizzes are included within each chapter to check your comprehension of the material. The correct answers are conveniently located after the last question. References are located at the end of each question.

QUICK QUIZ 1

1. The main categories of investment securities are:
   a. Corporate securities
   b. U.S. government securities
   c. State and municipal bonds
   d. Money market instruments
   e. All of the above

   Reference: Page 1-5

2. All corporations must issue:
   a. Preferred stock
   b. Common stock
   c. Bond debt
   d. Participating preferred stock
   e. All of the above

   Reference: Page 1-7

3. A key advantage of preferred stock is:
   a. It is honored before common stock in the event of corporate liquidation
   b. Usually preferred dividends must be paid before common dividends
   c. Preferred stock can carry with it a call provision
   d. Stipulates a specific dividend to be paid annually
   e. All of the above

   Reference: Page 1-8

ANSWERS: 1-e; 2-b; 3-d.

Debt Obligations   *Secured bonds* are those bonds that have property or other security as collateral put up to guarantee the bonds in the event of nonpayment. That is, in the event the bonds go into default because interest payments are not made, the corporation may be forced to forfeit certain properties. In general, secured bonds come in the form of *mortgage bonds, collateral trust bonds,* or *equipment trust certificates*. As each name implies, a lien is held by the bondholders or trustee representing the bondholders on property that will be taken in the event interest payments are not made. Thus, mortgage bonds represent a direct lien on buildings; for collateral trust bonds, other forms of collateral have been put up (usually securities of other companies); and equipment trust certificates have equipment or machinery as collateral backing up the bond.

Unsecured bonds are the most common form of bonds and are also referred to as *debentures*. Debentures generally have *no* specific property pledged as collateral. In short, debentures carry just the *general promise* of the corporation to pay its interest on time and pay the principal at maturity. Usually only very stable corporations with a high credit rating are able to issue debenture bonds. Zero coupon bonds, which pay all their interest at maturity, are now popular. Even though the interest is actually not paid until maturity (all at once), the "imputed interest" is taxed annually to the investor. Zero-coupon bonds are issued by corporations, municipalities and the U.S. Treasury (e.g., Separate Trading of Registered Interest and Principal of Securities — STRIPS), and they may be created by Broker/Dealers from other types of securities, including those issued by the federal government.

When pricing a zero-coupon at issuance, the issuer and the underwriter take into account several factors. They consider the interest rates being paid by regular debt obligations of similar safety and maturities, the premium investors might want in return for giving up a regular income stream, and the time value of money.

The more long-term debt (funded debt) a corporation has as a part of its capital structure, the more "leveraged" it becomes — and the more speculative a common stock investment in this company becomes.

Bonds, whether secured or unsecured, have certain features in common. One such feature is *redemption or maturity date*, which assures the investor that the initial par value of the bond (e.g., $1,000) will be paid back at the end of a specific time period (commonly, twenty years). In essence, the investor is only lending his or her money to the corporation for a specified length of time and collecting interest (generally, twice a year) throughout this period of time.

Most bonds include a *call feature* whereby the corporation may "call in" these bonds early (before maturity date) at a stipulated price. This feature can work to the advantage of the corporation and to the disadvantage of the investor. Refunding of bonds is a frequent financial maneuver employed by corporations when interest rate changes have taken place. This approach is used when a corporation has a high interest bearing bond outstanding and wishes to call in the bond – or purchase it in the open market – to retire (extinguish) it. If the company is still in need of

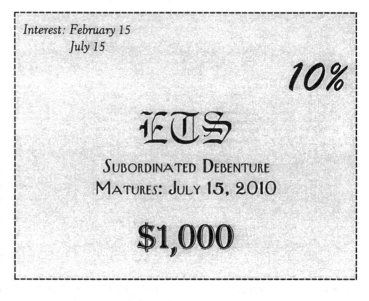

Interest: February 15
July 15

10%

𝕰𝕿𝕾

SUBORDINATED DEBENTURE
MATURES: JULY 15, 2010

$1,000

capital, it then "floats" (sells) a new bond issue at a lower current rate, thus reducing its overall cost of interest payments because the current rates are lower than the earlier rates. Since the majority of corporate bonds *do* carry a call feature now (corporations protecting themselves), there is frequently a limited period of time (e.g., five years) of *call protection* during which the corporation can not call in a bond.

Amortization of bonds refers to the fact that the principal amount of the indebtedness will be amortized, or written off, equally over the period of indebtedness.   (This is like amortizing a twenty-five-year mortgage on your house equally over the next twenty-five years.) Frequently corporations will set up a *sinking fund* to put aside funds *annually* so that, at the maturity date, the full amount for redemption will be available. Often this is a legal requirement of the bond indenture (agreement).

Conversion features are present on many bonds, just as they are on preferred stock. The format is the same; that is the investor may convert his or her bond into a stipulated number of common stock shares. If the common stock price rises to a high enough level, it is favorable to the investor to convert. Conversion is also a way for a corporation to get rid of some of its debt and transfer it to equity ownership in the corporation.

QUICK QUIZ 2

4.   _____ bonds have a corporate building or other forms of security pledged as collateral for the debt.

Reference: Page 1-9

   a.   Mortgage
   b.   Unsecured
   c.   Debenture
   d.   Secured
   e.   None of the above

5.   The most common form of corporate bond is a:

Reference: Page 1-10

   a.   Debenture bond
   b.   Mortgage bond
   c.   Refunding bond
   d.   Convertible bond
   e.   None of the above

6.   Purchasing in the open market or calling in existing bonds and issuing new bonds at a lower rate is an example of:

Reference: Page 1-10

   a.   Amortization
   b.   Conversion feature
   c.   Redemption bonds
   d.   Collateral trust bonds
   e.   Refunding (possibly using the call provision)

7.   The call feature protects the *corporation/investor* (circle correct answer).

Reference: Page 1-10

ANSWERS: 4-d; 5-a; 6-e; 7-corporation.

Special Securities

Stock rights are frequently issued to *existing* common stockholders of corporations allowing them to buy more common stock directly from the company at special prices. For instance, for every ten shares owned, an investor might be able to buy one more share if the corporation issues stock rights. Usually, the price at which the securities can be purchased is *below* the current market price so as to offer the investor an inducement (bargain) to buy. If the investor does not wish to exercise these rights, he or she may sell them to someone who does want to purchase the stock. A general formula is used for computing the *value of a right* should the investor want to sell them separately, although the actual price might differ from the calculated price because of commissions and such. This formula is for a right's value prior to the ex-date:

$$\frac{\text{Market price (M) - Subscription price (S)}}{\text{Number of rights needed (N)} + 1} = \text{Value of right}^{*}$$

Warrants are similar to rights, but they are not issued exclusively to existing shareholders. A company may sell warrants individually to raise money or attach them to preferred stock or bonds to sweeten these issues and thereby induce investors to buy them. Warrants allow for the purchase of shares at a predetermined price (just like rights) directly from the company itself. The *differences* between rights and warrants are:

- Warrants are not preemptive.
- Warrants are usually for a longer length of time and can be perpetual.
- The subscription price is higher than the market price of the underlying stock when the warrants are issued.

Options to buy common stock in corporations can take the form of *puts* and *calls*. A put option gives the holder the right to *sell* stock (usually one hundred shares) in a corporation at a predetermined price for a specified period of time. A call is the right to *buy* a stock at a predetermined price. The investor pays for the privilege of owning these options. For example, an investor purchases an option to buy one hundred shares of stock anytime within the next ninety days for $50 a share. To purchase this call option, he or she pays, say, $200, which will not be refunded. The $200 is the cost to purchase the option sometimes called the "premium." If the investor is right and the stock goes up within the ninety-day period in excess of $50, he or she can exercise the option to buy at $50. At this point, the investor can hold the stock or immediately sell it at a profit (over $50 per share). If, however, the investor chooses not to exercise the call option within ninety days, it is lost forever.

A put option is the opposite of a call option. A put option is the right to *sell* a stock at a predetermined price. An investor would choose to exercise this right if the current market price of a stock should fall below his or her option price. In essence, this option forces the person who sold the

---

*

The +1 is used in the formula when the calculation is before the ex-rights date – this is most often the case.
Note: *Cum-rights* means "with" rights and *ex-rights* means "without".

stock to pay the buyer more than it is currently worth. A *straddle* is a put option and a call option on the same stock. Performance is guaranteed by the Options Clearing Corporation (OCC).

Options are now written to cover bonds, interest rates, stocks, foreign currencies, indexes and almost anything else! Debt options are known as interest rate options and allow investors to purchase or sell U.S. Treasury bills, Treasury notes and Treasury bonds. An individual is given the opportunity to anticipate changes in foreign currency values (i.e., British Pounds, Japanese Yen, French Francs, etc.), through the purchase or sale of foreign currency options.

Lastly, an investor who predicts a change in overall market values or specific industry performance can attempt to take advantage of the potential change by taking a position with index options. Broad-based, e.g., Standard & Poor's, and industry-based, e.g., Computer, options are currently available.

Mortgage-backed securities have also become popular investments. These offer an individual interest in a pool of securities, generally government-backed securities, i.e., Government National Mortgage Association, Collateralized Mortgage Obligations, etc. They are very secure investments offering to repay interest and principal monthly. Interest rate changes can result in the refinancing of the underlying mortgage, in effect reducing the life of the CMO.

American Depository Receipts are issued through American banks to represent ownership in foreign companies whose securities have not been approved for trade domestically. All rights, except pre-emptive rights, are normally offered on ADRs. Each ADR represents ownership of a specific number of the foreign corporations stock, e.g. 10 shares. The ADR's price is sensitive to changes in currency exchange rates since it is traded in U.S. dollars. American Depository Shares (ADSs) now represent ownership directly (shares) in foreign corporations.

Restricted securities are common shares in a corporation that are not readily saleable by the owner. They are sometimes referred to as *nonmarketable securities* for this reason. The major reason common stock would be restricted or nonmarketable is that a public offering of the securities has never been made; that is, there has been no prospectus filed and no Securities Exchange Commission (SEC) review. There are specific SEC provisions whereby a corporation may issue a *limited* amount of securities before it must file a prospectus and follow the rules regarding public offerings. Such securities are referred to as restricted securities and usually carry a stamp or a "legend" right on the face of stock certificates stating that they cannot be resold except under certain exceptional circumstances.

QUICK QUIZ 3

8. Stock rights are issued to: Reference:
    a. Preferred stockholders   Page 1-12
    b. Convertible preferred stockholders
    c. Common stockholders
    d. Warrant holders
    e. Put and call holders

9. The basic formula for computing the value of a right prior to the   Reference:
    ex-date is: Page 1-12

10.   The two major differences between stock rights and stock warrants   Reference:
        are warrants are not _____ and they are for a _____ period   Page 1-12
        of time.
        a.   Preemptive/shorter
        b.   Preemptive/longer
        c.   Nonmarketable/shorter
        d.   Nonmarketable/longer
        e.   None of the above

11.   A put is an option to *sell/buy* one hundred shares of stock, and a   Reference:
        call is an option to *sell/buy* one hundred shares of stock (circle   Page 1-12
        correct answer).

                                                          m-s
                                Answers: 8-c; 9-n + 1; 10-b; 11-Sell/buy.

II. U.S. GOVERNMENT SECURITIES

Nonmarketable Issues

Nonmarketable issues is a term applied to certain securities that are *nontransferable*. The investor wishing to dispose of such securities must sell them back to the U.S. government and no one else. The two major forms of nonmarketable issues are Series EE and Series HH savings bonds. With Series EE type bonds, the investor pays $25 for a bond that matures for $50 approximately 12 years from time of purchase and can continue to earn interest for 30 years. In the early years, only small amounts of interest accrue; the bulk of the interest accrues in later years. Series EE bonds can be redeemed before maturity, but will receive a lower rate of return (giving the bondholder an incentive to hold bonds until maturity). The interest rate is determined every six months at 85% of the average rate for five-year marketable Treasury securities, thus it is "interest sensitive." Interest on Series EE bonds, incidently, can be reported annually by the taxpayer (accrued basis) or *deferred* until maturity for federal income tax purposes. Series HH bonds pay actual income and the government sends investors holding this type of bond a predetermined check twice a year.

With either type, if an investor wishes to cash in the bonds, he or she must sell them back to the U.S. government or its agent (e.g., bank) because they are nontransferable and nonmarketable. This fact also means that the bond holder *cannot* use Series EE or Series HH bonds as collateral for a loan at his or her local bank.

Marketable Issues

Treasury bills are the most frequently offered U.S. government marketable issue. An auction takes place, say, on Monday morning, run by the U.S. Department of Treasury, in certain selected cities around the country. All Treasury bills are auctioned off at the highest bids.

Treasury bills are bought on a discount basis; for example, a purchaser paying ninety-seven cents on the dollar at maturity gets one dollar back. Since the transactions take place in an auction market with many large financial institutions present and bidding, it is possible that each bidder will purchase Treasury bill blocks for a different amount of money. The bills are thus considered non-interest bearing (bought at a discount). Treasury bills have the shortest duration period of all U.S. government issues and usually mature between ninety-one days to one year (fifty-two weeks).

Treasury certificates are of the next shortest duration but will carry a stipulated rate of interest; that is, the buyer pays one hundred cents on the dollar and will get back more than one dollar at maturity. Certificates are generally one year to two years in duration.

Treasury notes carry a stipulated rate of interest and generally mature in one to ten years from the date of issue.

Treasury bonds are the longest term obligation offered by the U.S. government (thirty years) and also carry a specified rate of interest. This is known, when you hear daily financial reports of interest rates, as the "long bond."

Agency bonds are issues of selected agencies of the government that carry either a quasi-obligation or direct obligation of the U.S. government to see that they are paid. Examples of these agency bonds include obligations issued by the Federal Housing Administration, the Veterans Administration, the Tennessee Valley Authority, and such. Certificates of quasi-federal agencies such as Fannie Mae's are government guaranteed pass-through certificates, i.e., mortgage payments are passed through to institutional investors in FNMA certificates. Fannie Mae puts together pools of mortgage payments made by homeowners and passes these through to institutional investors.

QUICK QUIZ 4

12. Series EE and Series HH bonds are nontransferable and *can/cannot* be used as collateral for a loan (circle correct answer).

Reference: Page 1-14

13. Interest on Series EE bonds is taxed to a taxpayer under which of these methods?
   I.   Annual method
   II.   Deferred method
   III. Series EE bonds do not accrue interest
   IV.   Federal obligations are tax exempt
      a.   I only
      b.   III only
      c.   I and II only
      d.   II and III only
      e.   III and IV only

Reference: Page 1-14

14. Treasury bills are sold on a(n) _____ basis and _____ carry a specified rate of interest.
      a.   Auction/do
      b.   Negotiated/do not
      c.   Discount/do
      d.   Discount/do not
      e.   None of the above

Reference: Page 1-14

15. Treasury bills generally run from _____ to _____
      a.   Ninety-one days/fifty-two weeks
      b.   One year/two years
      c.   One year/five years
      d.   Five years/twenty years
      e.   Any of the above

Reference: Page 1-14

ANSWERS: 12-cannot; 13-c; 14-d; 15-a.

III. STATE AND MUNICIPAL BONDS

States and municipalities issue bonds (debt) to raise money for construction of needed highway systems, bridges, hospitals, and other projects – as well as to raise the general revenue needed by the state or municipality to survive. Municipal bonds are categorized as *general obligation bonds, revenue bonds,* and *industrial revenue bonds*.

With *general obligation bonds,* the full faith and credit (i.e., taxing power of the state or municipality) is placed behind the bond and therefore the bond is fully guaranteed. If the state or municipality does not have enough money to pay the interest on these bonds – and the principal when due – it must raise taxes to do so. General obligations bonds are the most secure type for an investor.

Revenue bonds are used to build projects that will generate revenue (i.e., a toll bridge or turnpike). The state or municipality collects revenues to pay back these bonds. Revenue bonds are called *limited obligation bonds.* It *must be understood* that if the revenue generated is *not* enough to pay the bond interest and principal when due, the state or municipality *does not* back these up. (Anyone not believing this should talk with those individuals who held Washington Public Power System Bonds some years ago!)

Industrial revenue bonds are a creative way to raise money by states and municipalities to attract industries. Generally, industrial parks and other project development costs are financed through these bonds. Unless otherwise stipulated, these bonds are just like revenue bonds and the revenue generated from the project must be enough to pay the bond interest or investors do not get paid.

The *tax status* of state and municipal bonds is important to understand. The *interest* paid on state and municipal bonds is generally exempt from federal income taxes. State and municipal bonds are generally subject to state income taxes, with one exception – if the investor resides in the state that has issued the bonds, they will be exempt from both state income tax and federal income tax. (For this reason, many state bonds are sold to residents of the state of issue.) For example, if a resident of Illinois purchases municipal bonds of the state of Illinois, the bonds are exempt from both Illinois state income taxes and federal income taxes. Please note that if the municipal bond is sold by the investor for a profit – a capital gain – this gain is *subject* to taxes just as any other investment. It is only the interest that is federal income-tax free.

A special tax status situation exists for U.S. Territorial government bonds, which are tax-free in all states. Puerto Rican bonds, for example, are also free of federal income taxes regardless of investor's resident state. These are known as triple exempt.

You should note that to maintain their tax exempt status municipal bonds must be public purpose bonds. If private purpose, the interest will be federally taxable.

QUICK QUIZ 5

16.   The state generally *does/does not* back up the obligations of a   Reference:
       revenue bond (circle correct answer).   Page 1-16

17. Municipal bonds may be categorized as _____.
    I.   General obligation bonds
    II. Limited obligation bonds
    III. Mortgage bonds
    IV. Industrial revenue bonds
        a.   I only
        b.   II only
        c.   I and III only
        d.   II and III only
        e.   I, II, and IV only

Reference:
Page 1-16

18. An investor sells a municipal bond for more than he or she paid
    for it three years from the date of purchase. This transaction
    will/will not have a *capital-gains* tax exposure (circle correct
    answer).

Reference:
Page 1-16

ANSWERS: 16-does not; 17-e; 18-will.

IV. MONEY MARKET INSTRUMENTS

In a *money market fund* investors purchase stock (shares) that represent short-term debt obligations of corporations and governmental units through a "pooled" fund to achieve a short-term return on their investment. The obligations held by the fund can range anywhere from thirty days to thirteen months to be considered money market investments. A slight variation of the money market fund approach is unit investment trusts, which purchase similar securities but package them as units ($1,000 units) for resale with only a minimum of administrative costs. Generally speaking, the *money market* is a short-term obligation (less than one year) and the *capital market* is a long-term obligation like stocks and bonds (more than one year).

Bankers acceptances are a form of finance usually used by large corporations with their banks. Bankers acceptances are used extensively in foreign trade to assist with credit guarantees. They work this way: a bank guarantees payment on behalf of the company with which it does business. However, the money is not due for a certain period of time (i.e., thirty days, forty-five days, sixty days). If the holder wants its money prior to this date, it can sell the bankers acceptances in the open market at a discount to private or institutional investors (like money market funds). What makes this type of investment secure is that the bank guarantees payment.

A Note on Money Market Investments

Increasing interest rates spurred the public to search for new means to earn "market rates" of interest and led to withdrawals from low yielding savings deposits. This is known as *disintermediation*.

Commercial paper is a term that refers to a type of short-term debt obligation of very credit-worthy corporations (AA or AAA credit rating). It is considered of "investment grade" (high quality), and a corporation might use it to raise money to meet payrolls or other working capital or liquidity needs for a short period of time. This market is available generally only to the largest corporations with the best credit ratings and individuals usually need one hundred thousand dollars or more to participate; that is, to purchase commercial paper notes. The maximum length of this indebtedness is nine months.

A *certificate of deposit* (negotiable) is *not* the receipt an individual receives when depositing money in a savings bank for six months, two years, and so forth. (Watch out for this one on the exam.) Certificates of deposit are large ($100,000 and up) notes issued by banks with a short-term maturity (less than one year) of three, six, or nine months.

Short-term debt obligations of corporations and governmental units *at issuance* are generally purchased by the largest financial institution, banks and money market funds. These purchasers see to it that the obligations are paid when due – and if not, default proceedings take place (a very rare occurrence with money market instruments). For instance, a municipality could borrow money for its short term needs until tax revenues come in (tax anticipation notes).

Debt obligations of corporations and governmental units with *short periods of time remaining to maturity* are a potential investment for individuals who wants their money at work only for the shortest periods of time before they get it back. Such investors purchase "paper" from existing holders who want their money immediately and can't wait for the maturity date of the obligation. One advantage of short periods of time to maturity is that potential changes in the interest rates and the value of the notes (principal) are lessened since maturity dates are shorter. Often types of securities considered in the general category of "money market" are U.S. treasury bills and Euro-dollars.

Debt obligations of U.S. government units subject to *repurchase agreements* are no different from any other form of money market instrument except for the fact that a repurchase agreement has been issued. Banks and brokers issue the repurchase agreement. These repurchase agreements stipulate that the debt will be repurchased (buy them back) at a specified date and price (usually between one and ninety days).

Author's Note to Candidates

Each chapter contains a "real life situation" applying some of the principles discussed within that chapter. Although written in a more relaxed manner for you here, please consider that the Series 6 test will present a number of "fact situations" for you to solve. A basic understanding of each chapter's concepts as well as the *application* of these concepts is crucial to your success.

REAL LIFE SITUATION

Guido Stugatz, retired librarian turned stockcar racer, seeks your advice on where to put $25,000 to work for six months to one year. He says he may need part of the money for the new dirt track he is developing. Your advice to Guido would be to:

Directions: *For each of the numbered recommendations that follow, please select A, B, or C as the evaluation you deem most correct. Place your selection on the line preceding each number.*

A. Worse than inappropriate. You'd better consider deep sea mining – you're not cut out for the investment business.

B. Inappropriate recommendation under the circumstances.

C. Suitable recommendation under the circumstances.

Answer

_____ 1. Buy real estate, it's the only good investment left.
_____ 2. Gold stocks will be "in" this year.
_____ 3. Open an Italian restaurant fast-food chain.
_____ 4. Invest in a money market fund.
_____ 5. Purchase an individual treasury bill – via his bank.
_____ 6. Make a commercial paper direct investment.

Answers: 1-B; 2-B; 3-A; 4-C; 5-C; 6-B.

CHECK YOUR UNDERSTANDING
(Circle One)

1. Corporations must have some form of debt in their capitalization.
    True/False

    Reference:
    Page 1-7

2. An investor can be a lender to a corporation as well as an owner.
    True/False

    Reference:
    Page 1-9

3. The use of debt in the capital structure of a corporation increases in the use of leverage.
    True/False

    Reference:
    Page 1-10

4. Money market funds typically take advantage of capital market type investments.
    True/False

    Reference:
    Page 1-17

5. Shorter term maturities on bond investments will provide the best investment in bonds to protect both interest payments and capital values.
    True/False

    Reference:
    Page 1-10

6. A call provision attached to preferred stock will further protect the preferred stockholder's investment and position in a company.
    True/False

    Reference:
    Page 1-8

7.   Stock rights and stock warrants provide the same basic advantages   Reference:
      to a holder of either.   Page 1-12
          True/False

8.   Securities that were not sold subject to a public offering are   Reference:
      considered restricted and, therefore, less marketable.   Page 1-13
          True/False

9.   General obligation bonds are often more secure for an investor   Reference:
      than revenue bonds.   Page 1-16
          True/False

10.   Bankers acceptances, commercial paper, and certificates of deposit Reference:
      should be looked on as risky and speculative to the prudent investor. Page 1-17
          True/False

Answers: 1-False; 2-True; 3-True; 4-False; 5-True; 6-False; 7-True; 8-True; 9-True;
10-False.

Author's Note to Candidates

If you didn't do well on the pretest at the beginning of the chapter, try it again now
that you have *completed* your study of Chapter 1.

STUDY NOTES

2

SECURITIES MARKET

PRETEST
(Circle one)

1. Which of the following represent prices quoted in the NASDAQ system?
    Reference: Page 2-6
    a. Actual trades that day, by NYSE members
    b. Wholesale prices quoted that day, by NASD members
    c. Retail prices quoted by NASD members on over-the-counter stock
    d. Previous trades that have taken place
    e. Foreign securities price quotes

2. Which of the following are classified as types of underwritings?
    Reference: Page 2-7
    a. Best efforts
    b. Standby
    c. All or none
    d. Firm commitment
    e. All of the above

3. A long-established company wishes to sell new securities to the public to raise money for a specific project. This offering is considered which of the following?
    Reference: Page 2-7
    a. Primary
    b. Secondary
    c. Best efforts
    d. Due diligence
    e. Negotiated

4. An outstanding block of securities is being redistributed in smaller blocks to the public. This would be:
    Reference: Page 2-7
    a. A primary issue
    b. A secondary issue
    c. A best efforts issue
    d. A rights offering
    e. A debenture offering

5.   An advertisement appearing in the newspaper listing the under-
      writers is referred to as a:
      a.   Due diligence listing
      b.   Effective prospectus
      c.   Competitive underwriting
      d.   Best efforts underwriting
      e.   Tombstone advertisement

Reference:
Page 2-9

6.   If you are charged a commission on a specific transaction and this
      commission appears in the confirmation statement, then the broker/
      dealer has probably acted in which of the following capacities?
      a.   Agency transaction
      b.   Dealer transaction
      c.   Principal transaction
      d.   On your behalf
      e.   On the behalf of the NASD

Reference:
Page 2-10

7.   If the record date for a corporate security is May 30 and an
      individual purchases this security on May 29, which of the
      following would occur?
      a.   The purchaser would be entitled to the dividend because he
            or she purchased prior to the record date
      b.   The purchaser would not be entitled to the upcoming dividend
      c.   It depends on the declaration date of the security
      d.   It depends on the payable date of the security, which is not
            given in the question
      e.   The purchaser is entitled to the dividend only if complete
            payment for the stock is made prior to May 30

Reference:
Page 2-11

8.   A corporate bond quoted at 101 3/4 would mean the purchaser
      must pay which of the following?
      a. $10.17
      b. $101.75
      c. $1,017.50
      d. $1,117.50
      e. $1,013.40

Reference:
Page 2-12

9.   A U.S. government bond is quoted at 90.8. This would be equal to
      which of the following figures?
      a. $90.08
      b. $90.80
      c. $900.80
      d. $902.50
      e. $925.00

Reference:
Page 2-12

10. A "listed" security would mean which of the following?   Reference:
     I.   Can be purchased only in the OTC market   Page 2-5
     II.   Can be purchased in an auction market
     III. Is traded on the NYSE only
     IV.   Is traded on an exchange
            a. I only
            b. I and II only
            c. II and III only
            d. II and IV only
            e. III only

11. The NASDAQ system generally would list: Reference:
     a. Actual securities trades that day   Page 2-6
     b. Approximate prices that securities can be purchased that day
     c. Those securities approved by the Federal Reserve Board listing
     d. The high and low purchase price for a stock that day
     e. b and d above

12. A securities offering that is being broken up and redistributed in   Reference:
     smaller blocks would be which of the following?   Page 2-7
     a. Primary offering
     b. New issue offering
     c. Secondary offering
     d. Standby underwriting
     e. Any of the above

13. An underwriting can be all of the following *except*:   Reference:
     a. Due diligence underwriting   Page 2-7
     b. Firm commitment underwriting
     c. Best efforts underwriting
     d. Standby underwriting
     e. All or none underwriting

14. A securities transaction where the broker has acted in an agency   Reference:
     capacity, would mean that: Page 2-10
     a. The securities can be purchased directly from inventory
     b. The broker/dealer has a financial interest in this security as
         well as you
     c. The broker/dealer is an agent for the issuing company
     d. The broker/dealer has gone out and purchased the stock
         for you and charged a commission
     e. None of the above

15. In a special cash account, securities would settle on:
     a.   Trade date plus 3 days
     b.   Date of trade
     c.   The record date
     d.   When a new owner is declared
     e.   When a "shareholder of record" is declared

     Reference:
     Page 2-11

16. The ex-dividend date would indicate which of the following?
     I.   The date on or after which, if you are the purchaser,
           you will not be entitled to the dividend
     II.   The date on or after which, if you are the seller,
           you will not be entitled to the dividend
     III. Generally the same as the trade date
     IV.   Generally two business days before the record date
           a.   I only
           b.   I and III only
           c.   I and IV only
           d.   II only
           e.   II and III only

     Reference:
     Page 2-11

17. A NYSE listed company goes ex-dividend on September 15. The
     record date (presuming all business days) would be:
     a.   September 11
     b.   September 12
     c.   September 15
     d.   September 17
     e.   September 22

     Reference:
     Page 2-11

18. *Good delivery* in a securities transaction would require all of the
     following *except*:
     a.   Securities are not mutilated
     b.   Names appear correctly
     c.   In units of 100 shares
     d.   A majority of registered co-tenants have signed it
     e.   Appropriate documentation is attached

     Reference:
     Page 2-12

19. A common stock quotation of the XYZ Company is 70 5/8. This
     would be equal to which of the following figures?
     a. $70.12
     b. $70.58
     c. $70.63
     d. $75.80
     e. $705.80

     Reference:
     Page 2-12

20.   Municipal bonds are generally quoted in: Reference:
       a.   1/8's   Page 2-12
       b.   1/16's
       c.   1/32's
       d.   After-tax effective yield
       e.   Only the "Bond Buyer" newsletter

ANSWERS: 1-b; 2-e; 3-a; 4-b; 5-e; 6-a; 7-b; 8-c; 9-d; 10-d; 11-b; 12-c; 13-a; 14-d; 15-a; 16-c; 17-d; 18-d; 19-c; 20-a.

OVERVIEW

It is essential for everyone that an orderly marketplace exist for the buying and selling of both corporate and government securities. Chapter 1 discusses corporate and government securities. This chapter provides an introduction to the marketplace and to established procedures for purchases and sales of these securities.

Author's Note to Candidates

Your thorough understanding of the two different types of markets, *exchanges* and over-the-counter, as well as the rules for the orderly operation of each, will be an important foundation for your study of the next five chapters. Please pay particular attention to the *financial commitment* agreed upon by each party as this chapter unfolds.

I. TWO MARKETS — EXCHANGES AND OVER-THE-COUNTER

Stock exchanges are considered *auction markets* because all the buyers and sellers are gathered together in one place. (This is just like an auction for real goods.) The New York Stock Exchange is the largest and most well-known of the stock exchanges. However, other stock exchanges exist such as the American Stock Exchange, the Midwest Stock Exchange, the Pacific Coast Stock Exchange, the Boston Stock Exchange, and the Philadelphia-Baltimore-Washington Stock Exchange.

Any company that wants its security traded on an exchange *must apply for listing*. Its stock then becomes "listed" on that exchange. There are stringent requirements to be met for listing — such that only large and "widely held" companies can qualify. There must be a minimum number of shares outstanding, minimum sales revenue, minimum capital in the company, and so forth. (And the New York Stock Exchange keeps raising the requirements!) The *nature of auction markets* is such that the *highest bidder* at any one moment will be the purchaser of that security.

The *over-the-counter* market (OTC) is a *negotiated market* because there is no single (physical) marketplace; that is, everyone does not gather in any one place like in exchanges. Rather it is a vast market connected by telephone lines. It is said to be a negotiated market because *individuals talking on the phone* and via computer negotiate prices for the purchase and sale of securities. There is *no requirement* for the stock to be listed as there is with the exchanges. *Any* stock that is traded between two individuals is considered to be traded over-the-counter if it is not traded on an exchange.

Since thousands of securities are traded in the over-the-counter market every day, it is necessary to have some *orderly manner* to keep track of prices, quantities, and such. The *National Association of Securities Dealers Automated Quotation System* (NASDAQ) was instituted for this purpose. The NASDAQ system uses tabletop computer terminals to give current quotes for securities in the over-the-counter market. It should be noted that often these are *just quotes* and *not actual transactions*. Prices quoted are *wholesale prices*. In contrast, prices quoted on exchanges and listed in newspapers are *actual* trade prices. Over 15,000 different securities are traded OTC (including all municipal and U.S. government securities), compared with 5,000 or so securities registered for listed trading on the various exchanges.

NASDAQ NATIONAL MARKET ISSUES

Fourth Market (INSTINET)

INSTINET is a market for institutional investors in which large blocks of stock (both listed and unlisted) change hands in privately negotiated transactions between banks, mutual funds, pension managers and other types of institutions, unassisted by a Broker/Dealer.

Registered with the SEC as a Broker/Dealer, INSTINET includes among its subscribers a large number of mutual funds and other institutional investors. All INSTINET members are linked by computer terminals. Subscribers can display bid and ask quotes, and their sizes, to others in the system.

II. NEW ISSUE MARKET

A *primary offering* is a stock offered to the public for the first time; that is, a *new issue*. Stock that has been previously outstanding but is being *resold* or redistributed in smaller blocks is considered a *secondary offering*.

Investment bankers are stock brokerage firms whose names you probably recognize (names such as Merrill Lynch; Prudential Securities; Smith Barney & Co.; Dean Witter, Inc.). These firms help bring to the public securities of companies that want to raise money. These investment bankers assist in an *underwriting*. They, of course, provide continuing services to their clients, such as investment advice and various securities products for sale. It is these firms that execute the buy and sell orders of their clients both on the exchanges and off the exchanges (OTC market). It is important to note that they are *not* commercial bankers.

Underwritings generally take the form of:

- Guaranteed or firm commitment underwritings
- Best efforts underwriting
- Standby underwritings (used in rights offering only)
- All or none underwriting

In *firm commitment underwritings*, investment bankers *guarantee* the amount of securities to be sold. If the total sales fall short, they are obligated for the difference. Investment bankers very rarely make mistakes here.

In *best efforts underwritings*, as the name implies, the investment brokers will do their best but *will not guarantee* how much they'll sell and will operate on a "best effort" basis; that is, will work for a commission only.

When *standby underwritings* are used in rights offering, an investment banker will stand by and purchase all the *unsold* rights. In such cases, a company selling securities can be assured that *all will be sold* because a standby underwriter will purchase all unsold amounts of the issue.

All or none underwriting occurs when the company raising the money must have all of the proceeds from the sake to undertake a specific project. Just a portion of the funds would not be beneficial to them. Therefore, if all of the issue is not sold, none of it will be (i.e., the money will be returned to the investors).

Note that a *due diligence* meeting takes place — usually during the cooling-off period (twenty days before the issue date) — when the underwriters (investment bankers) of the issue meet and discuss the status of the company and prospective sales results.

In all cases with a new issue, a *prospectus* must be delivered to the potential purchaser. The rule is that it must *precede* or *accompany every* solicitation for a new issue.

Registration ▷	20-Day Cooling Off	▷	Public Offering Price
(SEC) ▷	Due Diligence/Red Herring		Effective Date
			Final Prospectus

A "red herring" is a *preliminary* prospectus issued before the regular prospectus is effective. Its purpose is to allow investors to give an "indication of interest" to the underwriters. The red herring does not contain the final price of the new issue and all investors must be provided with the effective prospectus (when cleared by the SEC) before orders can be accepted.

QUICK QUIZ 1

1.   The exchanges are considered to be _____ markets while the OTC market is a _____ market.
Reference: Page 2-5

2.   Which of the following represent prices quoted in the NASDAQ system?
Reference: Page 2-6
   a.   Actual trades that day, by NYSE members
   b.   Wholesale prices quoted that day, by NASD members
   c.   Retail prices quoted by NASD members on over-the-counter stock
   d.   Previous trades that have taken place
   e.   Foreign securities quotes

3.   Which of the following are classified as types of underwritings?
Reference: Page 2-7
   a.   Best efforts
   b.   Standby
   c.   All or none
   d.   Firm commitment
   e.   All of the above

4.   A long established company wishes to sell new securities to the public to raise money for a specific project. This offering is considered which of the following?
Reference: Page 2-7
   a.   Primary
   b.   Secondary
   c.   Best efforts
   d.   Due diligence
   e.   Negotiated

5.   A prospectus must _____ or _____ every sales solicitation for   Reference:
       a new issue.   Page 2-8

                      ANSWERS: 1-auction, negotiated; 2-b; 3-e; 4-a; 5-precede, accompany.

Types of Underwritings

Competitive underwriting is one approach to the marketplace in which a corporation, or governmental body, calls in a number of underwriters and explains how much money must be raised and the type of securities to be offered. The underwriters then bid on the contract and the highest bidder buys it for resale to the public. A few states, as well as the federal government, issue their obligations (debt) directly without the aid (and cost) of investment bankers.

A *negotiated offering* is usually one in which *one* underwriter is involved and the price is negotiated between two parties only. The investment bankers then sell these new securities to the public. The difference between what they actually paid the issuing company and the total proceeds of the sale to the public is their profit.

For example, a firm wants to issue new securities in the amount of $50,000,000. It may be a competitive or negotiated offering. The underwriter might agree to pay this firm $47,000,000. The underwriter takes back $50,000,000 worth of "paper" and then sells the issue. If $50,000,000 is sold, as scheduled, then $3,000,000 is the underwriter's compensation. If only $45,000,000 is raised, then the underwriter loses $2,000,000.

A *tombstone advertisement* appears in the newspapers or financial magazines to inform the public of the underwriting (sale). It contains the familiar quotation, "This announcement constitutes neither an offer to sell nor a solicitation of an offer to buy these securities." If the ad appears during the cooling-off period, no price is shown; but after the effective date (actual date of sale) the price may be shown. A tombstone ad is not considered an offer to sell and thus is not considered a prospectus.

This announcement is neither an offer to sell nor a solicitation of an offer to buy these securities. The offer is made only by the Prospectus.

NEW ISSUE   November 24, 19__

800,000 Shares of Common Stock
800,000 Redeemable Warrants

GOLDEN EAGLE GROUP, INC.

Price $5.00 per Share and $0.10 per Warrant

NASDAQ SYMBOLS: GEGP and GEGPW

Copies of the Prospectus may be obtained from the undersigned only in States where the undersigned may legally offer these securities in compliance with the securities laws of such State.

Vantage Securities, Inc.

QUICK QUIZ 2

6.   An outstanding block of securities is being redistributed in smaller   Reference
      blocks to the public. This would be: Page 2-7
      a.   A primary issue
      b.   A secondary issue
      c.   A best efforts issue
      d.   A rights offering
      e.   A debenture offering

7.   An investment banker and a commercial banker are, in reality, one   Reference:
      and the same (circle correct answer).   Page 2-7
            True/False

8.   A period of twenty days before the actual issue date of the stock   Reference:
      is called the _____ _____ period and, during this time, a _____ _____   Page 2-7
      meeting between the members of the underwriting team usually takes place.

9.   An advertisement appearing in the newspaper listing the under-   Reference:
      writers is referred to as a: Page 2-9
      a.   Due diligence listing
      b.   Effective prospectus
      c.   Competitive underwriting
      d.   Best efforts underwriting
      e.   Tombstone advertisement.

                    ANSWERS: 6-b; 7-False; 8-cooling-off; due diligence; 9-e.

III.   MARKET TERMS

Bid price is the price you will receive when you sell a security. *Asked price* or *offering price* is the price you will pay if you want to purchase the security.
        Investment dealers who arrange for the purchase and sale of securities for their clients can act in either of two capacities:

- Agency relationship
- Principal or dealer relationship

        A broker/dealer wears two hats! An *agency transaction* means that the firm is acting as a broker and has gone out and *found* the stock for you, *delivered* it to you, and *charged* you a commission for its services. In a *principal transaction* the firm acts as a dealer, sometimes referred to as a *net transaction*, the firm has used its *own* securities and delivered them to you. No specific commission is paid on these transactions. In either type of transaction the price to the purchasing individual will be the same (i.e., fair market value on that date). The actual price of the stock to the broker/dealer, who uses its own securities, is not considered when the invoice (confirmation statement) is sent to the client.

There are a number of important dates in the securities industry:

RELATING TO THE PURCHASE AND SALE OF SECURITIES
- Trade date
- Settlement date

RELATING TO CORPORATE DIVIDENDS
- Declaration date
- Ex-dividend date
- Record date
- Payable date

Trade date is the date upon which the broker actually made the trade and the price is established for the investor (usually it is the same day the investor placed the order by phone or in person).

Settlement date is the date on which the money or securities is owed to the firm. This is *three business days after the trade date* (T+3).

Special Note: This is also called a *special cash account*. But the term *cash transaction* refers to a transaction completed that *same day*! This is confusing — note the difference, please, between special cash account and cash transaction. It should be pointed out that the most popular type of account is the *T+3* basis (delayed delivery means allowing up to two more business days for payment).

Declaration date is the date the company actually declares the dividend to be paid in the future to *shareholders of records* on a certain date.

On the *ex-dividend date* and thereafter, the stock sells ex-dividend, meaning without the dividend. Therefore, the purchaser will have bought it without the dividend. The ex-dividend date is automatically *two business days before the record date*. An exception is open-end investment companies which declare their own ex-dividend date.

Record date is the date upon which the corporation "goes into its records"; if the investor appears as a *shareholder of record* on that day, he or she is entitled to the declared dividend.

Payable date is the actual date the checks are mailed to individuals who are entitled to the dividend.

For example, a corporation announces (declaration date) that a $1 dividend will be paid to shareholders of record (record date) on September 15, and this dividend will be paid (payable date) on October 1. The record date is September 15 and the ex-dividend date is two business days before September 15 (assuming all are business days), or September 13. Therefore, anyone purchasing this security on September 13 or thereafter, bought it "ex-dividend" (i.e., without dividend). Anyone purchasing this stock prior to September 13, for instance, September 12, will be entitled to the $1 dividend. It should be noted however, that typically the stock drops in the price on the ex-dividend date by the amount of the dividend; therefore, there is relatively little advantage to either party.

Stock purchases after September 13 do not include the dividend

Good delivery of securities is always required of a seller. Good delivery usually means securities are:

- Not mutilated.
- In the correct name and signed by all owners appearing on the certificate (all joint owners must sign).
- In units of 100 shares (round lot); if not in the exact amount of shares sold.
- Accompanied by all appropriate records and documentation needed, attached and notarized with the signatures guaranteed by the transfer agent — NYSE firm or a commercial bank.

Security quotations are normally in fractions of 1/8 of one dollar, e.g., 50 + 1/8 = $50.125; 50 + 3/8 = $50.375.

Corporate issues, both stocks and bonds, are generally traded in 1/8's.

Corporate and municipal bonds are quoted as a percentage of par ($1,000). For example, a quote of 90 for a bond means $900 (i.e., 90% of $1,000 is $900). A quote of 97 would mean 97% of $1,000 or $970, 97 ½ would mean $975.

Government bonds are quoted in 1/32's (i.e., 50.16 means 50 + 16/32; 50 for a bond is 500, 16/32 equals ½ or $5; therefore, the price of this bond is $505).

QUICK QUIZ 3

10.   The price at which an investor can buy a security is considered the   Reference:
       _____ price, and the price at which he or she can sell a security   Page 2-10
       is considered the _____ price.

11.   If you are charged a commission on a specific transaction and this   Reference:
       commission appears in the confirmation statement, then the broker/   Page 2-10
       dealer firm has probably acted in which of the following capacities?
       a.   Agency transaction
       b.   Dealer transaction
       c.   Principal transaction
       d.   On your behalf
       e.   On the behalf of the NASD

12.   If the record date for a NYSE security is May 30 and an individual   Reference:
       purchases this security on May 29, which of the following would   Page 2-11
       occur?
       a.   The purchaser would be entitled to the dividend because he or
             she purchased prior to the record date.
       b.   The purchaser would not be entitled to the upcoming dividend.
       c.   It depends on the declaration date of the security.
       d.   It depends on the payable date of the security, which is not
             given in the question.
       e.   The purchaser is entitled to the dividend only if complete
             payment for the stock is made prior to May 30.

13.   A corporate bond quoted at 101 3/4 would mean the purchaser   Reference:
       pay which of the following?   Page 2-12
       a. $101.75
       b. $10.17
       c. $1,017.50
       d. $1,013.50
       e. $1,117.50

14.   A U.S. government bond is quoted at 90.8. This is equal to which   Reference:
       of the following?   Page 2-12
       a. $90.08
       b. $90.80
       c. $900.80
       d. $902.50
       e. $925.00

                         ANSWERS: 10-asked or offered, bid; 11-a; 12-b; 13-c; 14-d.

REAL LIFE SITUATION

Mr. P.J. Polluck, a commercial fisherman friend of yours, mentions to you that he likes to
read the stock exchange reports and securities information in the daily newspaper. Mr.

Polluck asks you some questions about the meaning of stocks quoted in the *Over The Counter* section of the newspaper.

Your reply to his questions are:

Directions: *For each of the numbered recommendations that follow, please select A. B, or C as the evaluation you deem most correct. Place your selection on the line preceding each number:*

A. Inappropriate, more answers like this and you'll be all wet!

B. Not a completely accurate statement, two or more shortcomings present.

C. An accurate statement under the circumstances.

Answer

_____ 1. Only listed securities are quoted in the paper and they are the most secure investments anyway.

_____ 2. Fish prices are bound to go up more than stock prices so he should use the financial pages for fish bait.

_____ 3. The *OTC* section lists wholesale prices quoted that day and not actual trades.

_____ 4. Mr. Polluck should be advised that OTC stocks are only for speculators who want to play the market daily.

_____ 5. The OTC market is a negotiated market and does not have the advantage of bringing buyers and sellers together for the highest bid and lowest offer auction to effect trades.

ANSWERS: 1-B; 2-A; 3-C; 4-A; 5-C.

CHECK YOUR UNDERSTANDING
(Circle one)

1. If a company wants its security listed on a stock exchange it must apply for listing on that exchange.
   True/False

   Reference: Page 2-5

2. Stocks to be sold on the over-the-counter market (OTC) are also required to be listed.
   True/False

   Reference: Page 2-5

3. NASDAQ quotes are not actual trades but rather wholesale prices quoted between members.
   True/False

   Reference: Page 2-6

4. Investment bankers are stock brokerage firms who assist in underwriting:
      True/False

Reference:
Page 2-7

5. A company can be assured all rights will be sold in a *standby*
   underwriting because an investment banker will purchase unsold
   amounts of the issue.
      True/False

Reference:
Page 2-7

6. Previously outstanding stock being resold in smaller blocks would
   be considered *best efforts*.
      True/False

Referenced:
Page 2-7

7. Prices are never shown in "tombstone advertisement," which
   informs the public of underwriting sales.
      True/False

Reference:
Page 2-9

8. The *record date* is an important date in the securities industry
   because shareholders of record on that day are entitled to the
   declared dividend.
      True/False

Reference:
Page 2-11

9. The date the company actually declares the dividend to be paid to
   shareholders of record on a certain date is known as the *dividend
   date.*
      True/False

Reference:
Page 2-10

10. "The term used for the price at which investors are willing to sell
    a specific security is the *ex-price*."
       True/False

Reference:
Page 2-10

ANSWERS: 1-True; 2-False; 3-True; 4-True; 5-True; 6-False; 7-False; 8-True; 9-False;
10-False.

Author's Note to Candidates

We covered many terms in this chapter. Go back now to the chapter
pretest and see if you have mastered the material. In succeeding
chapters follow the same procedure.

STUDY NOTES

*Interesting Fact: Lost opportunity: Coca Cola Co. once had
the chance to buy bankrupt Pepsi-Cola Co. for $1,000
— and turned it down.*

3

INVESTMENT RISKS,
PORTFOLIOS AND FINANCIAL
ANALYSIS OF CLIENTS

PRETEST
(Circle one)

1. An investor purchases a 10% corporate bond for $1,000 and inter-   Reference:
    est rates rise in the future. This investor would be most exposed to   Page 3-5
    which of the following risks?
    a. Financial risk
    b. Purchasing power risk
    c. Market risk
    d. Capital value risk
    e. Economic risk

2. In a period where a specific public corporation is doing very well   Reference:
    and making more profits than ever before, yet its stock suffers a   Page 3-6
    decline in the market place due to general overall market conditions,
    an investor would be exposed to:
    a. Financial risk
    b. Interest rate risk
    c. Purchasing power risk
    d. Market risk
    e. Economic risk

3. Utility stocks historically could be considered an example of   Reference:
    _____ issues.   Page 3-8
    a. Offensive
    b. Defensive
    c. Aggressive
    d. Secondary
    e. Consolidating

1

4.   The ability to convert an investment to cash without loss of
      principal would describe:

      Reference:
      Page 3-6

      a.   Marketability of the investment
      b.   Liquidity of the investment
      c.   Profitability of the investment
      d.   Management ability of the investment
      e.   Balanced portfolio

5.   A person in a 28% tax bracket is considering purchasing a tax-
      exempt municipal bond in the state in which he or she resides.
      The yield in the tax-exempt investment is 6%. What would
      be the taxable equivalent yield?

      Reference:
      Page 3-10

      a.   4%
      b.   6%
      c.   8.3%
      d.   15%
      e.   40%

6.   A traditional investment portfolio concentrating on high current
      income would be considered:

      Reference:
      Page 3-9

      a.   A growth type portfolio
      b.   A money-market type portfolio
      c.   A conservative type portfolio
      d.   An income type portfolio
      e.   A balanced portfolio

7.   A specialized portfolio is considered one where more than
      _____ is invested in one industry, geographic location,
      or special situation:

      Reference:
      Page 3-10

      a.   25%
      b.   15%
      c.   12%
      d.   10%
      e.   No minimum

8.   A client whose objective is *growth* of invested capital, and for
      whom current income is *not* a requirement, would consider which
      of the following?

      Reference:
      Page 3-11

      a.   Reinvestment of dividends but not capital gains
      b.   Reinvestment of capital gains but not dividends
      c.   Reinvestment of both capital gains and dividends
      d.   No reinvestment but acceptance of the income and placing
            this income in a savings account
      e.   Selection of a qualified bond and preferred stock portfolio

9. Which of the following would be considered working capital for an individual?

    a. Total assets minus total liabilities
    b. Current assets minus total liabilities
    c. Total assets minus current liabilities
    d. Current assets minus current liabilities
    e. Same as net worth for an individual

    Reference: Page 3-11

10. Discretionary income for an investor would be considered to be which of the following?

    a. Earned income only (not passive) minus all living expenses.
    b. Both earned and unearned income minus expenses but not including taxes.
    c. Both earned and unearned income minus expenses (including taxes).
    d. Adjusted gross income.
    e. Unearned or passive income only (interest on investments, etc.)

    Reference: Page 3-11

11. Which of the following, in order of importance, is the suggested approach to a client's financial well-being?

    I.   Cash savings account
    II.   Life insurance, disability insurance, property insurance
    III. Diversified portfolio of common stocks and bonds based on investment objectives
    IV.   Gift-giving program coordinated with estate planning

    a. I, II, III, IV
    b. I, II, IV, III
    c. II, III, I, IV
    d. II, I, III, IV
    e. III, I, II, IV

    Reference: Page 3-12

12. Management ability is considered a key ingredient in major businesses that prove successful. The risk faced by an investor that an individual business concern that he or she owns stock in could fail due to lack of management expertise would be considered:

    a. Financial risk
    b. Interest rate risk
    c. Market risk
    d. Economic risk
    e. Capital value risk

    Reference: Page 3-6

13.   The ability to convert your investment to cash, regardless of amount   Reference:
received, means that your investment possesses a high degree of: Page 3-6
   a.   Taxability
   b.   Marketability
   c.   Liquidity
   d.   Defensive ability
   e.   Balanced portfolio

14.   Portfolios of securities that are comprised mainly of aggressive-   Reference:
type investments with a high degree of "risk exposure" can, at   Page 3-7
times, offer the investor the potential of:
   a.   High reward
   b.   High defensive risk
   c.   High income
   d.   Low market risk
   e.   Little purchasing power risk

15.   A type of securities portfolio, considered stable historically, has   Reference:
been which of the following?   Page 3-9
   a.   Speculative portfolio
   b.   Income portfolio
   c.   Balanced portfolio
   d.   Aggressive growth portfolio
   e.   International portfolio

16.   Corporate bond prices, as well as municipal bond prices, have   Reference:
generally had which of the following relationships to interest   Page 3-6
rates?
   a.   Parallel relationship
   b.   Converse relationship
   c.   Reverse relationship
   d.   Inverse relationship
   e.   Little relationship

17.   Reinvestment of dividends received or of capital gains attained   Reference:
in a diversified investment program will allow the investor which   Page 3-11
of the following?
   a.   Deferral of all current taxation
   b.   No specific income tax advantages
   c.   The ability to attain growth as well as income from this
      investment program
   d.   The highest possible current net yield of an investment
      program
   e.   The lowest possible net yield on an investment program

18. Net worth as defined in a personal balance sheet would be:
    a. Current assets minus current liabilities
    b. Assets minus current liabilities
    c. Total assets minus total liabilities
    d. Current assets minus total liabilities
    e. Net discretionary income

Reference:
Page 3-11

19. To say a client was to die *intestate* would mean which of the following?
    a. Dying without a will
    b. Dying with a will
    c. Dying with no taxable estate
    d. Dying with a taxable estate
    e. Dying of a intestine ailment

Reference:
Page 3-13

ANSWERS: 1-d; 2-d; 3-b; 4-b; 5-c; 6-d; 7-a; 8-c; 9-d; 10-c; 11-a; 12-a; 13-b; 14-a; 15-c; 16-d; 17-b; 18-c; 19-a.

OVERVIEW

This chapter is essentially a *client-oriented* chapter. It addresses the agent's responsibility (1) to analyze a client's financial status, using specific financial statement tests, and (2) to determine the client's investment objectives and financial ability to meet these objectives. Inherent in delivering that service is an exact analysis of the risk/reward posture of the client and the client's financial ability to take significant risks. The establishment of an appropriate portfolio and measurement of all degrees of risk/reward is needed. The over-riding obligation is to provide clients with only investments "suitable" for them.

Author's Note to Candidates

This chapter is a living, breathing, everyday, *practical application* of what should take place in the securities market between a client and his or her professional advisor. It would only be prudent for both the client and registered representative to consider each element in this chapter as a personal question to be answered before investment goals can be established. The necessary *strategy* to attain these goals must be mapped out. This will be one of the most practical study chapters in your Series 6 preparation.

I.   KINDS OF INVESTMENT RISK

Financial risk is a term used to refer to the degree of likelihood that an individual business may or may not do well; that is, the possibility that it will go out of business. This risk applies to individual owners and/or investors in that business and sometimes is known as business and/or credit risk. Often this is also called *functional risk*.

Interest rate risk is sometimes called *capital value risk* and refers to two specific situations:

- If *interest rates rise*, the capital value (principal) will go *down* due to the lessened desirability of that investment because it carries too low an interest rate: Who would pay full value on old bonds paying 6% when new bonds pay 10%?
- If *wide fluctuations in interest rates* occur on borrowed money, it becomes difficult for companies that must borrow money to stay in business or to grow, which places a severe restriction on their financial capabilities.

Purchasing power risk is the risk associated with *inflation*. If invested dollars are not growing at least as fast as the inflation rate, then the investor is losing ground and losing purchasing power.

Market risk refers to the investment of securities quoted on the open market when, for one reason or another, a bad stock market exists and beyond the control of anyone, prices decline. Market risk is sometimes referred to as "beta risk." This is a risk even if a company is making more money than ever.

Economic risk is considered a new area of risk and occurs when general economic conditions affect individual investments (e.g., recession in the United States, unsettled world conditions, etc.).

Management ability of a company is crucial to the successful overall profitability and avoidance of the above risks. In a fast-changing world, effective management is more difficult than ever before and certainly demands a high level of day-to-day management expertise. Thus, management ability is a crucial area that an individual must assess *prior to* investing in any business.

The *risk of liquidating at inappropriate times* is always a concern for the investor who, because of a need for cash, might be forced to liquidate during a "down" period in the market. (It is an unsettling thought that it is usually when the market is down and the economy in a slump when investors need to cash in (liquidate) their investments!)

Liquidity, marketability, and *taxation* should all be closely analyzed prior to placement of investment monies. Liquidity and marketability are different concepts in that:

- *Liquidity risk* generally refers to the ability of converting an investment to cash quickly *without* loss of principal. Examples are demand deposits (checking accounts), savings accounts, savings bonds and even, sometimes, money market investments.
- *Marketability or redeemability risk* refers to the ease or difficulty of selling an investment at "market value". Even if an investor must take a loss, if he or she can sell a security fairly quickly, the security has high marketability. Examples are commonly traded bonds, common stock, mutual funds, etc.
- *Taxation* refers to ordinary income taxes, capital-gains taxes, tax deferral, or tax exemption generated from an investment. All investments should be analyzed on an *after* tax basis for the client.

AN EXAMPLE OF INVESTOR'S REACTIONS TO ECONOMIC CHANGES

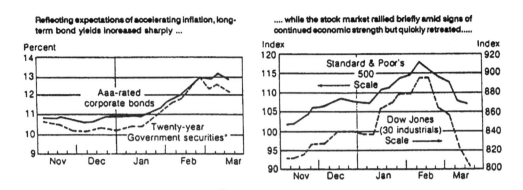

*This yield is adjusted to twenty-year maturities and excludes bonds with special estate tax privileges.

Sources: Federal Reserve Bank of New York, Board of Governors of the Federal Reserve System. Moody's Investors Service, Inc., Dow Jones and Company, Inc., and Standard & Poor's 500.

II.   RISK/REWARD CONCEPT

The *risk/reward ratio* refers to the degree of risk that specific clients wish to take in the achievement of their investment goals. As always the higher the risk, the higher the potential reward; however, the higher the risk, the greater chance of loss.

Diversification is one key element present in the portfolios of almost all serious investors. Diversification means spreading the potential up and down fluctuations in value over a large enough sampling of investments. Generally ten to fifteen stocks are needed to begin to get a "diversified portfolio" of individual securities. Even the high risk investors must protect themselves via diversification.

It is possible to *measure* the risk exposure for an entire portfolio (grouping) of securities. First the stocks can be listed as either inherently defensive or inherently aggressive types of investments. *Defensive types* of investments are considered to be those securities that will resist a downward movement in the market. Historically, such investments, like high grade utility stocks because of a heavy income component, have been considered "defensive" but today there are few truly defensive issues left. However, in an up market, defensive investments do not rise rapidly either. *Aggressive types* of portfolios of investments, on the other hand, are frequently comprised of the "glamour type" stocks, the latest "fad type" stocks, or new and untried companies in limited industries that, while they may rise quickly, can at the first sign of economic woes plummet just as quickly. (Be ready for a roller coaster ride at times with aggressive portfolios.)

An individually selected portfolio of securities can be difficult for an investor to manage because of a lack of expertise in managing and the need to make frequent decisions regarding purchases and sales. While an *account executive* with a brokerage house can provide this investment advice, it is the investor who generally must make the final decision as to buying and selling policies. (It should be noted that commissions are charged on both purchases and sales.)

QUICK QUIZ 1

1.   An investor purchases a 10% corporate bond for $1,000 and   Reference:
      interest rates rise in the future. This investor would be most   Page 3-5
      exposed to which of the following risks?
      a.   Financial risk
      b.   Purchasing power risk
      c.   Market risk
      d.   Capital value risk
      e.   Economic risk

2.   In a period when a specific public corporation is doing very well   Reference:
      and making more profits than ever before, yet its stock suffers a   Page 3-6
      decline in the market place due to general market conditions, an
      investor would be exposed to:
      a.   Financial risk
      b.   Interest rate risk
      c.   Purchasing power risk
      d.   Market risk
      e.   Economic risk

3.   Utility stocks have been historically considered an example of   Reference:
      _____ issues.   Page 3-7

4.   The ability to convert an investment to cash without loss of   Reference:
      principal would describe: Page 3-6
      a.   Marketability of the investment
      b.   Liquidity of the investment
      c.   Profitability of the investment
      d.   Management ability of the investment
      e.   Balanced portfolio
                                        ANSWERS: 1-d; 2-d; 3-defensive; 4-b.

III.   INVESTMENT PORTFOLIOS

There are seven categories of classification of diversified *investment portfolios* based upon the client's objectives:

1. *Money market portfolio*: Investment in exclusively *short term* debt obligations of the most credit worthy corporations and governments. Characteristics of money market portfolios are *high liquidity, minimum chance of loss,* and *return dependent on current interest rates.*

2. *Income portfolios:* Comprised of income securities that pay *high dividends* (stock) or high interest (bonds). Income portfolios are subject to wide fluctuations in income if the obligations are for long periods of time, e.g., 30 years. Capital value risk is a potential problem here.

3. *Conservative growth portfolio:* Generally considered to be securities of *larger corporations* and *blue-chip type stocks.* Bond investments play a less significant role in this type of portfolio than in an income portfolio.

4. *Aggressive growth portfolios:* Comprised almost exclusively of *common stock investments* in companies or industries that seem to be in a growth phase. A greater movement *away from established corporations* is a characteristic of this portfolio.

5. *Growth-income portfolios:* An attempt to not miss growth opportunities while keeping an eye *towards current income* is the "flavor" of this portfolio. A leaning toward *preferred stocks* and some *bond investments* is considered characteristic of this type of portfolio.

6. *Speculative portfolio:* Characterizes a total disregard for current income and more established corporations. Investment in common stock in small technological firms would be characteristic of speculative portfolios.

7. *Balanced portfolios:* Considered to be the most *stable* and are comprised of *common stock* and *bonds* as well as, on occasion, *preferred stock.* For example, a portfolio with 50% bonds would be considered balanced.

In contrast to a common stock portfolio, *a balanced and preferred stock portfolio* generates high income from the interest received on bonds and dividends received on preferred stocks. However, if interest rates rise, the basic dollar value of this portfolio (capital value) declines. There is an inverse relationship between bond prices and interest rates; that is, when interest rates rise, the prices on bonds decline and vice versa.

Some funds now offer "asset allocation funds" which maintain a predetermined ratio or mix of investments, e.g., stocks vs. bonds.

A mutual fund portfolio is considered *specialized* when 25% or more of the portfolio is invested in:

- One industry: such as aerospace, computer science, oil and gas. Sometimes these are called industry or "sector funds."
- One geographical location: such as the Sun Belt or Midwestern agricultural area.
- Special situations: an all encompassing term referred to a specific or unusual reason for investment merit; for example, citrus groves in Florida, Alaskan North Slope petroleum development, or avocado groves in Greece. How about railroad boxcar investing .... timber certificates ...?

Tax-exempt portfolios have become very popular lately. These portfolios are comprised of municipal bonds and other tax-exempt securities of municipalities and state governments. The yield (interest payments) to the investor is *after-tax*. A common equation used to compare before-tax yields with after-tax yields is:

$$\frac{\text{Tax-exempt yield}}{100 \text{ minus individual marginal tax rate}} = \text{Taxable equivalent}$$

This formula allows you to specifically analyze when a move from taxable income (e.g., corporate bonds) to non-taxable income (e.g., tax-exempt bonds) is best. The specific *marginal tax* should be used in this calculation. This is the tax bracket in which the investor's last dollars are taxed (highest).

QUICK QUIZ 2

5.   A person in a 33% combined tax bracket is considering purchasing   Reference:
a tax-exempt municipal bond in the state in which he or she resides.   Page 3-10
The federal income taxes and state income taxes will therefore be
avoided. The yield in the tax exempt investment is 6%. What would
be the non-tax exempt equivalent yield?

6.   A traditional investment portfolio concentrating on high current   Reference:
income would be considered: Page 3-9
    a.   A growth type portfolio
    b.   A money market type portfolio
    c.   A conservative type portfolio
    d.   An income type portfolio
    e.   A balanced portfolio

7.   A specialized portfolio is considered one which has more than   Reference:
_____% is invested in one industry, geographic location, or   Page 3-9
special situation.

ANSWERS: 5-9%; 6-d; 7-25%.

IV.   INVESTMENT OBJECTIVES AND SUITABILITY

The *investment objective* of a client concerns how much current income is needed, how stable the capital must remain, and what type of growth possibilities are expected. This objective determines for the registered representative the type of investments to recommend to the client. Generally, a client has a lump sum, frequently from savings accounts, that he or she wishes to invest in a diversified portfolio to meet these objectives. The client will develop an *accumulation program*, into which monthly or quarterly investments can be made, to add to this portfolio.

    If the objective is *growth*, there is no need for income and the automatic *reinvestment* of all dividends and capital gains distributions is the desired election on behalf of the client. If the client needs *current income* but also wants *growth*, then a consideration is *dividends* received in cash but capital-gain distributions *reinvested* for growth. You will remember from our earlier discussion that dividends and capital gains currently are taxed to the investor whether reinvested, taken in cash, or some of both.

Government economic policy is a major factor in the success. . . . and sustaining the success . . . . of the economy and securities markets. Congress has a major impact cn the economy via its *fiscal policies* of taxing and spending. Changes in taxes and spending programs are referred to as fiscal policy.

Likewise, the Federal Reserve Board has major impact on the securities markets by control of our nation's money supply, know as *monetary policy*. Changes in the money supply, mostly via the banking system, directly effect interest rates. The major controls "the Fed" has are:

- Changes in reserve requirements for banks;
- Changes in discount rate (loans it supplies to banks), and;
- Open market operations (buying and selling U.S. Government Bonds directly).

International monetary factors also have impact on U.S. and worldwide markets. Two major items are balance of payments policies (deficits) among trading nations and short/long-term changes in currency exchange rates.

V.   FINANCIAL STATEMENTS

The preparation of a *personal balance sheet*, as well as a *personal income statement*, is a necessary *beginning point* for both the client and the registered representative. These will make clear the client's *present* financial position as compared to his or her *desired* position, as well as indicating the amount of current income that can be earmarked for continuing investment. With the balance sheet, the difference between total assets and total liabilities is the client's personal *net worth*. This net worth should be calculated throughout the investment period to identify growth via the investment portfolio.

The *working capital* a client has available for investment is defined as *current assets minus current liabilities*. Table 3.1 offers an example of a personal balance sheet.

A personal income statement lists the client's total income from all sources. When normal expenses are subtracted a *discretionary income* remains. From this, the client might choose to use a portion for an investment portfolio.

The balance sheet will identify *retirement benefit programs* in which the client participates. Frequently, this money will *not* be available for investment, as it is already part of a present plan. However, a registered representative must explore completely the *maximum* use of available retirement programs. The inherent tax advantage of qualified retirement programs such as 401(k) plans (payments deductible and growth tax deferred) can be one of the prime accumulation solutions for a client.

If *lump sum* amounts are available for investment, it becomes easier for the registered representative to select a *specific portfolio* to try to satisfy the client's objectives. If, however, only current income is available, periodic investments and/or mutual fund accounts — in which immediate diversification can be achieved with only a small investment — are a valid consideration.

One service to investors is a "timing service" which alerts investors to anticipated market conditions for possible change in desired investment mix of investments.

Prior to a client considering the investment portfolio, some basic needs must be addressed. *Adequate cash savings* for liquidity and to meet emergency needs must be available. A general rule of thumb is that three-to-six months of *net income* comprise a sufficient amount. Certainly an adequate *insurance program*, property insurance liability coverage, and life insurance are all prerequisites to investing.

TABLE 3.1. Sample Personal Balance Sheet: Hans Christian Hasenpfeffer

As of December 31, 199_

Current Assets:		*Current Liabilities:*	
Cash (checking account)	$ 800	Credit cards	$ 1,000
Savings	6,000	Current outstanding bills	3,000
Money market fund	20,000	Current loan payments	6,000
Fixed Assets:		*Long-term Liabilities:*	
Automobiles	9,000	Residence mortgage	65,000
Residence	80,000	Apartment building mortgage	70,000
Household items	5,000	Automobile loan (3 years)	5,000
Apartment building	100,000		
Jewelry	9,000		
Stamp collection	15,000	*Total Liabilities:*	$150,000
Deferred Assets (other):			
Cash surrender value life insurance	16,000		
Expected inheritance (in probate)	46,000	*Net Worth:*	$221,800
Corporation pension (vested)	40,000	*Total Liabilities & Net Worth:*	$371,800
Keogh Plan	25,000		
Total Assets:	$371,800		

Many registered representatives overlook the importance of disability insurance in a client's overall financial plan. The existing assets of the client should be well protected and liability exposures should be guarded against via umbrella policies. Adequate life insurance to support the family in the event of death of the breadwinner is only prudent. These insurance coverages are considered to be of *primary* importance (i.e., before investments). A *properly executed will* for the passage of assets to appropriate family members, so that these assets will not pass under intestate laws (dying without a will), is needed.

Following this initial analysis, the registered representative and his or her client can assess the client's ability to accept risk and fluctuations in value. Fluctuations not only in income but also in the purchasing power of the income and the capital invested are a modern day concern. Any investment program should have an eye towards the *long-term results* and the ability of the client to stay with the program for a long period of time.

The client's specific *need for liquidity* and/or *tax relief* certainly should concern the registered representative. Liquidity needs might be for emergencies or other investments that come along and better meet the client's objectives than the present investments do. Tax relief is obviously a major concern of most investors in the United States today.

NYSE Rule 405 *"Know Your Customer"* rule requires reasonable efforts to obtain all financial information of a client in order to recommend suitable investments.

TELEPHONE SOLICITATIONS

The Telephone Consumer Protection Act of 1991 (TCPA), administered by the Federal Communications Commission (FCC), was enacted to protect consumers from unwanted telephone solicitations. The Act requires an organization that performs telemarketing (in particular, *cold calling*), which includes a Broker/Dealer that undertakes telemarketing, to:

- Maintain a *"do not call list"* of customers who do not want to be called;
- Institute a written policy (available on demand) on maintenance procedures for the *"do not call list"*;
- Train reps on usage of the list;
- Ensure that reps acknowledge and immediately record the names and telephone numbers of customers that ask not to be called again;
- Ensure that anyone making cold calls for the firm informs the customer of the name and telephone number or address of the firm;
- Ensure that telemarketers do not call customers within 12 months of a do-not-call request (within 12 months customers have a "private right of action" entitling them to recover monetary loss, $500 in damages per call violation or both); and
- Ensure that telephone solicitations occur only between the hours of 8:00 am and 9:00 pm of the time zone in which the customer is located.

The FCC rule exempts calls made to customers with whom there is an established business relationship or when the customer has invited or given express permission for the call.

QUICK QUIZ 3

8.   A client whose objective is *growth* of invested capital, and for   Reference:
whom current income is *not* a requirement, would consider which   Page 3-11
of the following:
   a.   Reinvestment of dividends but not capital gains
   b.   Reinvestment of capital gains but not dividends
   c.   Reinvestment of both capital gains and dividends
   d.   No reinvestment but acceptance of the income and placing
          this income in a savings account
   e.   Selection of a qualified bond and preferred stock portfolio

9.   Working capital for an individual would be considered which of   Reference:
the following: Page 3-11
   a.   Total assets minus total liabilities
   b.   Current assets minus total liabilities
   c.   Total assets minus current liabilities
   d.   Current assets minus current liabilities
   e.   Same as net worth for an individual

10.   Discretionary income for an investor would be considered to be   Reference:
which of the following: Page 3-11
   a.   Earned income only (not passive) minus all living expenses
   b.   Both earned and unearned income minus expenses but not
          including taxes
   c.   Both earned and unearned income minus expenses (including
          taxes)
   d.   Adjusted gross income
   e.   Unearned or passive income only (interest on investments, etc.)

11.   Which of the following, in order of importance, is the suggested   Reference:
approach to a client's financial well-being: Page 3-12
   I.   Cash savings account
   II.   Life insurance, disability insurance, property insurance
   III. Diversified portfolio of common stocks and bonds based on
          investment objectives
   IV.   Gift-giving program coordinated with estate planning
          a.   I, II, III, IV
          b.   I, II, IV, III
          c.   II, III, I, IV
          d.   II, I, III, IV
          e.   III, I, II, IV   ANSWERS: 8-c; 9-d; 10-c; 11-a.

REAL LIFE SITUATION

Hans Christian Hasenpfeffer, retired alpine mountain climber turned rabbit breeder, has been successful at his new avocation. Mr. Hasenpfeffer has asked for your advice and assistance with investments and is particularly interested in saving taxes and providing an inflation hedge.

You have constructed Mr. Hasenpfeffer's personal balance sheet and determined his net worth to be $221,800 (see page 3-12).

Please answer the following selections as to your advice to Mr. Hasenpfeffer:

Directions: *For each of the numbered recommendations that follow, please select A, B, or C as the evaluation you deem most correct. Place your selection in the line preceding each number.*

A. Worse than inappropriate. You'd better consider fixing ski bindings as a profession.

B. This recommendation would be inappropriate considering the circumstances involved.

C. Suitable advice under the circumstances.

Answer

_____ 1.   The personal feelings of Mr. Hasenpfeffer toward investments, specifically toward his risk/reward posture, are needed.

_____ 2.   Mr. Hasenpfeffer should definitely consider employment in a more stable industry if he wants to invest through you.

_____ 3.   Diversification of investments will not be quite so important to Mr. Hasenpfeffer because he has a substantial net worth.

_____ 4.   Mr. Hasenpfeffer should probably consider diversifying the categories of portfolios he might prefer.

_____ 5.   By having all of his investments in a tax-exempt portfolio, Mr. Hasenpfeffer will definitely be better off.

ANSWERS: 1-C; 2-A; 3-B; 4-C; 5-B.

CHECK YOUR UNDERSTANDING
(Circle one)

1.   Market risk means that the market for your product may dry up or competitors may force you to sell less profitably.
          True/False

Reference:
Page 3-6

2.   Interest rate risk is typically a greater consideration with bond   Reference:
      investments than common stock investments.   Page 3-6
           True/False

3.   The risk of leaving money in the savings bank at 4%-5% is   Reference:
      purchasing power risk.   Page 3-6
           True/False

4.   Personal taxes are a private matter and, generally, are not to be   Reference:
      discussed with investment advisers.   Page 3-6
           True/False

5.   Defensive type stock issues can be relied upon not to decrease   Reference:
      substantially in value.   Page 3-8
           True/False

6.   Growth type portfolios, where capital gains are the objective, can   Reference:
      partially solve the income tax problem because of the potential   Page 3-9
      favorable capital gains tax treatment.
           True/False

7.   The greatest risk in high grade corporate bond issues is the   Reference:
      potential capital value risk.   Page 3-9
           True/False

8.   Qualified retirement programs have a two-fold tax advantage.   Reference:
           True/False   Page 3-11

9.   A savings account is always a prerequisite to starting an investment Reference:
      portfolio.   Page 3-12
           True/False

10.   Adequate life insurance on the life of the investor is nearly always   Reference:
      a prerequisite to starting an investment portfolio.   Page 3-12
           True/False

ANSWERS: 1-False; 2-True; 3-True; 4-False; 5-False; 6-True; 7-True; 8-True; 9-True;
10-True.

4

OPEN-END INVESTMENT COMPANIES

PRETEST
(Circle one)

1. Which of the following classes of securities may open-end
    investment companies issue to their shareholders?
    Reference:
    Page 4-6
    a. Preferred stock
    b. Common stock
    c. Bonds
    d. Preferred and common stock only
    e. All of the above

2. The investment advisor to an open-end investment company
    would be paid through:
    Reference:
    Page 4-7
    a. Sales charges levied upon initial payments into the
        fund by shareholders
    b. The shareholders directly predicated on an agreed-upon
        fee
    c. A management fee, expressed as a percentage of the
        total fund assets
    d. The profits generated from the investment advice only
    e. The owners of the mutual fund directly

3. All of the following are basic reasons individuals consider the
    mutual fund concept, EXCEPT:
    Reference:
    Page 4-6
    a. Non-professional management of mutual fund assets
    b. Diversification of mutual fund assets
    c. Ease of accounting services provided by the mutual fund
    d. Ability to reinvest dividends and capital gains or a
        compounding of investment
    e. Increased protection against theft of security certificates

4.   Which of the following statements about the tax status of mutual   Reference:
fund distributions is/are correct?   Page 4-8
I.   Dividend distributions are ordinary income
II.   Dividend distributions are taxed as capital gains
III.   Capital gain distributions are taxed as ordinary
        income
IV.   Capital gain distributions are not taxable to the
        shareholder if reinvested in fund shares
        a.   I
        b.   II
        c.   II and III
        d.   II and IV
        e.   I and III

5.   Distribution of dividends of a mutual fund to a shareholder includes: Reference:
        a.   Income from dividends and interest, plus capital gains   Page 4-8
               during the year, less expenses
        b.   Income from dividends and interest, long term capital
               gains excluded, less expenses
        c.   Gross dividend income received during the year
        d.   Gross interest earnings received during the year
        e.   Both gross dividend income and gross interest earnings
               received during the year

6.   Short-term gains distributed by a mutual fund to a shareholder are: Reference:
        a.   Taxed at ordinary income rates   Page 4-8
        b.   Taxed as capital gains
        c.   Not taxed if reinvested in additional fund shares
        d.   Taxed according to status of shareholder (i.e., either as
               an individual or corporation)

7.   Unrealized appreciation in the value of a mutual fund portfolio is   Reference:
taxed to the shareholders: Page 4-8
        a.   Twice a year as dividend distributions are announced
        b.   Once a year as capital gain distributions are announced
        c.   Only when realized via the scale within the portfolio or
               a shareholder redeeming his shares
        d.   In no instance
        e.   Only if the mutual find is in a net operating profit position

8.   Which of the following may a shareholder, owning 525 shares of   Reference:
      the ABC Mutual Fund, do?   Page 4-8
      a.   Pledge the entire value of these shares as collateral for
            a loan
      b.   Redeem any portion of the shares
      c.   Request a stock certificate showing fund ownership rather
            than just confirmation statements
      d.   Rely upon the mutual fund management to provide year-end
            tax information
      e.   All of the above

9.   Which of the following could be common stock mutual funds?   Reference:
      a.   Growth fund   Page 4-10
      b.   Income fund
      c.   Special fund
      d.   Balanced fund
      e.   All of the above

10.   Dividends from a municipal bond fund are generally exempt from   Reference:
      which of the following forms of taxes?   Page 4-11
      I.   Federal income taxes
      II.   State income taxes
      III.   Capital gains taxes
      IV.   Alternative minimum taxes
             a.   I only
             b.   II only
             c.   I and II only
             d.   III only
             e.   IV only

11.   U.S. government securities funds have which of the following   Reference:
      advantages?   Page 4-11
      a.   High income
      b.   High risk
      c.   Exemption from U.S. government taxes
      d.   Exemption from state income taxes
      e.   All of the above

12.   Which of the following types of securities would a money market   Reference:
      fund generally have in its portfolio?   Page 4-11
      a.   Common stock, preferred stock, but no bonds
      b.   Preferred stock and bonds only for income
      c.   Short-term guaranteed debt obligations
      d.   U.S. government bonds
      e.   International debt instruments

13. Automatic reinvestment privilege offered by many open-end   Reference:
     investment companies could offer investors all of the   Page 4-9
     following, EXCEPT:
     a.   Fractional share ownership of shares
     b.   A compounding effect on the investment
     c.   Purchase of shares with no sales charge (at net asset value)
     d.   Deferral of income taxes on reinvested distributions
     e.   Precise accounting of share values and allocation of dividends
          versus capital gains.

14. Open-end investment companies are permitted to do all of the   Reference:
     following, EXCEPT: Page 4-6
     a.   Issue new shares at no less than the NAV per share
     b.   Issue preferred stock
     c.   Invest in long-term debt instruments
     d.   Continuously redeem their shares
     e.   Continuously offer their shares

15. Investors in open-end investment companies may receive a return   Reference:
     that represents all of the following, EXCEPT: Page 4-8
     a.   Unrealized gains in the portfolio will accrue to the
          investor's benefit upon share redemption
     b.   Unrealized gains in the portfolio will accrue to the
          investor's benefit upon share purchase
     c.   Annual dividend distributions in shares or cash
     d.   Annual capital-gain distributions in shares or cash
     e.   Possible redemption of fund shares in excess of cost basis

16. The ability to "swap" or exchange one type of investment company   Reference:
     (e.g., growth fund) for another (e.g., income fund) under the *same*   Page 4-10
     management is referred to as:
     a.   Reinvestment privilege
     b.   Accumulation privilege
     c.   Exchange privilege
     d.   Compounding effect of mutual fund investments
     e.   Not allowed after 1970

17. The portfolio of a money market fund would typically include all of   Reference:
     the following, EXCEPT: Page 4-11
     a.   Banker's acceptances
     b.   Commercial paper
     c.   Treasury bills
     d.   Municipal bonds
     e.   Eurodollar Certificates

18. Dividend distributions from municipal bond funds are exempt from: Reference:
     a.   Federal income taxes only   Page 4-11
     b.   State income taxes only
     c.   Federal estate taxes only
     d.   State estate taxes only
     e.   a and b above

19. Dividend distributions from federal securities funds (U.S.) are   Reference:
     exempt from: Page 4-11
     a.   Federal income taxes only
     b.   State income taxes only
     c.   Federal estate taxes only
     d.   State estate taxes only
     e.   a and b above

20. Money market funds are exempt from: Reference:
     a.   Federal income taxes   Page 4-11
     b.   State income taxes
     c.   Federal estate taxes
     d.   State estate taxes
     e.   None of the above

ANSWERS: 1-b; 2-c; 3-a; 4-a; 5-b; 6-a; 7-c; 8-e; 9-e; 10-a; 11-d; 12-c; 13-d; 14-b; 15-b; 16-c; 17-d; 18-a; 19-b; 20-e.

OVERVIEW

One of the most *popular* methods of investment for both middle-income and high-income investors is through *open-end investment companies*. This method meets the desired professional management, diversification, marketability and record-keeping needs of thousands of investors. This method of investing has become widely accepted since the 1950s and is the backdrop against which millions of dollars make their way into investment markets every day in the United States. This chapter examines the reasons for that popularity.

Author's Note to Candidates

Chapter 4 is the first of five consecutive chapters in your Series 6 study program concentrating on open-end investment companies as a mode of investment. This five-chapter sequence represents 35% of your Series 6 examination content. Need we say more??

I.   THE MUTUAL FUND CONCEPT

A fund that is *owned mutually by a large number of investors* exemplifies the basic concept under which open-end investment companies operate. The money paid in by these many shareholders is invested in securities that then make up the *investment portfolio* of a particular fund. Each investor has an *undivided interest* in the portfolio, which is represented by a specific number of shares.

At any one time, the total asset value of these shares equals the total net asset value of the investment portfolio. The *value of a share* is determined by computing the total value of the fund each day (by actual market value) less any liabilities and dividing this total by the number of outstanding shares. For example, if the total value of the portfolio is $2,000 and there are fifteen shares, the value per share is $133.33.

Each shareholder has both *full* and *fractional* shares representing his or her actual investment.

Open-end investment companies continually offer new shares to investors as money is received. To avoid diluting the value of the shares, an even exchange of money for the exact net asset value per share is made by the managers of the fund. That is, an investor who invests $400 (after sales charges) will receive the number of shares that $400 will buy. For example, if the net asset value (NAV) is $8.00 per share and the net investment equals $400.00, fifty shares will be purchased for this investment.

These new monies are then invested by the professional managers of the fund. Shares are considered Class A voting common stock; therefore, each shareholder has one vote per share owned. Open-end investment companies do *not* issue to shareholders preferred stock or bonds. (Do not confuse this with the fact that the investment portfolio might contain *investments* in preferred stock and bonds of corporations.) When an investor purchases *mutual funds*, the shares he or she receives represent an *undivided interest* in the fund.

Diversification is the benchmark of the mutual fund concept and permits the dispersion of risk among many different securities. This diversification can be spread among a variety of:

- Industries
- Companies in the same industry
- Types of securities or kinds of investment
- Different instruments (e.g., bonds, preferred stock, common stock, bankers' acceptances, commercial paper, etc.)

It should be noted that a mutual fund, by design, maintains a certain minimum cash position so that when *redemptions* of fund share are made, the actual securities in the portfolio will not have to be sold (i.e., cash is available for redemption up to a certain amount). Also note that a shareholder redeeming (selling) his or her share back to the mutual fund receives the precise net asset value of that share on the day it is redeemed.

The assurance of *professional management* is one of the major reasons individuals invest in a mutual fund. Technically proficient portfolio managers, who are full-time employees, study the market and recommend which securities should be bought or sold to achieve the specific objectives of that mutual fund. Since some mutual funds have *income* for an objective, some have *growth* for an objective, and so forth, well-informed, professional management is essential.

It is the investment advisor to the mutual fund who decides on the *appropriate timing* of investment (i.e., when to buy, sell, hold, etc.). The fund management arranges for distributions of dividends and capital gains and makes reports to shareholders for their individual tax reporting. (Dividends are taxed as *ordinary income* and long-term capital-gains distributions are considered *long-term capital gains* to the shareholder). The investment advisor is paid a fee (e.g., 1/2 of 1%) directly from the fund's assets (i.e., an expense of fund).

Most investors have neither the time nor the expertise to develop a sound portfolio for themselves and thus indirectly hire these professionals through the mutual fund concept. For individuals to accomplish the same objectives by investing individually, they would need:

- Large enough sums of money to achieve diversification in their own right
- Investment expertise
- Time to oversee portfolio transactions

QUICK QUIZ 1

1.   An individual may purchase open-end investment company shares   Reference:
      from any shareholder, much like common stock in corporations   Page 4-6
      (circle correct answer).
            True/False

2.   Which of the following classes of securities are open-end   Reference:
      investment companies allowed to issue to their shareholders?   Page 4-6
      a.   Preferred stock
      b.   Common stock
      c.   Bonds
      d.   Preferred and common stock only
      e.   All of the above

3.   The investment advisor to an open-end investment company is   Reference:
      paid through: Page 4-7
      a.   Sales charges levied upon initial payments in the fund
            by shareholders
      b.   The shareholders directly predicated on an agreed-upon fee
      c.   A management fee as an expense of the fund itself (e.g., .5%)
      d.   The profits generated from the investment advice only
      e.   The owners of the mutual fund directly

4.   All of the following are basic reasons individuals consider the   Reference:
      mutual fund concept, EXCEPT: Page 4-7
      a.   Non-professional management of mutual fund assets
      b.   Diversification of mutual fund assets
      c.   Ease of accounting services provided
      d.   Ability to reinvest dividends and capital gains or a
            compounding of investment
      e.   All of the above
                                                    ANSWERS: 1-False; 2-b; 3-c; 4-a.

II.   MEASURING PROFIT AND LOSS

Investment company shares (open-end investment companies) provide three areas for potential *investment return* to a shareholder:

1.   Dividend distributions
2.   Capital gains distributions
3.   Eventual sale of shares for (hopefully) more per share than originally paid

Dividend distributions are basically derived from dividend income received in the portfolio of common and preferred stock as well as the interest earned on holdings of debt obligations (i.e., bonded debt). Operating costs and fees are subtracted from this amount resulting in a *net dividend distribution* to shareholders.

Capital gains distributions are the profits resulting from the actual purchase and sale of securities — both stocks and bonds — during the fund year. Securities sold within *one year and one day* are considered *short-term* gains and/or losses to the portfolio and are *offset* against long-term gains or losses of the portfolio. If there are realized short-term gains these are taxed as ordinary income. These portfolio transactions are called *realized* gains or losses. Only *net* long-term gains are distributed to the shareholders, usually once a year, at the end of the fund's fiscal year. In a bad year, no capital-gains distributions may take place.

It is only the net realized gains or losses that are counted. *Unrealized* appreciation or depreciation on unsold securities do not enter into the capital-gains computation. However, unrealized appreciation or depreciation increases or decreases the *value* of the investment company shares and is reflected in the *price* of the shares.

One of the most popular features of open-end investment companies is the ability to *reinvest automatically* all dividends and capital-gains distributions into the purchase of additional shares. As mentioned, the purchase of fractional shares is allowed. Most funds allow the shareholder a *choice* of cash, reinvestment, or a combination of either.

Author's Note to Candidates

For taxation purposes, it makes no difference whether a shareholder chooses *reinvestment* of dividends or capital gains or *cash*. When dividends or capital gains are distributed, they are reportable by the shareholder whether or not that shareholder chooses to reinvest in additional shares or to receive cash. Thus, note that there is *no tax advantage* to reinvesting as described above.

QUICK QUIZ 2

5. Which of the following statements about the tax status of mutual fund distributions is/are correct?

    I.   Dividend distributions are taxed as ordinary income
    II. Dividend distributions are taxed as capital gains
    III. Capital-gains distributions are taxed as capital gains
    IV. Capital-gains distributions are not taxable to the shareholder if reinvested in fund shares

        a.   I
        b.   II
        c.   II and III
        d.   II and IV
        e.   I and III

    Reference: Page 4-8

6. Distribution of dividends of a mutual fund to a shareholder includes:

        a.   Income from dividends and interest, plus capital-gains profit during the year, less expenses
        b.   Income from dividends and interest, capital gains not included, less expenses
        c.   Gross divided income received during the year
        d.   Gross interest earnings received during the year
        e.   Both gross dividend income and gross interest earnings received during the year

    Reference: Page 4-8

7. Short-term gains distributed by a mutual fund to a shareholder are:

        a.   Taxed at ordinary income rates
        b.   Taxed before being netted against other capital losses
        c.   Not taxed if reinvested in additional fund shares
        d.   Taxed according to status of shareholder (i.e., either as an individual or corporation)
        e.   Not taxed as capital gains

    Reference: Page 4-8

8.   Unrealized appreciation in the value of a mutual fund portfolio is   Reference:
        taxed to the shareholders: Page 4-8
        a.   Twice a year as dividend distributions are announced
        b.   Once a year as capital gains distributions are announced
        c.   Only when realized via the sale within the portfolio or a
                shareholder redeeming his or her shares
        d.   In no instance
        e.   Only if the mutual fund is in a net operating profit position

                                                ANSWERS: 5-e; 6-b; 7-a; 8-c.

III.   MUTUAL FUND CONVENIENCES

Investors who choose to invest in mutual funds gain several *conveniences*. Among them:

- **Day-to-day investment decisions by professional fund managers**
- Increased protection against theft of security certificates
- Greater savings through investment of large mutual funds rather than small individual amounts
- **Opportunity for daily liquidity, including sales of partial shares**
- Acceptability of fund shares as collateral for bank loans
- Automatic reinvestment of dividends and capital gains
- Ability to exchange shares within the same "family" of fund management (exchange privilege) — although exchanges are taxable
- Automatic receipt of information on distributions during the tax year for inclusion on tax return
- **Less risk on diversification than on an individual portfolio**

Hundreds of mutual funds exist with *varying* investment policies and range from *small specific funds investing on one* industry to *large* diversified mutual funds investing in virtually *all* industries. The selection opportunity of an investor, therefore, is a wide one.

Examples of *common stock* funds are:

- Growth funds
- Growth and Income funds
- Income funds
- Special funds
- Balanced funds — although technically not a stock fund because these include bonds

Municipal bond funds now exist in which the entire portfolio is invested in municipal bonds that are *exempt* from *federal* income taxation and, *to a degree*, from *state* income taxation. The municipal bond fund management reports to shareholders each year what percentage is exempt from state income tax to a *resident* of that state. Municipal bond income from obligations of states other than the investor's residence state are generally *not exempt* form *state* income taxes, however, such income (e.g., a fund whose only investment is in obligations of California, New York, Massachusetts, etc.). These have become attractive to residents of those states. Municipal bond investments are sold on a *unit investment trust* basis. Thus municipal bond portfolios are not corporations but, rather, are trusts (unit investment trusts).

Unit investment trusts can also issue shares of beneficial interest (SBI) representing an undivided participation in a unit of specified securities.

In contrast, it should be noted that *federal obligations* (i.e., U.S. government securities) are *not* exempt from federal income taxes but *are* exempt from state income taxes. One of the reasons for the increasing popularity of U.S. government securities funds is that the income is exempt from state income taxes. U.S. government security funds are also considered to be almost *riskless* as to principal because the portfolio securities are *guaranteed* by the U.S. government.

Money market funds form a diversified portfolio of generally short-term *debt* instruments of highly reputable and creditworthy corporations, as well as bank obligations and debt instruments of the federal government. An example of the make-up of a money market fund is:

- Banker's acceptances   1.3%
- Certificate of Deposit   22.5%
- Commercial Paper   58.1%
- Eurodollar Certificates   16.2%
- Other short-term debt instruments and cash and receivables   1.9%

Money market funds have become extremely popular in the last few years and now make up more than one half of the total assets of *all* mutual funds!

MONEY MARKET MUTUAL FUNDS

Fund	Avg. Mat.	7Day Yld.	e7Day Yld.	Assets	Fund	Avg. Mat.	7Day Yld.	e7Day Yld.	Assets	Fund	Avg. Mat.	7Day Yld.	e7Day Yld.	Assets
DlyPaso f	51	2.41	2.44	2255	GrdCsFd	13	2.70	2.74	327	MdInInst	55	2.94	2.98	37
OWltrLg	61	2.79	2.82	8927	GrdCsMg	17	2.57	2.61	79	MonManGvt	42	2.19	2.21	78
OWltrUS	65	2.48	2.51	1043	HTInsgrCs	54	2.88	2.92	258	Mcn&ManPr	46	2.65	2.69	100
DelaCR f	63	2.60	2.63	780	HTInsgrGv	49	2.72	2.76	203	MonarchGfCsh	35	3.15	3.20	112
DelaTr	79	2.19	2.21	41	HanvCsh	62	2.91	2.95	618	MonMMgt f	68	2.30	2.33	133
DryBasic	59	1.66	1.73	434	HanvGov	85	2.70	2.74	477	MonMkTrst	61	3.10	3.15	898
DryBasGov	74	3.44	3.52	91	HanvUSTr	49	2.56	2.59	929	MonitorGvT	57	2.62	2.65	46
Dry100 US	86	2.71	2.75	3267	HanvTreas	69	2.62	2.65	401	MonitorMMT	51	2.84	2.88	311
DryGvt	80	2.73	2.77	692	Harbor	44	2.30	2.33	53	MonitorUST	54	2.82	2.86	192
DryInG	85	2.89	2.93	208	HelmsPr	61	3.11	3.15	898	MonitrMMI	51	2.74	2.77	21
DryInst	55	3.01	3.05	343	HelmsUS	48	2.88	2.92	430	MontGovRes	59	3.18	3.23	60
DryfLA	69	2.86	2.90	5667	HrtgCsh	79	2.61	2.64	894	MS Mony	46	2.99	3.03	453
DryMM	56	2.94	2.98		HiMrkDv	66	2.73	2.77	463	MutlOmah	54	2.38	2.41	160
DryWld	65	3.06	3.11	5887	HiMrkUS	65	2.62	2.65	134	NCC Govt	34	2.69	2.73	6
EalVCsh	33	2.67	2.71	125	HiMrkUST	79	2.59	2.62	237	NCC MM	23	2.71	2.74	41
ElfunMM	77	3.29	3.35	53	HilrdGovt	59	2.56	2.59	738	NYL Inst	65	2.97	3.02	68
EmblPr	69	3.05	3.10	548	HmestdDiv	67	2.94	2.98	73	NationsFdPr	66	2.94	2.98	268
EmblUS	56	2.68	2.72	554	HorznPr	54	3.38	3.43	10027	NationsFdTr	52	2.59	2.62	108
EnterMM	57	2.36	2.38	19	HorznTr	52	3.00	3.04	2846	NatwMM	43	2.81	2.83	476
EvarnM	75	3.21	3.26	349	Hummer	41	2.57	2.60	158	NeubCsh	43	2.75	2.79	258
FBL	46	1.57	1.58	30	IDS CshM	52	2.44	2.47	1128	NeubGvl	66	2.54	2.57	296
FFB Csh	55	2.82	2.86	496	IDS PLA	39	2.56	2.59	95	Newton	50	3.01	3.09	284
FFB US Gvt	69	2.83	2.87	183	IMGLiq	45	3.00	3.04	118	Nicholas	30	2.89	2.90	143
FFB US Tr	53	2.72	2.76	372	IndCaGv	71	2.36	2.38	281	OppMoney	64	2.71	2.75	752
FFBLexicn	66	2.80	2.84	59	IndCaMM	57	2.64	2.67	293	OvldExTrs	42	2.59	2.63	136
FMBInst	50	3.09	3.14	61	IndOnPr	45	2.82	2.86	418	OvldExMM	51	2.50	2.54	277
FdShtUS	50	3.09	3.14	1017	IndOnUS	57	2.66	2.69	238	PFAMCo MM	39	2.87	2.91	8
FedMstr	67	3.11	3.16	1068	InfnAlGv	43	2.86	2.89	45	PNC Gvt	49	2.89	2.93	154
FidInDom	49	3.17	3.22	693	InfnAlPr	27	2.84	2.87	31	PNC Prm	54	2.86	2.90	859
FidInGov	79	3.27	3.32	6099	InfCCR	74	2.52	2.55	424	PCHrtPr	54	3.06	3.10	10027
FidInMM	59	3.36	3.40	5328	InfInPeg	34	3.47	3.52	202	PCHrtTr	52	2.68	2.71	2846
FidInTr	71	3.20	3.25	2577	InstCsh	68	3.28	3.28	657	PacificGv	76	2.81	2.85	195
FidInTrII	51	3.15	3.20		InstFd	41	2.75	2.79	15	Pacifica	79	3.14	3.19	136
FidCsRes	65	3.16	3.21	1004	InstGov	25	3.04	3.09	248	PW Cash	53	3.00	3.04	3801
FidDMM	53	2.85	2.89	1603	InvCshGv	50	2.91	2.95	65	PW MstrM b	43	1.50	1.51	36

QUICK QUIZ 3

9.   Which of the following may a shareholder, owning 525 shares of   Reference:
     the ABC Mutual Fund, do?   Page 4-8
     a.   Pledge the entire value of these shares as collateral for a loan
     b.   Redeem any portion of these shares
     c.   Request a stock certificate showing fund ownership rather
          than just confirmation statements
     d.   Rely upon the mutual fund management to provide year-end
          tax information
     e.   All of the above

10. A mutual fund investing 25% or more of its funds in one specific   Reference:
     industry (e.g., computer sciences), yet diversifying its investment   Page 4-10
     among hundreds of such firms, is considered a:
     a.   Growth fund
     b.   Income fund
     c.   Specialized fund
     d.   Balanced fund
     e.   Any of the above

11. Dividends received from a municipal bond fund are exempt from   Reference:
     which of the following forms of taxes under all circumstances?   Page 4-11
     I.   Federal Income taxes
     II.   State income taxes
     III. Alternative minimum tax
           a.   I only
           b.   II only
           c.   I and II only
           d.   III only
           e.   II and III only

12. U.S. government securities funds have which of the following   Reference:
     advantages?   Page 4-11
     a.   High income
     b.   High risk
     c.   Exemption from U.S. government taxes
     d.   Exemption from state income taxes
     e.   All of the above

13.   Which of the following types of securities would a money market   Reference:
        fund generally have in its portfolio?   Page 4-11
        a.   Common stock, preferred stock, but no bonds
        b.   Preferred stock and bonds only for income
        c.   Short-term guaranteed debt obligations
        d.   U.S. government bonds
        e.   International debt instruments

                              ANSWERS: 9-e; 10-c; 11-a; 12-d; 13-c.

REAL LIFE SITUATION

Granville C. Ludwig, IV, age 42, former flute player turned streetcar conductor, seeks your advice about the type of mutual fund he should select to diversify his investments.

    Mr. Ludwig is quite conscious about the tax impact on his investments since he is in a high tax bracket as a result of the income he is receiving from a recent inheritance. He also prefers bond-type investments to stock-type investments. Your advice to Granville would be to:

Directions: *For each of the numbered recommendations that follow, please select A, B, or C, as the evaluation you deem most correct. Place your selection on the line preceding each number.*

A. Worse than inappro-   B. Inappropriate recom-   C. Suitable recommen-
    priate. You were   mendation under the   dation under the
    studying this assign-   circumstances.   circumstances.
    ment   when   you
    were sleeping!

Answer

_____ 1.   Concentrate on income funds since these will help most in his tax bracket.
_____ 2.   Money market fund
_____ 3.   Municipal bond fund
_____ 4.   A computer technology fund would be good since that is a fast-growing
               industry with little income but capital appreciation prospects.
_____ 5.   Forsake the mutual fund approach and start a flute manufacturing business
               in Vienna.

                              ANSWERS: 1-A; 2-A; 3-C; 4-B; 5-A.

CHECK YOUR UNDERSTANDING
(Circle one)

1. Open-end investment companies are usually not corporations but large partnerships.
   True/False

   Reference: Page 4-6

2. The actual purchase price per share of an open-end investment company is determined by supply and demand for that fund and not by the net asset value calculation.
   True/False

   Reference: Page 4-6

3. Open-end investment companies may purchase preferred stocks and bonds if their investment policy allows for such investments.
   True/False

   Reference: Page 4-6

4. Upon redeeming (selling) your mutual fund shares back to the fund, the bid price per share is the figure that determines your redemption value.
   True/False

   Reference: Page 4-6

5. Both dividend and capital-gains distributions from a fund are subject to full current ordinary income taxation.
   True/False

   Reference: Page 4-9

6. Mutual fund shares cannot be used for collaterizing bank loans.
   True/False

   Reference: Page 4-10

7. Income from a U.S. government securities fund will be exempt from state income taxes.
   True/False

   Reference: Page 4-11

ANSWERS: 1-False; 2-False; 3-True; 4-True; 5-False; 6-False; 7-True.

STUDY NOTES

5

COMPARING, BUYING, AND REDEEMING MUTUAL FUND SHARES

PRETEST
(Circle one)

1. The key to any mutual fund's investment success for its share-   Reference:
    holders is the quality of its management. Which of the following   Page 5-6
    is recognized as the most important measure of the quality of the
    management team?
    a.   Past management performance
    b.   Loss expense ratio
    c.   Moderate investment management fee
    d.   Level of risk exposure of the fund
    e.   Proximity to the New York Stock Exchange

2. Mutual funds publish their past performance histories. When   Reference:
    comparing funds, the *time frame* they may use is all of the   Page 5-6
    following, EXCEPT:
    a.   Last twelve months
    b.   Last five years
    c.   Last ten years
    d.   Any period of January 1 through December 31
    e.   Complete period since fund inception

3. When mutual funds show their past performance and when service   Reference:
    companies offer direct comparisons of different funds' performance   Page 5-6
    histories, which of the following applies?
    a.   Ten-year histories only are allowed
    b.   All comparisons must show sales charges deducted
    c.   All comparisons must be without reinvestment shown
    d.   Each comparison service must be registered with the NASD
    e.   None of the above are correct

1

4.   When mutual funds show past performance, the net amount   Reference:
      invested at the beginning of the period shown must reflect which   Page 5-6
      of the following?
      a.   The highest sales charge that is in effect
      b.   The lowest sales charges that is in effect
      c.   The average sales charges
      d.   The median sales charge
      e.   None of the above

5.   The annual management fee paid to the fund advisor is paid from: Reference:
      a.   The sales charge   Page 5-9
      b.   The auditor's expense fee
      c.   The gross income of the fund
      d.   The assets of the fund
      e.   An assessment on the shareholders directly

6.   The price received for mutual fund shares redeemed by an   Reference:
      investor is based on: Page 5-12
      a.   The offered price per share
      b.   The net asset value per share
      c.   The median between the bid and asked price per share
      d.   The net asset value per share plus the sales charge
      e.   The asked price per share

7.   The signature guarantees for investors wishing to redeem fund   Reference:
      shares can be made by which of the following?   Page 5-17
      I.   A national bank
      II.   An NYSE brokerage firm
      III.   An NASD broker/dealer if acceptable to the transfer
             agent
      IV.   The transfer agent itself
             a.   I
             b.   I and II
             c.   I, II and III
             d.   I, II and IV
             e.   All of the above

8.   A mutual fund with a per share asked price of $20.00 and bid   Reference:
      price of $18.30 would have a sales charge of: Page 5-13
      a.   8.5%
      b.   9.2%
      c.   17%
      d.   18.3%
      e.   20%

9. Mutual fund historical figures usually:
    I.   Include reinvestment of dividends and capital gains
    II.   Are not allowed to include dividends and capital
          gains reinvestments
    III. Are permitted for select time periods only
    IV.   Can be shown for any time period
          a.   I and III only
          b.   I and IV only
          c.   II and III only
          d.   II and IV only
          e.   None of the above

    Reference:
    Page 5-6

10. Comparisons of most mutual funds and their past histories are
    available from:
          a.   The SEC division of enforcement
          b.   The NASD mutual fund divisions
          c.   The state insurance department
          d.   The state securities department
          e.   Private service companies such as Johnson Charts, etc.

    Reference:
    Page 5-6

11. Service features included in many mutual funds are all of the
    following, EXCEPT:
          a.   Withdrawal plan
          b.   Exchange privilege
          c.   Plan completion insurance for periodic payment plans
          d.   Reports telling an investor when to invest
          e.   Fund accounting reports

    Reference:
    Page 5-7

12. The reinvestment privilege allows an investor (by law) to:
          a.   Reinvest dividends at the offering price
          b.   Reinvest dividends at the asked price
          c.   Reinvest dividends and capital gains at the NAV price
          d.   a and b above only
          e.   No legal requirement (fund can select)

    Reference:
    Page 5-6

13. One indicator of a mutual fund's management from the stand-
    point of cost control is:
          a.   Expense ratio
          b.   Cost ratio
          c.   Historical ratio
          d.   Reinvestment ratio
          e.   Current ratio

    Reference:
    Page 5-7

14.   *Indexing*, when applied to a management advisor's fee in mutual   Reference:
       funds, means: Page 5-9
       a.   The investor gets the market using an index such as
             Standard & Poor or NYSE index
       b.   The investor gets the market using an index such as the
             Consumer Price Index
       c.   Allowing a portion of the management fee to be determined
             by management's performance relative to a "market index"
       d.   If performance was less than the market, no fee
       e.   Is not allowed by the SEC

15.   A mutual fund that has a sales charge will allow purchases of   Reference:
       shares at: Page 5-12
       a.   A variable rate based directly on the market
       b.   A fee related to the prime rate
       c.   The asked or offered price per share
       d.   The bid or NAV price per share
       e.   None of the above

16.   An investor who wants to buy fund shares might experience a   Reference:
       "distribution" or sales process (between the fund and investor)   Page 5-11
       which could be:
       a.   From the fund to the investor directly (no middle person)
       b.   From the fund to an underwriter to the investor
       c.   From the fund to the underwriter to a dealer to the investor
       d.   From the fund to the underwriter to a plan company to
             the investor
       e.   All of the above

17.   The underwriter of fund shares is also called: Reference:
       a.   Open-end management company   Page 5-12
       b.   Distributor
       c.   Custodian
       d.   Agent
       e.   Broker

18.   A mutual fund that has, at the time of investor purchases, an   Reference:
       asked price of $12, a bid price of $10.98, and an underwriter's   Page 5-13
       concession or dealer's reallowance of $.98. How many shares
       can an investor purchase to invest $1,000?
       a.   1200 shares
       b.   100 shares
       c.   83.3 shares
       d.   91.1 shares
       e.   10.98 shares

19.   Which of the following is a valuable feature for an investor who is   Reference:
      considering adding additional money in the near future if the fund   Page 5-14
      permits?
      a.   The conversion privilege
      b.   The withdrawal privilege
      c.   Plan completion insurance
      d.   A letter of intent
      e.   Dividends and capital gains in cash

20.   Which of the following best describes the *right of accumulation*   Reference:
      feature?   Page 5-15
      a.   Lower sales charges on new purchases under the break-
            point system adding together all fund shares under the
            same management but different funds
      b.   The legal right of shareholders to invest more money in
            their fund at any time
      c.   The legal right to force a fund to reinvest dividends and
            capital gains even if it does not offer such an option
      d.   The right to defer taxation on "all accumulations"
      e.   None of the above.

ANSWERS: 1-a; 2-d; 3-b; 4-a; 5-d; 6-b; 7-c; 8-a; 9-a; 10-e; 11-d; 12-e; 13-a; 14-c; 15-c;
16-e; 17-b; 18-c; 19-d; 20-a.

OVERVIEW

It is important for the registered representative to explain thoroughly to a client the procedure for purchasing mutual fund shares, the associated sales charges, and the specific vernacular used by the investment industry. Since all mutual funds shares are "purchased to be sold," a thorough explanation of the value upon redemption of fund shares should be included. Once an investor understands the basics of purchasing and redeeming mutual fund shares, the next subject to be addressed is *which* mutual fund should be purchased. Chapter 4 discussed the different objectives of the various mutual funds available for purchase. After establishing a client's investment objectives and preparing a list of funds that meet these objectives, a *comparison* of the funds in consideration should be made. This chapter addresses that comparison, as well as describing the methods used in buying and redeeming mutual fund shares.

Author's Note to Candidates

Your knowledge of standards used for comparing mutual funds, as well as of the specifics regarding the purchase and redemption of mutual funds, is both a legal requirement and an obligation to your clients. This chapter, in particular, contains *specific, practical sales tools* to help you become more successful in your sales.

I.   COMPARISON OF MUTUAL FUNDS

The *basis of comparison* for open-end investment companies should include examination of the *investment objectives, investment policies, quality of management*, and other *risk factors* involved in fund selection. While the investment objectives and investment policies are straightforward and fully detailed in the prospectus for each fund, the quality of management and the potential risk to the client are *not* so easily measured.

Past management performance of a mutual fund is the *cornerstone* used by many investment advisors to judge whether or not a particular fund's management is among the best available. Accurate comparison of *past performance* of mutual funds is important to both the registered representative and the client. It is imperative that only funds with *similar investment objectives* be compared and that a *comparable time frame* be used. The time periods allowed by the SEC and NASD for comparing performance are:

- Latest twelve months (calendar year)
- Last five years
- Last ten years
- Full period since inception of the fund (from first year of business to current)

A mutual fund yield must be computed in a uniform manner as determined by the SEC.

It is also important to note if the company comparison states whether dividends and capital gains are automatically reinvested or paid in cash. Reinvestment of dividends can be at either the bid price (NAV) or the asked price. Usually, fund charts *assume reinvestment* of all distributions. (This usually makes performance look better.) Keep in mind that the rules of comparison between funds dictate that *assumptions be identical.*

It should be noted that — if fund distributions are reinvested — the individual shareholder bears the *tax liability* for *both* dividends and capital-gain reinvestments out of private funds. Therefore, the accumulation of fund assets is *before taxes*; that is taxes have to be paid out of separate funds to allow this accumulation.

It is also considered important by investment analysts that all *sales charges* be shown and identified in each comparison. Services often used for this information are Morningstar Reports, Johnson Charts, and Donoghue Reports; all of which report what sales charges are deducted in the beginning. An additional requirement when comparing mutual funds is that the *highest* sales charge be shown — *not* the average or those that were subject to *breakpoints* (lower sales charges).

Information on a mutual fund's *historical performance* can be obtained from the *prospectus* itself, *shareholder reports* and numerous *information services*. These services are usually third-party, independent services that assist in the analysis process. They operate, generally, as subscription services and provide useful data.

Additional Factors

The comparison of mutual funds demands more than just a mathematical comparison and a comparison of historical performance. Service features that are valuable privileges to the investor, and should be considered in comparisons, are:

- Withdrawal plans
- Automatic reinvestment program for dividends and capital gains
- Exchange privileges (converting from one fund to another under the same management)
- Special features such as contractual plan insurance
- Minimum purchase requirements, convenience of purchase, and so forth

---

Author's Note to Candidates

In regard to automatic reinvestment of dividends to shareholders, some mutual funds offer this feature at the asked price or offering price (including sales charge). Others offer this feature at the bid price or net asset value (without sales charges). Reinvestment at net asset value is *more* favorable to the investor because sales charges are *avoided* on these reinvestments. Capital gains reinvestments are always at net asset value.

Expense Ratio   Certain expenses may be *deducted directly* from the fund — which, remember, is the shareholder's money. These expenses are fully disclosed in the fund's prospectus and include such items as the auditor's expense, cost of preparation of the annual report, the custodian's fees for safekeeping of securities, and the annual management fee. Often investors relate the expense of a fund to its assets; that is, its *expense ratio*. The expense ratio should be as *low* as possible.

Goals and Objectives   The investor should analyze a fund's past performance in the light of how closely it achieved the announced goals and objectives. However, past performance *cannot* assure what will happen in the future. Predicting a mutual fund's ability to achieve its objectives in the future is very difficult and never certain. The most important measurement, however, is investment return to the shareholder!

Chart 5.1   Mutual Funds Charts demonstrate the cumulative value of reinvesting distributions.

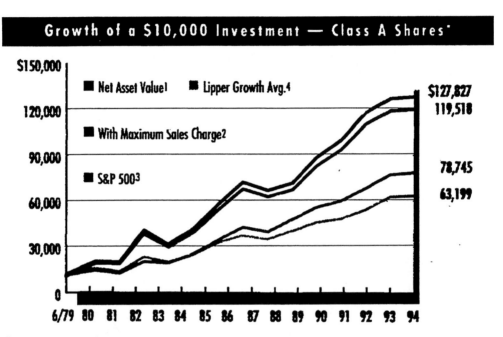

Growth of a $10,000 Investment — Class A Shares*

- ■ Net Asset Value1
- ■ Lipper Growth Avg.4
- ■ With Maximum Sales Charge2
- ■ S&P 5003

$150,000 / 120,000 / 90,000 / 60,000 / 30,000 / 0

6/79 80 81 82 83 84 85 86 87 88 89 90 91 92 93 94

$127,827
119,518
78,745
63,199

All performance is historical and is not indicative of future results.

* Used with permission of The New England, Boston, MA

Turnover Ratio   This ratio measures the number of times the portfolio is "turned over" or sold during a period of time, usually one year. A turnover ratio of 1.5:1 would indicate that the entire portfolio turned over one-and-one-half times during the year. This is a high ratio. Usually it is expressed as a percentage, i.e., 150%. The measurement is important because the fund must pay *commissions* on every sale and purchase. This can reduce the shareholder's financial return.

Asset Size   Often, the larger the fund, the better economies of scale. Larger purchases and sales of portfolio securities permit lower commissions, better buying power, and such. Efficiency of portfolio management seems to favor the larger funds, at least up to a limit.

Table 5.1 Comparison with standard statistical measures.

Investment Results   Total Returns for Periods Ended 12/31/91

	One-Year	Five-Year	Ten-Year
Growth Fund	56.72%	142.09%	619.87%
Lipper Growth Fund Index[1]	36.13	94.49	319.70

Calculations are based on net asset value assuming the reinvestment of all distributions for the periods indicated. Please consult your fund prospectus for the annual breakdown of capital and income components. All results illustrate past performance. The investment return and principal value of an investment will fluctuate, so an investor's shares, when redeemed, may be worth more or less than the original cost.

*Standard & Poor's 500 Stock Index is an unmanaged index representing the performance of 500 major companies, the majority of which are listed on the New York Stock Exchange.
*Lipper Analytical Services is a leading independent mutual fund tracking service. Lipper returns do not reflect sales charges.

Investment Results with Maximum Sales Charge
Average Annual Total Returns for Periods Ended 12/31/91

	One-Year	Five-Year	Ten-Year
Growth Fund	46.46%	17.75%	21.01%

The maximum sales charge for New England Growth Fund is 6.50%.

Annual Performance   12/31/76–12/31/91

	Growth Fund	S&P 500*		Growth Fund	S&P 500*
1976	+18.15%	+23.81%	1984	-6.45%	+6.22%
1977	-0.15	-7.19	1985	+34.91	+31.64
1978	+26.87	+6.52	1986	+18.58	+18.62
1979	+27.32	+18.45	1987	+18.47	+5.21
1980	+48.85	+32.45	1988	+1.45	+16.50
1981	+3.14	-4.88	1989	+22.25	+31.59
1982	+78.65	+21.50	1990	+5.14	-3.12
1983	+11.21	+22.46	1991	+56.72	+30.40

NOTE:
Funds may compare their results with standard statistical measures — as here with Standard & Poor's 500 Index and above with the Lipper Growth Fund Index.

The *annual management fee*, often one-quarter to one-half of one percent of net asset value (.5%), is a *fixed item*. Additional management fees may *not* be taken by fund management. It has become popular recently to have a base fee *and* an additional fee paid via *indexing*. With indexing, the fund performance is compared to a standard reference such as Standard & Poor's Index or New York Stock

Exchange average. If the fund's performance exceeds these indexes by a certain amount, an additional management fee is paid to the management company as an incentive.

An increasing number of funds are operating as 12(b)-1 plans. The SEC allows these funds to deduct as much as .75% (and .25% for service) of average net assets to cover commissions, advertising and marketing expenses whether actually used by the fund or not. These must be disclosed in the prospectus.

QUICK QUIZ 1

1. The key to any mutual fund's investment success for its share-   Reference:
    holders is the quality of its management. Which of the following   Page 5-6
    is recognized as the most important measure of the quality of the
    management team?
    a.   Past management performance
    b.   Loss expense ratio
    c.   Moderate investment management fee
    d.   Level of risk exposure of the fund
    e.   Proximity to the New York Stock Exchange

2. Mutual funds publish their past performance histories. When   Reference:
    comparing funds, the *time frame* they may use is all of the   Page 5-6
    following, EXCEPT:
    a.   Last twelve months
    b.   Last five years
    c.   Last ten years
    d.   Any period of January 1 through December 31
    e.   Complete period since fund inception

3. When mutual funds show their past performance and when   Reference:
    service companies offer *direct* comparisons of different funds'   Page 5-6
    performance histories, the following applies:
    a.   Ten-year histories only are allowed
    b.   All comparisons must show sales charges deducted
    c.   All comparisons must be without reinvestment shown
    d.   Each comparison service must be registered with the NASD
    e.   None of the above are correct

4. When mutual funds show past performance, the net amount   Reference:
    invested at the beginning of the period shown must reflect which   Page 5-6
    of the following?
    a.   The highest sales charge that is in effect
    b.   The lowest sales charge that is in effect
    c.   They must average the sales charges
    d.   They must use the median sales charge
    e.   None of the above

5.   The annual management fee paid to the fund advisor is paid from: Reference:
  a.   The sales charge   Page 5-9
  b.   The auditor's expense fee
  c.   The gross assets value of the fund
  d.   The net asset value of the fund
  e.   An assessment on the shareholders directly.

ANSWERS: 1-a; 2-d; 3-b; 4-a; 5-d.

II.   PURCHASING FUND SHARES

Fund shares are purchased at the *asked* or *offering* price. All open-end investment company shares are ultimately purchased from the fund. All redemptions are ultimately from the fund also. Therefore, the fund itself is the central *clearing house* for all of its own shares.
  The process involved in the sale of fund shares from the fund to the investor may take different forms. The possibilities are:

- From the fund to the investor directly (no middle person) — **A**
- From the fund to an underwriter to the investor — **B**
- From the fund to the underwriter to a dealer to the investor — **C**
- From the fund to an underwriter to a plan company to the investor — **D**

MAJOR DISTRIBUTION ARRANGEMENTS:

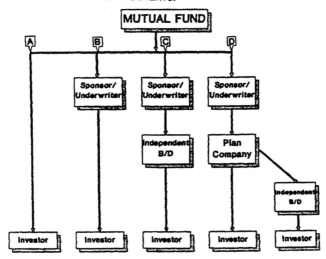

Note that in the different methods of fund purchase all are through an underwriter. Another term for an underwriter is a *distributor* or *sponsor* of a specific mutual fund's shares. The underwriter can sell directly to investors or through other investment dealers, such as major brokerage houses. A fund underwriter may have any number of dealers operating under a *dealer agreement* for the sale of fund shares to each dealer's clients. The dealer is paid a commission or *dealer's reallowance*, which is part of the *sales charge*.

It should be noted that the price to the investor is the same under any of the above methods; that is, the investor pays the public offering price or asked price per share. A portion of this sales charge is "reallowed" to the dealer involved.

The fund itself deals with only its "underwriter" which often is the same organization, company, etc. Sales charges, where applicable, are deducted by the underwriter. Shares are issued in the name of the ultimate purchaser (investor) and, upon redemption, all net proceeds are paid to the investor. Intervening sales organizations such as *underwriters, or dealers* merely help to sell funds — and receive a commission for their service.

It should also be noted that a dealer ordering mutual fund shares from the fund (or underwriter) can only place a specific order if (1) a customer has given the dealer a specific order or (2) it is for the dealer's own personal investment and *not* for an inventory account. All orders, of course, are paid for in cash.

A dealer, thus, cannot speculate in mutual fund shares; that is, buy them in hopes they will go up and then sell them to clients with a built-in profit (as they can on regular securities).

III.   MUTUAL FUND PRICING

All mutual fund shares are priced by calculation of the *net asset value* (NAV) per share, which is as stipulated in the prospectus but usually at the *close* of business on every business day. All securities in the mutual fund portfolio are valued as of the close of business and the total value is divided by the total number of outstanding shares. This calculation gives the *actual* dollar and cents value per share.

For example, at the close of business today:

$$\frac{\text{Portfolio value (\$10,000,000)[1]}}{\text{Number of outstanding shares (1,000,000)}} = \$10 \text{ NAV per share}$$

Daily changes in the net asset value result from changes in the value of the fund portfolio. *Additions* to the net asset value result from increases in the quoted values of the securities, dividends, and interest received in the fund portfolio. *Deductions* from the net asset value result from decreases in the value of the securities and any expenses assessed. The net asset value becomes the *bid price* for a mutual fund share. On any given day, the bid price of a mutual fund becomes the *transaction price* for shareholders who redeem their shares. Prices of mutual fund shares are found in the financial pages of most major newspapers.

---

[1]   Less accrued expenses.

Sales Charges and Quantity Discounts

For mutual funds that have *sales charges* (and many do!), the *asked* or *offering* price per share is arrived at by *adding* the sales charges to the bid price. The prospectus of a mutual fund provides a detailed explanation of the calculation of sales charges. The maximum sales charge is 8½% of the public offering price. Almost all funds are substantially less than that due to marketplace competition, e.g., 4%.

TABLE 5-2.

MUTUAL FUND QUOTATIONS

	NAV	Offer Price	NAV Chg.
GIEA t	11.39	11.93	-.09
GllnA p	10.50	10.94	...
GIGIA p	8.68	9.09	-.01
GrthA p	18.69	19.57	+.01
HilnA p	7.93	8.26	...
IncA p	9.73	10.14	...
InvGA p	10.40	10.83	...
MHIA p x	10.48	10.92	...
NTxA p	11.68	12.17	+.01
NYTA p x	10.47	10.91	...
RgFA p	16.56	17.34	...
STGIA p	9.68	9.98	...
USGA p	9.99	10.41	...
AsstB t	11.31	11.31	-.02
ATLB t	12.33	12.33	-.01
BlueB t	16.43	16.43	-.05
CalTB t	11.40	11.40	...
CapAB t	10.50	10.50	-.06
DvGB t	21.58	21.58	-.05
EuGB t	7.18	7.18	-.01
GrthB t	18.50	18.50	+.02
GIEB t	11.36	11.36	-.09
GllnB t	10.48	10.48	...
GIGIB t	8.62	8.62	-.01
HilnB t	7.92	7.92	+.01
IncB t	9.73	9.73	...
InvGB t	10.40	10.40	...
MHIB t x	10.48	10.48	+.01
NTxB t	11.68	11.68	+.01
NYTB t x	10.47	10.47	+.01
RgFB t	16.48	16.48	+.01
STGIB t	9.66	9.66	+.01
USGB t	10.00	10.00	+.01
DvGD p	21.64	21.64	-.05
GllnD t	10.49	10.49	...
HilncD p	7.93	7.93	+.01
NTxD p	11.68	11.68	+.01
STGID p	9.66	9.66	...
USGD p	9.99	9.99	...

	NAV	Offer Price	NAV Chg.
Pilgrim Grp:			
AUS I-A	7.29	7.29	...
ARS I	7.22	7.22	...
ARS I-A	7.23	7.23	...
ARS II	7.27	7.49	...
AdjUS	7.27	7.27	...
AdjUSII	7.30	7.53	...
AUSIII	7.29	7.67	...
CpUtl p	10.12	10.43	...
GNMA	13.80	14.23	+.02
HiYld p	5.79	5.97	...
MagC	12.62	13.28	-.05
STMMII	8.10	8.10	...
ShiTr p	7.24	7.46	-.01
Pillar Funds:			
EqAgA	10.72	NL	-.08
EqGrA	10.49	NL	-.01
EqInA	10.65	NL	-.01
FxdInA	10.31	NL	+.01
STInvA	10.02	NL	...
Pioneer Fund:			
EqInc p	14.95	15.86	-.03
Bond p	9.37	9.81	+.01
CapGr p	13.94	14.79	+.11
MuBd p	10.28	10.76	+.01
Europ p	14.94	15.85	+.07
Fund p	22.18	23.53	-.03
Pionr II p	19.60	20.80	-.02
PThre p	19.58	20.77	+.04
US Gv p	10.19	10.67	...
Piper Jaffray:			
Balan p	12.10	12.60	-.03
EmGr	16.32	17.00	-.09
Govt	...	...	...
GrInc	10.05	10.47	-.02
InstGv	...	...	...
MNTE	10.73	11.18	+.01
NatTE	10.87	11.32	+.01
PacEurG	10.11	10.11	+.02

	NAV	Offer Price	NAV Chg.
RchTng	17.83	NL	-.03
Rey BC	15.43	NL	-.56
Rightime Group:			
BlueC p	30.52	32.04	-.06
RT fp	36.18	NL	-.01
GvSc p	13.10	13.75	+.03
Grth p	27.93	29.32	-.03
MidCap p	28.52	29.94	-.10
SocAw p	30.77	32.30	-.10
Rimco Bd	10.21	10.31	...
Rimco Stk	10.16	10.26	+.02
RiverInE	10.56	11.06	+.03
RiverGVI	9.74	9.96	...
RivCapEq	11.45	11.80	+.01
RivCapFI	10.29	10.61	+.01
RobSEG p	16.31	NL	-.06
RobSVP	10.71	10.71	+.01
Rochester Fds:			
Convt p	11.18	11.56	+.01
RoMu p	17.60	18.33	+.01
LtdNY p	3.16	3.22	...
TxMod p	10.06	10.85	-.03
Rodney Square:			
DivIn p	13.08	13.55	...
Gwth p	16.13	16.80	-.06
IntlEq p	9.57	9.97	+.03
Rushmore Group:			
AGas	10.54	NL	-.04
Nova	9.95	NL	...
SMP Id	17.12	NL	-.01
OTC Id	15.07	NL	-.06
USGLg	10.43	NL	+.01
US Gov	10.51	NL	+.02
MD TF	10.53	NL	+.01
VA TF	10.74	NL	...
SBSF Cv	11.01	11.01	-.01
SBSF Gr	15.68	15.68	-.04
SEI Funds:			
Bond p	10.74	NL	+.01

	NAV	Offer Price	NAV Chg.
Divers	9.57	10.05	-.03
Progrs	14.32	15.03	-.03
TaxEx	10.84	11.01	...
USGv p	5.25	5.53	+.01
St FarmFds:			
Balan	31.18	31.18	-.02
Gwth	22.96	22.96	-.06
Interm	10.46	10.46	...
Muni	8.34	8.34	+.01
StStreet Resh:			
Exc	206.53	206.53	-.56
Gth	113.14	113.14	-.64
Inv	9.35	9.79	-.06
Steadman Funds:			
Am Ind	1.39	NL	-.01
Assoc	.74	NL	...
Invest	1.36	NL	...
Ocean	2.62	NL	-.03
Stein Roe Fds:			
Cap Op	25.24	NL	-.15
GvtInc	10.34	NL	+.01
HYMu	11.55	NL	+.01
Income	9.52	NL	...
IntBd	8.90	NL	...
IntMu	11.18	NL	...
MgdM	9.12	NL	+.01
PrimE	14.25	NL	-.01
Specl	22.46	NL	-.10
Stock	26.34	NL	-.12
TotRet	26.96	NL	-.04
StratDv	28.40	NL	-.03
Strat Gth	20.20	NL	-.01
Strong Funds:			
Advtg	10.02	NL	...
CmStk	14.63	NL	+.02
Discov	15.57	NL	...
GovSc	10.43	NL	+.01
Inco	9.36	NL	...

To calculate the percentage of sales charges for a mutual fund, use the formula:

$$\text{Percent sales charge} = \frac{\text{Asked price - Bid price}}{\text{Asked price}}$$

For example:

Bid price = $9.15

Asked price = $10.00

$$\text{Percent sales charge} = \frac{\$10.00 - \$9.15}{\$10.00} = \frac{.85}{\$10.00} = 8\tfrac{1}{2}\%$$

Many mutual funds offer *quantity discounts* when large dollar amounts are invested. These discounts are referred to as *breakpoints* and are fully disclosed in the company's prospectus. Table 5.3 below is a sample of a typical quantity discount.

These breakpoints or quantity discounts are allowed to any person who wishes to invest; they are not available to investment clubs banding together for the purpose of purchasing securities. However, a fiduciary, such as a pension, profit-sharing account, or custodial account is considered "any person," and can purchase mutual fund shares and receive breakpoint savings on sales charges.

Reduced Sales Charges   Associated with quantity discounts are *reduced sales charges*, which are available when *lump sums* are invested (see Table 5.3) or when a *letter of intent* (LOI) is used. With a LOI, the investor can contribute additional money and qualify for reduced sales charges:

- Within *thirteen months* of a specific purchase
- By *back dating ninety days* from a specific purchase

Even though an investor has signed an LOI indicating the contribution of additional money, the underwriter or distributor still *deducts* the *entire* sales charge. The portion of the sales charge that would be saved *if* further money were contributed is used to purchase additional fund shares. These shares are held in escrow. When the investor deposits more money to meet the LOI requirements, these shares are turned over to him or her. For example:

TABLE 5.3   Quantity Discount Table (breakpoints)

Amounts Invested	Sales Charge
$0 to $9,999	8½%
$10,000 to $24,999	7%
$25,000 to $49,999	6%
$50,000 to $99,999	4%
$100,000 to $249,000	3%
$250,000 and above	2%

SITUATION:
        Sales charge = 8½%
        Breakpoint for $10,000 = 7%
        Investment = $5,000 (1,000 shares at $5 per share)
        LOI (for thirteen months) = $5,000
RESULT:
        8½% ($425) is deducted for sales charge
        1½% ($75) is used to purchase fifteen additional shares in escrow

Fifteen shares are turned over to investor when an additional $5,000 is contributed *and* the additional $5,000 is accepted at the lower sales charge.

Note that the investor is *not* obligated to invest more money. If no additional money is contributed, the higher sales charge is paid. Please note also it is only the underwriter or distributor, and not the investor who is obligated by the LOI (to accept the total amount of money at a lower sales charge).

Right of Accumulation (ROA)   Many mutual funds offer what is called a *right of accumulation*. This term refers to the shareholder's opportunity to count the current total dollar value of all shares owned in several funds under the same management toward the purchase of additional shares to gain the breakpoint savings.

For example, if a shareholder owns $8,000 of a specific fund (valued on the net asset that day), but $10,000 offers a breakpoint for lower commissions, then all new contributions by that shareholder receive the discounted value (lower sales charge) as soon as the $10,000 level is reached. This right of accumulation usually extends for the *lifetime of ownership* (never less than 10 years) and is *not* limited to the thirteen months, as in a LOI. The Right of Accumulation privilege with some fund groups can include other family members.

Investors may have different accounts funded by a particular mutual fund group. Most mutual funds allow a combination of fund shares held by a single individual to be totaled when considering discounted sales charges under *either* the right of accumulation or the LOI.

Please note that the main difference between these two privileges, other than limited time frame of LOI, is that with LOI the investor has achieved the lower sales charges on the *entire* investment. With ROA, it is the lower sales charges on only new money coming in.

Dollar Cost Averaging   A favored form of investment for individuals who are investing from their current income is *dollar cost averaging* (DCA). Dollar cost averaging occurs when a fixed amount at fixed intervals is invested, without concern for the daily value of fund shares. This method assures that the average cost per share will *always* be below the average price per share during the same time period.

The major *benefit* of dollar cost averaging is that more shares are purchased when per share values are low and fewer when per share values are high, which is exactly the correct thing to do and happens automatically. Many investors like the dollar cost averaging approach because it uses their current income to purchase securities and it removes the need to decide when to *buy*. In contrast, a *shortcoming* of dollar cost averaging is that it does *not* tell the investor when to *sell* his or her fund shares. Therefore, if the investor liquidates during a down period in the market, there is no guarantee that he or she will be able to sell the total shares for as much as they cost originally.

This is tricky, isn't it — the difference between "average cost" per share and "average price" per share? Maybe Table 5.4 will help.

TABLE 5.4   Dollar Cost Averaging

If $100 per month is invested at intervals when the per share value is:		
Per share value	Amount Invested	Shares Purchased
$10.00	$100.00	10
$9.00	$100.00	11.1
$5.00	$100.00	20
$10.00	$100.00	10
$20.00	$100.00	5
Total: $54.00	Total Invested: $500.00	Total Shares Purchased: 56.1

The average *cost* per share = $8.91 ($500 ÷ 56.1 shares)
The average *price* per share over this period = $10.80 ($54 ÷ 5)
Note: The end result is what the investor wants — the lowest possible average *cost* per share.

QUICK QUIZ 2

6.   The conversion privilege for a mutual fund refers to the fact that   Reference:
      shares of one fund may be converted to shares of another fund   Page 5-7
      under the same management with no sales charge.
           True/False

7.   Under the distribution method of mutual funds, dealers may order   Reference:
      mutual funds for only two reasons: Page 5-12
      a.   For their own personal investment
      b.   Because their clients gave them orders
           True/False

8.   Dealers may not inventory mutual fund shares and then sell them   Reference:
      to their customers.   Page 5-12
           True/False

9.   A mutual fund has a net asset value of $9.15 and an asked price   Reference:
      of $10.00 per share. The percentage sales charge of this mutual   Page 5-13
      fund is _____.

10.   A *letter of intent* usually covers what period of time?   Reference:
                                                                                Page 5-14

11.   An investment club can purchase mutual fund shares on a re-   Reference:
       duced sales charge basis (breakpoint) if the total purchase is   Page 5-14
       sizable enough.
           True/False

12.   The *right of accumulation* refers to the opportunity of the share-   Reference:
       holder to include existing fund shares with new purchases for   Page 5-15
       breakpoint and reduced sales charge purposes.
           True/False

13.   An investor using the *dollar cost averaging* approach to invest-   Reference:
       ment can always be sure that the average price per share is less   Page 5-15
       than the average cost per share.
           True/False

   ANSWERS: 6-True; 7-True; 8-True; 9-8½%; 10-thirteen months; 11-False; 12-True;
13-False.

IV.   REDEMPTION OF OPEN-END INVESTMENT COMPANY SHARES

An investor may sell (redeem) his or her mutual fund shares back to the mutual fund at any time. Normally the investor does not have the actual certificates but instead has a confirmation statement showing the total number of shares owned. In this case, a written request to the transfer agent of the mutual fund, along with a signature guaranteed by a NYSE firm, or a national bank is required. Actually, anyone acceptable to the transfer agent can guarantee the customer's signature. A state bank or NASD member is permitted to do so only if the transfer agent consents. National banks and NYSE members are always permitted to guarantee signatures.

If an investor wants actual certificates, he or she must request them. (A possible use for certificates is collateral for a loan.) When selling, the investor must include the certificates (signed on the back or signed with a stock power) and the signature guarantee. In addition, the investor might include a written request to the transfer agent including the intent to redeem.

An investor redeeming mutual fund shares sells at the next *computed* redemption price (net asset value or bid price), determined after receipt of the redemption request. All redemption requests are time-stamped so that no question will arise regarding the exact dollar amount due per share. Occasionally, mutual funds have a *redemption fee* which is a percentage (1%; 2%) of the amount redeemed. The mutual fund itself is required to make payment to the shareholder within *seven calendar days* after the proper presentation of the signed shares and/or written request. (Remember this point; it is important — seven calendar days.)

If an investor deals with an underwriter who has agreed to "repurchase" mutual fund shares, the net asset value is calculated by the same procedure described above.

All redeemed shares may *not* be resold by the mutual fund and are physically destroyed; that is, shares are canceled. Any new purchasers of that fund are issued *new* shares; that is, shares never owned before. Remember, the fund underwriter is ultimately the final authority for all purchases and redemptions of its shares.

V.   CLASSES OF FUND SHARES

Some mutual funds offer classes of shares that allow for different sales charges and fees. The following is an example of how a fund may classify shares as *Class A, Class B, Class C or Class D* shares.

- Class A shares have a *sales load* — that is, the charge is paid at purchase; the charge is the difference between the purchase price and the net amount invested.
- Class B shares have a *back-end load* — that is, the charge is paid at redemption; the charge is a contingent deferred sales load.
- Class C shares have a *level load* — that is, the charge is an annually paid asset-based fee.
- Class D shares have both an asset-based fee and a contingent deferred sales charge.

The class of shares determines the type of sales charge only; all other rights associated with ownership of mutual fund shares remain the same across each class.

A fund that has deferred sales charge *or* 12(b)-1 fee of more than .25 of 1% of net assets cannot be described by salespeople as "no load" the NASD has ruled. To do so would be a violation of the Rules of Fair Practice.

QUICK QUIZ 3

14.   Mutual funds are required to redeem fund shares tended to it with-   Reference:
        in a period of _____ _____ days.   Page 5-17

15.   The price received for redeemed mutual fund shares by an investor   Reference:
        will be based on: Page 5-17
        a.   The offered price per share
        b.   The net asset value per share
        c.   The median between the bid and asked price per share
        d.   The net asset value per share plus the sales charge
        e.   The asked price per share

16.   The signature guarantees for investors wishing to redeem fund   Reference:
        shares can be made by which of the following?   Page 5-17
        I.   A national bank
        II.   An NYSE brokerage firm
        III.   An NASD broker/dealer if acceptable to the transfer agent
        IV.   The transfer agent itself
               a.   I
               b.   I and II
               c.   I, II and III
               d.   I, II and IV
               e.   All of the above

                                ANSWERS: 14-seven calendar; 15-b; 16-c.

REAL LIFE SITUATION

Ms. Trevor Tripe, former dairy queen turned equestrienne, made your acquaintance at a recent horse auction and wanted some "new investments befitting her stature in life." Ms. Tripe wanted some "fundamentally strong" recommendations as to mutual fund investing. Your first round of advice to Ms. Tripe was:

Directions: *For each of the numbered recommendations that follow, please select A, B, or C as the evaluation you deem most correct. Place your selection on the line preceding each number.*

A. Totally inappropriate, you should get a job cleaning out the stables.	B. Inappropriate, one or more shortcomings are present.	C. A suitable recommendation under the circumstances.

Answer

_____ 1.   After selecting a group of funds the objectives of which are the same as hers, a comparison of past performance, expense ratios, and management fees should be made.

_____ 2.   Quite possibly a venture into the restaurant business would be "made to order" for her desires of a new investment befitting her stature in life.

_____ 3.   A vital consideration: if an open-end investment company, is the fund willing to buy back its shares in the future (redeem them)?

_____ 4.   Most mutual funds have the same sales charge and performance is somewhat similar, so it shouldn't be too difficult a decision for her to make as to which fund.

_____ 5.   Just as in horse breeding, past performance and current management are difficult to measure but worth the effort if you intend to be a winner.

ANSWERS: 1-C; 2-A; 3-A; 4-A; 5-C.

CHECK YOUR UNDERSTANDING
(Circle one)

1.   A requirement when comparing mutual funds is that the highest sales charges be shown.
      True/False

Reference:
Page 5-7

2.   The annual management fee is one of the expenses that may be deducted directly from the fund.
     True/False

Reference: Page 5-9

3.   Dealers routinely maintain an inventory of mutual fund shares for speculation.
     True/False

Reference: Page 5-12

4.   The calculation of sales charges is explained in the prospectus of a mutual fund.
     True/False

Reference: Page 5-13

5.   *Breakpoints* or *quantity discounts* are allowed to any investors including investment clubs.
     True/False

Reference: Page 5-14

6.   A *letter of intent* is one method of qualifying for reduced sales charges.
     True/False

Reference: Page 5-14

7.   The *right of accumulation* usually extends for the life of ownership, whereas the letter of intent is limited to thirteen months.
     True/False

Reference: Page 5-15

8.   Mutual fund shares can be redeemed by the investor only at specified times.
     True/False

Reference: Page 5-17

9.   A shareholder can expect payment from a mutual fund four to six weeks from proper presentation of signed shares and/or written request.
     True/False

Reference: Page 5-17

10. The pricing of mutual funds starts with the calculation of net asset value (NAV) per share, which is determined at the close of every business day.
     True/False

Reference: Page 5-12

ANSWERS: 1-True; 2-True; 3-False; 4-True; 5-False; 6-True; 7-True; 8-False; 9-False; 10-True.

STUDY NOTES

6

THE OPERATION OF OPEN-END INVESTMENT COMPANIES

PRETEST
(Circle one)

1. The officers of a mutual fund are appointed by: Reference:
    Page 6-3
    a.   A majority vote of shareholders
    b.   A majority vote of the Board of Directors
    c.   The Board of Directors or its delegates
    d.   A shareholder committee
    e.   The NASD

2. The investment management company that provides advice to   Reference:
    the fund via an advisory contract would generally be compensated: Page 6-4
    a.   By an annual fee negotiated at the beginning of the year
    b.   By a salary plus bonus system
    c.   By the Board of Directors directly
    d.   By the shareholders directly
    e.   By a percentage of the average daily net assets of the
         fund to which they are providing advice

3. All of the following are rights of open-end investment company   Reference:
    shareholders except: Page 6-4
    a.   The right to elect officers of the fund
    b.   The right to approve investment advisory agreements
    c.   The right to vote by proxy
    d.   The right to receive audited annual reports
    e.   The right to approve any change in the investment policy of the fund

4.   If the bid price (NAV) of a particular mutual fund is $14, the   Reference:
        underwriter's concession is $.80, and the total sales charges is   Page 6-6
        $1, a purchaser paying $10,000 into the fund would receive how
        many shares?
        a.   633 shares
        b.   666 shares
        c.   681 shares
        d.   714 shares
        e.   Cannot be determined from information given

5.   The custodian and transfer agent fees, which are set by contract,   Reference:
        are paid from: Page 6-6
        a.   Sales charges of the mutual fund
        b.   The annual management fee
        c.   Directly from the assets of the fund
        d.   Directly by the Board of Directors
        e.   Directly by the shareholders at the end of the year

6.   A majority of the non-affiliated directors must specifically approve   Reference:
        which of the following?   Page 6-4
        a.   The fund's auditors
        b.   The fund's investment advisory contract
        c.   The fund's officers
        d.   The appointment of the fund's custodial bank
        e.   All of the above

7.   The basic investment policy of a mutual fund can only be changed   Reference:
        by: Page 6-3
        a.   The Board of Directors
        b.   The investment advisor
        c.   Majority vote of the officers
        d.   The shareholders
        e.   All of the above

8.   Generally, employees of the management company (investment   Reference:
        advisor) to a mutual fund can also be: Page 6-4
        a.   Employees of the SEC
        b.   Employees of the auditing firm
        c.   Employees of the custodian bank
        d.   Employees of the NASD
        e.   None of the above

9.   The fund is required to report its portfolio holdings to shareholders: Reference:
      a.   Annually   Page 6-4
      b.   Semi-annually
      c.   Bi-annually
      d.   Only when a major change takes place
      e.   At no specific time

10.   Such expenses as printing sales literature and distribution costs for   Reference:
      the sales solicitation in a mutual fund organization are borne by: Page 6-6
      a.   The shareholders directly by assessment
      b.   The shareholders indirectly because these are expenses
            of the fund itself
      c.   The investment management firm
      d.   The custodian bank
      e.   The underwriter or sponsor or through a 12(b)1 plan

                ANSWERS: 1-c; 2-e; 3-a; 4-b; 5-c; 6-b; 7-d; 8-e; 9-b; 10-e.

OVERVIEW

This chapter examines the *structure and operation* of open-end investment companies and discusses the functions of the *Board of Directors* and the *management company*. The *rights of shareholders* is an important topic covered in the chapter, as well as the *procedures* used by underwriters and transfer agents with regard to the cancellation of fund shares and the issuance of new shares.

Author's Note to Candidates

An understanding of the internal operation of an investment company will provide insight into the functions of an investment company, the investment advisory contract, and the procedures for issuing and redeeming mutual fund shares through the use of transfer agents.

I.   THE BOARD OF DIRECTORS AND THE INVESTMENT MANAGEMENT COMPANY

The Board of Directors has responsibility for the overall operation of an open-end investment company. Like any corporation, the Board of Directors *appoints the officers* of the firm or, in this case, of the fund itself. The Board also is responsible for the investment management (advisory contract) of the fund. The Board of Directors must follow the objectives of the company as well as the policies. There is, however, one function the Board of Directors *cannot* perform. They cannot change the basic investment objectives of the fund. Only a *majority* vote of the outstanding shares can change the investment policies — since this is such a far-reaching decision.

The *investment management team* is responsible for *supervising* the investment portfolio to make sure that the basic investment objectives of the fund are followed precisely. *Internal operating committees* (such as a committee of Board or officers of the fund) all assure that the *implementation* of policy decisions by the Board of Directors is carried out.

The choice of a *management company* is most crucial for the Board of Directors and indeed the shareholders, of an open-end investment company. The management company is the organization that advises the fund *what* securities to buy and sell and *when*. Usually an *investment advisory contract* exists between the management company and the fund itself. This is often a one- or two-year contract. Frequently, there are "interlocking directorates"; that is, the directors of one company serve on the Board of Directors of other firms in which they have a financial interest. Also, there would be a conflict of interest for the fund to employ anyone connected with the auditing (accounting) firm or the custodian (bank) of the fund. These relationships are prohibited. Since the investment advisory contract is of such importance, it must be approved by a *majority vote* of the Board of Directors and a majority of the non-affiliated directors and a majority vote of the outstanding shares. It is interesting to note that interlocking directorates exist; that is, members of the Board of Directors of the fund are also members of the investment advisory management company. However, as mentioned, a majority of the *outside* directors (non-affiliated) *must* approve the *investment advisory contract* and it must be submitted for shareholder approval the first time.

One of the key reasons that the work of the investment management firm is very closely related to the operation of the fund is the substantial fee to the investment advisor involved. (Think of it. One-half of one percent of a $100,000,000 fund is $500,000 annually and one-half of one percent of $1,000,000,000 under a management is $5,000,000.) Frequently the management fee is scaled down with the size of the fund. In all cases, however, the method used to calculate the management fee is fully identified in the prospectus. It is customary to establish a *ceiling* on expenses of the fund and on the management. These limits are specified in the prospectus as a *protection* to shareholders. The *expense ratio* (expenses as a percentage of total assets) is an important *indicator* of how well the fund is managed.

II.   RIGHTS OF SHAREHOLDERS

One of the major rights of shareholders has already been mentioned, namely, the right of the shareholders to change the basic investment policy of a mutual fund by a majority vote. Shareholders have other voting rights, including the right:

- To approve the investment advisory agreement via proxy (mail) or in person
- To elect the Board of Directors
- To select or ratify an independent auditing firm

When the fund is a corporation (most frequent), the shareholders are solicited annually to allow a certain designated individual of the company (often the secretary) to vote their shares via *proxy*. Each proxy solicitation states the management's opinion on how the shareholders should vote. Some funds are organized as business trusts and, as such, do not have annual meetings.

A report must be sent semi-annually to all shareholders. The report must list the current holdings of the fund and report all salient items taking place during that year. Also, investment companies must provide the SEC with an audited annual report (not semi-annual).

QUICK QUIZ 1

1. The officers of a mutual fund are appointed by: Reference:
    a. A majority vote of shareholders   Page 6-3
    b. A majority vote of the Board of Directors
    c. The Board of Directors or its delegates
    d. A shareholder committee
    e. The NASD

2. The investment management company that provides advice to the   Reference:
    fund via an advisory contract would generally be compensated: Page 6-4
    a. By an annual fee negotiated at the beginning of the year
    b. By a salary plus bonus system
    c. By the Board of Directors directly
    d. By the shareholders directly
    e. By a percentage of the average daily net assets of the
        fund to which they are providing advice

3. All of the following are rights of open-end investment company   Reference:
    shareholders *except*:   Page 6-4
    a. The right to elect officers of the fund
    b. the right to approve investment advisory agreements
    c. The right to vote by proxy
    d. The right to receive audited annual reports
    e. The right to approve any change in the investment policy
        of the fund

                                            ANSWERS: 1-c; 2-e; 3-a.

CHART 6.1

Organization of Mutual Fund

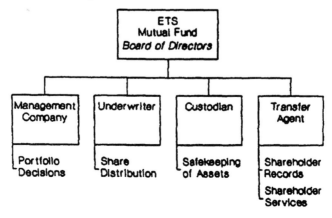

III.   FUNCTIONS OF THE UNDERWRITER

An *underwriter* is frequently referred to as a *sponsor* or *distributor*. This person, or organization, is responsible for selling fund shares to the public either though dealer agreements or directly to the investors.

One method of distribution is called *wholesaling*. Underwriters employ wholesalers, who aid in the distribution through securities dealers. It is these dealers who solicit and accept orders from their customers and place the orders directly with the fund underwriter.

The compensation of a fund underwriter is an important item. The underwriters are normally paid from the sales charge itself. For example:

Underwriter's concession	1½%
Dealers concession or reallowance	7%
Total sales charge	8½%

One of the most important functions of the underwriter is the preparation of sales literature, which must conform with all regulatory requirements. It is also the responsibility of the underwriter to *pay all sales expenses*, including the printing and distribution of sales literature and prospectuses.

IV.   CUSTODIAL AND TRANSFER FUNCTIONS

Whom do you think actually receives safeguards, the physical assets of the fund (securities, money, etc.)? The *custodian* — which is usually a national bank or trust company — assumes these responsibilities. For safety purposes, it would be *unwise* for the fund, in its business offices, to provide custodial functions. The custodian bank is paid a fee for its services.

Of equal importance is the transfer function by the *transfer agent*. The transfer agent, usually a separate organization, is designated to:

- Issue new shares
- Cancel redeemed shares
- Pay dividends and capital-gains distributions
- Maintain records on names, addresses, number of shares owned, and such, of fund shareholders
- Issue period reports and proxy solicitation on behalf of the fund

The transfer agent is sometimes called the *shareholder servicing agent* because it provides the aforementioned services to the fund's shareholders. Transfer agents also are paid an *annual fee* for their services directly from the fund. Please note that both the custodian's fee and the transfer agent's fee are direct expenses of the fund; that is, they are paid from shareholder's money.

QUICK QUIZ 2

4.   If the bid price (NAV) of a particular mutual fund is $14.00, the   Reference:
      underwriter's concession is $.80, and the total sales charge is   Page 6-6
      $1.00, a purchaser paying $10,000 into the fund would receive
      how many shares?
      a.   633 shares
      b.   666 shares
      c.   681 shares
      d.   714 shares
      e.   Cannot be determined from information given

5.   Issuing new fund shares and canceling old shares are functions   Reference:
      of the _____.   Page 6-6

6.   The custodian and transfer agent fees, which are set by contract,   Reference:
      are paid from: Page 6-6
      a.   Sales charges of the mutual fund
      b.   The annual management fee
      c.   Directly from the assets of the fund or some funds, the
            management fee includes all expenses
      d.   Directly by the Board of Directors
      e.   Directly by the shareholders at the end of the year

                    ANSWERS: 4-b; 5-transfer agent; 6-c.

REAL LIFE SITUATION

Hadley V. Hadrumple, III, haberdasher turned bank vice president has become convinced
that you can provide him an entree to mutual fund business for his bank. Unschooled as
Hadley is in the needs of a mutual fund, he asked you what a bank can, customarily, do
for a mutual fund organization. He "presses" you for information on exactly what a
commercial bank can offer. Your advice is:

Directions: *For each of the numbers recommendations that follow, please select A, B, or
C as the evaluation you deem most correct. Place your selection on the line preceding
each number:*

A. Inappropriate —
    about as embarrass-
    ing as bending over
    and splitting your
    pants at an Ameri-
    can Banker's Asso-
    ciation Meeting for
    Hadley.

B. Somewhat inappro-
    priate but not really
    wrong (somewhere
    between a very
    narrow tie, and a
    very wide tie for
    Hadley)!

C. Appropriate advice
    and recommenda-
    tion under the cir-
    cumstances.

Answer

_____ 1.   Mutual funds need a custodian not only to hold cash and securities for safekeeping but also to assist as "payables" and "receivables" on the securities transactions.

_____ 2.   Mutual funds do need transfer agents to issue new shares, cancel redeemed shares, allocate dividends and capital gain distributions, and generally service shareholders.

_____ 3.   With money coming in daily and valuable securities purchased daily, a "bank" needs to be a functional part of the mutual fund procedure.

_____ 4.   Custodian fees are the responsibility of each individual shareholder directly and each shareholder must use his or her bank for this service.

_____ 5.   His bank can probably get the "investment management contract" to advise the fund on purchases since this is usually a minor contract award by the fund.

ANSWERS: 1-C; 2-C; 3-C; 4-A 5-A.

CHECK YOUR UNDERSTANDING
(Circle one)

1.   The responsibility for the operation of the investment company lies with the Board of Directors.
     True/False

Reference:
Page 6-3

2.   The management company advises the fund which securities to buy and sell and when to execute the transactions.
     True/False

Reference:
Page 6-4

3.   The transfer agent has the option of sending periodic reports to shareholders.
     True/False

Reference:
Page 6-4

4.   The person or organization responsible for selling fund shares to the public is an underwriter.
     True/False

Reference:
Page 6-6

5.   Custodian and transfer agent fees, set by contract, are direct   Reference:
      expenses of the mutual fund.   Page 6-6
         True/False

6.   The payment of sales expenses, including printing and distribution   Reference:
      of sales literature and prospectus, is a function of the management   Page 6-6
      company.
         True/False

7.   An important indicator of how well the fund is managed is the   Reference:
      expense ratio (expenses as a percentage of total assets).   Page 6-4
         True/False

8.   One of a shareholder's major voting rights is to approve the invest-   Reference:
      ment advisory contracts.   Page 6-4
         True/False

9.   The transfer agent and custodian are always the same company.   Reference:
         True/False   Page 6-6

10.   The Board of Directors *cannot* change the basic investment objec-   Reference:
      tives of the fund, only the majority vote of outstanding shares can   Page 6-3
      change investment objectives.
         True/False

ANSWERS: 1-True; 2-True; 3-False; 4-True; 5-True; 6-False; 7-True; 8-True; 9-False;
10-True.

STUDY NOTES

STUDY NOTES

*"A professional is someone who can do his best
work when he doesn't feel like it."*
Alistair Cooke

7

FORMS OF MUTUAL FUND OWNERSHIP AND TAX TREATMENT

PRETEST
(Circle one)

1. Under which of the following forms of ownership will a decedent's ownership interest in property be passed to that decedent's heirs or designees through his or her estate?
    a. Joint tenants with right of ex-survivorship
    b. Joint tenants with right of survivorship
    c. Tenants by the entirety
    d. Tenants in common
    e. None of the above

    Reference:
    Page 7-4

2. Which of the following is a form of joint ownership only allowed between husband and wife?
    a. Joint tenants without right of survivorship
    b. Joint tenants with right of survivorship
    c. Tenants by the entirety
    d. Tenants in common
    e. None of the above

    Reference:
    Page 7-4

3. Under a Uniform Gifts to Minors Act transfer, the gift would be:
    I.   Revocable
    II.   Irrevocable
    III. Registered as a custodianship
    IV.   Registered as a guardianship
        a. I and II
        b. I and IV
        c. II and III
        d. II and IV
        e. II, III and IV

    Reference:
    Page 7-4

1

4. Which of the following forms of joint ownership of mutual funds will allow a joint tenant to sell a fractional interest in the property without permission of the other tenants? Reference: Page 7-4
    a.   Joint tenant with right of survivorship
    b.   Tenants by the entirety
    c.   Fractional interest joint tenancy
    d.   Tenants in common
    e.   Under no circumstances

5. Upon the death of one of the joint tenants in JTWROS the property interest of that joint tenant is distributed to: Reference: Page 7-4
    a.   The heirs of the estate
    b.   By will of the joint tenant
    c.   The other joint tenant(s)
    d.   Whoever is designated by state law
    e.   None of the above

6. Under the Uniform Gift to Minors Act, which of the following statements is correct? Reference: Page 7-4
    I.   If the donor is named as custodian, income is taxable to the donor
    II.   Only mutual funds shares can be used as qualifying gifts
    III. A minor doesn't have to file an income tax return regardless of income
    IV.   Gifts to minors are not gift-tax items
        a.   I
        b.   III
        c.   IV
        d.   I, II, III and IV
        e.   None of the above

7. Closed-end investment company shares can be purchased: Reference: Page 7-10
    a.   Directly from the fund itself
    b.   From other shareholders through a brokerage house
    c.   By writing to the underwriter
    d.   For the net asset value
    e.   Without normal sales commissions levied

8.   An individual wishing to sell closed-end investment company   Reference:
      shares must: Page 7-10
      a.   Tender to the fund for redemption
      b.   Send to the transfer agent for redemption
      c.   Redeem at net asset value per share minus a redemption
            fee if applicable
      d.   Find a purchaser for these shares
      e.   Be assured of a profit if held for more than twelve months
            and one day

9.   Under the Uniform Gift to Minors Act, what exclusion allowance   Reference:
      (in dollars) is applicable annually to a gift to a minor from one   Page 7-4
      parent (no joint gift) before the gift is subject to gift taxes?
      a. $10,000
      b. $5,000
      c. $30,000
      d.   A dollar amount according to a government table
      e.   None

10.   To apply the conduit tax principle to mutual funds, a minimum of   Reference:
      90% of which of the following must be passed to shareholders?   Page 7-6
      a.   All gross income
      b.   Net investment income
      c.   Net investment income and realized capital gains
      d.   Net investment income and unrealized and realized capital gains
      e.   All income and all capital gains (realized and unrealized)

            ANSWERS: 1-d; 2-c; 3-c; 4-d; 5-c; 6-e; 7-b; 8-d; 9-a; 10-c.

OVERVIEW

Like any property, there are many different ways that mutual funds can be owned (e.g., individually, joint ownership, trust accounts). Mutual funds are very attractive as gifts because management of assets is built in. There are a number of unique tax principles that apply to mutual fund ownership that will be discussed in detail in this chapter. Also included here is a discussion of the differences between open-end and closed-end investment companies.

Author's Note to Candidates

The exact tax treatment of mutual fund ownership is a matter of importance to all prospective clients. The *taxation* of distributions and the *redemption* of mutual fund shares will be part of your Series 6 test. This chapter will provide the answers.

I.   MUTUAL FUND OWNERSHIP

Joint ownership of mutual fund shares is possible just like any other type of property. Two such forms of joint ownership are:

    1.   Joint tenants with the right of survivorship
    2.   Tenants in common

The term *joint tenants with the right of survivorship* (JTWROS) applies to *undivided* property owned by two or more individuals. As the title implies, at the death of one of the joint tenants, the property is *automatically* owned by the other tenant or tenants. Because the *entire* property automatically goes to another at death, this property does not go through probate and heirs of the decedent (who are not joint tenants) have no right to claim ownership. The *tax* consequences, while living, are divided *equally* among joint tenants. At death, if joint owners are spouses, then one-half is included in estate of deceased for estate tax purposes (if non-spouses, based upon percentage of contribution).

Joint tenancy with the right of survivorship can be created between husband and wife. This is JTWROS by *tenants by the entirety*. Note that tenants by the entirety can apply between legally *married* spouses only. Under JTWROS and tenants by the entirety, the property cannot be sold without the permission of other joint tenants.

Tenants in common is fund ownership in which each of two or more individuals has a *fractional interest*. Each tenant has a *specific, designated* interest — just as in a "partnership," where one partner can sell his or her share *without* permission of the other partners, so it is with tenants in common. At the death of one of the tenants, the other tenant or tenants do *not* come into ownership. Rather, the fractional interest may be left to whomever the deceased designates. *Taxation*, under tenants in common, is *proportionally* determined by fractional interest of ownership.

Another, and by far the *most common form* of mutual fund ownership, is *individual ownership*. This form also applies to *trusts* that own mutual fund shares registered to the trust. In this manner, the trust holds all the rights of a shareholder.

A special law influencing a type of ownership is the *Uniform Gifts/Transfers To Minors Acts*. This law permits the establishment of a custodian account for a minor in which mutual fund shares are often a suitable investment. All states have some type of Uniform Gifts to Minors Acts by which property is given *irrevocably* to a minor and placed in a custodial account until the minor reaches the age of majority (eighteen in many states). The donor may *not change his or her mind about the gift*. *However, the donor* may be named as custodian for the account. (If the grantor names himself/herself as custodian the value of the account will be taxed in the grantor's estate for estate tax purposes.) The account assets can be used for the benefit of the minor *only*, and *must* be turned over to the minor at the age of majority. One of the most important aspects of this arrangement is that income and profits in a Uniform Gifts to Minors account are taxable to the minor and not to the donor. This can result in income tax savings. However, if the minor is under age 14, unearned income in excess of a permitted amount (e.g., $1,300 per year, as indexed) is taxed at the parent's maximum marginal rate.

Since a Uniform Gifts to Minors account is truly a gift, normal gift-tax rules apply; that is, $10,000 may be given to one person in one year with no gift tax implication ($20,000 if joint husband and wife gift). All gifts of more than $10,000 per year per person are subject to gift tax and a federal gift tax return must be filed.

An example of how mutual funds are registered under the Uniform Gifts to Minors Acts would be: Carleton Fisk as custodian for Jamie Fisk under the New Hampshire UGMA.

QUICK QUIZ 1

1. Under which form of ownership will a deceased person's fund ownership be passed to heirs or designees?

    Reference: Page 7-4

    a. Joint tenants without right of survivorship
    b. Joint tenants with right of survivorship
    c. Tenants by the entirety
    d. Tenants in common
    e. None of the above

2. The form of joint ownership that can be used *only* between husband and wife is:

    Reference: Page 7-4

    a. Joint tenants without right of survivorship
    b. Joint tenants with right of survivorship
    c. Tenants by the entirety
    d. Tenants in common
    e. None of the above

3. Corporations, partnerships, or trusts may own mutual fund shares as an investment.

    Reference: Page 7-4

    True/False

4. Under a Uniform Gifts to Minors Acts transfer, the gift is:

    Reference: Page 7-4

    I.   Revocable
    II.   Irrevocable
    III. Registered as a custodianship
    IV.   Registered as a guardianship
        a. I and III
        b. I and IV
        c. II and III
        d. II and IV
        e. II, III, and IV

ANSWERS: 1-d; 2-c; 3-True; 4-c.

II.   FEDERAL INCOME TAXATION OF MUTUAL FUNDS

Subchapter M of the Internal Revenue Code describes regulated investment companies that qualify for a special tax treatment of mutual funds and their shareholders. This treatment is called the *conduit* or *pipeline principle*. According to this principle, a mutual fund that distributes at least *90%* of all *net investment income* to its shareholders will *not* be taxed on that investment income. So only the shareholders will be taxed except for the amount the fund does not distribute. Remember that *all* distributions from mutual funds are tax-reportable income to the shareholders.

Chart 7.1

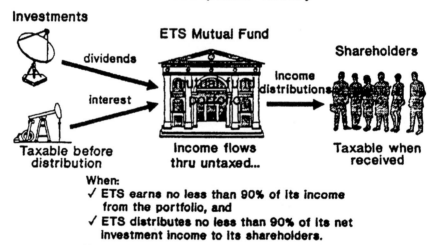

Taxation of Mutual Fund Distributions
Regulated Investment Companies
Conduit/Pipeline Theory

When:
✓ ETS earns no less than 90% of its income from the portfolio, and
✓ ETS distributes no less than 90% of its net investment income to its shareholders.
If not regulated, all income is taxed before distribution.

Dividend distributions from net investment income of mutual funds are taxed as ordinary income to the shareholder. Capital gains distributions are taxed as long-term capital gains. Capital gains may be offset with other capital losses by the investor.

As a matter of practice, most mutual funds make dividend distributions quarterly and capital-gain distributions only once, by regulation, at the end of the fiscal year. In all cases, the type of distribution is clearly reported to the shareholder. The shareholder is *responsible* for reporting dividend distributions and capital-gains distributions for federal taxation (if applicable). Federal regulations require that the mutual fund report to the Internal Revenue Service *all* distributions so that the IRS can cross-check to assure that each shareholder is reporting income properly.

When a mutual fund makes a capital-gains distribution to its shareholder, it is a *long-term* capital-gains distribution. This approach assures the long-term capital-gains taxation status. Because the holding period is already attained, it is not necessary for the shareholder to qualify for it. This step especially affects shareholders who have recently purchased their mutual fund shares (less than one year and one day). They received a capital-gains distribution, but it is still *long-term* capital gains because the fund held it for the required length of time.

As a practical matter, most mutual funds have short-term gains and losses during the year as well as long-term gains and losses. However, any net short-term gains (after offset against short-term losses) will not be paid out as long-term capital-gains distribution. They must be designated as a dividend since such a payment is considered ordinary income for taxation purposes.

If a mutual fund was to declare a capital gains dividend but not distribute it, the fund will notify the shareholders of the amount. The mutual fund will pay the federal income tax on the undistributed amount and the shareholder will receive a credit for taxes paid.

TAX EXEMPT MUNICIPALS

The Tax Reform Act of 1986 designates four categories of municipal bonds. The tax treatment varies among those categories. When a mutual fund passes through interest from bonds, it is exempt or taxed to the shareholder depending on its character.

Public purpose bonds issued after that date will continue to be income tax exempt. "Public purpose" includes bonds issued to meet essential government functions such as highway construction or school financing. Interest on non-public purpose bonds (used to finance housing and student loans, for example) will be partially income tax-exempt. The interest will be "excludible" for regular income tax purposes, but will be treated as a preference item in computing alternative minimum tax.

Taxable municipals are bonds issued to finance non-essential purposes such as upgrading pollution control facilities, building a sports stadium, or financing loans to farmers. They may be exempt from state or local income tax, but they will be subject to federal income tax.

QUICK QUIZ 2

5.   Which of the following forms of mutual fund joint ownership will allow a joint tenant to sell a fractional interest without permission of the other tenants?   Reference: Page 7-4
   a.   Joint tenant with right of survivorship
   b.   Tenants by the entirety
   c.   Fractional interest joint tenancy
   d.   Tenants in common
   e.   Under no circumstances

6.   Upon the death of one of the joint tenants in JTWROS, the property interest of that joint tenant is distributed to: Reference: Page 7-4
   a.   The heirs of the estate

> b.   By will of the joint tenant
> c.   To the other joint tenant or tenants
> d.   Whoever is designated by state law
> e.   None of the above

7.   Under the Uniform Gift to Minors Act, which of the following statements is correct?   Reference: Page 7-4
>   I.   If the donor is named as custodian, income is taxable to the donor
>   II.   Only mutual funds shares can be used as qualifying gifts
>   III. A minor doesn't have to file an income tax return regardless of income
>   IV.   Gifts to minors are not gift-tax items
>   a.   I
>   b.   III
>   c.   IV
>   d.   I, II, III, and IV
>   e.   None of the above

8.   Subchapter _____ of the Internal Revenue Code pertains to regulated investment companies and allows an investment company to pass along to shareholders at least _____ of its net investment income and capital gains.   Reference: Page 7-6

9.   An individual purchases mutual fund shares in October, and in December receives a capital-gain distribution. This capital-gain distribution would be taxed to the shareholder as _____.   Reference: Page 7-7

10.   Interest on non-essential municipal bonds is subject to federal income tax.   Reference; Page 7-7
>   True/False

ANSWERS: 5-d; 6-c; 7-e; 8-Subchapter M, 90%; 9-long-term; 10-True.

III.   MUTUAL FUND REDEMPTIONS

When a shareholder redeems from the fund, the fund has *seven calendar days* within which to make payment. The redemption is at next closing price (NAV). Federal taxation of mutual fund redemptions is the same as that which covers the sale of any other security; that is, if the fund shares are sold for more than their purchase price, then tax must be paid. Each shareholder must identify the total *cost basis* of all shares owned. All payments for the purchase of fund shares at different times must be identified as such.

Automatic reinvestment of dividends and capital-gains distribution will *add* to the total amount of fund shares owned by the shareholder. However, the distributions are taxed during the years they were reinvested so no taxation would apply at redemption (i.e., they will add to the *cost basis* of the shareholder). On the other hand, any rise in the actual price of these shares will be subject to tax. If the shareholder liquidates within a one year and one day period, *short-term* capital gains will apply (ordinary income). If the holding period is more than one year and one day, *long-term* capital gains will apply. Any shareholder liquidating only a portion of his or her shares must identify those shares being liquidated to ascertain:

- The *cost basis* of those specific shares, and
- The *holding period* of those specific shares.

Capital losses can be claimed by a shareholder if the value of shares redeemed is less than the cost basis. Capital losses are first offset against capital gains, and then, if capital losses exceed capital gains, a maximum of $3,000 per return including joint return is allowed per year against other taxable income. This $3,000 can be used year after year until the loss is dissipated.

An investor should maintain *precise recordkeeping* to identify the *cost basis* and *holding period* of mutual fund shares. It is possible for a shareholder to generate gains or losses on first-in, first-out method (FIFO), last-in, first-out method (LIFO), or identify the actual shares being sold. If precise records are not maintained, the investor will have to report the sale on a FIFO basis, or if the shareholder qualifies, an *average basis*. Once the shareholder elects to use the average basis method it will apply to all sales of shares of the same mutual fund, even if they are held in different accounts.

The IRS has a *wash sale rule*, which essentially *disallows* capital losses when securities are sold specifically for the purpose of claiming a capital loss. The provision of the rule is that thirty days *before* or *after* a liquidation of mutual funds shares for a loss, the shareholder may *not repurchase* these shares and still claim the loss. For individual securities, the rule goes so far as to say "substantially identical property" cannot be purchased within this sixty-one day period — or even an option to purchase these securities. An example of "substantially identical" would be the purchase of convertible bonds in the same corporation. This would disallow the loss deduction. Actually, the rule covers 61 days — 30 days before and after as well as the actual trade date.

IV.   OPEN-END AND CLOSED-END INVESTMENT COMPANIES

Although open-end investment companies make up more than 90% of the mutual funds available, closed-end investment companies also purchase securities for their shareholders. Open-end investment companies *continually* offer shares to the public, but closed-end investment companies have only a fixed number of shares outstanding. The closed-end investment company does have a public offering initially just like any other public security. Additional shares may be offered in future years under certain circumstances, but the investment company itself does *not* continually offer shares.

Another important distinguishing characteristic of the closed-end investment company is that it will *not* generally redeem its shares. After the initial offering, the purchase and sale of closed-end investment company shares is treated like any other security; that is, supply and demand dictate the price. Should a person wish to purchase shares of a closed-end investment company, he or she must find another individual who owns them and purchases from them, just as in normal stock purchases. The price paid for the shares is the price supply and demand dictate and is probably not exact net asset value as it is with open-end companies. Brokerage firms execute these transactions for clients and charge a commission. A shareholder who wishes to sell closed-end investment company shares must sell through normal channels and generally pays a commission for the service. Closed-end funds have a tendency to trade at a discount from the NAV.

Table 7.2

Management Company Comparison Open-End vs. Closed-End	
Open-End Characteristics	Closed-End Characteristics
1. Capitalization structure consists entirely of voting common stock.	1. Capitalization structure may consist of common stock, preferred stock and bonds.
2. Shares are purchased from the fund at an offering price determined by the NAV.	2. Shares are purchased through the open market (exchange or OTC) at a market price determined by sellers.
3. The offering price includes a sales charge.	3. A commission is added to the market price.
4. Shares are redeemed by the fund at the NAV and a check is sent within 7 calendar days.	4. Shares are sold in the open market at a price determined by purchasers. There is no guarantee of a buyer.
5. Shares cannot be priced below NAV.	5. Shares are commonly sold at prices below NAV.

QUICK QUIZ 3

11.   Wash sales are those made within a period of _____ days before or after the liquidation and, if the wash sale rule applies, any capital loss will be _____.

Reference: Page 7-9

12.   Mutual fund shares *liquidated* at a profit after being held more than one year and one day will be subject to _____ _____ *taxation*.

Reference: Page 7-7

13.   Mutual fund shares *liquidated* at a profit after being held less than one year and one day are subject to _____ _____ taxation.

Reference: Page 7-7

14.   Closed-end investment company shares can be purchased:
      a.   Directly from the fund itself

Reference: Page 7-10

b.   From other shareholders through a brokerage house
c.   By writing to the underwriter
d.   For the net asset value
e.   Without normal sales commissions

15.   An individual wishing to sell closed-end investment company   Reference:
shares must: Page 7-10
a.   Tender (remit) to the fund for redemption
b.   Send to the transfer agent for redemption
c.   Redeem at net asset value per share minus a redemption
fee if applicable
d.   Find a purchaser for these shares
e.   Be assured of a profit if held for more than twelve months
and one day

16.   Closed-end investment companies have a _____ number of shares   Reference:
outstanding.   Page 7-10

ANSWERS: 11-30, disallowed; 12-long-term capital gains; 13-short-term (ordinary income); 14-b; 15-d; 16-fixed.

REAL LIFE SITUATION

Sir Marco Bolo, a retired round-the-world sailor, asks for advice on the difference between open-end and closed-end investment companies.

Mr. Bolo tells you that he does not have an account at a brokerage house at this time but does want to invest in some "investment company shares." Your advice to Mr. Bolo would be:

Directions: *For each of the numbered recommendations that follow, please select A, B, or C as the evaluation you deem most correct. Place your selection on the line preceding each number:*

A. Inappropriate, he has   B. Reasonable advice   C. Excellent advice un-
come to someone   but two or more short-   der the cir-
who is all wet!   comings exist.   cumstances.

Answer

_____   1.   You purchase investment company shares through any bank.
_____   2.   Investment company shares are not as good as government bonds and you
can buy these from the federal reserve.

_____ 3.   There is no difference, essentially, between open-end and closed-end except whether the fund will accept you because of high entry requirements.

_____ 4.   Be careful about this investment because investment expertise is needed.

_____ 5.   Closed-end companies, once their shares are sold, trade in the "open market" and continued purchases and sales would indicate that the services of a brokerage house would be required.

_____ 6.   Many investors favor open-end companies because of the ease of purchasing and redeeming.

ANSWERS: 1-B; 2-B; 3-A; 4-B; 5-C; 6-C.

CHECK YOUR UNDERSTANDING
(Circle one)

1.   Mutual fund taxation is better than any other form of investment.   Reference:
     True/False   Page 7-6

2.   The term *tenants in common* applies in a situation where an   Reference:
     individual owns an interest in a partnership can "will it" to heirs.   Page 7-4
     True/False

3.   The conduit tax treatment of mutual funds seeks to prevent   Reference:
     double taxation.   Page 7-6
     True/False

4.   Capital gains distributions are more desirable, from a tax stand-   Reference:
     point, than dividend distributions.   Page 7-6
     True/False

5.   Dividend distributions from a municipal bond fund can retain the   Reference:
     same character (federal income tax free) to the shareholder.   Page 7-7
     True/False

6.   If an individual sells mutual fund shares within six months,   Reference:
     favorable tax treatment still applies.   Page 7-7
     True/False

7.   All distributions of interest from municipal bond funds are tax   Reference:
     exempt.   Page 7-7
     True/False

8.   When selling closed-end investment company shares, the fund   Reference:
      must redeem within seven calendar days.   Page 7-10
           True/False

9.   The *wash sale rule* covers, essentially a 61-day period of time.   Reference:
           True/False   Page 7-9

10.   Closed-end investment companies have greater tax advantages to   Reference:
      an investor than do open-end investment companies.   Page 7-10
           True/False

ANSWERS: 1-False; 2-True; 3-True; 4-True; 5-True; 6-False; 7-False; 8-False; 9-True;
10-False.

STUDY NOTES

STUDY NOTES

8

THE MUTUAL FUND PROSPECTUS,
TYPES OF ACCOUNTS,
AND SALES CHARGE REFUNDS

PRETEST
(Circle one)

1. The prospectus of an investment company will include: Reference:
    I.   A list of securities owned by the fund   Page 8-8
    II.   The fund's assets and liabilities
    III. Income and expense items of the fund itself
    IV.   Income and expense items of the management company
              a.   I
              b.   II
              c.   I and III
              d.   I, II, and III
              e.   I, II, III, and IV

2. Which of the following statements about mutual fund prospectuses   Reference:
    is/are correct?   Page 8-6
    I.   All prospectuses must be cleared through the SEC
    II.   All open-end investment companies must file a
          registration statement with the SEC
    III. Prospectuses need not be given to individuals
          who have invested in mutual funds before
              a.   I and II
              b.   I, II, and III
              c.   I and III
              d.   II and III
              e.   III only

1

3.   To which of the following shareholders is plan completion insurance   Reference:
     valuable?   Page 8-14
     a.   Those who cannot afford to continue their investment
     b.   Those who become disabled
     c.   Those who die
     d.   Those affected when the fund goes bankrupt
     e.   The market goes down

4.   Which of the following methods are permissible for *receiving*   Reference:
     payments under a mutual fund withdrawal plan?   Page 8-12
     I.   Regular payments of a fixed dollar amount (fixed
           dollar amount)
     II.   Regular payments whereby a fixed number of shares
           are redeemed (variable dollar amount)
     III. Regular payments of a fixed percentage of share-
           holder's total holdings (variable dollar amount)
           a.   I
           b.   II
           c.   I and II
           d.   I and III
           e.   I, II, and III

5.   Which of the following statements most accurately portrays the   Reference:
     relationship of a mutual fund registration statement and a mutual   Page 8-6
     fund prospectus?
     a.   The prospectus and registration statement are the same thing
     b.   The prospectus is a synopsis and part of the registration statement
     c.   The registration statement is a synopsis of the prospectus
     d.   The prospectus is a required document but the registration
          statement is not
     e.   A copy of the registration statement must be given each
          prospective investor

6.   The method used to calculate the sales charge on open-end   Reference:
     investment company purchases is: Page 8-9
     a.   Explained in the beginning of the prospectus
     b.   A level charge
     c.   The same for all funds
     d.   Regulated by the SEC
     e.   All of the above

7.   All the following are contained in a mutual fund prospectus *except*:   Reference:
     a.   A listing of the Board of Directors and their business   Page 8-8
          affiliations
     b.   A balance sheet of the fund
     c.   A listing of the holdings of the fund
     d.   An income and expense statement of the management company
     e.   An income and expense statement of the fund itself

8.   A mutual fund account in which a single purchase is made and   Reference:
     no subsequent purchases are contemplated is: Page 8-11
     a.   An open account
     b.   A voluntary accumulation account
     c.   A single purchase account
     d.   A contractual plan account
     e.   A periodic payment plan account

9.   A *pre-authorized check plan* with the shareholder's bank is used to: Reference:
     a.   Put more money into the fund   Page 8-11
     b.   Take money out of the fund (withdrawal plan)
     c.   Guard against "bounced checks"
     d.   Keep more accurate records of payments
     e.   Establish credit with the mutual fund

10. Which of the following must be pointed out to the investor when   Reference:
     comparing a withdrawal plan to an annuity?   Page 8-12
     a.   The withdrawal plan may be more favorable
     b.   The annuity may be more favorable
     c.   The annuity may involve more favorable taxation treatment
     d.   A withdrawal plan and an annuity are not the same
     e.   a, b, and c above

11. When a shareholder participates in a withdrawal plan, which of   Reference:
     the following tax principles apply?   Page 8-13
     I.   Distributions representing dividend payments will be
           taxed as ordinary income
     II.   Distributions representing capital-gains payments will
           be taxed as capital gains
     III. Distributions representing capital will be taxed as capital
           gains

IV.   All distributions are income tax free up to the shareholder's cost basis (total amount paid in)
   a.   I
   b.   I and II
   c.   IV
   d.   I, II, and III
   e.   I and III

12.   "Money market" type mutual funds offer all of the following services *except*:

Reference:
Page 8-13

   a.   Check writing privileges
   b.   Daily compounding of dividends
   c.   Daily compounding of capital gains
   d.   Calculation of both realized and *unrealized* appreciation or depreciation of fund assets
   e.   Tax-free accumulation of income

13.   When plan completion insurance is used with a periodic payment plan (contractual plan) mutual fund, the insurance proceeds are paid to:

Reference:
Page 8-15

   a.   The custodian of the mutual fund
   b.   The accountants of the mutual fund for distribution
   c.   The beneficiary named by the fund
   d.   The beneficiary named by the shareholder
   e.   The shareholder's estate

14.   An investor who owns a contractual mutual fund plan with plan completion insurance may transfer this ownership to another individual if:

Reference:
Page 8-15

   a.   The transfer is for a good purpose (e.g., estate planning purposes)
   b.   The mutual fund approves of the transfer
   c.   The new owner proves insurability to the plan completion insurance company
   d.   All of the above conditions are met
   e.   Not permitted under any circumstances

15.   Which of the following taxes applies to life insurance death *benefit* under plan completion insurance?

Reference:
Page 8-15

   a.   Income taxes
   b.   Estate taxes (if applicable)
   c.   Gift taxes (if applicable)
   d.   Inheritance taxes (if applicable)
   e.   None of the above

16.   Which of the following statements is true of a contractual mutual   Reference:
      fund plan?   Page 8-14
      a.   Normally two (2) prospectuses are used
      b.   Level sales charges are payable in the first forty-five days
      c.   Level sales charges are payable in the first eighteen months
      d.   Plan completion insurance is mandatory
      e.   An investor who wants the plan completion insurance option
            has to qualify for this option

17.   The full refund period under a contractual mutual fund plan is: Reference:
      a.   Fort-five days from the first payment   Page 8-16
      b.   Forty-five days from the mailing of the letter from the
            custodian bank
      c.   Forty-five days from the receiving of the letter from the
            custodian bank
      d.   Eighteen months from the inception of the plan
      e.   None of the above

18.   Under 50% front-end load plans, an investor may cancel his or her   Reference:
      plan within eighteen months and receive back: Page 8-16
      a.   All money paid
      b.   All money paid less 15% of payments
      c.   All money paid less 45% of payments
      d.   Current value of shares plus 15% of payments
      e.   Current value of shares plus all sales charges that exceeded
            15% of payments

19.   Which of the following is the most advantageous plan for an   Reference:
      investor who wishes to make payments for a period of more than   Page 8-11
      five years but less than fifteen years?
      a.   Open account with one purchase
      b.   Voluntary accumulation account
      c.   Periodic payment plan account
      d.   Contractual plan *with* refund features
      e.   Contractual plan *with* refund features and plan completion
            insurance

20.   Under the "spread load" regulations of the Investment Company   Reference:
      Amendments Act of 1970, a periodic payment plan mutual fund   Page 8-16
      must limit its sales charges to:
      a.   50% in the first year

b.   Forty-five days of the first year
c.   An average of 16% over forty-eight payments
d.   An average of 15% over forty-eight payments
e.   No particular amount if a refund provision is part of the plan

ANSWERS: 1-d; 2-a; 3-c; 4-e; 5-b; 6-a; 7-d; 8-a; 9-a; 10-d; 11-b; 12-e; 13-a; 14-e; 15-e; 16-a; 17-b; 18-e; 19-b; 20-c.

OVERVIEW

The prospectus is the most important single legal document in the mutual fund world. This chapter explains the information that must be contained in the prospectus and how the prospectus must be used by a registered representative dealing with clients. Also covered here are different types of accounts available for investing money in a mutual fund and taking money out. Finally, special contractual mutual fund plans, their sales charges, and refund requirements are covered.

Author's Note to Candidates

It is axiomatic that if a representative wants to avoid suits by clients and loss of registration, a thorough knowledge of the prospectus and its uses is essential. Special client protection requirements, such as refunds of sales charges on contractual plans, make this chapter one of the most practical chapters for your study.

I.   THE PROSPECTUS

Under the Securities Act of 1933, all new issues of a mutual fund must issue a *prospectus*, which is a synopsis of the registration statement (it is actually *part* of the registration statement). The prospectus must be filed with the SEC. This prospectus contains important information about the offering. It is a legal document and must *precede* or *accompany* all sales presentations. This rule is a basic rule of the mutual fund world because mutual funds are new issues.

The prospectus is designed to inform the client about all the facts of the proposed investment. A brief history of the company is included. The regulators (SEC) determine what must be in the prospectus, which tends toward the potential negative aspects of the investment (i.e., risk level). Every *prospectus* must be cleared through the SEC, but the SEC does *not* approve any securities. A statement at the bottom of every prospectus explains to the public that the SEC does not approve the securities being offered in the prospectus (see sample).

SAMPLE PROSPECTUS

EDUCATIONAL TRAINING SYSTEMS, INC. FUND FOR INCOME
116 Middle Road, Southborough, Massachusetts 01772-0410
(508-481-3578)
July 1, 199_

ETS, INC. FUND FOR INCOME (the "Fund") is an open-end diversified management investment company. The shares of the Fund may be redeemed at any time at the investor's request. Redemptions will be made at the next determined net asset value. (See "Determination of Net Asset Value" and "Redemption of Shares.")

The primary investment objective of the Fund is to earn a high level of current income. To the extent possible, in view of that objective, the Fund also seeks growth of capital as a secondary objective. The Fund emphasizes investment in lower-grade, high-yielding debt securities, generally purchased at a discount from par value, to try to achieve these objectives. Since the price of lower-grade debt securities tends to fluctuate more than investment grade debt securities, the net asset value of the Fund's share's reflected under "Selected Per Share Data and Ratios." Because of the emphasis placed upon high-yielding securities by the Fund, investors should differentiate between it and investment companies emphasizing high grade debt securities, and it should be used by investors only for the portion of their resources that they wish to commit to such a portfolio which may be accompanied by higher risk. There can be no assurance that the objectives of the Fund will be realized.

This prospectus sets forth concisely the information about the Fund that a prospective investor should know before investing. A Statement of Additional Information, dated April 28, 199_, has been filed with the Securities and Exchange Commission and is incorporated herein by reference in its entirety. The Statement of Additional Information is available at no charge upon written or verbal request to the Fund at the address or telephone number indicated above.

THESE SECURITIES HAVE NOT BEEN APPROVED OR DISAPPROVED BY THE SECURITIES AND EXCHANGE COMMISSION NOR HAS THE COMMISSION PASSED UPON THE ACCURACY OR ADEQUACY OF THIS PROSPECTUS. ANY REPRESENTATION TO THE CONTRARY IS A CRIMINAL OFFENSE.

The prospectus for an open-end investment company contains a description of the type of investment company, the specific investment *objectives* of the fund, and *policies* and restrictions on shareholders. The prospectus also contains the *exact method* for computing the public offering price.

In addition, the following information is all contained in the prospectus:

- Sales charges, deferred sales charges, 12(b)-1 charges, and redemption fees
- Management fees
- Breakpoints for quantity discounts

- Right of accumulation
- Letter of intent requirements
- Transfer rights within a family of funds (conversion privilege)

SUMMARY OF CONTENTS

I.   **The Fund, Its Investment Objectives and Policies** (Page 3)

The Fund is an open-end diversified investment company and has been in continuous operation since August 20, 1970. One class of equal shares — the only authorized class — represents the entire beneficial interest in the assets of the Fund. The Fund may issue an unlimited number of shares. When issued, shares are fully paid and non-assessable. Shareholders have no pre-emptive privileges.

II.   **Investment Management and Fees** (Page 7)

E.T.S. Management Company, Inc. ("ETS"), a subsidiary of ETS Consolidated is Investment Advisor for the Fund, pursuant to an Investment Advisory Agreement. ETS is paid for the performance of its duties under the Advisory Agreement a management fee and recurring charge which vary according to the average daily net assets of the Fund.

III. **Purchase of Shares** (Pages 9)

The minimum initial purchase is, with certain exceptions, $200. The sales price includes a sales charge of 4.00% of the sales price (4.17% of the net amount invested) in transactions involving an aggregate of less than $10,000. Reduced sales charges are available with regard to larger purchases and certain other transactions.

IV.   **Principal Underwriters** (Page 8)

The Fund has entered into a Co-Underwriting Agreement with ETS Management Company, Inc. and ETS Corporation, 116 Middle Road, Southborough, Massachusetts 01772, as Co-Underwriters.

V.   **Redemption of Fund Shares** (Page 11)

Shares are redeemable at no charge at the redemption value next determined after the receipt of the redemption order in proper form from the investor. The redemption value, the net asset value adjusted for fractions of a cent, is computed at the close of the New York Stock Exchange.

The prospectus also outlines the accounting methods used for per-share income allocation on (1) interest income and (2) per-share capital increases or decreases due to realized and unrealized appreciation and depreciation in the funds' assets. The redemption procedure is fully detailed. The price calculation per share (net asset value) is also described in the prospectus.

The *history* and *organization* of the fund are covered in the prospectus (but without pictures). Minimum investment requirements for the shareholders and an explanation of the withdrawal plan (with requirements) are also described.

Charts, tables, and graphs that are pertinent to the investment are presented in the prospectus. The prospectus must contain the most *current financial statements* of the fund, including:

- Schedule of investments in the fund portfolio
- Statement of the assets and liabilities of the fund
- The income and expense statement of the fund
- Statement of increases or decreases in the value of the fund for the reported period
- Report by an outside accounting firm

The SEC now requires all mutual funds to consolidate all fees and expenses in one location in a uniform tabular-form. There are three sections, one listing all non-recurring shareholder's fees (sales charges, redemption fees), the second listing recurring expenses against the fund's assets or income (12(b)-1 fees), and the third showing the expenses on a hypothetical $1,000 investment over one-, three-, five-, and ten-year periods.

FEE TABLE

The following table has been prepared to assist the investor in understanding the various costs and expenses a shareholder of the Fund will directly or indirectly bear.

SHAREHOLDER TRANSACTION EXPENSES (Non-Recurring)

Maximum Sales Load Imposed on Purchases
(as a percentage of offering price) 4.00%

Exchange Fee $5.00

ANNUAL FUND OPERATING EXPENSES (Recurring)
(as a percentage of average net assets)

Management Fees 69%
12b-1 Fees 11%
Other Expenses 19%

Total Fund Operation Expenses 99%

EXAMPLE	1 year	3 years	5 years	10 years
You would pay the following expenses on a $1,000 investment, assuming (1) 5% annual return and (2) redemption at the end of each time period:	$94	$114	$135	$196

QUICK QUIZ 1

1. An effective prospectus of the investment company must precede   Reference:
    or accompany all offers by mail to clients about the purchase   Page 8-6
    of shares.
        True/False

2. The Securities and Exchange Commission approves the accuracy   Reference:
    the statements in a prospectus before the prospectus can be   Page 8-6
    considered effective.
        True/False

3.   The prospectus of an investment company will include: Reference:
      I.   A list of securities owned by the fund   Page 8-8
      II.   The fund's assets and liabilities
      III.   Income and expense items of the fund itself
      IV.   Income and expense items of the management company
             a.   I
             b.   II
             c.   I and III
             d.   I, II, and III
             e.   I, II, III, and IV

4.   An effective prospectus must precede or accompany every sales   Reference:
      presentation where that specific mutual fund is discussed.   Page 8-6
             True/False

5.   Which of the following statements about mutual fund prospectuses   Reference:
      is/are correct?   Page 8-6
      I.   All prospectuses must be cleared through the SEC
      II.   All open-end investment companies must file a
             registration statement with the SEC
      III.   The SEC approves the information contained in a
             prospectus prior to its being cleared
      IV.   Prospectuses need not be given to individuals who
             have invested in other mutual funds before
             a.   I and II
             b.   I, II and III
             c.   I and III
             d.   I and IV
             e.   I, II, III, and IV

                        ANSWERS: 1-True; 2-False; 3-d; 4-True; 5-a.

II.   TYPES OF ACCOUNTS AND SERVICES

An *open account* or *accumulation account* is one in which dividend and capital gain distributions may be reinvested to compound growth. There are requirements as to the minimum number of shares to be purchased or minimum dollar amounts required for investment. Ownership of fractional shares is permitted in funds that have reinvestment privileges. Dividend distributions usually occur quarterly and capital-gains distributions at the end of the fund's fiscal year.

Automatic reinvestment of capital-gain distributions and dividends is *not* required by any funds but, obviously, they wish to promote reinvesting of distributions so the shareholder account and the fund, grow in total assets. The prospectus will detail whether dividends are reinvested at net asset value or at a higher offering price. Capital gains, by law, must be reinvested at NAV (no sales charge).

Most funds have a minimum initial investment (e.g., $1,000). The accumulation plan is popular because additional investments by shareholders can be made whenever desired. Usually these plans have a *level sales charge*, which is deducted as each payment is made. When a "breakpoint" is reached, the sale charge drops to the next level for which the total investment in that fund qualifies.

A voluntary accumulation plan usually offers reinvestment of dividend and capital-gains distributions. However, it is only a contractual plan that offers *plan completion insurance*, which is a form of decreasing term life insurance. This insurance pays only if the individual dies, at which time the payment is made to the fund custodian and *not* to a designated beneficiary. A shareholder can leave the paid up fund shares to whomever he or she may choose through a will, joint tenancy with right of survivorship, and such.

A *service feature* of these plans is a pre-authorized check plan, in which an individual authorizes a bank to pay automatically a fixed amount to the mutual fund at fixed intervals (e.g., $100 a month) from their checking account.

QUICK QUIZ 2

6. A financial statement (i.e., balance sheet and income statement)   Reference:
    in the prospectus must be _____.   Page 8-8

7. Plan completion insurance would be of value to a shareholder in   Reference:
    which of the following situations?   Page 8-14
    a.   If the shareholder could not afford to continue his or
         her investment
    b.   If the shareholder became disabled
    c.   If the shareholder were to die
    d.   If the mutual fund went bankrupt
    e.   The market goes down

8. Voluntary accumulation plans involve a _____ sales charge.   Reference:
                                                                            Page 8-11
                                                 ANSWERS: 6-current; 7-c; 8-level.

III.   WITHDRAWAL PLANS

Withdrawal plans are similar to those of any type of savings or investment fund in which an individual, as the owner, can take out any amount of money at any time. Withdrawal plans are really a *convenience* offered to fund shareholders. Withdrawal plans usually require a *minimum* investment (e.g., $10,000) before the fund management will withdraw money from the account to pay to the shareholder.

Withdrawal plans may be set up by one large payment or by payments accumulated over a number of years as in a voluntary accumulation plan. The purpose is to service shareholders who have a need for a flow of income. However, additional payments to the fund, even during the withdrawal payment period, are allowed under certain circumstances. A sales charge is levied when the money is deposited, but no sales charge is levied when money is taken out (withdrawals), although some funds may have a small *redemption* charge.

It must be pointed out by the registered representative that a withdrawal plan is *not a life annuity* and that an individual eventually may exhaust both the principal and earnings by excessive withdrawals.

Withdrawal plans can be set up on behalf of an investor under the following arrangements:

- Dividend distributions can be automatically sent to the shareholder and, if the shareholder desires additional income, shares can be liquidated
- All distributions can be reinvested and specific shares redeemed for each payment

An investor may specify the dollar amount needed (e.g., $500 per month). A varying number of shares would be redeemed every month to equal the dollar amount needed. An investor may request that a certain number of shares be liquidated each month; therefore, the income received would vary. This plan differs from a variable annuity — for withdrawal plans are *not* annuity payments, and a withdrawal plan can be exhausted.

To review, the types of withdrawal plans available are:

- Fixed dollar payments (monthly)
- Fixed percentage payments (e.g., 12% of fund annually or 1% per month)
- Fixed number of shares liquidated each month
- Liquidation over a fixed period of time (e.g., 10% of value of the fund for ten years)

Note that withdrawal payments are in cash and that the actual assets of the fund (securities) are never distributed.

The *taxation* of withdrawal plans is the same as taxation of dividend or capital-gains distributions or redemptions of fund shares (i.e., all amounts *over* cost basis are taxable). It is the responsibility of the fund or designated agent to detail to the client the exact nature of all distributions and redemptions under a withdrawal plan, and a report of payments is sent to the Internal Revenue Service (Form 1099). Therefore, the shareholder knows how much of each payment represents dividend distributions, capital-gains distributions and actual redemption of fund shares. It is the taxpayer's responsibility to calculate the cost basis for each share and to report any gains.

Sales literature for withdrawal plans must clearly detail to clients that it is only their own money that may be taken out. Payments may be *more than, less than,* or *equal to* growth in the fund. Under no circumstances is preservation of principal guaranteed when using a withdrawal plan.

Other services offered by *some* money market funds are:

- The ability to write checks directly on the fund
- Daily dividend reinvestment
- Daily receipt of dividends
- Telephone transfers (small extra charge)
- Complete confirmation statements
- Maintaining a fixed allocation (asset allocation) among different fund types
- Conversion privilege to other funds

QUICK QUIZ 3

9. Mutual fund withdrawal plans are similar to annuities.   Reference:
    True/False   Page 8-12

10. Under a mutual fund withdrawal plan, a fixed number of shares   Reference:
    may be automatically redeemed or a fixed dollar amount can be   Page 8-12
    redeemed at specified times.
    True/False

11. A shareholder can choose whether the mutual fund withdrawal   Reference:
    plan sends him or her actual securities or cash payments.   Page 8-13
    True/False

12. Proceeds from mutual fund withdrawal plans are taxed like   Reference:
    _____.   Page 8-13

ANSWERS: 9-False; 10-True; 11-False; 12-redemptions.

IV.   CONTRACTUAL PLANS

Contractual plans are sometimes referred to as *periodic payment* plans. The investor commits to making fixed payments over a fixed period of time. Note that the investor is not legally committed to make additional payments, but the structure of the plan is such that it is to his or her advantage to continue payments. The usual procedure is to have the shareholder determine a total investment goal (e.g., $10,000, $25,000). A fixed time period is set to achieve this goal (e.g., ten years or fifteen years). Contractual plans are federally regulated by the Investment Company Act of 1940 (1940 Act) and the Investment Company Amendments Act of 1970 (1970 Act).

Characteristics

Contractual plans have the following specific characteristics:

1. There are percentage *sales charges* levied against every payment in contractual plans. In contractual or periodic payment plans, the sales charges are higher in early years and lower in later years.

2. On rare occasions a lump sum purchase (single pay) is made in a contractual plan. Normally, the open account type of plan is used for such a purpose.

3. There are *custodial* fees as in most mutual funds.

4. Dividends and capital gains are *reinvested* because compounding of the investment is the primary objective.

5.   *Partial liquidation* is allowed and reinstating the plan, by making all missed payments, is permitted. Full cancellation usually does not involve reinstatement privileges and the investor is not able to resume the plan. *Partial* liquidations are limited to once a year and reinvestment is not allowed within 90 days of the partial liquidation in order to be allowed *reinstatement* privileges.

6.   Contractual mutual fund plans involve heavy sales charges in the early years, thus penalizing those shareholders who do not keep up payments or who cancel.

An example of such sales charges is 20% in the first three years; 4% in the fourth through ninth year; and 2% in the tenth year and so on (1970 Act).

A prospectus must clearly detail the entire contractual plan program. The specific separate prospectus used for contractual plans is referred to as a *plan prospectus*. It outlines the requirements of the investment plan and is an addition to the prospectus of the mutual fund itself. (This is interesting, the investor gets two prospectuses: one detailing the plan and one detailing the fund itself.)

Plan completion insurance is a feature of contractual plans. It functions as group decreasing term insurance. If an investor dies before the period of expected payments has been completed, the death benefit to the fund is the amount yet to be paid by the deceased shareholder. The insurance provides that payments be made *at once in total* to the fund custodian. In this way, the contractual mutual fund is paid up. The plan completion insurance is written on the life of the original contractual plan shareholder and the coverage is *non-transferable*. Since the fund shares will be paid up at death, the total value will be included in the estate of the deceased. The decedent can leave the fund shares to chosen heirs.

Capital-gains and dividend reinvestment tax information will be reported to the contractual plan holder, just as with other types of mutual funds. If the individual with plan completion insurance dies, the plan is paid up via the insurance proceeds.

Operation

The actual operation of a contractual plan, then, is divided into two elements:

1.   The mutual fund is the underlying asset, purchased as payments are made. This mutual fund may include other investment arrangements (i.e., voluntary accumulation plan).

2.   The plan sponsor or plan company is involved in the sale of the administration of the plan as well as in the collection of the sales charges.

The plan *custodian* is responsible for the *safe keeping* of assets and the *accounting* of the mutual fund shares as purchased.

The contractual plan shareholder is not provided with mutual fund certificates, unless specifically requested. This is customary in the mutual fund industry. However, a plan certificate will be issued to the contractual plan holder identifying the type of plan, pertinent information, and such. All mutual fund shareholders can request actual certificates if desired.

A periodic payment or contractual-plan investor may make a collateral assignment or may *transfer* fund shares to someone else. A trust may be the owner of a contractual mutual fund plan on behalf of the trust beneficiary, just as a trust may own any other property. The beneficiary must be designated when the trust is originally written. If plan completion insurance is used, the custodian will pay up the fund shares and the total value will be turned over to the trust for administration or liquidation of the total plan values.

Sales charges on contractual plans are now closely regulated by Section 27A of the Investment Company Act of 1940 (50% plans) and by Sections 27F and H of the **Investment Company Amendments Act** of 1970 (20% plans). These plans are considered front end load or penalty plans because the high sales charges in the early years impose a penalty on the shareholder upon early liquidation. The 50% plan allows for 50% of the first year's payments to be deducted as sales charges. This means that only 50% of payments go into the fund.

Section 27H of the 1970 Act allowed for *spread load payment plans* whereby a maximum of 20% may be charged on any one payment, and therefore no more than 20% in total the first year. However, there is a maximum of 64% that may be charged in the first four years, so many mutual funds have gone to a 20-20-20- and 4 plan; that is, 20% the first year, 20% the second year, 20% the third year, and 4% the last year. This meets the requirements of an *average of 16%* over the first forty-eight payments. Note that this is forty-eight payments and not forty-eight months, even though payments are usually monthly. If payments are more frequent than monthly, the forty-eight payment rule still applies. Please note that under all contractual plans sales charges over the life of the plan are limited to 9%.

Refunds

Contractual mutual funds plans *must* offer a "withdrawal privilege" to the investor. Within forty-five days of the date of mailing the cancellation privilege letter by the custodian bank, the investor may cancel and receive a full refund of all sales charges. The custodian will mail a registered letter containing this withdrawal privilege when the plan is originally written. The forty-five days begin on the date of the *mailing* of the letter. Within that period of time, the investor may cancel the plan and receive a refund of all sales charges plus the current value of the account. The value of the account may have gone up or down depending upon investment performance. Therefore, it is possible to make a profit upon canceling the plan within forty-five days. The sales charges are the *difference* between gross payments remitted to the plan company and the "net amount invested" in the fund.

Another refund provision is the *limited right* to get a partial refund within eighteen months of adoption of the plan. This is called the "surrender right." This generally takes place after the forty-five days have expired and is applicable to 50% front end load plans only (1940 Act). This provision allows a refund of all sales charges that *exceed* 15% of gross payments during an eighteen-month period. As always, the existing value of the account will be returned to the shareholder plus any refund of sales charges that exceed 15%. A further requirement upon a 50% plan holder is that a reserve must be set up by the plan company in case the shareholder should cancel; that is, all sales charges over 15% must be retained by the plan sponsor in the event of surrender within the first eighteen months. After eighteen months of plan operation, the reserve can be released.

Because of the high penalty against a shareholder who cancels the plan in the early years, some state have *prohibited* the sale of front end load contractual plans, particularly the 50% type plans. Because of the heavy requirements of refunds and reserve requirements for refunds, 50% front end load plans have quickly faded from the scene.

QUICK QUIZ 4

13. In a contractual or period payment plan, two separate prospectuses   Reference:
    are presented. The first is a _____ prospectus and the second   Page 8-14
    is an _____ prospectus of the mutual fund itself.

14. Contractual mutual fund plans are generally written covering a   Reference:
    period of time of either _____ years or _____ years and most   Page 8-14
    commonly the periodic payments are monthly.

15. Plan completion insurance is life insurance of a _____ _____   Reference:
    nature and the death benefit is paid to the _____.   Page 8-14

16. If a contractual planholder has completion insurance, upon death   Reference:
    the new value of the fund shares that are now completely paid up   Page 8-15
    will not be subject to income taxation.
            True/False

17. The Investment Act of 1940 limited the first year sales charge   Reference:
    under contractual mutual fund plans to a maximum of _____.   Page 8-15

18. The Investment Company Amendments Act of 1970 (Section 27H)   Reference:
    limited sales charge on any one payment or in any one year to a   Page 8-15
    maximum amount of _____.

19. The total that may be charged under a *spread load payment plan*   Reference:
    in the first four years cannot exceed _____ percent and there-   Page 8-15
    fore cannot exceed an annual average of _____ percent over this
    four year time (assuming monthly payments).

20. The forty-five day period that allows a full refund of all sales   Reference:
    charges starts when the notice of this right is _____.   Page 8-15

21. It is/is not (circle one) possible to make a profit using the full   Reference:
    refund cancellation privilege within forty-five days.   Page 8-15

22. In a 50% front end load contractual mutual fund plan, a share-   Reference:
    holder has a _____ month period in which to cancel the plan,   Page 8-15
    and all sales charges in excess of _____ will be refunded plus
    the current existing value of the fund.

ANSWERS: 13-plan, actual; 14-10, 15; 15-decreasing term, custodian; 16-True; 17-50%;
18-20%; 19-64%, 16%; 20-mailed; 21-is; 22-eighteen months, 15%.

REAL LIFE SITUATION

Mr. Vasco De Rama, round-the-world sailor turned professional roller skater, has been investigating the advantages of mutual funds and solicits your advice as to which type of fund would best suit his needs. Mr. De Rama wishes to invest $5,000 when he receives an inheritance from his sailing brother. He would also like to set aside $100 per month for this purpose. Your advice to Mr. De Rama would be to:

Directions: *For each of the numbered recommendations that follow, please select A, B, or C as the evaluation you deem most correct. Place your selection on the line preceding each number.*

A. Worse than inappropriate. Advice like this is usually reserved for Saturday night roller skating parties.

B. Inappropriate, two or more shortcomings exist.

C. Best recommendation under the circumstances.

Answer

_____ 1. Tell Mr. De Rama that mutual fund investing is only for well-heeled investors and he needs more funds than he has even to open an account.

_____ 2. Consider a contractual plan that would "force" him to invest the $100 per month as planned.

_____ 3. Establish one fund with the $5,000/$10,000 dollars and a second fund for monthly investments so he can diversify more.

_____ 4. Purchase a fund with the accumulated money now but save the $100 per month in a bank and invest it at the end of the year.

_____ 5. Return to round-the-world sailing to gain added notoriety.

_____ 6. A voluntary accumulation account should be considered, allowing for the monthly investments as well as the $5,000/$10,000 under a letter of intent for lower sales charges if the fund selected has a breakpoint at $10,000.

ANSWERS: 1-A; 2-A; 3-B; 4-B; 5-A; 6-C.

CHECK YOUR UNDERSTANDING
(Circle one)

1. The mutual fund prospectus is a required legal document.   Reference.
   True/False   Page 8-6

2.   The purpose of the prospectus is to inform the client of the risk   Reference:
      nature of the investment.   Page 8-6
         True/False

3.   A statement of assets and liabilities of the management company   Reference:
      does not need to be included in the prospectus.   Page 8-8
         True/False

4.   In an open account, dividend and capital gains can not be reinvested.   Reference:
         True/False   Page 8-11

5.   A voluntary accumulation plan is the most popular form of mutual   Reference:
      fund.   Page 8-11
         True/False

6.   A minimum investment of $10,000 is usually a requirement for a   Reference:
      withdrawal plan.   Page 8-12
         True/False

7.   It is optional for the fund agent to send to the IRS a report of   Reference:
      distributions and redemptions under a withdrawal plan.   Page 8-13
         True/False

8.   A concept of contractual and periodic payment plans is that the   Reference:
      sales charges are high at the start and lower in later years.   Page 8-14
         True/False

9.   A shareholder may request a refund from a contractual mutual   Reference:
      fund plan within forty-five days of mailing the letter from the   Page 8-16
      custodian bank.
         True/False

10.   The method used to calculate the sales charge on open-end invest-   Reference:
      ment company purchases is explained in the prospectus.   Page 8-7
         True/False

   ANSWERS: 1-True; 2-True; 3-True; 4-False; 5-True; 6-True; 7-False; 8-True; 9-True;
10-True.

STUDY NOTES

"A hot product always burns the one with limited
knowledge on how to handle it."
D.M. Doyle

9

VARIABLE ANNUITIES

PRETEST
(Circle one)

1. Under which of the following annuity contracts are investment risks assumed by the contract owner:
   a. Fixed annuity contracts
   b. Variable annuity contracts
   c. Investment risk annuity contracts
   d. Fixed annuity contracts during the payout period
   e. Endowment annuity contracts

   Reference:
   Page 9-7

2. When an owner/annuitant elects the annuity payout provisions of an annuity contract (fixed or variable), the principal or capital sum value is affected in which of the following manners?
   a. The principal is held by the insurance company for payment in total at the death of the annuitant.
   b. The principal cannot be transferred but may be used as collateral for loans, etc.
   c. The principal guarantees the monthly payments and, therefore, if principal is withdrawn by the annuitant the monthly payments will be proportionately reduced.
   d. The status of the principal to the annuitant/owner is completely dependent upon whether it is a fixed annuity monthly payment or a variable annuity monthly payment.
   e. The principal or capital sum is, in essence, given up to the insurance company in return for the guarantee of payments.

   Reference:
   Page 9-8

3. Variable annuity contracts are generally funded by:
   a. The general account method
   b. The variable annuity contract account method
   c. The separate account method
   d. The wrap-around account method
   e. The close-end investment method

   Reference:
   Page 9-9

1

4.   The legal form of the separate account is usually: Reference:
      a.   A mutual life insurance company   Page 9-9
      b.   A stock life insurance company
      c.   A multi-state life insurance company
      d.   A bank
      e.   Unit Investment Trust (UIT)

5.   The measurement of investment return under a variable annuity con- Reference:
      tract during the accumulation phase is/are which of the following?   Page 9-10
      I.   Dividend and interest income is credited to a
            separate account
      II.   Dividend and interest income is credited to a general
            account
      III. Only realized capital gains are credited to increase
            the separate account value
      IV.   Both realized and unrealized gains or appreciation are
            credited to the separate account by the accounting
            system
            a.   I and II
            b.   I and IV
            c.   II and III
            d.   II and IV
            e.   III only

6.   The variable annuity separate account may possibly be reduced in   Reference:
      value by a form of corporate (insurance company) taxation under   Page 9-12
      which of the following circumstances?
      I.   Net income and realized capital gains and all monies
            held by the separate account under tax-qualified
            plans, may be taxed
      II.   Parent insurance company may owe taxes
      III. If insurance company losses money (claims) but they still owe
            taxes, the IRS could take from separate account
            a.   I only
            b.   II only
            c.   III only
            d.   I and III
            e.   None of the above

7.   An investor, who wishes to purchase a variable annuity contract   Reference:
      and sends a payment to the insurance company, but does not   Page 9-12
      want annuity payments for some number of years, will have his
      or her account credited with:
      a.   The number of accumulation units determined by that payment
      b.   The number of annuity units purchased by that payment
      c.   The number of shares purchased by that payment
      d.   The number of combination units purchased by that payment
      e.   Accumulation units and annuity units are the same thing, and
            the number purchased will depend upon the payment made

8.   Which of the following statement(s) is/are true about the valuation   Reference:
      methods used for accumulation units and annuity units under   Page 9-14
      variable annuity contracts?
      I.   The accumulation unit uses no assumed interest
             rate for its calculation
      II.   The annuity unit calculation generally uses no
             assumed interest rate for its calculation
      III.   The annuity unit generally uses an assumed interest
             rate in its calculation that is built into the annuity
             rate options offered in the contract
             a.   I and II
             b.   I and III
             c.   I only
             d.   III only
             e.   All of the above

9.   The settlement option selected by a contract holder who wishes to   Reference:
      receive payments for life, plus payments continuing to a surviving   Page 9-17
      spouse, would be:
      a.   Straight life annuity
      b.   Joint and survivor annuity
      c.   Ten year certain and continuous annuity (10 C&C)
      d.   Unit refund annuity
      e.   Combination fixed and variable annuity

10.   An individual with a variable annuity contract who elects the maxi-   Reference:
      mum payments per month for life with no payments to survivors   Page 9-16
      would choose:
      a.   Straight life annuity
      b.   Joint and survivor annuity
      c.   Ten year certain and continuous annuity
      d.   Unit refund annuity
      e.   Combination fixed and variable annuity

11.   Which of the following are *guarantees* in variable annuity contracts?   Reference:
      a.   Mortality   Page 9-17
      b.   Expense
      c.   Termination or surrender right
      d.   Non-forfeiture or paid-up provision
      e.   All of the above

12.   All the following are methods of purchasing variable annuities *except:*Reference:
      a.   An immediate annuity contract where a lump-sum purchase   Page 9-18
           is made and annuity payout begins immediately (within one
           or two months)
      b.   Single payment deferred annuity — lump-sum payment with
           no further payments
      c.   Periodic payment deferred annuity
      d.   Irregular purchase payments to a deferred annuity contract
           (e.g., some payments this year, some payments next year,
           etc.) within minimums set forth in the contract
      e.   Social Security election — variable Social Security payments
           under a variable annuity contract rather than fixed

13.   The major concept(s) in determining the premium rate base for all   Reference:
      annuity contracts are: Page 9-7
      I.   Mortality assumption
      II.   Expense assumption
      III.   Waiver of premium assumption
      IV.   Interest assumption
             a.   I and II
             b.   I, II, and III
             c.   I, II and IV
             d.   IV only
             e.   None of the above

14.   Under which of the following types of annuity contacts does the   Reference:
      insurance company assume the risk of investment return and, if   Page 9-7
      earnings are less, the loss?
      a.   Fixed annuity contracts
      b.   Variable annuity contracts
      c.   Variable life insurance contracts
      d.   Whole life insurance contracts
      e.   Investment annuity contracts

15. Income from premiums is earned from investments in the separate account is generally:

    a. Distributed as interest
    b. Profit to the insurance company
    c. Distributed as a capital gain
    d. Distributed as a dividend
    e. Reinvested to provide greater return inside the separate account

Reference: Page 9-10

16. Which of the following statements regarding variable annuities is/are correct?

    I. A prospectus is not required — just the policy itself
    II. Variable annuities cannot be used in Keogh or IRA plans
    III. Variable annuity separate account investment performances is not as good as mutual fund performance on the whole
    IV. Variable annuity contract in the "accumulation" phase can be surrendered for cash

        a. II only
        b. II and III
        c. IV only
        d. II, III, and IV
        e. I, III, and IV

Reference: Page 9-9

17. Which of the following statements regarding an assumed interest rate (AIR) is/are correct?

    I. The settlement options (annuity payout options) contain an assumed interest rate
    II. The settlement options (annuity payout options) do not contain an assumed interest rate
    III. The accumulation unit value contains an assumed interest rate
    IV. The accumulation unit value does not contain an assumed interest rate

        a. I and III
        b. I and IV
        c. II and III
        d. II and IV
        e. None of the above are correct

Reference: Page 9-14

18.   Which of the following variable annuity settlement options is most   Reference:
        appropriate for a healthy employee electing early retirement who   Page 9-17
        wishes payments to continue to his or her spouse at death?
        a.   Straight life annuity with two named payees
        b.   Life annuity with contingent beneficiary
        c.   Unit refund annuity with spouse beneficiary
        d.   Fixed period annuity (employee and spouse's lifetime)
        e.   Joint and survivor annuity

19.   The annuity settlement option that translates to "Please pay me   Reference:
        $1,000 per month until the money runs out" is: Page 9-17
        a.   Life annuity
        b.   Fixed period annuity
        c.   Fixed amount annuity
        d.   Specified sum life annuity
        e.   Specified sum period annuity

20.   If a variable annuity contract contained a special death benefit and   Reference:
        the investor paid in $1,000 per month for ten years and died at   Page 9-17
        the end of ten years when his "contract value" was $100,000,
        the amount paid would be:
        a. $93,000
        b. $100,000
        c. $111,600
        d. $120,000
        e. $128,400

ANSWERS: 1-b; 2-e; 3-c; 4-e; 5-b; 6-e; 7-a; 8-b; 9-b; 10-a; 11-e; 12-e; 13-c; 14-a; 15-e;
16-c; 17-b; 18-e; 19-c; 20-d.

OVERVIEW

This is the first of two chapters devoted to variable annuity study. Chapter 9 details the variable annuity contract, the separate account system, and the technical aspects of variable annuity contracts. The actual workings of accumulation units and annuity units will be discussed in detail. Particular attention should be paid to discussion of the valuation method of accounts and the annuitant's right to select different payout options.

Author's Note to Candidates

In general, two major financial products that have had an indelible impact in the last decade are (1) *money market funds* (previously covered) and (2) *deferred annuities* (both fixed and variable). It is important to understand how variable annuities accept payments and why deferred annuities are considered a valid savings accumulation device by many investors. This chapter reviews the variable annuity contract itself. The end of this chapter reviews a most intriguing concept — Variable Life Insurance.

The general definition of an *annuity* is "a series of payments over a specific or indefinite period of time." However, the term has been adapted by insurance companies to mean "payments for a lifetime." This second definition represents a specialized use of the term, since historically only a life insurance company could issue a life annuity contract. Banks now will be able to do so under certain circumstances.

Fixed Annuities Contracts

The traditional annuities offered by insurance companies guarantee fixed dollar payments, usually monthly, for a lifetime. The insurance company, in pricing its product, takes into consideration three major variables:

- Mortality
- Interest
- Expenses

Mortality, in terms of an annuity contract, means just the *opposite* as it does with life insurance; that is, the longer a person lives, the *more* the insurance company pays out. This fact is taken into consideration when lifetime payments are guaranteed.

Interest here refers to the amount of interest *earnings* an insurance company acquires during the time it has premiums to work with. Premium income is invested to provide a greater return to the policyholder and to the company.

The third variable in computation is *expense assumptions*, which are the projected expenses of selling and servicing an annuity contract.

The expected number of time payments is calculated (based on mortality tables). Expenses *add* to the premiums assessed. Interest (earnings) assumed are *subtracted* from the total premium. With *fixed annuities*, the investment risk is assumed by the insurance company that is, if the company earns more than it expected to, it keeps the excess; if the insurance company earns less than the assumption, it must stand the loss. Under all annuity contracts, the annuitant decides *when* to start receiving payments — often at retirement age. When a payout option is selected, the *principal* of the contract must be *given up* to the insurance company in return for the *guarantee* of a series of payments (usually monthly) under one of the annuity options. (See "settlement options" later in this chapter.)

Variable Annuities

The *variable annuity contract* operates in the same manner as the fixed annuity contract except that one of the three elements of the premium functions differently. That element is *interest*. (Remember that mortality, interest, and expense make up "the cost" of an annuity contract.) With fixed annuities, the interest is guaranteed by the insurance company. With variable annuities, the interest rate is only - *assumed*. *Excess* investment earnings benefit the policyholder. However, if interest (earnings) is *less* than the assumed amount, the value of the contract is less. In a variable annuity, there is *no* guaranteed rate of return to the policyowner.

A variable annuity policyholder who elects a settlement or payout option (e.g., at retirement) gives up the right to the principal of the contract in return for the guarantee of monthly payments. Thus a guarantee of monthly payments is provided, but — under a variable annuity — the *amount* of payment will vary.

Please note that it is possible to have a *combination* fixed and variable annuity contract. For example, 50% of premium payments might go to a fixed contract (guaranteed return) and 50% of the payments to a variable annuity contract (return not guaranteed). Many investors feel that the fixed return will provide a minimum base guarantee and, if the portfolio performs well, the variable return portion can provide a hedge against inflation.

Table 9.1

Annuity Comparison

Fixed vs. Variable

Fixed Annuity	Variable Annuity
• Guarantees:	• Guarantees:
✓ Mortality (-)	✓ Mortality (-)
✓ Expense (-)	✓ Expense (-)
✓ Interest (+)	
• Location of Assets	• Location of Assets
✓ General Account	✓ Separate Account
• Insurance company assumes the investment risk	• Annuity holder assumes the investment risk

Separate Accounts

A special *separate account* system is established by the insurance company for use with variable annuity contracts because the rate of return on a variable annuity contract *varies* with the portfolio performance in this separate account. It should be noted that under fixed annuity contracts, the insurance company's general assets back up the guaranteed rate of return so this guarantee is considered part of the "general account." The net amount (after sales charges, if any) of payments to a variable annuity contract is placed directly into this separate account. Most separate accounts are Unit Investment Trusts (UITs) for this purpose.

Investments in the separate account are in conformance with investment objectives spelled out in the prospectus (as in a mutual fund prospectus). Variable annuities can be used to fund Keogh and IRA plans. The separate account is managed by professional managers (usually from within the insurance company). All investments are made directly in the name of the separate account and precise accounting of all investments is maintained. All gains, losses, income, and expenses are credited or debited to the separate account.

Many companies choose to have a separate account that is used to fund more than one variable annuity contract — or other equity type products that the company offers. This is quite feasible because UIT form is in use. UIT is actually a trust and is measured in units (generally $1,000) on a "net basis." This procedure allows an insurance company to have only one funding medium (large unit investment trust) to fund a number of products it offers. The single fund or trust sometimes is easier to manage than a number of smaller funds.

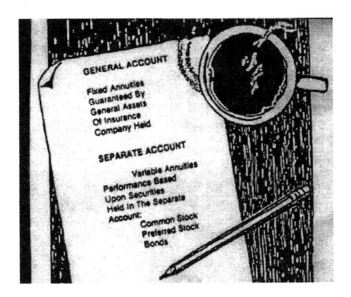

Professional management is similar to mutual fund professional management. A *Board of Managers* oversees the investment portfolio and investment advisory contracts.

Computation of Investment Return

The separate account computes its investment return by *adjusting* account values specifically for all dividend income, interest income, and realized capital gains (or losses). Any unrealized appreciation or depreciation is part of the computation. As a result the *exact* portfolio value must be *computed daily*. In this manner, a per unit value can be computed each day for use in:

- Payment of proceeds to contract holders surrendering
- Crediting of "accumulation units" to contract holders making payments
- Determining the value of the "annuity units," which are used for monthly payments to annuitants.

QUICK QUIZ 1

1. Under which of the following annuity contracts are investment risks   Reference:
    assumed by the contract owner?   Page 9-7
    a.   Fixed annuity contracts
    b.   Variable annuity contracts
    c.   Investment risk annuity contracts
    d.   Fixed annuity contracts during the payout period
    e.   Endowment annuity contracts

2. When an owner/annuitant elects the annuity payout provisions of an   Reference:
    annuity contract (fixed or variable), the principal or capital sum value   Page 9-8
    of this contract is affected in which of the following manners?
    a.   The principal is held by the insurance company for payment
          in total at the death of the annuitant
    b.   The principal cannot be transferred but may be used as
          collateral for loans, etc.
    c.   The principal guarantees the monthly payments; therefore,
          if principal is withdrawn by the annuitant the monthly
          payments will be proportionately reduced
    d.   The status of the principal to the annuitant/owner is completely
          dependent upon whether it is a fixed annuity monthly
          payment or a variable annuity monthly payment
    e.   The principal or capital sum is, in essence, given up to the
          insurance company in return for the guarantee of payments

3. Variable annuity contracts are generally funded by which of the   Reference:
    following methods?   Page 9-9
    a.   The general account method
    b.   The variable annuity contract account method
    c.   The separate account method
    d.   The wrap-around account method
    e.   The closed-end investment method

4. The legal form of the separate account is usually: Reference:
    a.   A mutual life insurance company   Page 9-9
    b.   A stock life insurance company
    c.   A multi-state life insurance company
    d.   A bank
    e.   Unit Investment Trust (UIT)

5. The measurement of investment return under a *variable annuity*   Reference
    contract, during the accumulation phase, is/are which of the   Page 9-10
    following?
    I.   Dividend and interest income are credited to a
          separate account
    II.   Dividend and interest income are credited to a
          general account
    III. Only realized capital gains are credited to increase
          the separate account value
    IV.   Both realized and unrealized gains or appreciation
          are credited to the separate account by the
          accounting system
          a.   I and II
          b.   I and IV
          c.   II and III
          d.   II and IV
          e.   III only

                                                ANSWERS: 1-b; 2-e; 3-c; 4-e; 5-b.

INVESTMENT OBJECTIVES AND POLICIES OF VARIABLE ANNUITIES

During the accumulation period, variable annuity contract holders will see the value of their accounts *vary*, depending upon portfolio performance. As with other equity-based investments, keeping pace with inflation is often an investor's goal. When the variable annuity contract holder elects retirement income payments under one of the variable annuity settlement options, the payments will vary with the performance of the portfolio. The longer the annuitant lives, the more payments the annuitant will receive. Also, in this longer period of time the payments have the ability to increase or decrease depending upon performance. The design of this type of investment is an income that is sensitive to inflation after the annuitant starts receiving payments. Of course, the opposite could be true also.

The investment policy of the variable annuity itself depends on the general investment posture outlined in the prospectus. As with all investment company products, when selling a variable annuity, the prospectus must precede or accompany all sales presentations. The investment philosophy of variable annuity companies is usually *conservative* and *long-term oriented*. These contracts often cover thirty to forty years or more.

Variable annuities are often used in retirement planning under tax-qualified plans (i.e., IRA, pension, profit-sharing plans), enhancing the long-term capital growth nature of the investment. Companies with variable annuity contracts not under any plan "qualified" with the IRS — have *no* special taxation advantages (other than the fact that during the accumulation period taxation is deferred).

An insurance company must report net gains of the separate account (after expenses) — and must report these gains for taxation at the corporate rate of the insurance company. Therefore, the insurance company may pay taxes on the performance of the separate account used under variable annuity contracts on funds that do not represent "tax-qualified money." This requirement is not considered a major disadvantage because:

1.   Insurance company taxation is different from normal corporate taxes, and
2.   Internal accounting steps can be taken to minimize taxation (Insurance company taxation is complex!)

Valuation of Variable Annuity Contracts

Most forms of investment are usually measured in terms of shares. Variable annuity contracts, however, are measured in terms of *units*. This difference is only a matter of terminology. *Separate account value* is computed each day. Instead of a "per share value," the account value becomes a "per unit value." Those contracts that are not in the payout phase are accumulating and the unit measurement on these accounts is called an *accumulation unit*.

When a payment arrives at the variable annuity company, the sales charges (if any) are subtracted, and the net amount is invested in a separate account. The separate account has an accumulation unit value for that day. *Forward pricing* occurs because the money may arrive during the day, but the exact number of units purchased will not be computed until the end of the business day. Therefore, instead of contract holders being credited with "number of shares owned," they are actually credited with "number of accumulation units owned."

Thus, the actual *value* of accumulation units changes every day depending upon portfolio performance. Investors own more accumulation units by paying in money and buying more units each time. Over a period of time, it is hoped that the accumulation unit's value will continue to rise. The value to a contract holder at any given time is the total number of accumulation units owned times the current value of accumulation unit.

For example, Jake Jones has paid in $15,000 over a period of ten years to the ABC Variable Annuity Company. After sales charges, the net amount invested has credited Jake with 14,200 accumulation units. Jake wants to know the current value of his account as of January 1, 199_.

Total Accumulation Units Owned	Value of Accumulation as of 1/1/9_	Total Value of Jake's Contract
14,200	$1.15	$16,330.00

When a contract holder tells the insurance company that he or she wants to receive monthly payments (e.g., in retirement), there is an accounting change from what is known as *accumulation units* to what becomes known as *annuity units*. (Don't worry about this — just concentrate on the words and their meaning.) "Accumulation" means during the accumulation phase, and "annuity" means during the annuity, or payout phase. The actual procedure is:

1. The total value of the annuitant's contract is assessed; that is, the number of accumulation units are multiplied by the current value (see Jake Jones example).
2. To this total dollar value is applied the annuity rates guaranteed in the contract for the option selected. Step 1 (contract value) X Step 2 (annuity rate) = the first monthly payment.
3. Divide the initial monthly payment by the value per annuity unit.

The result is the number of annuity units.

The number of annuity units remains fixed forever; it is the value of the annuity unit that varies with portfolio performance and determines the dollar amount of the annuity payment.

Accumulation Units to Annuity Units (Annuitizing the Contract)

The accounting method used when changing from accumulation units to annuity units, is fully detailed in the variable annuity prospectus. Guaranteed annuity rates are listed at the back of the contract and differ depending upon the option selected. For example:

Step 1: Total number of accumulation units owned is 12,000.
Current value of accumulation unit quoted by company is $1.67.
Total value of contract = 12,000 X $1.67 or $20,040.00.

Step 2: $20,040.00 is applied to purchase life annuity.
Guaranteed annuity rate in contract is $7 per $1,000. (back of contract)
$20.040 X 7 = $140.28 per month.

Step 3: If the current value of an annuity unit quoted by the company is

$1.40 then $\frac{($140)}{$1.40}$ = 100. Therefore one hundred annuity units will be paid monthly.

Note: The *number* of annuity units remains fixed (the *value* of the annuity unit fluctuates with portfolio values). So, if in the second month, the value of the annuity unit rises to $1.43, the payment is 100 annuity units X $1.43 or $143.00 for that month's payment.

When most variable annuity companies are first established, they fix the accumulation unit at $1 (for convenience). The major pricing ingredients, as discussed earlier, are incorporated into annuity contracts. With variable annuities, the annuity rate table (in the back of the contract) builds into the rate an *assumed interest rate* (AIR). This assumed interest rate is used for the convenience of the annuitant so that annuity payments will fluctuate less dramatically. This assumed rate is a very conservative rate (usually 3½%, 5%, 7%).

Let's review. The calculation of the number of annuity units each person receives will determine the fixed number of units to be received monthly for the remaining period of the contract. The first monthly payment is the number of annuity units times the current value of the annuity unit.

For example, ABC Variable Annuity Company has an AIR of 3½% in all of its settlement option rates (i.e., assumes a 3½% investment return). An annuitant, after electing an option, starts to receive monthly payments.

- If the separate account earns 3½% per annum, payments will remain level.
- If the separate account earns in excess of 3½%, payments will gradually increase.
- If the separate account earns less than 3½%, the payments will gradually decrease.

Therefore, in retirement, a person receiving monthly payments will know the *number* of annuity units paid every month (e.g., 500 units per month), but the *value* of the annuity unit will go up and down with the portfolio performance. Hence, with a variable annuity the investor will always receive a payment. However, if the annuity unit value decreases (because of poor portfolio performance), the payments will become smaller.

Chart 9.2

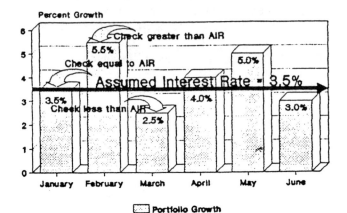

Growth vs. AIR

QUICK QUIZ 2

6.   A variable annuity contract can be used to attempt to keep pace   Reference:
      with inflation before retirement, however, it is of no use after   Page 9-12
      retirement.
              True/False

7.   The variable annuity separate account may possibly be reduced in   Reference:
      value by a form of corporate (insurance company) taxation under   Page 9-12
      which of the following circumstances?
      I.   Net income and realized capital gains and all monies
             held by the separate account under tax-qualified
             plans, may be taxed
      II.   Parent insurance company may owe taxes
      III.   If insurance company losses money (claims) but they still owe
             taxes, the IRS could take from separate account
                 a.   I only
                 b.   II only
                 c.   III only
                 d.   I and III
                 e.   None of the above

8.   An investor, who wishes to purchase a variable annuity contract   Reference:
      and sends a payment to the insurance company but does not want   Page 9-12
      annuity payout payments for some number of years, will have his
      or her account credited with:
          a.   The number of accumulation units purchased by that payment
          b.   The number of annuity units purchased by that payment
          c.   The number of shares purchased by that payment
          d.   The number of combination units purchased by that payment
          e.   Accumulation units and annuity units are the same thing,
                and the number purchased will depend upon the payment made

9.   Which of the following statements is/are true about the valuation   Reference:
      methods used for accumulation units and annuity units under   Page 9-14
      variable annuity contracts?
      I.   The accumulation unit uses no assumed interest
            rate for its calculation
      II.   The annuity unit calculation generally uses no assumed
            interest rate for its calculation
      III. The annuity unit generally uses an assumed interest
            rate in its calculation that is built into the annuity
            rate options offered in the contract
            a.   I and II
            b.   I and III
            c.   I only
            d.   III only
            e.   All of the above
                                    ANSWERS: 6-False; 7-e; 8-a; 9-b.

Variable Annuity Settlement Options

Settlement or *payout options* are included in all annuity contracts (fixed or variable). Payout options are rates, *guaranteed* to the contract holder, on which annuity payments are based if the contract owner wishes to move from accumulating the money to paying it out (monthly). In the past few years, insurance companies' newest or most current annuity rates have been higher than past rates and thus more favorable to the contract holder. Therefore, "current rates" are being offered to existing contract holders to place annuity contracts on a payout basis. Current rates are those which the company offers to new policyholders (rates have risen over the years).
          The standard settlement options are:

    •   Straight life annuity
    •   Joint and survivor annuity
    •   Life annuity with period certain
    •   Unit refund annuity
    •   Fixed period annuity
    •   Fixed amount annuity
    •   Combination fixed and variable annuity

With *straight life annuity*, payments are guaranteed (generally monthly) for the annuitant's life. *No* refund or other return is available when the annuitant dies. This option favors an annuitant who lives a long period after electing the option (far outstripping the principal paid for the contract). It does *not* favor an annuitant who does not live to at least "life expectancy." This option offers the *highest* possible monthly payment, but at the death of the annuitant, it's all over — in more ways than one!!

Joint and Survivor annuity is a customary choice for husband and wife (but such a relationship is not required). Payments are made to the annuitant for life. At the death of that annuitant, the survivor (e.g., spouse) receives equal or reduced payments (depending on the option selected) for the rest of his or her lifetime. This is a desirable option if continued "family income" is needed. Please note that if the second named annuitant dies first, the first annuitant continues to receive payments, but they will end at his or her death. (Joint and 100% survivor annuity will provide the same monthly payment to the survivor; with *joint and 1/2 survivor annuity* the monthly payments are *reduced* to 1/2 to the survivor.)

Life annuity with period certain is applicable when an annuitant wants life income payments and at least a minimum amount paid in the event of early death. The most common form of this annuity is *ten year certain and continuous*; that is, a life annuity for the annuitant's lifetime with at *least* ten years' payments in the event the annuitant dies within ten years. This option is sometimes referred to as 10 C&C.

Unit refund annuity provides another method to calculate the certain period for variable payout option. The accumulated amount is divided by the first monthly payment, the result is the number of months certain. When this option is offered, the calculation method is specified in the contract.

Fixed period annuity does not consider mortality (annuitant's lifetime) at all to figure payment. With fixed period annuity payments are made over a fixed *period* of time (e.g., ten years, twenty years), whether the annuitant lives or not.

Fixed amount annuity occurs when a *fixed amount* is paid for as long as it lasts (e.g., $1,000 a month until principal and interest are dissipated). This type also is not based on mortality. It should be noted that the fixed period and fixed amount options provide that the remaining payments be made to a designated recipient should the annuitant die before the principal and interest are exhausted.

Combination fixed and variable annuity requires issuing two monthly checks to an annuitant. The fixed annuity payment is made from the general account of the insurance company and the variable annuity payment from the separate account. Actually two separate annuity contracts exist, one under fixed annuity and one under variable. This approach also allows the annuitant the right to select among all fixed annuity options and all variable annuity options at the time of retirement.

Contractual Guarantees of the Annuity Contract

All annuity contracts, as previously discussed, are based on mortality, interest, and expenses. The mortality guarantee in the contract means that if mortality is adverse to the insurance company (everybody is living long and collecting annuity payments) it will *not* affect policyholders. The insurance company must stand the mortality loss. The same guarantee holds with expenses; that is, a maximum level of expenses is acceptable, and any expenses exceeding this amount will *not* be charged against the annuity contract.

Many variable annuities offer a *death benefit* during the accumulation period. The death benefit is either the total of all payments into the contract or the current accumulated value, whichever is greater. This option could be valuable to a contract holder who dies before the payout begins.

Annuity contracts, both fixed and variable, have *non-forfeiture* provisions, which state that the annuitant has the right to surrender the contract for cash at any point during the accumulation phase or the right to consider the contract "paid up" at any point during the accumulation phase (if above a certain minimum value). This *paid up right* prevents the insurance company from forcing an annuitant to make more payments than necessary into the contract. The right to terminate the policy and surrender for cash is fully spelled out in the prospectus and in the actual contract.

During the accumulation period, contract holders may wish to *surrender* their contract. As discussed, the value of any contract is the total number of accumulation units multiplied by the current value of an accumulation unit. Occasionally there will be surrender charges or redemption fees. Many times contract holders may wish to exercise a loan provision (if available in the contract). Some contracts provide for these and some do not. Actually, a loan provision is a partial redemption and redemption fees sometimes apply. Whether the amount taken out can be replaced at a later date is dependent upon contract provisions.

Many companies allow an owner to split the contribution (e.g., 50% fixed/50% variable or 75% fixed/25% variable) within specified limits. Many contracts allow the contract holder to change between fixed and variable and vice versa (often limited to once a year). At retirement, or payout time, the contract owner can choose between fixed annuity options, variable annuity options, or a combination of both.

Method of Purchasing Variable Annuities

A *single premium immediate annuity* is purchased with one lump-sum payment (minimum is usually $10,000). This method allows the variable annuity company to begin payout under a settlement option. The number of annuity units are calculated according to the option selected and payments begin immediately.

One of the most popular types of purchase plans for financial planning is the *single payment deferred annuity* in which a lump-sum purchase is made but the contract remains in the accumulation phase (i.e., no payout). After a deduction of sales charges (if any), accumulation units are credited. As previously discussed, reinvestment of all investment income and capital gains is automatic with annuity contracts. This condition is different from that of an open-end investment company, where dividend and capital gains may be taken in cash. Any payments from the annuity contract to the contract holder during the "accumulation phase" are considered partial redemptions. (See taxation principles in the next chapter for the tax treatment of partial redemptions — a very important subject.)

For contract owners who wish to pay over a period of time, a *periodic payment deferred annuity* is available in which a series of payments (e.g., monthly, quarterly) are made to a contract. This option is attractive to an individual who wants to accumulate values overs an extended period of time. Accumulation units are credited (after the deduction of sales charges) each time a payment is made. Once again, gains or losses are adjusted automatically within the separate account fund.

QUICK QUIZ 3

10.   The settlement option selected by a contract holder who wishes to   Reference:
       have payments for life, plus payments continuing to a living spouse,   Page 9-17
       would be:
       a.   Straight life annuity
       b.   Joint and survivor annuity
       c.   Ten year certain and continuous annuity (10 C&C)
       d.   Unit refund annuity
       e.   Combination fixed and variable annuity

11.   An individual with a variable annuity contract who elects the maxi-   Reference:
       mum payments per month for life with no payments to survivors,   Page 9-16
       would choose:
       a.   Straight life annuity
       b.   Joint and survivor annuity
       c.   Ten year certain and continuous annuity
       d.   Unit refund annuity
       e.   Combination fixed and variable annuity

12.   Which of the following is/are *guarantees* in variable annuity   Reference:
       contracts?   Page 9-17
       a.   Mortality
       b.   Expense
       c.   Termination or surrender right
       d.   Non-forfeiture or paid up provision
       e.   All of the above

13.   Many investors owning variable annuity contracts during the   Reference:
       accumulation phase may wish to change the nature of their invest-   Page 9-18
       ment (i.e., variable to fixed, fixed to variable, or a combination of
       the two). Many insurance companies have attempted to satisfy
       this investment need by allowing the conversion from the
       variable annuity separate account to a fixed rate of return (general
       account).
               True/False

14.   All the following are methods of purchasing variable annuities *except*Reference:
   a.   An immediate annuity contract where a lump-sum purchase   Page 9-18
          is made and annuity payout begins immediately (within
          one or two months)
   b.   Single payment deferred annuity — lump-sum payment with
          no further payments
   c.   Periodic payment deferred annuity
   d.   Irregular purchase payments to a deferred annuity contract
          (e.g., some payments this year, some payments next year,
          etc.) within minimums set forth in the contract
   e.   Social Security election — variable Social Security payments
          under a variable annuity contract rather than fixed

ANSWERS: 10-b; 11-a; 12-e; 13-True; 14-e.

VARIABLE LIFE INSURANCE

Variable Life Insurance policies have become increasingly important in the investment world. Individuals are attempting to take advantage of appreciation in other investments through their life insurance policies. This becomes a possibility with the introduction of Variable Life Insurance. To better understand the newer breed of life insurance first consider the whole life insurance policy.

I. WHOLE LIFE INSURANCE

Whole life insurance, also known as *ordinary* or *straight life*, is the simplest form of permanent insurance. The whole life policy contains a fixed minimum death benefit which is paid at the time of the insured's death. This death benefit is the insurer's "amount at risk."

   Most straight life policies carry a level premium throughout the life of the contract. Part of the premium is used to pay the *mortality, interest, expense, etc. charges* with the remainder becoming *cash value*. Since the risk of death increases with age, an insured is overpaying substantially in the early years of a policy. However, the insurer's "amount at risk" is proportionately high in the early years and to offset this, an excessive mortality charge is applied. Mortality charges increase over time but the premiums remain level, meaning, hopefully to the insurer, that overpayment in the beginning years of the policy will make up for the deficiencies charged in later years.

   Although the policyholder does not pay the full amount at risk, the contract is designed to provide cash value accumulation which will at least equal the death benefit at completion of the contract. Whole life policies guarantee minimum cash values and the insurer is at risk for any amount that the investment return does not cover the guaranteed cash value. Whole life protection continues, as does premium payments, to age 100. The cash value will equal the face amount and the benefit will be paid whether or not the insured has died.

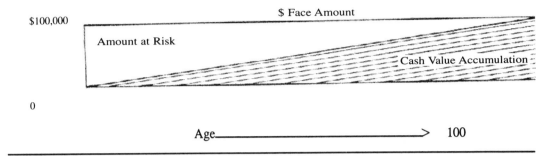

As cash values buildup in a policy, the owner is generally allowed to borrow against it at a *guaranteed interest rate*. This rate is usually less than other rates in the market. The amount of the loan is deducted from the current cash value resulting in a reduced investment return in the policy. The loan may be repaid at the option of the policyowner. Interest is paid by the owner or deducted from future cash value accumulation. Should the policy be terminated or death occur before the loan is repaid, the benefits are reduced by the outstanding loan and interest balance.

II. UNIVERSAL LIFE INSURANCE

This was one of the first policies to "unbundle" the three elements of the permanent life policy. That is, separate and written fees (premiums) for the cost of:

- Death benefits
- Cash values
- Other costs

The biggest change was the policyowner controls *when* and *how much* premium, up to the full amount, *they* choose to send in to the insurance company including skipping premiums for a few years!

Death benefits in Universal Life policies may be either level or increasing. The death benefit is provided by a Renewable Term policy which generally cannot decrease below a minimum specified amount as long as minimum premiums or minimum cash values exist (to pay the "cost" of the death benefit). The overall death benefit may increase if the cash value appreciates.

A *level benefit* policy maintains only enough insurance in excess of cash values to keep a level death benefit. If cash values increase substantially and a minimum amount of insurance must still be carried ("the corridor"), the death benefit may increase. The *increasing benefit* policy maintains a fixed amount of insurance which increases death benefits as the cash value increases.

UNIVERSAL LIFE

LEVEL BENEFIT

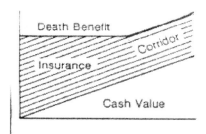

1. . . . YEARS. . . .

INCREASING BENEFIT

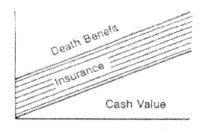

1. . . . YEARS. . . .

Premium payments are flexible. The amount of insurance is selected by the policyowner and the premium, above a set minimum, is determined. The frequency and amount of payments may *vary* based upon the policyowner's needs. These payments are deposited into the cash value account and the cost of the Term insurance is deducted on a monthly basis. There is a guarantee on a minimum amount of growth, generally 4 to 4½%, in the cash value account since it earns interest at money market rates.

Loans are usually allowed in <u>Universal policies</u>, however the policy death benefit is *reduced* by the amount of the loan. Interest is charged to the account and growth in the cash value account may be reduced while the loan is outstanding. A fundamental ingredient with increasing benefit Universal Life policies is that the premium for the Term insurance increases with age thereby resulting in larger deductions from the cash value account to pay the death benefit costs.

III. VARIABLE LIFE INSURANCE

This is the most important life insurance policy to know for your test. The combination of whole life insurance with the growth potential of investments resulted in the creation of Variable Life insurance. Policyowner's have a *guaranteed minimum death benefit* which may be increased through appreciated cash value.

Premiums are *level* and these "fixed premiums" must be paid every year (or borrowed from cash values). The big difference is the policyowner directs the money into a selection of funds or investment choices. The cash value fluctuates up and down depending upon the performance of the separate account. The insured bears the risk of this investment and it is possible the actual return will be less than what is anticipated. Loans may be available, but only to a percentage (e.g., 75% after the contract has been in force for 3 years) of actual cash value since this cash value will fluctuate.

Voting Rights of Policyholders

Variable Life insurance is related to a variable annuity and as a result, shares many of the same characteristics. A Variable Life product must be registered with the SEC and all selling agents must be NASD registered through a Series 6, 7 or equivalent examination. Also, a prospectus is required to be delivered *prior to or at the time* of any sale or presentation of sales literature. Contained within the prospectus are the voting rights of the policyholders. Contract holders actually instruct the insurance company how to vote on key items such as:

- Changes in the investment policy
- Managers of the portfolio
- Auditing firm

Mention should be made of the insurance company's right to reject coverage for any individuals who do not qualify.

Settlement Options

The policyholder or beneficiary (if given the freedom to do so) may choose the settlement option. If an option is not chosen, the insurance company will distribute the benefits in a lump sum. This would allow the beneficiary the ability to manage the proceeds in an attempt to exceed the returns guaranteed by the insurer. Other options may be chosen, which include:

- Fixed period
- Life income
- Life income with refund
- Interest
- Specified amount
- Joint and Survivor life income

A *Fixed Period* option results in the proceeds and any interest earned to be paid out over a fixed period of time. The longer an individual wishes payments to be made, the lower each payment will be. Any interest earned in excess of the amount guaranteed will increase the amount of each payment, not extend them.

Life Income options can only be offered by insurance companies since it guarantees an income for life even if the principal investment is used up. This option is identical to a Life Annuity under variable annuities. Income is guaranteed for the life of the beneficiary when, upon death, payments cease unless the option is modified with a *Period Certain* clause. The Life Income option offers the *greatest cash flow* per payment.

If a *Life Income with Refund* option is chosen, payments will continue for the life of the beneficiary with any proceeds that remain at the beneficiary's death being paid to a contingent beneficiary. A *Cash Refund* option provides a lump sum payment of the remainder to the beneficiary, whereas an *Installment Refund* will continue the payments to any subsequent beneficiaries until the principal and interest are exhausted.

The *Interest* option guarantees the beneficiary a steady stream of income which may increase. At the completion of the interest period, the proceeds of the policy are paid to the beneficiary.

Should the beneficiary wish to establish the size of the payments, the *Specified Amount* option would be chosen. Payments will last until the principal and interest are depleted. If interest above the guaranteed amount is earned, the payment period will be extended.

A *Joint and Survivor Life Income* option will provide income for the life on the last surviving beneficiary. This means that when the primary beneficiary dies, payments will continue to the contingent beneficiary until their death. It may be possible to modify this option with a Period Certain clause.

Not all options may be available from a particular insurer. As was true of variable annuities, Variable Life, being an insurance product, can provide income for life. This cannot be inferred on non-insurance based products.

Contractual Provisions

Insurance contracts, whether Traditional or Variable, have different provisions which automatically apply and others which may be added. These range from basic loan privileges to various riders which may be used to modify the contract.

As was mentioned earlier, policyholders have the right to borrow against the cash value of the contract. The interest rate charged on the loan is generally lower than those charged on loans from other commercial lenders. The loan and interest charges will lower the cash value of the contract.

Supplementary benefits may be added to existing policies to satisfy special needs of an individual. These are known as insuring agreements or riders and most often require additional premiums.

The most common additions to life policies are Term Riders. When a person has temporary needs to satisfy, a Term rider may be attached. A Term policy lasts for a limited period of time and usually does not build up cash value, but the premium is less than if the coverage was permanent insurance.

When cash value is generated Nonforfeiture provisions become useful. The cash value is considered to be an asset of the policyowner and should the policy be terminated for reasons other than death or complete depletion of cash value, the policyowner can usually choose one of the following Nonforfeiture options:

- Cash payment
- Extended Term insurance
- Reduced Paid-Up insurance

Take note that cash values in Variable Life policies fluctuate as the fund or funds appreciate and depreciate on a daily basis. This could result in little or no cash value in a poor investment climate.

A provision specific to Variable Life policies is the ability of the contractholder to direct to which fund the premium is invested. The policyowner also retains the right to change fund investments on new premiums as well as a limited ability to transfer between funds during the life of the policy. Another provision also allows for conversion into a whole life policy for a minimum of 24 months from the date of the contract.

Sales Charges and Expenses

The *prospectus*, which must be delivered prior to or accompany any sales literature or offer of a Variable Life policy, specifies the amount of the sales and investment charges as well as any expenses on the policy. Although charges may vary dramatically between insurance companies and Variable policies, the maximum sales charge calculated over a 20-year period is 9%. The limit on sales charges in the first policy year is equal to 50% of the premium paid. If a policyholder has been charged the maximum sales charges, a refund (at least partial) will be allowed if the policy is surrendered within the first two years of the policy issue date: Year 1 = Cash Value + (S.C. - 30%); Year 2 = Cash Value + (S.C. - 10%).

Other charges are identified in the prospectus and may include *mortality costs, investment management fees, and administrative expenses.* Contained within the policy's provisions is an expense guarantee which guarantees the expenses of the policy will not increase even if expenses to the insurance company increase.

Valuing a Variable Life Policy

The *advantage* of a Variable Life policy is that the death benefit may be increased with good investment performance. Although there is a minimum death benefit below which the policy cannot fall, any excess is determined by the performance of the securities within the portfolio of the fund the policyholder has chosen. In addition, any outstanding loan or overdue premium will reduce the amount of benefits at death. Death benefits must be *calculated annually* and reported to policyowner.

Cash values, which are calculated no less than *monthly*, are not guaranteed. If the fund is performing positively, the cash value will increase as premiums are paid when due. The cash value will be reduced by any investment or management charges applying to the investment account.

Tax Treatment of Variable Life Insurance

During the life of the policy, nondeductible premiums are paid to the insurance company. The "inside build-up" of cash value is allowed to grow tax-deferred until the policy is surrendered. Any net investment income and realized capital gains generated by the funds under the policy are tax-deferred until the policyowner cashes in the contract.

If a withdrawal is made, it is taxed first as ordinary income then as a return of investment. It is also subject to a 10% penalty if made before the policyholder reaches age 59 1/2. There are exceptions to this penalty.

Upon death, the policy proceeds, if paid in a lump sum to the beneficiary, are income tax exempt. If another option is chosen, a portion of the proceeds may be taxable. When the Interest option is chosen, the interest earned on the proceeds sent by the insurance company to the beneficiary is taxable as ordinary income.

QUICK QUIZ 4

1.   The insurer's "amount at risk" is less in the early years of a policy   Reference:
      than in the later years.   Page 9-20
            True/False

2.   The cash value is designed to equal the face amount of the policy   Reference:
      at conclusion of the contract.   Page 9-20
            True/False

3.   Which of the following is/are element(s) of a permanent whole life   Reference:
      policy?   Page 9-21
            I.   Death benefit
            II.   Cash value
            III.   Level premium payment
            IV.   Mortality expense
                a. I and II only
                b. I, II and III only
                c. I, III and IV only
                d. II only
                e. All of the above

4.   All of the following are true of a Variable Life Insurance policy,   Reference:
      EXCEPT: Page 9-22
                a. Death benefits may actually exceed the face amount
                b. Policyowners may direct the premium into a specific fund
                c. A minimum rate of growth is guaranteed in the cash value
                d. A minimum death benefit is guaranteed as long as premiums
                   are current
                e. All of the above

5.   Which settlement option would offer the greatest cash flow?   Reference:
                a. Life Income   Page 9-23
                b. Life Income with 10 years guaranteed
                c. Life Income with Refund
                d. Joint and Survivor Life Income
                e. Joint and 1/2 Survivor Life Income

6.   The maximum average sales charge calculated over a 20-year   Reference:
      period on a Variable Life policy is: Page 9-25
                a. 50%
                b. 20%
                c. 16%
                d. 9%
                e. 5%

7. Death benefits for a Variable Life policy must be calculated no less   Reference:
    than: Page 9-24
    a. Annually
    b. Semi-annually
    c. Quarterly
    d. Monthly
    e. Daily

8. Cash values for a Variable Life policy must be calculated no less   Reference:
    than: Page 9-24
    a. Annually
    b. Semi-annually
    c. Quarterly
    d. Monthly
    e. Daily

9. The "inside build-up" in a Variable Life policy is tax-deferred until   Reference:
    the policy is surrendered.   Page 9-25
         True/False

10. Withdrawals from a Variable Life policy made before the insured   Reference:
    reaches age 59 1/2 may be subject to a penalty tax of: Page 9-25
    a. 0%
    b. 5%
    c. 10%
    d. 28%
    e. 50%
         ANSWERS: 1-False; 2-True; 3-b; 4-c; 5-a; 6-d; 7-a; 8-d; 9-True; 10-c.

REAL LIFE SITUATION

Mr. Abercrombie F. Papoofnick, pastry chef turned clothing store operator, has asked you about your business, since he has noticed your are purchasing his most expensive clothing. He asks your advice on how deferred variable annuities operate because his stockbroker speaks very highly of them. He is confused by the terms *accumulation unit, annuity unit* and *assumed interest rate.*

     Mr. Papoofnick wants to know "what's in store" for him should he purchase such an annuity. Your advice would be:

Directions: *For each of the numbered recommendations that follow, please select A, B, or C as the evaluation you deem most correct. Place your selection on the line opposite each number.*

A. "Unsuitable" advice, you need to go back for a better fit!

B. Not completely accurate information under the circumstances.

C. Suitable and correct advice under the circumstances.

Answer

_____ 1.   All of these three items are just technical jargon and they don't mean much.

_____ 2.   Accumulation units are purchased instead of shares and they fluctuate in value based on an underlying portfolio (called a separate account).

_____ 3.   Annuity unit is the term used to designate when a contract is converted to a payout status under an annuity option.

_____ 4.   The only important consideration is what happens during accumulation. The annuity rates, annuity units calculation, and assumed interest rates make no difference.

_____ 5.   The assumed interest rate (AIR) is built into the rates for settlement options and has no effect on the contract during the accumulation phase.

ANSWERS: 1-A; 2-C; 3-C; 4-B; 5-C.

_____

CHECK YOUR UNDERSTANDING
(Circle one)

1. Issuing a life annuity contract is a procedure allowed to life insurance companies only.
        True/False

Reference:
Page 9-7

2. With fixed annuities, the investment risk is assumed by the buyer.
        True/False

Reference:
Page 9-7

3. The rate of return on both variable and fixed annuities is guaranteed by the insurance company.
        True/False

Reference:
Page 9-7

4. A unit investment trust is the most prevalent form of separate account system for variable annuities.
        True/False

Reference:
Page 9-9

5. Once an annuitant begins receiving payments from a variable annuity, the payment is fixed for the remainder of the annuitant's life.
        True/False

Reference:
Page 9-14

6. Variable annuity contracts, like many other investments, are measured in terms of shares.
    True/False

    Reference: Page 9-9

7. As the performance of a variable annuity portfolio improves, additional annuity units are credited to the contract holder's account.
    True/False

    Reference: Page 9-14

8. A joint and survivor annuity is the most common settlement option for an annuitant who wants his or her spouse to receive an income in the event of death.
    True/False

    Reference: Page 9-17

9. A single annuity contract may be a combination of both a fixed annuity and a variable annuity.
    True/False

    Reference: Page 9-18

10. A death benefit option with a variable annuity pays the *greater* of either the total of all payments made into the contract or the current value of the contract.
    True/False

    Reference: Page 9-17

ANSWERS: 1-True; 2-False; 3-False; 4-True; 5-False; 6-False; 7-False; 8-True; 9-False; 10-True.

STUDY NOTES

STUDY NOTES

10

SALES CHARGES AND TAX TREATMENT OF VARIABLE ANNUITIES

PRETEST
(Circle one)

1. Generally, variable annuities have what type of sales charges?
    a. High front end load charges
    b. Level 8.5% plans
    c. Either moderate amounts, e.g., 4%-5%, or no up front sales charges at all
    d. Only no loads—front and back
    e. Insurance company pays all sales charges

    Reference:
    Page 10-7

2. Redemptions of variable annuities with no up front sales charges especially in the first few years, could have:
    a. Restrictive, i.e., not allowed, by company
    b. Government prohibitions
    c. Government prohibitions for maximums only
    d. Government prohibitions for minimums only
    e. Redemption fees graded downward the longer the investment is held

    Reference:
    Page 10-7

3. Some charges (fees) inherent to variable annuities that are not present with mutual fund investments could be:
    a. Mortality expense fee
    b. Lifetime expense guarantee fee
    c. Neither of the above
    d. Both a. and b.
    e. No difference between variable annuities and straight mutual funds

    Reference:
    Page 10-7

1

4.   Another name for back-end sales charges, if none charged up   Reference:
      front, is: Page 10-8
      a.   Contingency fee (mandatory)
      b.   Contingency fee (if needed)
      c.   Contingent deferred sales charges
      d.   Phantom sales charge
      e.   Asset based sales charge

5.   In which manner is all interest and earning income as well as   Reference:
      realized capital gain income treated under non-qualified variable   Page 10-9
      annuity contracts?
      a.   Automatically reinvested in the separate account and
            capital-gain taxed to the owner
      b.   Automatically reinvested in the separate account and tax-
            deferred to the owner
      c.   Depends upon whether received in cash by the contract
            owner or reinvested
      d.   No reinvestment of earnings is allowed under annuity taxation
      e.   None of the above

6.   In a non-tax qualified deferred variable annuity contract, the   Reference:
      contract owner is taxed basis?   Page 10-9
      a.   Ordinary income tax annually on net investment income only
      b.   Ordinary income tax annually on net investment income and
            capital-gain tax on realized capital gains
      c.   Ordinary income tax annually on net investment income and
            capital-gain tax on unrealized capital gains
      d.   Annual taxation is deferred if no withdrawals are made
      e.   Identical to mutual fund taxation

7.   A deferred variable annuity contract holder with accumulated fund   Reference:
      assets over a ten-year period wishes to make a partial withdrawal.   Page 10-10
      Income taxation will be which of the following?
      a.   If the withdrawal amount exceeds the cost-basis, this
            excess is taxed at capital-gains rates
      b.   If the withdrawal amount exceeds the cost-basis, this
            excess is taxed at ordinary income tax rates
      c.   No taxation occurs if contract is still in the accumulation phase
      d.   Partial withdrawals will be considered payment of earnings
            up to the amount of the excess of funds available over
            the cost basis
      e.   None of the above

8. In which manner is a variable annuity contract under a settlement   Reference:
    option, where annuity payments are being made monthly, taxed   Page 10-10
    to the annuitant?
    a.   Under the exclusion allowance principal
    b.   Only on amounts up to the cost of the contract
    c.   Predicated on life expectancy via the insurance company tables
    d.   Taxed only when the total amount of payments exceeds
          the cost-basis
    e.   None of the above

9. Should a deferred variable annuity contract holder die during the   Reference:
    accumulation phase of the contract, and the proceeds of that con-   Page 10-12
    tract be paid to a beneficiary, which of the following taxation rules apply?
    I.   The estate of the deceased will escape taxation on
          this contract since it goes directly to a named
          beneficiary
    II.   The total value of the lump-sum proceeds will be
          taxed in the estate of the deceased
    III. The beneficiary receiving the contract takes the
          donor's cost-basis for income tax purposes
    IV.   The beneficiary receiving the contract will have the
          current value at the date of the deceased's death
          as the cost-basis
          a.   I only
          b.   I and II
          c.   II and III
          d.   I and III
          e.   All of the above

10. Unfunded deferred compensation plans between an employer and   Reference:
    an employee generally have which of the following taxation   Page 10-14
    precepts applied?
    I.   When the employee's rights become non-forfeitable
          and funded, taxation can apply to the employee currently
    II.   Deferred compensation payments at retirement,
          disability, or death are taxed as ordinary income
    III. Such plans do not require IRS approval
    IV.   It is possible to be discriminatory (selective) with-
          out adverse tax impact
          a.   I only
          b.   I and II
          c.   II and III
          d.   I and III
          e.   All of the above

11.   Which of the following statements about exclusion ratio is correct?   Reference:
    a.   The exclusion ratio determines the amount of each annuity   Page 10-11
        payment that is income tax free
    b.   The exclusion ratio determines the amount of each annuity
        payment that is taxed as ordinary income
    c.   The exclusion ratio determines the amount of each annuity
        payment that is taxed at capital-gain rates
    d.   The exclusion ratio does not affect taxation — it is based
        on life expectancy
    e.   If the annuity contract is purchased with after-tax dollars the
        exclusion ratio does not apply

12.   The principle behind taxation on annuity payments is that *part* of   Reference:
    each payment is the return of one's own money (and is income   Page 10-11
    tax free) and *part* of each payment is the result of earnings (and
    is taxed as ordinary income). The exclusion ratio, once figured,
    means that the annuitant can treat part of each annuity payment as
    return of principal up to:
    a.   The total amount he or she has invested in the contract
    b.   The average life expectancy (government tables) has been
        reached
    c.   The point that the total amount excluded under the exclusion
        ratio is equal to what the contract's value was at the inception
        of the annuity
    d.   No limit, as long as annuity payments are received
    e.   The mortality value of the contract using government
        mortality tables

13.   The tax *benefit* to the variable annuity insurance company, under   Reference:
    tax qualified plans, is essentially which of the following?   Page 10-11
    a.   During the accumulation phase, there is no corporate income
        tax exposure to investment earnings and gains
    b.   During the accumulation phase, there is no individual policy-
        holder income tax exposure to investment earnings and gains
    c.   If a plan loses its tax qualified status because of violating
        IRS rules, the owner can be subject to taxation on the growth
        (earnings and gains)
    d.   During the annuity payout phase, there is no corporation
        income taxation of investment earnings and gains
    e.   During the annuity payout phase, there is no policyholder
        income taxation on investment earnings and gains

14.   If the mortality experience of a specific variable annuity company   Reference:
       is more favorable than the industry average and the mortality   Page 10-8
       experience is more favorable than contemplated by the company's
       rates, the annuity income payments to contract holders under an
       annuity payout option will:
       a.   Tend to increase as a result of the favorable mortality
       b.   Tend to decrease as a result of the favorable mortality
       c.   Only increase if the mortality savings are substantial and
             consistent
       d.   Only decrease if the mortality savings are substantial and
             consistent
       e.   Not actually be affected

15.   Some deferred annuity contracts—to discourage early withdrawals   Reference:
       of money from the company—have adopted which of the following   Page 10-8
       provisions?
       a.   Waiver of premium provision
       b.   Redemption fee provision
       c.   Assignment provision
       d.   Sales charges graded down in later years
       e.   Level sales charge

16.   Should a variable annuity contract holder become *disabled* under   Reference:
       a periodic-payment variable annuity contract with the death benefit   Page 10-8
       provision, he or she will experience which of the following?
       a.   The periodic premiums will automatically be paid
       b.   No special benefit will be paid
       c.   The value of the contract will be frozen
       d.   The value of the contract will be the total current value
             or all premiums paid in, whichever is greater
       e.   None of the above

17.   Life expectancy used for federal taxation of variable annuity   Reference:
       benefits is based on: Page 10-10
       a.   IRS life expectancy tables
       b.   Federal Reserve life expectancy tables
       c.   SEC life expectancy tables
       d.   NASD life expectancy tables
       e.   Insurance company life expectancy tables

18.   Payments to a variable annuity contract under a tax qualified plan   Reference:
affect the "separate account" taxation in which of the following   Page 10-13
manners?
    I.   Tax qualified contributions will incur no taxation at
        the separate account or corporation level
    II.   The "separate account" must be registered as tax qualified
    III. Separate account taxation or taxation at the corporate
        level can apply only where the account has more
        than 10% non-tax, qualified contributions
      a.   I only
      b.   I and II
      c.   II and III
      d.   II only
      e.   III only

19.   An investor, redeeming a variable annuity contract, will have *any*   Reference:
gain on this contract taxed at: Page 10-10
      a.   Ordinary income rates
      b.   Short-term capital-gain rates
      c.   Long-term capital-gain rates
      d.   Deferred income rates
      e.   Rates that allow for exclusion ratio

20.   Which computation basis is used, if the recipient redeems a   Reference:
contract for its current value, under the general rule regarding   Page 10-13
cost-basis to an heir receiving a variable annuity contract from
an estate of a deceased?
      a.   Deceased's cost-basis plus "fresh-start addition"
      b.   Deceased's cost-basis
      c.   Stepped-up cost basis, i.e., fair market value at the date
          of death
      d.   No cost-basis at all because the heir never paid anything
          for it
      e.   Redemption will be income tax free because it is received through
          an estate, i.e., cost-basis is irrelevant

ANSWERS: 1-c; 2-e; 3-d; 4-c; 5-b; 6-d; 7-d; 8-a; 9-c; 10-e; 11-a; 12-a; 13-a; 14-e; 15-b; 16-b; 17-a; 18-a; 19-a; 20-b.

OVERVIEW

For any potential investor, two major points to investigate when considering the purchase of variable annuity contracts are sales charges and taxation treatment. This chapter reviews in detail the sales charges and legal requirements of variable annuity companies and their sales representatives. Also included is a discussion of the tax treatment of variable annuities during both the accumulation period and the payout period.

Author's Note to Candidates

It is always required that sales charges be fully disclosed to each client. Therefore, an understanding of these charges is necessary. As with other investment contracts, variable annuity sales charges are not to be shied away from, because it is often the case that "you get what you pay for." One of the most practical aspects of variable annuity contracts, and indeed all fixed and deferred annuity contracts, is the potential tax savings to a client during the accumulation phase. However, there are also potential tax disadvantages of annuity contracts (e.g., ordinary income at payout, no stepped-up basis at death). Both the advantages and the disadvantages should be reviewed with the client. This chapter provides the necessary information for you to conduct such a review.

SALES CHARGES

Variable annuity contracts because of marketplace competition generally have low (e.g., 4%-5%) sales charges or none at all.

Some companies have little or no sales charge at the inception of a contract. Often however, a fee must be paid upon contract redemption — for *either* partial or complete redemption. These redemption fees may be scaled down over a period of time. For instance, a 5% charge may be applied on amounts redeemed in the first two years; 2% on amounts redeemed in years three, four, five; and 1% of all redemptions after five years. Any redemption charges are applied *only* to the amount redeemed and *not* to the entire value of the contract.

To the extent sales charges exist, *break-points* and *rights of accumulation* exist with variable annuities as they do with open-end investment companies. Remember, that break-points allow a lower sales charge on *quantity* purchases and rights of accumulation permit an investor to total all investments under the same management to achieve break-point savings on later investments.

Other Charges and Deductions

All fees are outlined clearly in the *prospectus*. The *investment management fee* is outlined. In addition, there may be extra contract fees with variable annuities because of other guarantees in the contract. *Mortality guarantees* and *expense guarantees* are available that protect the contract in the event of adverse experience with either mortality or expense to the insurance company. (Conversely, any favorable experience will not directly benefit the contract either.) A fee is paid to the insurance company in return for these guarantees.

Some variable annuity companies offer a *built-in death benefit*, which states that should the contract holder die prior to retirement, the value of the contract will be either the current market value or total payments placed in the fund, whichever is *greater*. The company charges a fee for this potential risk.

In addition, many states have *premium taxes* (usually 1% to 2%) on annuity payments. In states where these apply, the insurance company pays the tax and then usually deducts it as an expense of the fund.

Redemption fees are more common now with variable annuities and deferred annuities than in the past. These fees are also detailed in the prospectus.

Any *brokerage fees* paid as commissions for securities transactions in the separate account are also an expense.

A few variable annuity and deferred annuity contracts provide a *waiver of premium benefit*. In which case, if a contract holder becomes disabled, the normal premiums are paid by the insurance company. There is an extra charge for this benefit. Occasionally, waiver of premium is a special election in which the fee is paid only by those contract holders electing the waiver of premium provision.

Contingent deferred sales charges are sometimes charged by an annuity company for early surrender or withdrawal of funds, i.e., all amounts withdrawn within first five years — 6% sales charge; amounts withdrawn years six to ten — 4% sales charge; all amounts withdrawn after ten years — no sales charge. The purpose of these deferred sales charges is to force retention of the investor's money longer and to pay distribution (commissions, etc.) expenses.

QUICK QUIZ 1

1.   Variable annuities do not require a prospectus.   Reference:
           True/False   Page 10-7

2.   Generally, variable annuities have what type of sales charges?   Reference:
      a.   High front end load charges   Page 10-7
      b.   Level 8.5% plans
      c.   Either moderate amounts, e.g., 4%-5%, or no up front
            sales charges at all
      d.   Only no loads—front and back
      e.   Insurance company pays all sales charges

3.   Redemptions of variable annuities with no up front sales charges   Reference:
      especially in the first few years, could have: Page 10-7
      a.   Restrictive, i.e., not allowed, by company
      b.   Government prohibitions
      c.   Government prohibitions for maximums only
      d.   Government prohibitions for minimums only
      e.   Redemption fees graded downward the longer the invest-
            ment is held

4.   Some charges (fees) inherent to variable annuities that are not   Reference:
      present with mutual fund investments could be: Page 10-7
      a.   Mortality expense fee
      b.   Lifetime expense guarantee fee
      c.   Neither of the above
      d.   Both a. and b.
      e.   No difference between variable annuities and straight
            mutual funds

5.   Another name for back-end sales charges, if none charged up   Reference:
      front, is: Page 10-8
      a.   Contingency fee (mandatory)
      b.   Contingency fee (if needed)
      c.   Contingent deferred sales charges
      d.   Phantom sales charge
      e.   Asset based sales charge

                              ANSWERS: 1-False; 2-c; 3-e; 4-d; 5-c.

TAX TREATMENT OF NON-QUALIFIED VARIABLE ANNUITIES

The term *non-qualified variable annuity contract* refers to those contracts owned by individuals or institutions that have *no* special tax treatment; that is, they are *not* investments under a Keogh plan, IRA plan, pension, profit-sharing, or other IRS qualified plan. What follows is an explanation of the taxation on this type of variable annuity contract.

Annual Tax Treatment

During the *accumulation phase*, there is *no* taxation to the contract holder. All net investment income and realized capital gains are automatically reinvested within the separate account and no taxation is assessed to the taxpayer each year. Note the difference between this variable annuity accumulation phase and that of open-end investment companies, where taxation is present annually.

Taxation upon Redemption

Under the IRS Code, deferred annuities generally allow an annuitant to defer taxation of the accumulated earnings until the annuity payments begin. In order to discourage the use of deferred annuities as a short-term investment, the taxation rules were changed under TEFRA for contracts entered into after August 13, 1982. For post-August 13, 1982 contracts, partial withdrawals before the annuity starting date will be considered payment of accumulated earnings and will only be treated as a non-taxable distribution out of principal after all accumulated earnings are withdrawn. Loans received by the annuitant are treated as withdrawals. Withdrawals of accumulated earnings from post-August 13, 1982 contracts may be subject to a 10% penalty tax, unless certain stipulated conditions are met.

Taxation of the Variable Annuity Company

The insurance company's separate account (non-qualified account) is fully taxed at insurance company rates (different from normal corporate rates)to the extent they are <u>not</u> allocated to reserves. However, they are normally allocated to reserves (policyholder money) so generally no taxes due with variable annuity investments until money is withdrawn by the investor.

Although insurance company taxation is complex, suffice it to say that many companies can minimize this tax impact on their non-qualified separate accounts. Payments to the separate account that represent "qualified money" (e.g., Keogh, IRA, pension contributions) do *not* result in company taxation.

Taxation under Settlement Options

When an annuitant/contract holder elects to move from the accumulation phase to the annuity payout phase, the contract, as discussed earlier, changes from accumulation units to annuity units. The value of a fixed number of annuity units are paid monthly to the annuitant. The taxation of these payments in retirement is based on the *annuity taxation principle*, which states that a portion of each payment will be *excluded* from taxation as a "return of principal" (annuitant's own money). Remember, no capital gains — ever! The amount excluded is called the *exclusion ratio*. The remaining portion is taxed as ordinary income. Calculation of the exclusion ratio is as follows:

$$\frac{\text{Investment in Contract}}{\text{Expected Return}^1} = \text{Exclusion Ratio}$$

The "life expectancy" of the annuitant is not based on insurance company life expectancy tables but on U.S. Treasury (IRS) tables. TRA '86 has changed the amount of the distributions that may be tax free. The amount of tax free recovery is limited to annuitant's investment in the contract. Payments thereafter are all taxable income. However, if annuity payments cease before the entire investment is recovered, the amount of the unrecovered investment is allowed as a deduction to the annuitant for the last taxable year. The rule applies for annuity starting dates after December 31, 1986.

When a variable annuity contract moves from the accumulation stage to the annuity stage, at the election of the owner, it is said that the contract becomes "annuitized." Remember, once an annuity option is selected and payments begin (annuitized), it is *irrevocable*. It should be reemphasized that a surrender of an annuity contract, at any point prior to the election of the annuity option, exposes the owner to potential ordinary income tax. The owner will receive the cost basis (investment in the contract) tax-free. The amount received in excess of the cost basis is taxable income. All earnings are

---

[1]   Amount of monthly payments times life expectancy of annuitant.

taxed at current income (ordinary income) rates.   To prevent a severe tax impact in any one year, contract holders should surrender portions of contracts over a long period of time, or elect to surrender major portions during years in which they have other losses to offset these gains.

    There is a potential 10% penalty if the annuity date is before age 59½. If the contract is being paid-out over a lifetime, even if started before age 59½, the 10% penalty can be avoided. This is one of the exceptions to the 10% penalty rules.

CHART 10.1

Non-Qualified Plan Taxation

Accumulation Period
- Contributions via "after tax" dollars
- Inside growth not taxable

↓

Payout Period
- distributions are not taxable to amount of cost basis
- Inside growth is fully taxable

Annuity Taxation Principle

Expected Return	
Inside growth is fully taxable	cost basis is non-taxable

QUICK QUIZ 2

6.   Under non-qualified variable annuity contracts, all interest and earnings income, as well as realized capital-gains income, is treated in which of the following manners?

Reference: Page 10-9

    a.   Automatically reinvested in the separate account and capital-gain taxed to the owner

    b.   Automatically reinvested in the separate account and tax-deferred to the owner

    c.   Depends upon whether received in cash by the contract owner or reinvested

    d.   No reinvestment of earnings is allowed under annuity taxation

    e.   None of the above

7.   In a non-tax qualified deferred variable annuity contract, the contract   Reference:
      owner has annual taxation predicted on which of the following?   Page 10-9
      a.   Ordinary income tax annually on net investment income only
      b.   Ordinary income tax annually on net investment income and
            capital-gain tax on realized capital gains
      c.   Ordinary income tax annually on net investment income and
            capital-gain tax on unrealized capital gains
      d.   Annual taxation is deferred if no withdrawals are made
      e.   Identical to mutual fund taxation

8.   A deferred variable annuity contract holder who has accumulated   Reference:
      fund assets over a ten-year period wishes to make a partial with-   Page 10-9
      drawal. Income taxation will be which of the following?
      a.   If the withdrawal amount exceeds the cost basis, this excess
            is taxed at capital-gains rates
      b.   If the withdrawal amount exceeds the cost basis, this excess
            is taxed at ordinary income tax rates
      c.   No taxation occurs if contract is still in the accumulation phase
      d.   Partial withdrawals will be considered payment of earnings
            up to the amount of the excess of funds available over the
            cost basis
      e.   None of the above

9.   A variable annuity contract under a settlement option, in which   Reference:
      annuity payments are being made monthly, is taxed to the   Page 10-10
      annuitant in which of the following manners?
      a.   Under the exclusion allowance principle
      b.   Only on amounts up to the cost of the contract
      c.   Predicated on life expectancy via the insurance company
            tables
      d.   Taxed only when the total amount of payments exceeds
            the cost basis
      e.   None of the above
                                          ANSWERS: 6-b; 7-d; 8-d; 9-a.

_____

DEATH BENEFIT DURING THE ACCUMULATION PERIOD

The *death benefit* under a variable annuity contract during the accumulation period is either the *current value* of the contract or, with some annuity companies, the *greater of either* the current value of the contract or the total payments made by the owner. In either case, if the deceased owned the contract, the total value is includable in the estate for estate tax purposes. A beneficiary can receive the total lump-sum benefits. There is *no* favorable stepped-up cost-basis to the beneficiary; that is, if lump-sum proceeds are cashed, the difference between the total proceeds received and the cost basis of the original owner (deceased) will be immediately taxed as ordinary income to the beneficiary. Please note this special rule.

TAX TREATMENT DURING THE ACCUMULATION PHASE OF TAX QUALIFIED ACCOUNTS

The insurance company itself calculates accumulation unit values under separate accounts for monies invested on a *tax-qualified* basis (e.g., Keogh, IRA, pension, 401(k)). The investment gains in this account are *not* subject to taxation as with any qualified plan.

Other non-qualified plans, such as payroll deduction plans, can use variable annuity or deferred annuity funding. A corporation can allow individuals to have payroll deductions for a personally owned deferred annuity account as a fringe benefit. No special taxation rules apply here. These plans are treated as non-tax qualified, i.e., after tax dollars.

Annuity contracts differ from other securities when calculating the *cost-basis* for individuals inheriting these contracts from an estate and, also, the cost-basis (for income tax purposes) to the estate itself. The general rule (after May, 1980) is that the securities value is "stepped-up" at the death of the owner. That is, the *income tax* cost basis to the estate and subsequently to the recipient of securities is "the fair market value on date of death, " or alternative valuation date (six months later), if elected. This rule is favorable *except* for *deferred* annuity contracts, which do *not* qualify for this treatment. The cost-basis to a recipient receiving deferred annuity contracts from an estate is the deceased's cost-basis (which is probably much lower than date of death value).

This cost-basis discussion applies to income taxation only. The difference between the total amount received upon surrender and the deceased's cost-basis is subject to ordinary income taxes. It does *not* affect *estate taxation*. The estate has the full fair market value of all annuity contracts taxed in the deceased's estate if the deceased owned the contract prior to death.

CHART 10.2

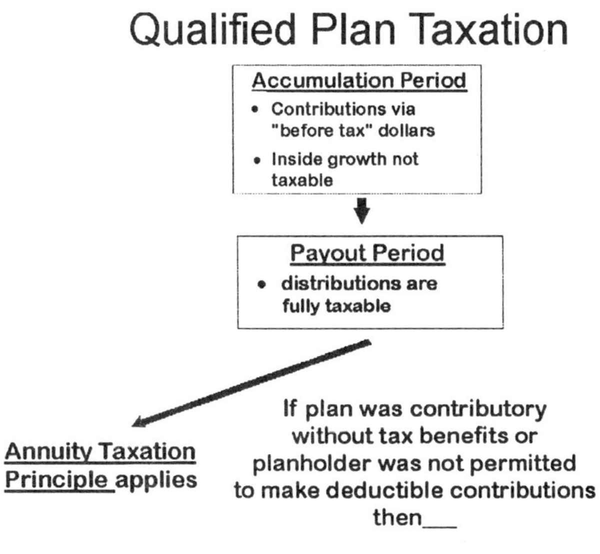

Qualified Plan Taxation

Accumulation Period
- Contributions via "before tax" dollars
- Inside growth not taxable

↓

Payout Period
- distributions are fully taxable

Annuity Taxation Principle applies

If plan was contributory without tax benefits or planholder was not permitted to make deductible contributions then___

DEFERRED COMPENSATION

Deferred compensation is a written and binding agreement entered into by an employer and an employee (usually highly paid) for the deferral of part of the employee's compensation until retirement, disability, or death — whichever occurs first. Most deferred compensation plans are now *non-qualified*; that is, they are informal and are not approved by the IRS. This means they receive *no* special tax treatment.

The advantage of informal or "pick and choose" deferred compensation plans is that the employer can select the employees to which he or she is willing to offer this benefit. Generally, the benefits are outlined in the agreement and cover such benefits as retirement, disability, or death benefits. If an employee, however, were to leave an employer prior to retirement, disability, or death; often all rights are forfeited unless there is a vesting schedule.

Many of these plans are *unfunded* (i.e., employer sets aside no funds). Funded plans can carry with them adverse tax impact: if the employee has complete non-forfeiture rights and if the funds are set aside and the employer no longer has control, the employee can be taxed on this money. (This is just what one doesn't want to happen!) It is only the general *promise* of the corporation to pay the benefits in the contract that allows non-qualified, informal deferred compensation plans still to have a place in America!

The corporation does not set aside money or other assets so the above mentioned adverse tax impact will not take place. However, it *is* a legally binding promise to pay should the employee meet the terms of the contract and keep working for that firm until retirement, disability, or death. As you can see, the employee is reliant upon the corporation's solvency far into the future. Corporate failure could lead to a loss of deferred compensation payments. Under these plans, only when the employee actually receives the deferred compensation payments are they taxed and then only the amount actually received each year.

QUICK QUIZ 3

10.   Should a deferred variable annuity contract holder die during the accumulation phase of the contract, and the proceeds of that contract be paid to a beneficiary, which of the following taxation rules apply?   Reference: Page 10-12

    I.   The estate of the deceased will escape taxation on this contract since it goes directly to a named beneficiary

    II.   The total value of the lump-sum proceeds will be taxed in the estate of the deceased

    III.   The beneficiary receiving the contract takes the donor's cost basis for income tax purposes

    IV.   The beneficiary receiving the contract will have the current value at the date of the deceased's death as the cost basis

        a.   I only

        b.   I and II

    c.   II and III
    d.   I and III
    e.   All of the above

11.   Which of the following taxation precepts are generally   Reference:
    applied with unfunded deferred compensation plans between   Page 10-14
    employer and an employee?
    I.   When the employee's rights become non-forfeitable
        and funded, taxation can apply to the employee currently
    II.   Deferred compensation payments at retirement,
        disability, or death are taxed as ordinary income
    III. Does not require IRS approval
    IV. It is possible to be discriminatory (selective) without
        adverse tax impact
        a.   I only
        b.   I and II
        c.   II and III
        d.   I and III
        e.   All of the above

ANSWERS: 10-c; 11-e.

REAL LIFE SITUATION

Mr. Axewell Aileron, owner of a private aircraft flying service, occasionally flies you and other professionals to business meetings. He also is a 50% partner in a French restaurant with his daughter, Entrecote.

    You have frequented their restaurant and have given financial advice, when asked, to Entrecote. She has discussed how long everyone in her family seems to be living; you mention that a variable annuity might be appropriate for some of her family members.

    Entrecote tells you that last February she inherited a variably annuity contract from her mother's estate. She is quite familiar with income taxes and asks to be "briefed" on how this variable annuity contract works. Your advice to Entrecote is:

Directions: *For each of the numbered recommendations that follow, please select A, B, or C as the evaluation you deem most correct. Place your selection on the line opposite each number.*

A. You have served up a bad steak, less than tasty!	B. Inappropriate advice; one or more shortcomings exist.	C. Suitable and correct advice under the circumstances.

Answer

_____   1.   Variable annuities completely avoid income taxes, whether received through inheritance or otherwise.

_____   2.   A deferred annuity contract like hers does not receive any "step-up" cost-basis at death, so she will be exposed to ordinary income taxes upon redemption on the difference between the current value and her mother's original cost-basis (possibly quite low).

_____   3.   The best solution to avoiding income taxes would be to select a payout (annuity) option, if the insurance company will permit, and receive monthly payments.

_____   4.   She should redeem immediately and invest in rare French wines because variable annuities are not good for people who live a long time.

_____   5.   There will be no way for her to achieve capital-gain treatment on a variable annuity contract, but continued income tax deferral is a valuable feature of these contracts.

ANSWERS: 1-A; 2-C; 3-B; 4-A; 5-C.

CHECK YOUR UNDERSTANDING
(Circle one)

1.   A variable annuity must always have a sales charge, which is disclosed in the prospectus.
        True/False

Reference:
Page 10-7

2.   The sales charge on a voluntary deferred annuity must be the front-end load type.
        True/False

Reference:
Page 10-7

3.   With a built-in death benefit, generally if the contract holder of a variable annuity dies before retirement, the value of the contract will be either the current market value or total payments placed in the fund, whichever is greater.
        True/False

Reference:
Page 10-12

4.   During the accumulation phase, annual taxation on non-qualified variable annuity contracts exists only on the realized capital-gain portion.
        True/False

Reference:
Page 10-9

5.   A partial withdrawal from a non-qualified annuity is taxed as income   Reference:
      to the extent that the accumulation exceeds the cost-basis.   Page 10-9
           True/False

6.   Insurance company taxation is generally not a factor for either   Reference:
      qualified or non-qualified variable annuity accounts.   Page 10-10
           True/False

7.   The annuity taxation principle states that a portion of each payment   Reference:
      will be excluded from taxation as a return of principal.   Page 10-10
           True/False

8.   Once all originally invested principal has been paid out, the tax-   Reference:
      free portion of the monthly annuity payment is no longer tax exempt   Page 10-10
           True/False

9.   Once a contract holder has moved from the accumulation phase   Reference:
      to the annuity or "payout" phase, he or she cannot go back.   Page 10-10
           True/False

10.   Deferred compensation would be an excellent retirement option for   Reference:
      a thirty-five-year-old executive who is not really sure if his or her   Page 10-14
      company will still be around in thirty years to pay its normal retire-
      ment benefits.
           True/False

ANSWERS: 1-False; 2-False; 3-True; 4-False; 5-True; 6-True; 7-True; 8-True; 9-True; 10-False.

STUDY NOTES

<u>STUDY NOTES</u>

11

QUALIFIED PLANS:
IRA AND PLANS FOR
SELF-EMPLOYED INDIVIDUALS

PRETEST
(Circle one)

1. Each of the following are acceptable as funding instruments for an IRA *except*:
   a. Mutual fund programs
   b. Face amount certificates
   c. Government bonds
   d. Retirement-income policies
   e. Flexible premium annuities

   Reference:
   Page 11-6

2. Individual Retirement Account funding instruments are restricted by:
   a. The Reform Act of 1976
   b. The Revenue Act of 1978
   c. The Employment Retirement Income Security Act of 1974
   d. The Self-Employed Individual Tax Retirement Act of 1962
   e. The Keogh Act

   Reference:
   Page 11-6

3. Trustee and custodial plans are permissible funding instruments for an IRA. Examples of these plans would include:
   a. Savings accounts
   b. Series HH bonds
   c. Series EE bonds
   d. Flexible premium annuities
   e. Retirement-income endowments

   Reference:
   Page 11-6

1

4.   An individual IRA participant may contribute up to what percentage   Reference:
      of income to his or her plan (limit $2,000)?   Page 11-8
      a.   100% of total income
      b.   10% of total income
      c.   100% of earned income
      d.   10% of earned income
      e.   None of the above

5.   SIMPLE IRAs allow an employee to defer, as a tax incentive, their   Reference:
      wages into an employer paid SIMPLE IRA of up to _____ of wages?   Page 11-8
      a. $30,000
      b. $15,000
      c. $9,500
      d. $7,500
      e. $6,000

6.   Contributions made to an IRA in excess of the allowable limits are   Reference:
      subject to: Page 11-8
      a.   Removal
      b.   6% penalty tax
      c.   50% penalty tax
      d.   No penalty but no tax deduction
      e.   Plan disqualifications

7.   Premature distributions from an IRA Plan would be subject to: Reference:
      a.   50% penalty tax   Page 11-9
      b.   25% penalty tax
      c.   No penalty tax
      d.   10% penalty tax
      e.   5% penalty tax

8.   Distributions from an individual retirement account are taxed as: Reference:
      a.   Capital gains   Page 11-10
      b.   Ordinary income
      c.   An annuity
      d.   Not taxed
      e.   Taxed at 50%

9.   Premature distributions from an IRA prior to age 59½ subjects the   Reference:
      distribution to a 10% penalty tax *except*:   Page 11-10
      a.   In the event of partial disability
      b.   If economic need is established
      c.   If only a partial distribution
      d.   In the event of death
      e.   None of the above

10. If IRA benefits are distributed in the form of annuity payments and the full amount of the individual payments is not distributed in the year due, a tax is imposed of:
Reference: Page 11-11
   a.   10%
   b.   20%
   c.   30%
   d.   40%
   e.   50%

11. When all pension plan contributions are put into an annuity or a life insurance contract, the plan is said to be:
Reference: Page 11-13
   a.   Fully funded
   b.   Fully insured
   c.   Split funded
   d.   Split insured
   e.   None of the above

12. Face amount certificates are considered under the law as being:
Reference: Page 11-13
   a.   Life insurance contracts
   b.   Variable investments
   c.   Equity instruments
   d.   Annuities
   e.   Trusted accounts

13. When a portion of a qualified plan contribution is placed in an annuity and the balance is placed in another type of investment medium, the plan is referred to as:
Reference: Page 11-13
   a.   Split funded
   b.   Split insured
   c.   Combination insured
   d.   Uninsured
   e.   Fully invested

14. A face amount certificate is considered an investment contract between the purchaser and the _____ issuing the certificate.
Reference: Page 11-13
   a.   Individual
   b.   Employer
   c.   Company
   d.   Mutual fund
   e.   Government

15. The pension plan benefit or contribution limit for a self-employed person is determined by:

Reference: Page 11-15

    a. Schedule C income
    b. Earned income
    c. Compensation
    d. Covered payroll
    e. IRA contributions

16. Investment income realized from voluntary contribution is not taxed to the participant until the plan benefits are actually distributed; however, voluntary contributions are:

Reference: Page 11-17

    a. Tax deductible
    b. Not tax deductible
    c. Penalized
    d. Non-vested
    e. None of the above

17. A sole proprietor with no employees with Schedule C income of $125,000 may contribute what amount for his/her Keogh pension?

Reference: Page 11-15

    a. $30,000
    b. $31,500
    c. $15,000
    d. $90,000
    e. $25,000

18. Who among the following would not be eligible to borrow from a qualified plan?

Reference: Page 11-16

    a. A regular corporation president
    b. A minority stockholder-employee
    c. A corporation employee
    d. A partnership employee
    e. A sole proprietor

19. Which of the following is a tax advantage of a qualified retirement plan?

Reference: Page 11-17

    a. Death benefits are excluded from a deceased employee's estate
    b. Employer contributions are taxable income to employees
    c. Investment earnings accrue on a tax-deferred basis
    d. Distributions from a qualified plan are exempt from taxation as ordinary income
    e. None of the above

20.   All of the following are tax benefits of a partnership qualified plan,   Reference:
       except: Page 11-16

    a.   Participants are not subject to current taxation on annual
        contributions

    b.   Plan investment earnings accrue without current income
        tax liability

    c.   Pension plan death benefits are included in a deceased
        participant's taxable estate

    d.   Distributions are subject to income taxation when received

    e.   A participant's non-deductible contribution can be recovered
        income tax-free

ANSWERS: 1-d; 2-b; 3-a; 4-c; 5-e; 6-b; 7-d; 8-b; 9-d; 10-e; 11-b; 12-d; 13-a; 14-c; 15-b;
16-b; 17-e; 18-e; 19-c; 20-c.

OVERVIEW

A "qualified plan" is a retirement plan that qualifies for various tax advantages. Any individual who has earned income may establish an Individual Retirement Account (IRA). Through an IRA an individual will benefit by tax savings while building a retirement fund.

    From 1962 until 1984 self-employed persons (sole proprietors or partners) could establish Keogh (HR10) plans. These had some of the advantages of corporate plans — but some limitations also. However, since 1984 self-employed plans have become very similar to corporate plans. In the second part of this chapter, please note that there are some remaining differences, which are pointed out.

    It is important that registered representatives understand the tax treatment of plan contributions, plan investment earnings, and plan distributions.

Author's Notes to Candidates

In this chapter we will explore the various facets of IRA and self-employed individuals' Plans. Much of this material will look familiar to you; however, please do not underestimate its difficulty. You should reference this material with any new legislative changes in amounts and requirements that have recently passed. Your company can provide this material.

I.   INDIVIDUAL RETIREMENT ACCOUNT (IRA)

The purpose of an IRA

That tax deferred IRA account was everything
it was cracked up to be!

Individual retirement accounts allow for tax-deductible contributions to retirement programs for employees whether covered or not by a private, qualified pension or profit-sharing plan. These contributions are allowed to accumulate on a tax deferred basis; that is, the contributions and investment income will not be taxed until distributed to the individual.

The Funding of an IRA

The Revenue Act of 1978 restricts "the ways individual retirement accounts can be funded." The Revenue Act provides that *no* fixed premium contract can be used. This prevents the use of regular annuities, endowments, or fully insured plans (e.g., retirement income insurance policies). The only insurance-type contracts to remain following these revisions are *flexible premium annuities*. Most insurance companies offer these now.

Trustee and custodial plans are permissible funding instruments for an IRA. These plans include savings accounts, mutual fund programs, face amount certificates, and insured credit union accounts. There are several restrictions that apply to this type of funding medium. For example, the contribution must be made in cash with a maximum limit of $2,000. (Spousal IRAs, to be covered later in this assignment, permit $4,000). In addition the account must be non-forfeitable, provide no life insurance coverage, and the commingling of funds with any personal property is not allowed.

Government bonds offer an additional type of funding instrument. These special bonds were created under the Second Liberty Bond Act and meet all of the requirements of the Internal Revenue Code. If this type of funding instrument is used there is no need for a special plan or trust agreement. The provisions of this bond issue are that interest is accumulated and paid at redemption, which may take place at any time. The maximum purchasable amount coincides with the contribution limitations provided by an IRA Plan. These bonds are *not* transferrable and may *not* be used as collateral.

You've got to deal with one of these traditional institutions if you want an <u>IRA</u>!

Mutual Fund   **Insurance Company**   **Bank**   **U.S. Government**

QUICK QUIZ 1

1. Each of the following are acceptable as funding instruments for an   Reference:
    IRA *except*:   Page 11-6
    a. Mutual fund programs
    b. Face amount certificates
    c. Government bonds
    d. Retirement-income policies
    e. Flexible premium annuities

2. Individual Retirement Account funding instruments are restricted by: Reference:
    a. The Reform Act of 1976   Page 11-6
    b. The Revenue Act of 1978
    c. The Employee Retirement Income Security Act of 1974
    d. The self-employed individual's Tax Retirement Act of 1962
    e. The Keogh Act

3. Trusteed and custodial plans are permissible funding instruments   Reference:
    for an IRA. Examples of these would include: Page 11-6
    a. Savings accounts
    b. Series HH bonds
    c. Series EE bonds
    d. Flexible premium annuities
    e. Retirement-income endowments

4. The government bonds used to fund an IRA are/are not transferable   Reference:
    and may/may not be used as collateral (circle correct answers).   Page 11-6

                          ANSWERS: 1-d; 2-b; 3-a; 4-are not, may not.

Contributions to an IRA

A qualified IRA participant may contribute up to 100% of *earned income* before taxes or $2,000, whichever is less. In addition, an individual participant having a legally married spouse may elect a non-working spousal option and contribute a maximum of $4,000. In a spousal IRA, the amount of the contribution credited to each party can be designated but no participant may be credited with more than $2,000.

IRAs and TRA '86

The Tax Reform Act of 1986 made major changes in the deductibility of IRA contributions. Deductible IRA contributions are restricted to:

- Individuals who are not participants in an employer-maintained retirement plan.
- Any other individual, as long as the individual (or married couple if a joint return is filed) has adjusted gross income below a specified limit. If the AGI exceeded this limit, the $2,000 IRA limit is reduced under a formula that eventually permits no deduction.

If either spouse is an active participant in an employer plan, then both spouses are subject to the participation restriction. Persons who are not eligible to make deductible contributions may make non-deductible contributions and still gain the benefit of tax deferred growth.

After January 1, 1997, *SIMPLE IRAs*, now allow small employers of under 100 employees to contribute to an employee's IRA. These are now known as SIMPLE IRAs (Savings Incentive Match Plan for Employees). Employees may defer salary up to $6,000 per year in such a plan (up to 3% of pay). Vesting is immediate.

Taxation of Contributions to an IRA

Contributions up to the limits established (the lesser of 100% of earned income or $2,000 — or $4,000 if the spousal option is elected) are tax deductible. These limits apply to all funding media. Contributions in excess of allowable limits are subject to an annual (non-deductible) 6% penalty tax for the year in which they are made — and each year thereafter until the excess is removed. If not withdrawn, excess IRA contributions may be deducted in a subsequent year — when an individual's deductible contribution is less than the maximum allowable deduction. In the event of excess contributions, the excess may be withdrawn at any time without being included in gross income, if no tax deduction was previously allowed (i.e., participant deposited more than allowable limit but didn't try to deduct for excess on income tax return).

The deadline for establishing a new IRA, or contributing to an in-force IRA, is the due date for filing your income-tax return for the taxable year. For example, an IRA may be established as late as April 15, for the preceding taxable year. Any allowable contributions made within this period would be fully tax deductible for the filing year.

Rollover IRA is a means of investing certain *qualified plan* distributions from either qualified pension, profit-sharing, IRA or 403(b) tax-sheltered annuities. The purpose of a rollover IRA is to defer taxation on such distributions and/or to avoid tax penalties resulting from any premature plan distributions before age 59½. To qualify as a *rollover*, money or property that has been distributed must be reinvested within sixty days. A distribution from an IRA may be partially rolled over within sixty days of receipt. The amount rolled over will not be taxed, but any amount retained will be taxed in the year received. After January 1, 1993, unless a rollover is effected through a trustee-to-trustee transfer, the distribution amount is subject to a mandatory income tax withholding of 20%. In other words, the check can no longer be made out to you and signed over to the new trustee — unless you want 20% withheld.

What are you doing
between 59½ and 70½?

Taking out my IRA
proceeds, of course.

Plan distributions that are transferred to a rollover IRA are "frozen in" until age 59½. No parts of the distribution can be withdrawn, borrowed, pledged, or hypothecated in any way. Any such premature distribution, except electing a lifetime annuity payout before age 59½, would be subject to a 10% penalty tax. In the case of a loan, the entire plan is disqualified. A tax-deferred rollover may be made only *once* each year. Also, such transfers must be made into a separate rollover IRA and cannot be commingled with the assets of an IRA to which an individual is contributing annually. There is no restriction on owning both a rollover IRA, which is holding assets of a tax-deferred transfer, and a regular IRA, to which an individual is making annual contributions. A trustee to trustee transfer from a qualified plan to an IRA is not considered a "rollover."

Taxation During the Accumulation Period

One of the primary tax advantages provided by an IRA is the deferment of taxation on contributions made to the program from earned income. These contributions and the interest earnings will accumulate tax deferred throughout the accumulation period.

QUICK QUIZ 2

5.   An individual IRA participant may contribute up to what percentage   Reference:
of income to his or her plan (limit $2,000)?   Page 11-8
    a.   15% of total income
    b.   10% of total income
    c.   100% of earned income
    d.   10% of earned income
    e.   None of the above

6.   SIMPLE IRAs allow an employee to defer, as a tax incentive, their   Reference:
wages into an employer paid SIMPLE IRA of up to _____ of wages?   Page 11-8
    a. $30,000
    b. $15,000
    c. $9,500
    d. $7,500
    e. $6,000

7.   Contributions made to an IRA in excess of the allowable limit are   Reference:
subject to: Page 11-8
    a.   Removal
    b.   6% penalty tax
    c.   50% penalty tax
    d.   No penalty but no tax deduction
    e.   Plan disqualifications

8.   Premature distributions from an IRA Plan would be subject to: Reference:
    a.   50% penalty tax   Page 11-9
    b.   25% penalty tax
    c.   No penalty tax
    d.   10% penalty tax
    e.   5% penalty tax

ANSWERS: 5-c; 6-e; 7-b; 8-d.

Taxation During Payout Period

Distributions from an individual retirement account must begin after age 59½ but before age 70½. These distributions are taxed as ordinary income including a lump-sum distribution.

Exceptions to this early distribution rule, i.e., penalty waived, are death, disability, or lifetime payout (annuity) of funds. New rules allow penalty to be waived if distribution is for medical expenses because of unemployment (twelve weeks or longer and eligible for unemployment compensation) or for medical expenses that exceed 7.5% of adjusted gross income. Any "premature distribution" from an IRA, prior to age 59½, subjects the distribution to a 10% penalty tax. (This is on top of any increase in an individual's regular income tax that may result from including the distribution in gross income.) In addition to being imposed on an actual distribution, the penalty tax is also imposed on any "constructive" distribution resulting from a disqualification of an IRA. For example, if an individual borrows money from the IRA, the plan will be disqualified as of the first day of the taxable year in which the loan was made, *and* the individual will be treated as if the entire assets of the plan had been distributed. However, if an individual borrows money, using a portion of the IRA as security, *only* the portion used as security is treated as a distribution.

In addition to penalizing a distribution that is made too early, the law also penalizes one that is made too late in life. To encourage the use of IRAs for retirement purposes, the law requires an individual to start drawing retirement benefits *no later than* April 1 following the year in which age 70½ is reached. If the benefits are taken in a lump sum, the entire amount must be distributed before this date. If the benefits are distributed in the form of annuity payments, the full amount of each payment must be distributed in the year when due. Violation of this rule results in a 50% tax being imposed on the difference between the minimum and actual payment. For example, if an individual receives an annual annuity payment of $1,000, which is less than a minimum required payment of $1,500, a tax of $250 ($1,500 - $1,000 x 50%) must be paid. This tax will be waived where excess accumulations are due to reasonable cause and steps are being taken to correct it.

QUICK QUIZ 3

9. Distributions from an individual retirement account are taxed as:
   Reference:
   Page 11-10
   a. Capital gains
   b. Ordinary income
   c. An annuity
   d. Not taxed
   e. Taxed at 50%

10. Premature distributions from an IRA prior to age 59½ are subject to a 10% penalty tax *except*:
    Reference:
    Page 11-10
    a. In the event of partial disability
    b. If economic need is established
    c. If only a partial distribution
    d. In the event of death
    e. None of the above

11. If IRA benefits are distributed in the form of annuity payments and the full amount of the individual payments is not distributed in the year due, a tax is imposed of:
    Reference:
    Page 11-11
    a. 10%
    b. 20%
    c. 30%
    d. 40%
    e. 50%

12. The penalty tax mentioned in question #11 will be waived when excess accumulations are due to _____ _____ and steps are being taken to _____ the excess.

Reference:
Page 11-8

ANSWERS: 9-b; 10-d; 11-e; 12-reasonable cause, correct.

II. RETIREMENT PLANS FOR SOLE PROPRIETORS AND PARTNERS

Background

For many years in the United States there has been general recognition that employers should be encouraged to provide retirement benefits for their employees. Tax incentives were offered to employers as well as to their employees who participated in the plans.

The legislation that provided the tax incentives recognized stockholders as employees if they were performing personal service in an incorporated business. However, owners of unincorporated businesses were deemed to be "self-employed" (not employees) and thus not eligible for tax advantaged retirement plans. Thus, there was little incentive for these individuals to establish retirement programs for their employees.

The plight of the self-employed was understood by Representative E.J. Keogh of New Jersey who dedicated his congressional career to rectifying the situation. In 1962 he introduced House Resolution 10 (HR-10), the Self-Employed Individual's Retirement Act, which was enacted into law.

This Act enabled sole proprietors and partners to establish retirement plans for themselves and their employees. The tax benefits were significant, but not as liberal as the benefits provided by corporate plans. The rules were stringent — allowing little flexibility for self-employed individuals establishing such plans.

Initially, the allowable tax deductible deductions were quite small, but the amount was increased periodically.

Parity between corporate plans and plans for self-employed persons was achieved with the passage of the Tax Equity and Fiscal Responsibility Act of 1982 (TEFRA). This Act essentially provided equal benefits for plan years beginning in 1984 and after.

I'm a split funded plan

Funding

A funding agency is an organization that provides facilities for the accumulation and/or administration of assets for the ultimate payment of benefits under a pension plan. Funding agencies include life insurance companies, corporate fiduciaries, and individuals acting as trustees.

A funding instrument (or medium) is an agreement or contract specifying the conditions under which assets are accumulated or administered by a funding agency. The most common funding media are annuity and life insurance contracts, mutual funds, bank trust funds, and face amount certificates.

Annuity and life insurance contracts are the funding media offered by insurance companies. When all plan contributions are put into annuities or life insurance contracts, the plan is said to be fully insured. When only a portion of the plan contributions are placed in annuity or life insurance contracts and the balance placed in other investments, the plan is referred to as combination-funded or split-funded plan.

A mutual fund is a funding medium where contributions are made to an investment company, which then invests the money into a large and diversified portfolio of stocks and/or bonds. The investment company thus has pooled funds of many contributions for investment.

Bank trust funds also provide a medium for investing plan contributions. A bank-trusteed retirement plan can provide for a variety of investments. For example, they can invest funds utilizing their own investment facilities; or they can act as other financial organizations, such as insurance companies or investment companies.

U.S. Government bonds provide another medium for the investment of funds. An interesting feature of the bond purchase plan for IRAs only is that there is no need for a detailed plan document, as is necessary with other funding media.

Face amount certificates are considered under the law to be annuities. Put simply, a face amount certificate is an investment contract between the purchaser and the company issuing the certificate. It is a promise to pay the certificate's face amount at maturity. The plan document used when purchasing face amount certificates is of the same general type as the one used when purchasing annuity or life insurance contracts from an insurance company. Face amount certificates are deemed to be securities if the maturity is greater than 24 months.

QUICK QUIZ 4

13.   When all contributions are put into an annuity or a life insurance   Reference:
      contract a plan is said to be: Page 11-13
      a.   Full funded
      b.   Fully insured
      c.   Split funded
      d.   Split insured
      e.   None of the above

14.   Face amount certificates are considered under the law as being:
   a.   Life insurance contracts
   b.   Variable investments
   c.   Equity instruments
   d.   Annuities
   e.   Trust accounts

   Reference:
   Page 11-13

15.   When a portion of plan contributions is placed in an annuity and the balance is placed in another type of investment medium, the plan is referred to as:
   a.   Split funded
   b.   Split insured
   c.   Combination insured
   d.   Uninsured
   e.   Fully invested

   Reference:
   Page 11-13

16.   A face amount certificate is considered an investment contract between the purchaser and the _____ issuing the certificate.
   a.   Individual
   b.   Employer
   c.   Company
   d.   Mutual fund
   e.   Government

   Reference:
   Page 11-13

   ANSWERS: 13-b; 14-d; 15-a; 16-c.

Eligibility and Vesting

Employees are eligible to participate when they meet the eligibility requirements specified in the plan. These requirements may include both minimum age and years of service, but not to exceed age 21 or the completion of one year of service. The plan may require the completion of two years of service, but it must then give the participant a nonforfeitable right to 100% of the accrued benefit.

   Vesting requirements are no longer as stringent as they formerly were, but must meet minimum ERISA requirements (See Chapter 12).

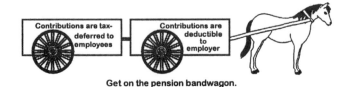

Get on the pension bandwagon.

Contributions

A proprietor or partner may contribute and deduct annually an amount up to 25% of earned income, not to exceed $30,000 (Keogh). Earned income is defined as net earnings after business deductions (including contributions made to a qualified plan) resulting from "personal services rendered."

Illustrating the calculation of a proprietor's qualified plan contribution:

Joe Richard's proprietorship has three employees and "Schedule C income" (business income after all deductions except those for plan contributions) is $150,000. The Richard plan calls for contributions of 10% of compensation (for regular employees) or earned income (for the proprietor).

Plan Participant	Compensation or Earned Income	Plan Contribution
Owner	$133,000	$13,300
#1	10,000	1,000
#2	12,000	1,200
#3	15,000	1,500

The proprietor's contribution is determined by this method:

1. Subtract employee's contributions from Schedule C income ($150,000 - $3,700 = $146,300)
2. Divide the result by 1 plus the percentage to be contributed ($146,300/1.10 = $133,000)
3. Apply the percentage to the owner's earned income (.10 x $133,000 = $13,300).[1]

Margie's Gas Station   Margie   Margie's Towing Service

If you own more than 0% of any business, employees in all of them have to be included in the plan.

---

[1]   Only the first $150,000 of earned income is to be considered in calculating contributions.

Special Rules

There are several rules that apply to qualified plans for a partner or proprietor:

1. Plan contribution is based on "earned income" rather than "compensation". (See above)
2. A partner or proprietor may not borrow from their qualified plan, although regular employees may borrow against their account if permitted by the plan document.
3. A business generally cannot take a deduction for the cost of pure life, health, or accident insurance for a partner or proprietor. The cash value portion of the premium can be deduction.
4. If a qualified plan covers a partner or proprietor who controls another business (more than 50% ownership) then the plan must cover the employees of the controlled business or a comparable plan must be provided for employees of the controlled business.

Taxation of Qualified Plans

Note: The Internal Revenue Code as well as Internal Revenue Service regulations and rulings have been changing frequently in recent years. The reader should check with his or her broker/dealer for recent changes.

The term "qualified plan" indicates that the plan qualifies for certain tax advantages, i.e., contribution is tax deductible. This section will discuss separately the tax treatment of contributions, accumulations, death benefits, and distributions.

Contributions

We have discussed earlier the deductibility of contributions to qualified plans for self-employed persons up to the lesser of 25% of earned income or $30,000. It is equally important to note that any contribution made on behalf of a plan participant is not currently taxed to that person. If a self-employed person contributes more than he can deduct in a year he is subject to a 10% penalty on the excess.

Accumulations

When the contribution is invested for a plan participant, the investment earnings accrue on a tax-deferred basis. That is, there is no year-by-year income tax liability on plan investment earnings.

Distributions

The general rule is that all distributions from a qualified plan are subject to taxation as ordinary income. If any plan participant has a cost-basis because of non-deductible contributions he or she is entitled to recover the cost basis free of income taxation. This will be discussed in greater detail in the following chapter.

QUICK QUIZ 5

17. Which of the following could participate in a partnership qualified plan?
    a. All partners without exception
    b. Partners who perform personal service
    c. Inactive or "silent" partners
    d. Limited partners
    e. Employees only

    Reference:
    Page 11-16

18. A sole proprietor with no employees with Schedule C income of $125,000 may contribute what amount for his/her Keogh pension?
    a. $30,000
    b. $31,250
    c. $15,000
    d. $90,000
    e. $25,000

    Reference:
    Page 11-15

19. Who among the following would not be eligible to borrow from a qualified plan?
    a. A regular corporation president
    b. A minority stockholder-employee
    c. A corporation employee
    d. A partnership employee
    e. A sole proprietor

    Reference:
    Page 11-16

20. A sole proprietor who has a pension is also a 60% partner in another business. Select the correct statement regarding the partnership:
    a. Must provide the same plan or a comparable plan to employees of partnership
    b. No plan required
    c. Either business may have a plan, but not both of them
    d. There is no requirement or prohibition
    e. None of the above

    Reference:
    Page 11-16

21. All of the following are tax benefits of a partnership qualified plan, *except*:
    a. Participants are not subject to current taxation on annual contributions
    b. Plan investment earnings accrue without current income tax liability
    c. Pension plan death benefits are included in a deceased

    Reference:
    Page 11-16

participant's taxable estate
    d.   Distributions are subject to income taxation when received
    e.   A participant's non-deductible contribution can be recovered
income tax-free

ANSWERS: 17-b; 18-e; 19-e; 20-a; 21-c.

REAL LIFE SITUATION

Garabaldo Bonati is an actuary for Divine Mutual Life Insurance Company. As an employee of Divine Mutual he participates in the company retirement program, which is considered qualified by the IRS. Two nights during the week, and on weekends, Garabaldo performs roller blader exhibitions. Garabaldo earns $19,000 a year at Divine Mutual and $53,000 per year as a roller blader. He has come to you for advice concerning his retirement program. Your advice to Garabaldo would be:

Directions: *For each of the numbered recommendations that follow, please select A, B, or C as the evaluation you deem most correct. Place your selection in the line preceding each number.*

A. For Garabaldo, this selection would be worse than losing a skate during a performance.

B. It is possible that this recommendation could be considered, but there are some serious short-comings.

C. Considering the circumstances involved, this is a suitable recommendation.

Answer

_____ 1.   Start a pension plan based on the earnings received as a roller blader.
_____ 2.   Start an IRA based on the earnings from Divine Mutual and start a pension plan based on the earnings from the part-time profession.
_____ 3.   Begin contributing to an IRA Plan.
_____ 4.   Invest in the establishment in which he performs.
_____ 5.   Quit working as an actuary for Divine Mutual and pursue international roller blading.

ANSWERS: 1-C; 2-C; 3-B; 4-A; 5-A.

CHECK YOUR UNDERSTANDING
(Circle one)

1.   A SIMPLE IRA program allows employee deferral of wages up to $15,000.
       True/False

Reference:
Page 11-8

2.   Contributions for a non-working spouse may be made by the   Reference:
        employed worker up to an additional $2,000.   Page 11-8
            True/False

3.   Following the Revenue Act of 1978 insurance companies are still   Reference:
        able to provide funding instruments for an IRA.   Page 11-6
            True/False

4.   An owner/employee may contribute and deduct annually an amount   Reference:
        up to 25% of earned income, subject to a maximum, to a Keogh   Page 11-15
        plan.
            True/False

5.   Qualified plan death benefits are excluded from a participant's estate.Reference:
            True/False   Page 11-17

6.   Sole proprietors and partners must install equal or comparable   Reference:
        plans in all businesses that they control.   Page 11-16
            True/False

7.   Premature distributions from a qualified plan are subject to a 50% Reference:
        penalty tax.   Page 11-10
            True/False

8.   Contributions made on behalf of an owner/employee that are   Reference:
        greater than those permitted are called excess contributions and   Page 11-16
        are subject to a 10% penalty tax.
            True/False

9.   Lump-sum distribution from qualified plan where no employee   Reference:
        contributions are taxed as ordinary income.   Page 11-17
            True/False

10.   IRAs may be rolled-over no more than once every three years.   Reference:
            True/False   Page 11-9

ANSWERS: 1-False; 2-True; 3-True; 4-True; 5-False; 6-True; 7-False; 8-True; 9-True;
10-False.

STUDY NOTES

STUDY NOTES

12

PENSION, PROFIT SHARING, AND TAX-DEFERRED ANNUITY PLANS

PRETEST
(Circle one)

1. An employer's contribution to a defined contribution pension plan is: Reference:
    Page 12-6
    a.   An amount that varies from year to year
    b.   A predetermined percentage of salary/earnings
    c.   Related to corporate profits
    d.   Uniform for all employees
    e.   Based upon the benefits selected

2. Some defined contribution pension plans require: Reference:
    Page 12-6
    a.   Employee to participate
    b.   No contributions in some years
    c.   No contributions on the part of the employer
    d.   Participation only when voted each year by Board of
         Directors
    e.   None of the above

3. If a participating insurance contract is used as a funding medium   Reference:
    for a defined contribution plan, any dividends must: Page 12-7
    a.   Lower the employer's cost of the program in future years
    b.   Be paid immediately to plan participants
    c.   Be paid immediately to the employer
    d.   Remain in the trust
    e.   None of the above

4. All of the following statements are correct concerning defined   Reference:
    contribution pension plans, *except*:   Page 12-7
    a.   Benefits may be actuarially determined
    b.   Benefits will be directly dependent upon the length of service
    c.   The employee's sex is not a factor
    d.   Benefits will be linked to the contributions made on the
         employee's behalf
    e.   None of the above

1

5.   The type of formula where each plan participant receives the same   Reference:
      benefit regardless of earnings would best describe: Page 12-8
      a.   Flat amount per year of service
      b.   Flat percentage of earnings
      c.   Variable benefit
      d.   Percentage of earnings per year of service
      e.   Flat amount formula

6.   When a defined benefit pension plan is used, dividends received   Reference:
      on participating insurance contracts can: Page 12-8
      a.   Not be used to offset employer contributions
      b.   Be used to offset employer contributions
      c.   Must remain in the trust
      d.   Eliminate the necessity of future contributions
      e.   Are paid directly and immediately to the employee

7.   A profit-sharing plan must provide a definite predetermined formula Reference:
      for allocating the contributions made to the plan among the partic- Page 12-11
      ipants and for distributing the funds accumulated under the plan
      after any of the following events *except*:
      a.   Fixed number of years
      b.   The attainment of a stated age
      c.   Disability
      d.   Retirement
      e.   All of the above are correct

8.   If a defined contribution program is established for an S   Reference:
      Corporation, the maximum allowable deduction would be: Page 12-12
      a.   25% of compensation
      b. $1,500
      c.   25% or a maximum of $22,500
      d.   10% or a maximum of $1,500
      e.   10% or a maximum of $7,500

9.   The Internal Revenue Code provides for the deductibility of contrib- Reference:
      utions to a plan made by an employer. The liability for payment to   Page 12-11
      a plan by an employer must be established by:
      a.   His actual contribution
      b.   The close of the fiscal year
      c.   Up to the actual filing of the tax return
      d.   At any time
      e.   None of the above

10. A defined contribution plan and a profit sharing plan allow for deductibility up to a maximum of what percentage of total compensation?
    a. 25%
    b. 20%
    c. 15%
    d. 10%
    e. 5%

Reference:
Page 12-12

11. Lump-sum distributions are taxed:
    a. Partly ordinary income, partly capital gains
    b. Taxation depends on the year of distribution
    c. Taxation depends on the age of recipient
    d. As ordinary income, not capital gains
    e. Based on life expectancy

Reference:
Page 12-13

12. The exclusion allowance provided by a tax-sheltered annuity plan amounts to 20% of adjusted pay after:
    a. The exclusion
    b. The reduction
    c. Gross income
    d. Net income
    e. None of the above

Reference:
Page 12-15

13. A simple salary deduction is not enough for qualification of a tax deferred annuity plan. To qualify there must be a written agreement between the employer and the employee to actually:
    a. Exclude the amount involved
    b. Deduct the amount from gross income
    c. Deduct the amount from net income
    d. Provide a reduction after the allowance has been applied
    e. Reduce the employee's salary

Reference:
Page 12-16

14. If contributions are made to the trust for the purpose of investing in a mutual fund there is an additional excise tax of _____ on excess contributions.
    a. 30%
    b. 20%
    c. 15%
    d. 10%
    e. 6%

Reference:
Page 12-15

15. Corporate qualified 401(k) plans allow for the contributions to be:
    a. Before tax dollars
    b. After tax dollars

Reference:
Page 12-14

c.   Tax deferred except for highly paid group
d.   No tax advantage
e.   In lieu of Social Security taxes

16.   Under a defined benefit pension plan, highly paid employees would   Reference:
be most enthusiastic about which one of the following four major   Page 12-9
types of benefit formulae?
a.   Flat amount formula
b.   Flat percentage of earnings formula
c.   Flat amount per year of service formula
d.   Variable benefit formula
e.   None of these

17.   Variable benefit plans proposed for some pension plans would   Reference:
relate to which of the following?   Page 12-9
I.   Flat percentage of earnings plans
II.   Index-linked benefit plans
III.   Market-linked benefit plans
IV.   Variable annuity contract plans
a.   I only
b.   II only
c.   II and III
d.   IV only
e.   All of the above

18.   Vested benefits to employees who are participants in profit sharing   Reference:
plans would be generally available upon the occurrence of which   Page 12-13
of the following?
I.   Death
II.   Disability
III.   Severance of employment (voluntary)
IV.   Severance of employment (involuntary)
a.   I only
b.   II only
c.   II and III
d.   II, III, and IV
e.   All of the above

19.   The general rules for a profit sharing plan to be qualified with the   Reference:
IRS include: Page 12-11
I.   The plan MUST be definite but does not have to
be in writing
II.   There must be substantial and recurring contributions
III.   There must be an allocation formula in writing
IV.   Voluntary contributions are prohibited

a.   I only
b.   II only
c.   II and III
d.   II, III, and IV
e.   All of the above

20.   The "party in interest" rule that exists under the ERISA legislation   Reference:
prohibits transactions involving all the following *except*:   Page 12-16
a.   The employer
b.   A person owning 50% of the business
c.   The bank trustee servicing the plan
d.   Any employee or participant in the plan (non-owner)
e.   An insurance agent who sells insurance to the plan

ANSWERS: 1-b; 2-a; 3-d; 4-c; 5-e; 6-b; 7-e; 8-c; 9-b; 10-a; 11-d; 12-b; 13-e; 14-e; 15-a; 16-b; 17-c; 18-e; 19-c; 20-d.

OVERVIEW

In the previous chapter we discussed IRAs and plans designed for unincorporated businesses. In this chapter we will discuss corporate pension plans that are qualified. The Internal Revenue Service and ERISA (Employment Retirement Income Security Act) have placed limitations on a plan's deductibility and subsequent qualification. The formation of the pension program relating to employer/employee contributions and deductibility of these contributions, together with benefit payment schedules, are closely regulated by the IRS and ERISA.

We will discuss in some detail a *defined contribution plan*, where the employer's contribution to the retirement program purchases unknown benefits. A *defined benefit plan*, where benefits are determined by a benefit formula, will also be discussed. The various intricacies of a corporate deferred-payment *profit-sharing plan* are addressed in detail. A tax-deferred annuity plan as established under Internal Revenue Code Section 403(b) concludes the chapter.

Author's Note to Candidates

This chapter addresses the many and varied forms of qualified corporate pension plans. This material, though familiar to many, is challenging and may require careful study on your part. Pension planning represents a highly technical area of our industry and forms a significant percentage of your study for the Series 6 Examination.

I.   CORPORATE PENSION PLANS

Defined Contribution Plans

In a *defined contribution plan* the employer's contribution is fixed and is usually expressed as a percentage of the compensation of covered employees. Contributions to this type of plan are often *contributory*, requiring the employee to participate. A contributory plan is one where the employees are required to put in funds also. One of the primary distinctions of a defined contribution plan is that retirement *benefits can only be estimated* and are dependent upon the performance of the funding medium. As a result, uniform benefit levels are very difficult to design into this type of program.

I don't know what this will be worth to you in retirement, but it's building up pretty well.

If participating insurance contracts are used as a funding medium, any dividends paid must *remain in the trust* and cannot be used to lower the employer's cost of the program in future years. Pension benefits are *actuarially* determined and, therefore, the sex of the employee will have a substantial effect on the benefits provided due to the fact that females live longer. Federal rules limit the amount of adjustments for sex now. In addition, benefits will be directly dependent upon the length of time the employee is covered under the plan and the amount that is contributed on his or her behalf. A defined contribution plan allows maximum deductions to the lesser of $30,000 or 25% of compensation.

QUICK QUIZ 1

1.   An employer's contribution to a defined contribution pension   Reference:
      plan is: Page 12-6
      a.   An amount that varies from year to year
      b.   A predetermined percentage of salary/earnings
      c.   Related to corporate profits
      d.   Uniform for all employees
      e.   Based upon the benefits selected

2.   Some defined contribution pension plans require: Reference:
      a.   Employee to participate   Page 12-6
      b.   No contributions in some years
      c.   No contributions on the part of the employer
      d.   Participation only when voted each year by Board of
            Directors
      e.   None of the above

3.   If a participating insurance contract is used as a funding medium   Reference:
      for a defined contribution plan, any dividends must: Page 12-7
      a.   Lower the employer's cost of the program in future years
      b.   Be paid immediately to plan participants
      c.   Be paid immediately to the employer
      d.   Remain in the trust
      e.   None of the above

4.   All of the following statements are correct concerning defined   Reference:
      contribution pension plans *except*:   Page 12-7
      a.   Benefits may be actuarially determined
      b.   Benefits will be directly dependent upon the length of service
      c.   The employee's sex is not a factor
      d.   Benefits will be linked to the contributions made on the
            employee's behalf
      e.   None of the above

                                    ANSWERS: 1-b; 2-a; 3-d; 4-c.

Defined Benefit Plans

Don't worry about it, I promised you $500 a month in retirement, and I'm obligated for that amount.

When a *defined benefit plan* is used, retirement benefits are defined and a contribution is made sufficient enough to assure that the funds will be available to provide the pre-determined retirement benefits. The rate of contribution will vary with the earnings of the funding medium chosen and the earnings of the participating employee (benefit formula).   With the retirement benefit being predetermined, *uniform* benefit levels can be designed into this type of program (often benefiting owners and highly paid employees).   With a defined benefit pension plan, dividends received on participating insurance contracts *can be used* to offset future contributions that would be made by the employer.

Author's Note: The maximum benefit is the lesser of 100% of average compensation for the three highest paid years or $90,000. Since 1988 this figure has been adjusted for inflation each year.

Defined benefit pension plans utilize several types of formulas to determine retirement benefits of employees. The most common formulas are:

- Flat Amount Formula — Each plan participant receives the same benefits regardless of earnings. A comparison can be made to a medical insurance plan in that every participant is treated equally.
- Flat Percentage of Earnings — Based on, for example, "last five years" or "highest three years" so that benefits reflect the earnings level of different employees.
- Flat Amount Per Year of Service — The phrase "years of service" is defined as meaning the years the employee has worked for the corporation since the plan itself went into effect. With this type of formula the employee receives at retirement a flat dollar amount that is paid for each year of service.
- Variable Benefit Plans — Designed to provide protection against inflation. There are two major types of variable benefit plans:
  Index-Linked— the benefit varies according to some indicator, such as the "cost of living index."
  Market-Linked — the benefit varies according to the performance of the portfolio underlying the assets in the trust.

The amount of contributions required to support the level of benefits in a defined benefit pension plan are based upon actuarial assumptions.

There are two rules that are pertinent to the limits for contributions and the allowable deductions under the terms of a defined benefit plan. These rules are:

- Rule #1 — An amount equal to the unfunded cost of past and current service credits for all plan participants. This amount must be distributed as a percentage over remaining service for each employee.
- Rule #2 — Normal cost of plan plus an amount to fund any past service credits over a ten-year period.

QUICK QUIZ 2

5.   The type of formula where each plan participant receives the same   Reference:
     benefit regardless of earnings would best describe: Page 12-9
     a.   Flat amount per year of service
     b.   Flat percentage of earnings
     c.   Variable benefit
     d.   Percentage of earnings per year of service
     e.   Flat amount formula

6.   When a defined benefit plan is used, retirement benefits are _____   Reference:
     and a contribution is made sufficient to assure that the funds will   Page 12-8
     be available to provide a _____ retirement benefit.

7.   When a defined benefit pension plan is used, dividends received   Reference:
     on participating insurance contracts can: Page 12-8
     a.   Not be used to offset employer contributions
     b.   Can be used to offset employer contributions
     c.   Must remain in the trust
     d.   Eliminate the necessity of future contributions
     e.   Are paid directly and immediately to the employee

ANSWERS: 5-e; 6-defined, predetermined; 7-b.

Illustrated below is a comparison between a defined contribution plan and a defined benefit plan. This example is intended to depict the difference between the two programs and the various contribution decisions that must be made.

Two owner/employees own a corporation and each earn $30,000 per year. One owner/employee is fifty years old, the other is thirty and they are considering a pension plan in which they are willing to spend approximately $6,000 per year. Tables 12.1 and 12.2 show the results that can be obtained using a defined contribution plan and a defined benefit plan, both assuming an interest rate of 5%.

TABLE 12.1   DEFINED CONTRIBUTION PLAN
Pension formula would call for 10% of earnings as the contribution.

Age	Salary	Years to Retire	Contribution	Amount at Retirement
30	$30,000	35	$3,000/yr	$270,000
50	$30,000	15	$3,000/yr	$65,000

TABLE 12.2   DEFINED BENEFIT PLAN
Pension formula would call for a pension benefit of about 30% of salary equaling $9,000 per year.

(Approximately $105,000 is needed to provide an annuity of $9,000 per year for 18 years)

Age	Salary	Years to Retire	Contribution	Amount at Retirement
30	$30,000	35	$1,150/yr	$105,000
50	$30,000	15	$4,850/yr	$105,000

You will note that the two plans illustrated here each require the corporation to contribute $6,000 per year. The *defined contribution plan* obviously *favors* the younger owner/employee at the expense of the older individual. The *defined benefit plan* program provides more equity in a situation such as the one illustrated by providing an equal dollar amount for both individuals at retirement. It *favors older* employees.

CORPORATE DEFERRED PAYMENT PROFIT-SHARING PLANS

OK, I'll put some of the profits in — but I'm not promising how much.

The Internal Revenue Code defines a *profit-sharing plan* as a plan established and maintained by an employer to provide for the participation in his or her profits by the employees or their beneficiaries. The plan must provide a definite predetermined formula for *allocating* the contributions among the participants and for distributing to them the funds accumulated under the plan. These distributions are made after a fixed number of years, the attainment of a stated age, or upon the prior occurrence of some event such as a layoff, illness, disability, retirement, death, or severance of employment.

There is *no* requirement for a definite predetermined contribution formula; however, there *is* a requirement for *substantial and recurring contributions* to be made from profits to meet the requirements for plan permanence. A corporation's Board of Directors may use a discretionary formula that allows for flexibility and payments that do not exceed the amount currently deductible for a corporation by the Internal Revenue Service. Discretionary formulas usually impose maximums and minimums, such as from 10% to 30% of profits, which are determined by the Board of Directors. Definite predetermined formulas promote increased morale among employees and improve plan security.

When contribution allocation formulas are used by the employer, they must be decided upon the basis of how the contributions are to be divided among the plan participants. The two types of contribution allocation formulas are:

- *Compensation Formula* — a proportion of the participant's compensation to the total eligible compensation; for example, employee A earns $10,000 per year and the total eligible compensation is predetermined as $100,000. Here, employee A would receive 10% of the allowable contribution.

- *Compensation and Service Formula* — a unit credit is given for each year of service in addition to unit credits for each unit of compensation (for example, $100). In this case employee B has thirty years of service and earns $15,000 per year. This employee gets 30 units for service and 150 units for compensation for a total of 180 units. His or her percentage would be 180 divided by the total number of units credited.

A profit-sharing plan must be in writing and communicated to the employees. A trust *must* be used and voluntary employee contributions may not exceed 10%.

___

QUICK QUIZ 3

8.   A profit-sharing plan must provide a definite predetermined formula   Reference:
      for allocating the contributions made to the plan among the partici-   Page 12-11
      pants and for distributing the funds accumulated under the plan
      after any of the following events *except*:
      a.   Fixed number of years
      b.   The attainment of a stated age
      c.   Disability
      d.   Retirement
      e.   All of the above are correct

9.   When contribution allocation formulas are used by the employer,   Reference:
      they must be decided upon the basis of how the contributions are   Page 12-11
      to be divided among the plan participants. Two types of contribu-
      tions allocation formulas are _____ and _____ _____ _____.

ANSWERS: 8-e; 9-compensation, compensation and service.

___

A profit-sharing plan provides a maximum deduction of 15% of covered payroll (covered in the plan).

Combination plans provide that the total contribution for a combined pension and profit-sharing plan cannot exceed 25% of covered payroll. The profit-sharing portion cannot exceed 15%.

If a defined contribution plan is established in an S Corporation, the maximum allowable deduction is the same as for (regular) C Corporations or Limited Liability Corporations (LLC). A defined benefit program provides for the use of a special government table. This table uses a percentage of compensation based on the participant's age and provides the maximum contribution amount.

Contributions made for an employee are non-taxable to the employee until he or she constructively receives the benefits. Earnings on contributions made to the trust will accumulate tax-free on a deferred basis. ERISA requires prudent investment on the part of the trustees and further requires bonding. Funds deposited with a trust must be invested for the *exclusive benefit* of the participants and their beneficiaries. A fair rate of return and diversification of investments is required. Additionally, there are restrictions for investing in the stock of the parent corporation, including a percentage limitation. The IRS must be notified if such investments take place.

Tax Treatment during Payout Period

Section 72 of the Internal Revenue Code provides that if a retired employee receives distributions in the form of periodic payments, the amounts are not attributable to the employee's own contributions. They will be taxed as ordinary income in accordance with the annuity principle. The cost basis for an employee would be the employee's total investment into the plan. This includes the employee's own contributions, and the total amount of PS58 term cost (covered later) that the employees reported as income over the years in which the plan was in effect.

If distributions are made from a non-contributory plan, no cost basis has been established and entire payments are taxed as ordinary income when received.

The annuity principle provides that the percentage of each benefit payment representing a return of the *employee's* contribution, would be *excluded* from income tax.

The portion of each payment that represents a return of the employer's contribution is *taxable* as ordinary income. For example, if a retiree were receiving $1,000 per month as a total benefit payment and, using the annuity exclusion ratio, two-thirds of this payment represents a return of the

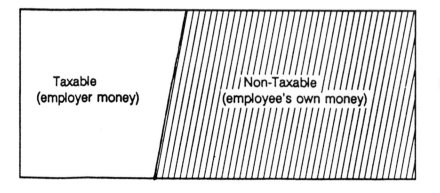

Taxable
(employer money)

Non-Taxable
(employee's own money)

Exclusion ratio

employee's contributions, then $666 of each monthly payment is excluded from income taxation, and the remaining one-third is subject to income taxation. After the retiree receives his/her cost basis tax-free, the entire payment becomes taxable income.

Tax Treatment of Lump Sum Payouts

There is *no* income tax due on any amount that the employee can include in his or her *cost basis*. All amounts over the cost basis are ordinary income.

Derivatives of Profit Sharing Plans

There are a number of special plans that are sophisticated derivatives of profit-sharing plans. We will describe some of them:

- 401(K) plans — new plans after January 1, 1997 known as SIMPLE 401(K) plans. These are profit-sharing plans with provisions to accept employee contributions, which are deductible. In some of these (cash or deferred accounts, CODA) the employee has the option of accepting the employer's contribution or deferring it.

- Stock bonus, and ESOP (employee stock ownership plan) differ from conventional profit-sharing plans because the plan assets are invested *primarily* in securities of the employer. Employers benefit by "cashless" contributions (stock) which are deductible. Employees enjoy ownership of the company where they are employed.

- Thrift plans (employees savings or investment plans) are defined contribution plans to which employees make voluntary contributions with matching employer contributions. Thrift plans have lessened in popularity as 401K plans have become more widely used.

QUICK QUIZ 4

10. If a defined contribution program is established for an S corporation, the maximum allowable deduction would be: Reference: Page 12-12
    a. 25% of compensation
    b. $1,500
    c. 25% or a maximum of $22,500
    d. 10% or a maximum of $1,500
    e. 10% or a maximum of $7,500

11. In which type of plan does a participant have an option of receiving the employer contribution in cash?   Reference: Page 12-14
    a. Thrift plans
    b. 401(k) CODA plans

     c.   ESOP plans
     d.   Tax-sheltered annuities
     e.   Defined benefit plans

12.   A defined contribution plan and a profit-sharing plan allow deduct-   Reference:
      ibility up to a maximum of what percentage of total compensation? Page 12-12
     a.   25%
     b.   20%
     c.   15%
     d.   10%
     e.   5%

13.   Lump-sum distributions are taxed: Reference:
     a.   Partly ordinary income, partly capital gains   Page 12-13
     b.   Taxation depends on the year of distribution
     c.   Taxation depends on the age of recipient
     d.   As ordinary income, not capital gains
     e.   Based on life expectancy

ANSWERS: 10-c; 11-b; 12-a; 13-d.

III.   TAX SHELTERED ANNUITY PLANS

Since 1942 under Section 501(C)(3), employees of eligible non-profit organizations have been able to take advantage of tax-deferred or tax-sheltered annuities. Section 403(b) granted authority for tax sheltered annuities and was amended to include employees of public school systems. SIMPLE 401(K) plans can now be used as 403(b) plans. To participate, a person must be a bona fide employee; a contract must be purchased by the employer; the rights must be non-forfeitable and the maximum exclusion allowance must be honored. *Any* employee of a qualified organization may participate, even seasonal and part-time employees; however, the person must be an *actual* employee not an independent contractor.

      Any annuity can be used to fund the plan as long as it is *not transferrable* and the employee's rights are non-forfeitable. The employer must be the applicant. The exclusion allowance is 20% of the adjusted pay after the reduction. This actually amounts to one-sixth of gross pay prior to the reduction. Any contribution by the employer to a qualified pension reduces the exclusion amounts. The exclusion amount can be increased by credit for past service. The maximum amount of this elective deferral under a salary reduction plan is $9,500. If any amount has been electively deferred under another plan the remainder, to $9,500, can be contributed to a TSA.

      As long as the participant is living and not receiving benefits, there are no income-tax consequences as long as contributions are within the exclusion allowance. Excess contributions to a trust for the purpose of investing in mutual funds, carry an additional excise tax of 6% on the excess. The proceeds at retirement are taxed as ordinary income. Taxes after death are generally the same to the beneficiary as they would have been to the deceased. Proceeds from pure life insurance death benefits are received income tax free. A special subclass of 501(C)(3), excluding school employees, can have the proceeds excluded from their estate, as long as there is a stipulated beneficiary. Refund payments are not considered as transfers for gift-tax purposes.

To qualify for a tax-sheltered annuity there must be a written agreement between the employer and employee to reduce the employee's salary. A simple reduction is not enough for qualification. Any contributions being made on the employee's behalf to a qualified plan will proportionately reduce the exclusion amount allowed by a tax-sheltered annuity. Part-time employees are eligible but their past service must be proportionately reduced to reflect that only part-time service was rendered. The IRS has held that salary reductions for tax-sheltered annuities, while reducing income subject to federal withholding taxes, could not reduce the amount of Social Security taxes. If an employer also has a pension plan, and the employee chooses to participate in a tax-sheltered annuity, then the amount of the salary reduction does not reduce the amount of salary used to figure pension benefits.

Hospitals are 501(C)(3) organizations.

What, reduce my salary .... OH ... to save taxes, OK, in that case.

IV.   ERISA CONCEPTS

The Employee Retirement Income Security Act, called ERISA is key federal legislation to protect workers whose employers maintained pension or profit sharing plans "qualified" with the IRS. The interest of the Act was to better financially secure workers' (employees') benefits and to prohibit many abuses that existed within these plans.

Party-in-interest: ERISA prohibits transactions between the trust established for pension programs and parties-in-interest. Those considered to be parties-in-interest are:

- Fiduciary: defined as person occupying a position that requires a high degree of trust.
- Any person owning over 50% of the business (direct ownership or indirect ownership).
- A relative of any of those listed above.
- Any personnel servicing the plan (e.g., you).
- The employer.

ERISA provides that plan fiduciaries must be named. In addition, there are requirements that prudent investment must take place on the part of the trustees and that the fiduciaries be bonded.

Fiduciary: Defined as a person occupying a position that requires a high degree of trust

Any person owning over 50% of the business (direct ownership or indirect ownership)

A relative of any of those listed above.

Any personnel servicing the plan.

The employer.

There are various transactions that are prohibited when involving parties-in-interest to a plan. These prohibited transactions include:

- Furnishing of goods and services by the parties-in-interest to the plan.
- Acquisition of securities of the parent company over the allowable limit.

- Credit extension or loans.
- Transfer to, or using of, the assets included in the plan.
- Sale or lease of property.

You mean I engaged in a prohibited transaction?

The limitation placed on the acquisition of securities by the trust of the parent corporation is 10% of the plan's assets. If any of the above listed prohibited transactions are encountered, there is an excise tax of 5% on the amount of money involved in the particular transaction. This is charged directly to the "interested party."

Vesting — TRA '86 imposed two vesting standards:

- 100% vesting after 5 years of service, or
- 3 to 7 years vesting (20% vesting after 3 years of service and increasing 20% per year until fully vested after 7 years of service).

A plan may require a 2-year waiting period for plan entry, with 100% immediate vesting upon entry. "Top heavy" plans must provide a faster vesting schedule.

QUICK QUIZ 5

14. The exclusion allowance provided by a tax-deferred annuity plan amounts to 20% of adjusted pay after:

    Reference: Page 12-15

    a. The exclusion
    b. The reduction
    c. Gross income
    d. Net income
    e. None of the above

15.   A simple salary deduction is not enough for qualification of a tax-   Reference:
      sheltered annuity plan. To qualify there must be a written agree-   Page 12-16
      ment between the employer and the employee to actually:
      a.   Exclude the amount involved
      b.   Deduct the amount from gross income
      c.   Deduct the amount from net income
      d.   Provide a reduction after the allowance has been applied
      e.   Reduce the employee's salary

16.   If contributions are made to the trust for the purpose of investing   Reference:
      in a mutual fund there is an additional excise tax of _____ on   Page 12-15
      excess contributions.
      a.   30%
      b.   20%
      c.   15%
      d.   10%
      e.   6%

17.   Corporate qualified 401(k) plans allow for the contributions to be: Reference:
      a.   Before tax dollars   Page 12-14
      b.   After tax dollars
      c.   Tax deferred except for highly paid group
      d.   No tax advantage
      e.   In lieu of Social Security taxes

                                    ANSWERS: 14-b; 15-e; 16-e; 17-a.

_____

_____

REAL LIFE SITUATION

Renaldo Spugazzi is the senior owner/employee of the Arabian Navel Lint Brush
Corporation. Renaldo has just celebrated his fifty-seventh birthday together with the other
owner/employee of the corporation who recently turned thirty years of age. Both of the
owner/employees earn $30,000 per year and are considering the establishment of a
pension program. They have decided the contribution that is affordable would be $6,000
per year. Renaldo has come to you for advice concerning their proposed pension program.
Your advice would be:

Directions: *For each of the numbered recommendations below, please select A, B, or C
as the evaluation you deem most correct. Place your selection on the line preceding each
number:*

A. For Renaldo, this selection would be worse than babies being born without navels.

B. This recommendation would be inappropriate considering the circumstances involved.

C. Considering the circumstances, this is undoubtedly the best recommendation.

Answer

_____ 1.   Establish a defined contribution pension program calling for 10% of earnings as the contribution level.

_____ 2.   Establish a Keogh program based on each owner/employee's earnings.

_____ 3.   Establish a profit-sharing program for both Renaldo and the other owner/employee.

_____ 4.   Start making contributions to a tax-sheltered annuity program for both owner/employees.

_____ 5.   Outline and establish a defined benefit pension program for both Renaldo and the other owner/employee.

ANSWERS: 1-B; 2-B; 3-B; 4-A; 5-C.

CHECK YOUR UNDERSTANDING
(Circle one)

1.   A defined benefit pension plan utilizing the flat amount per years of service formula would provide that each employee would receive at retirement a flat dollar amount that is paid for each year of service.
Reference: Page 12-9
True/False

2.   Variable benefit plans are recent developments and are designed to provide protection against the increased cost of living.
Reference: Page 12-9
True/False

3.   A defined contribution plan specifies a dollar benefit in retirement.
Reference: Page 12-7
True/False

4.   A profit-sharing plan must be in writing and communicated to the employees. Voluntary employee contributions must not exceed 10%.
Reference: Page 12-11
True/False

5.   Combination plans provide that the total contribution for a combined pension and profit-sharing plan cannot exceed 25% and the profit-sharing portion cannot exceed 15%.
Reference: Page 12-12
True/False

6.   If a defined contribution program is established for an S Corporation, the allowable maximum deduction would be 25% of compensation.   Reference: Page 12-12
        True/False

7.   Section 72 of the Internal Revenue Code provides that if a retired employee receives distributions in the form of periodic payments they will be taxed as capital gains in accordance with the annuity principle.   Reference: Page 12-13
        True/False

8.   There is a special ten-year look-back rule applied to aggregate distributions where an employee has received more than one lump sum distribution in that time period from a pension program.   Reference: Page 12-13
        True/False

9.   Under the terms of a tax-deferred annuity plan, the exclusion allowance is 20% of the adjusted pay after the reduction.   Reference: Page 12-15
        True/False

10.   ERISA prohibits transactions between the trust established for pension programs and parties-in-interest. A fiduciary, any person owning over 50% of the business, any relative of either, personnel servicing the plan, and the employer are all considered parties-in-interest.   Reference: Page 12-16
        True/False

ANSWERS: 1-True; 2-True; 3-False; 4-True; 5-True; 6-True; 7-False; 8-False; 9-True; 10-True.

STUDY NOTES

13

FEDERAL SECURITIES REGULATIONS

PRETEST
(Circle one)

1. When a new issue is being offered to a prospective buyer, what must be delivered either prior to the sales interview or during the sales interview?

    Reference: Page 13-6

    a. The registration
    b. The convention blank
    c. A prospectus
    d. A balance sheet
    e. An income statement

2. The fact that a registration statement for a security has been filed or is in effect with the Securities Exchange Commission implies:

    Reference: Page 13-7

    a. That the registration statement is true
    b. That the SEC approves these securities
    c. That the registration statement is accurate
    d. All of the above
    e. None of the above

3. A notice, circular, advertisement, or letter is not considered an offer to sell a security, provided this type of communication contains:

    Reference: Page 13-7

    a. Only explanatory information
    b. Descriptions of various products and services
    c. An invitation to inquire for additional information
    d. All of the above
    e. None of the above

4.　Any communication used by a person to offer to sell or include the　　　Reference:
sale of securities of any investment company — including communi-　　Page 13-8
cations between issuers, underwriters, and dealers — and designed
to be communicated to prospective investors is included under the term:
　　a.　Sales literature
　　b.　Prospectus
　　c.　Authorized communication
　　d.　Unauthorized communication
　　e.　Financial information

5.　If an advertisement appears in a bona fide newspaper, contains only　　Reference:
information the substance of which is included in the prospectus,　　　Page 13-9
and states conspicuously from whom a prospectus containing more
information can be obtained, this advertisement is considered:
　　a.　Authorized
　　b.　A prospectus
　　c.　Unauthorized
　　d.　A registration statement
　　e.　Financial information

6.　Any person engaged in the business of buying and selling securities　　Reference:
for his or her own account may be best defined as:　　　　　　　　　Page 13-10
　　a.　A broker
　　b.　A dealer
　　c.　A registered representative
　　d.　An account representative
　　e.　A registered broker

7.　It is unlawful for any person either directly or indirectly to use any　　Reference:
deceptive or manipulative device when communicating information　　Page 13-11
through the mails, interstate commerce, or any facility of a national
security exchange. This rule covers:
　　a.　Only securities that are registered on a national exchange
　　b.　Only OTC securities
　　c.　Any security whether registered on a national exchange or not
　　d.　Only securities prescribed by the SEC
　　e.　Only legal list securities

8. A notice in writing, indicating to the customer whether the broker/
    dealer is acting as an agent for the customer or as a principal, the
    date and time of the transaction, and whether or not there was any
    odd-lot differential or equivalent being paid by the customer is
    known as a:
    a. Confirmation statement
    b. Financial disclosure
    c. Registration statement
    d. Financial statement
    e. Disclosure statement

Reference:
Page 12

9. A broker/dealer may be registered by filing with the SEC. Within
    how many days of the date of filing the application must the com-
    mission grant registration or institute proceedings to determine
    whether registration should be denied?
    a. Ten days
    b. Twenty days
    c. Thirty days
    d. Forty days
    e. Forty-five days

Reference:
Page 13-12

10. The SIPC is designed to provide protection for the customer who
    deals with an investment firm. If the customer has on deposit a
    combination of cash and securities, this protection amounts to a
    maximum total of:
    a. $500,000
    b. $400,000
    c. $100,000
    d. $50,000
    e. $40,000

Reference:
Page 13-12

11. The phrase "Any person directly or indirectly owning, controlling
    or holding with power to vote 5% or more of the outstanding voting
    securities of a company; any officer, director, co-partner, or employee;
    an investment advisor or member of the advisory board of an
    investment company" best defines which of the following terms?
    a. Affiliated person
    b. Interested person
    c. Broker
    d. Dealer
    e. Underwriter

Reference:
Page 13-14

12.   The phrase "Any security, other than short-term paper, under the terms of which the holder is, upon its presentation to the issuer, entitled to receive approximately his or her proportionate share of the issuer's current net assets or cash equivalent," best defines which type of security?

Reference: Page 13-16

    a.   Growth security
    b.   Income security
    c.   Redeemable security
    d.   No-load security
    e.   Certificate

13.   The phrase "An investment company that is organized under a trust indenture, that does not have a Board of Directors and issues only redeemable securities representing an undivided interest in a unit of specified securities" best defines what class of investment company?

Reference: Page 13-16

    a.   Open-end
    b.   Closed-end
    c.   Diversified
    d.   Management
    e.   Unit investment trust

14.   A management company that is offering for sale, or has outstanding any redeemable security of which it is the issuer, is:

Reference: Page 13-16

    a.   A management company
    b.   A closed-end company
    c.   A face-amount certificate company
    d.   A diversified company
    e.   An open-end company

15.   With the exception of short-term credits, which are necessary for the clearance of transactions, it is illegal for a registered investment company to purchase any security:

Reference: Page 13-17

    a.   That is unapproved
    b.   On margin
    c.   Short
    d.   That is not a legal list security
    e.   That is growth oriented

16. No person may serve as an investment advisor with a registered investment company without:

    a.   Prior approval of the SEC
    b.   Prior approval of the NASD
    c.   Prior approval of the Board of Directors
    d.   A written contract
    e.   An established commission schedule

Reference:
Page 13-18

17. A registered closed-end investment company can issue a senior security if it has an asset coverage of at least:

    a.   300%
    b.   200%
    c.   150%
    d.   100%
    e.   90%

Reference:
Page 13-19

18. A registered investment company may not distribute long-term capital gains to its investors more often than once:

    a.   Every six months
    b.   Quarterly
    c.   Annually
    d.   Biannually
    e.   Monthly

Reference:
Page 13-19

19. The Securities and Exchange Commission has power to make rules and regulations applicable to registered investment companies. If the NASD were to make a rule that contradicted an SEC regulation, which would have precedence?

    a.   NASD
    b.   SEC
    c.   Each would have equal weight
    d.   One would cancel out the other
    e.   A court decision would determine applicability

Reference:
Page 13-20

20. It is unlawful for any registered investment company issuing periodic payment plan certificates to charge a sales load that exceeds _____ of the total payments to be made.

    a.   50%
    b.   20%
    c.   16%
    d.   15%
    e.   9%

Reference:
Page 13-21

ANSWERS: 1-c; 2-e; 3-d; 4-a; 5-b; 6-b; 7-c; 8-a; 9-e; 10-a; 11-a; 12-c; 13-e; 14-e; 15-b; 16-d; 17-a; 18-c; 19-b; 20-e.

OVERVIEW

This chapter presents information on federal regulations within the investment industry. The need for such industry regulations became apparent during the Great Depression. Security registration requirements, exchange regulations, investment company regulations and such provide the degree of scrutiny necessary to ensure proper industry supervision.

Regulations regarding sales literature, registration requirements, duties of broker/dealers, disciplinary actions, and the composition of margin accounts are all discussed in this chapter. Each one affects an agent's conduct and practice within the investment industry.

Author's Note to Candidates

Because of the complexity of the material covered here careful study of this chapter is required. The regulations that govern the security industry will dictate your conduct and your familiarity with these rules is essential for passing the exam. Your first exposure to federal regulations may be difficult, but after you have had a chance to digest and review the material your efforts will be rewarded.

I.   SECURITIES ACT OF 1933

A closer look at the first major securities act in the United States and its components is the perfect way to begin a study of the laws and their meaning. We have highlighted them for you. The 1933 Act is considered the "Paper Act" (regulated the securities themselves) and the Securities Exchange Act of 1934, the "People Act" (regulated the people themselves).

Section 5 — Prohibitions Relating to Interstate Commerce and the Mails

When a new issue is offered to the public, a *prospectus* must be delivered to the potential buyer. Prior to the delivery of a prospectus however, a *registration* for the new security must be in effect with the SEC. If this registration statement is not in effect, the broker/dealer is *prohibited* from using any means of communication related to interstate commerce or the use of the mails as a means of conveying information about the security.

Section 12 — Civil Liabilities Arising in Connection with Prospectuses and Communications

If a communication to sell a security contains an *untrue* statement of a material fact, or a material *omission*, the person purchasing the security may *sue* to recover the amount paid for the security, *plus interest*. Any income received while holding, or from selling, such a security is deducted from the amount paid to the suing party.

Section 17 — Fraudulent Interstate Transactions

It is unlawful for any person to employ a scheme to defraud, or obtain money or property, by making an *untrue* statement of a material fact, or by making a material *omission*. Section 17 specifically applies to using interstate commerce and the mails.

Section 23 — Unlawful Representations

The fact that a registration statement for a security has been filed or is in effect and the SEC has not issued a stop order of one type or another, does *not* mean that the commission has found the registration statement true and accurate. The SEC does not pass upon the merits of, or give approval to, any security. Therefore, it is unlawful for a broker/dealer to *represent* to any potential purchaser that the SEC approves a particular security or has passed positive judgment on its merits.

Advertising Related Rules

Rule 134 — Communications not Deemed a Prospectus   The term *prospectus* usually does not apply to a notice, circular, advertisement, letter, or other communication published or transmitted after a registration statement has been filed. The following information is permitted in non-prospectus communications:

- Name of the issuer of the security
- Full title of the security and the amount being offered
- Brief description of the general type of business of the issuer

An example of this type of communication is: "For more complete information about Company X, including charges and expenses, send for a prospectus by returning this coupon to (Company X's address). Read it carefully before you invest or send money."

Rule 135A — Generic Advertising   A notice, circular, advertisement, letter, or other communication is *not* considered an *offer to sell* a security, provided the communication is limited to any one or more of the following:

- Explanatory information
- The mention or explanation of an investment company of different types (balanced fund, growth fund, income fund, etc.)
- Offers, descriptions, and explanation of various products and services not constituting a security that would require registration
- An invitation to inquire for additional information

Rule 156 — Investment Company Sales Literature   This rule prohibits the use of sales literature that is misleading and is sent through the mails as an instrument of interstate commerce. Sales literature is considered misleading if it contains an *untrue* statement of material fact or *omits* a material fact. The determination of whether a statement is considered "material" is dependent on an evaluation of the *context* in which the statement is made.

Certain factors are relevant in determining whether or not a material fact can be considered misleading. They are:

- The *absence* of explanations, qualifications, or limitations on statements made
- *General* economic or financial conditions

Representations about past or future investment performance can be deemed misleading because of statements or omissions made involving a material fact, including situations in which:

- Portrayals of past income, gain, or growth of assets convey an impression of the net investment results achieved by an actual or hypothetical investment that are not justified under the circumstances
- Predictions are made about future investment performance

A statement about the characteristics or attributes of an investment company can be misleading because of:

- Reference to services to be provided or methods of operation that do not give equal prominence to risks or limitations associated with the investment
- Exaggerated or unsubstantiated claims about management skills or government supervision
- Unwarranted or incompletely explained comparisons with other investment vehicles or indexes

A violation:

"And I predict......."

The term *sales literature* includes any communication used by any person to offer to sell, or induce the sale of, securities of any investment company. Communications between issuers, underwriters, and dealers are included in this definition of sales literature if they can be reasonably expected to be shared with prospective investors, or are designed to be employed in either writing or *oral* form in the sale of securities.

If a mutual fund is going to advertise its total return, the method for the calculation of the yield must be standardized. This uniform yield must be presented for no less than the current and prior five years.

Rule 434d — Investment Company Prospectus Advertising   It should be noted here that if an advertisement does comply with the provisions of this rule (434d) that it will not be construed as a prospectus. It is important that the fund sponsor comply or be subject to the stricter prospectus rules. An advertisement is considered a prospectus if it:

- Deals with an investment registered under the Investment Company Act of 1940, which is selling or proposing to sell its securities in accordance with a registration statement that has been filed
- Appears in a bona fide newspaper or magazine or is used on radio or television
- Contains only information the substance of which is included in the prospectus
- States clearly from *whom* a prospectus containing more complete information can be obtained and states that an investor should read that prospectus carefully before investing
- Contains the following statement (if used prior to the effectiveness of the company's registration statement) and is known as a "Red Herring":

"A registration statement relating to these securities has been filed with the Securities and Exchange Commission, but has not yet become effective. Information contained herein is subject to completion or amendment. These securities may not be sold, nor may offers to buy be accepted, prior to the time the registration statement becomes effective. This prospectus shall not constitute an offer to sell or an offer to buy, nor shall there be any sale of these securities in any state in which such offer, solicitation or sale would be unlawful prior to registration or qualification under the securities laws of any such state."

QUICK QUIZ 1

1. When a new issue is being offered to a prospective buyer, what must be delivered either prior to the sales interview or during the sales interview?

   Reference:
   Page 13-6

   a.   The registration
   b.   The convention blank
   c.   A prospectus
   d.   A balance sheet
   e.   An income statement

2. The fact that a registration statement for a security has been filed or is in effect with the Securities Exchange Commission implies:

   Reference:
   Page 13-7

   a.   That the registration statement is true
   b.   That the SEC approves these securities
   c.   That the registration statement is accurate
   d.   All of the above
   e.   None of the above

3.   A notice, circular, advertisement, or letter is not considered an offer   Reference:
        to sell the security, provided this type of communication contains: Page 13-7
        a.   Only explanatory information
        b.   Descriptions of various products and services
        c.   An invitation to inquire for additional information
        d.   All of the above
        e.   None of the above

4.   Any communication used by a person to offer to sell or induce the   Reference:
        sale of securities of any investment company — including communi-   Page 13-8
        cations between issuers, underwriters, and dealers — and designed
        to be communicated to prospective investors, is included under
        the term:
        a.   Sales literature
        b.   Prospectus
        c.   Authorized communication
        d.   Unauthorized communication
        e.   Financial information

5.   If an advertisement appears in a bona fide newspaper, contains only   Reference:
        information the substance of which is included in the prospectus,   Page 13-9
        and states conspicuously from whom a prospectus containing more
        information can be obtained, this advertisement is considered:
        a.   Authorized
        b.   A prospectus
        c.   Unauthorized
        d.   A registration statement
        e.   Financial information

ANSWERS: 1-c; 2-e; 3-d; 4-a; 5-b.

II.   SECURITIES EXCHANGE ACT OF 1934

Section 3 — Certain Definitions Under the Act ("People Act")

Broker: Any person engaged in the business of effecting transactions in securities for the accounts of others (does not include a bank). Acts in an agency relationship.

Dealer: Any person engaged in the business of buying and selling securities for his or her *own* account, through a broker or otherwise (also does not include a bank). Acts as a principal.

Security: Any note, stock, treasury stock, bond, debenture, certificate of interest; participation in any profit-sharing agreement or in oil, gas, or other mineral royalty or lease; any collateral trust certificate, pre-organization certificate or subscription, transferrable share, investment contract, floating-trust certificate, certificate of deposit for a security; or, in general, any instrument commonly known as a "security"; or any security of interest or participation in, temporary or interim certificate for, receipt for, warrant or right to subscribe to or purchase any of the above mentioned items. The term security shall *not* apply to *currency* or any note, draft, bill of exchange, or banker's acceptance that has a *maturity* at the time of issuance or *within nine months* of issuance.

Person Associated with a Broker or Dealer: Any partner, officer, director, or branch manager of a broker or dealer (or any person occupying a similar status or performing similar functions); any person directly or indirectly controlling, controlled by, or under common control with a broker or dealer; or any employee of these whose functions are solely clerical or ministerial.

A person — or an entire broker/dealership — is subject to a "statutory disqualification" from the NASD for a serious violation of the rules.

Section 10 — Regulation Controlling the Use of Manipulative and Deceptive Devices

It is unlawful to use any deceptive or manipulative device when communicating information through the mails, using interstate commerce, or any facility of a national security exchange. This rule covers any security whether registered on a national exchange or not, and the SEC may prescribe regulations it feels appropriate to the public interest or for the protection of investors.

Rule 10b-5 — Employment of Manipulative and Deceptive Devices   It is unlawful for any person, either directly or indirectly, to use any means of interstate commerce or the mails, or a facility of any national securities exchange, to employ any device, scheme, or artifact to defraud; or to make any untrue statement of a material fact or any material omission.

Rule 10b-10 — Confirmations of Transactions   At or before the completion of a transaction, the broker/dealer must provide a *confirmation statement* (a notice in writing), which gives the following information:

- Whether the broker/dealer is acting as an agent for the customer, as an agent for some other person, as an agent for both a customer and another person, or as a principal for his or her own account
- The date and time of transaction
- Whether any "odd lot" differential or equivalent fee is to be paid by the customer

A broker or dealer may effect transactions for or with the account of a customer without giving or sending written notification if:

- Such transactions are effective pursuant to a periodic plan or an investment company plan
- The broker or dealer gives or sends to the customer within five business days after the end of each quarterly period a written statement disclosing each purchase or sale

and each dividend or distribution credited to or reinvested for the account of the customer during that period

Section 15 — Registration and Regulation of Brokers and Dealers

A broker or dealer may be registered by filing with the commission an application for registration. Within *forty-five* days of the application filing date, the commission will grant registration or institute proceedings to determine whether the registration should be denied. It is unlawful for a broker/dealer who is *unregistered* to make use of the mails or any other means of interstate commerce to affect any securities transactions.

Section 15(c)(1) — Manipulative, Deceptive, or Fraudulent Devices or Contrivances   No broker or dealer who is member of an exchange may use any manipulative, deceptive, or other fraudulent device or contrivance. This applies also to dealers in municipal securities. The SEC rules are designed to:

- Prevent deceptive or manipulative acts
- Prevent quotations that are fictitious
- Provide safeguards for financial responsibility of brokers and dealers
- Provide safety of customer's deposits or credit balances
- Require the maintenance of reserves for customer's deposits and credit balances
- Establish minimum financial responsibility requirements for all brokers and dealers

Section 15(c)(7) — Discretionary Accounts   This section tightly regulates the broker's conduct where a discretionary account exists. These accounts allow purchases and sales in a customer's account without the customer's knowledge. *All* records of each transaction must be kept and the customer notified promptly. The transactions must not be excessive in light of the account's financial resources and character. Because of potential abuses with discretionary accounts, some brokerage houses prohibit discretionary accounts.

III.   SECURITIES INVESTOR PROTECTION CORPORATION (SIPC)

The Securities Investor Protection Corporation was instituted for protection in the event of a brokerage firm going out of business. Protection is provided on a *per separate customer* basis. For example, an individual's account and another account with his or her spouse are considered two separate accounts and each is fully covered. Protection limits are:

- $500,000 for a combination of cash and securities
- $100,000 for cash only (the maximum that SIPC will ever pay for cash is $100,000)

Many brokerage houses purchase additional private insurance for excess amounts over the SIPC rules to further protect customers. Brokerage houses pay into the SIPC fund based on their *gross revenue* and not upon their profits and assets. No public money is involved.

QUICK QUIZ 2

6. Any person engaged in the business of buying and selling securities for his or her own account may be best defined as:

    a.   A broker
    b.   A dealer
    c.   A registered representative
    d.   An account representative
    e.   A registered broker

Reference: Page 13-10

7. It is unlawful for any person either directly or indirectly to use any deceptive or manipulative device when communicating information through the mails, interstate commerce, or any facility of a national security exchange. This rule covers:

    a.   Only securities that are registered on a national exchange
    b.   Only OTC securities
    c.   Any security whether registered on a national exchange or not
    d.   Only securities prescribed by the SEC
    e.   Only legal list securities

Reference: Page 13-11

8. A notice in writing, indicating to the customer whether the broker/dealer is acting as an agent for the customer or as a principal, the date and time of the transaction, and whether or not there was any odd-lot differential or equivalent being paid by the customer is known as a:

    a.   Confirmation statement
    b.   Financial disclosure
    c.   Registration statement
    d.   Financial statement
    e.   Disclosure statement

Reference: Page 13-11

9. A broker/dealer may be registered by filing with the SEC. Within how many days of the date of filing the application must the commission grant registration or institute proceedings to determine whether registration should be denied?

    a.   Ten days
    b.   Twenty days
    c.   Thirty days
    d.   Forty days
    e.   Forty-five days

Reference: Page 13-12

10. The SIPC is designed to provide protection for the customer who deals with an investment firm. If the customer has on deposit a combination of cash and securities, this protection amounts to a

Reference: Page 13-12

maximum total under SIPC of:
  a. $40,000
  b. $50,000
  c. $75,000
  d. $150,000
  e. $500,000   ANSWERS: 6-b; 7-c; 8-a; 9-e; 10-e.

IV.   INVESTMENT COMPANY ACT OF 1940

Section 2(a) — General Definitions of Investment Company Operations

Affiliated Person: Any person directly or indirectly owning, controlling, or holding with power to vote, 5% or more of the outstanding voting securities of a company; any officer, director, partner, co-partner, or employee; an investment advisor or member of the advisory board of an investment company.

Face Amount Certificate: Any certificate, investment contract, or other security that represents an obligation on the part of the issuer to pay a *stated sum* on fixed or determinable dates more than *twenty-four months* after the date of issuance, in return for payment of *periodic installments*.

Interested Person: When used with respect to an investment company this includes:

- Any affiliated person of the company
- Any member of the affiliate's immediate family
- Any person who has been a legal counsel to the company during the last two fiscal years
- Any broker/dealer registered under the Securities Exchange Act of 1934
- Any person whom the commission determines to be an interested person who has, during the last two fiscal years, maintained a material business or professional relationship with the company

When used with respect to an investment advisor or principal underwriter for any investment company, "interested person" refers to:

- Any affiliated person of the investment advisor or principal underwriter
- Any member of the affiliate's immediate family
- Any person who knowingly has a direct or indirect beneficial interest
- Any person or partner or employee of the investment company during the last two fiscal years
- Any broker/dealer registered under the Securities Exchange Act of 1934
- Any person determined by the commission to have a material business or professional relationship during the last two fiscal years with the investment advisor or principal underwriter

Author's Note

An affiliated person is an interested person, but an interested person is not necessarily an affiliated person.

Periodic Payment Plan Certificate: Any certificate, investment contract, or other security providing for a series of periodic payments by the holder and representing an undivided interest in certain specified securities, or in a unit or fund of securities, purchased wholly or partly with the proceeds of the payments.

Principal Underwriter: Any underwriter who, as a principal, purchases from an investment company or has a contract providing the right to purchase from an investment company; or who, as an agent for the company, sells or has the right to sell any security to a dealer or to the public; or both. This definition does not include a dealer who purchases from an investment company through a principal underwriter acting as an agent for the investment company.

Redeemable Security: Any security, other than short-term paper, under the terms of which the holder, upon presentation to the issuer, is entitled to receive approximately his or her proportionate share of the issuer's current net assets or the cash equivalent.

Sales Load: The difference between the price of a security to the public and the net portion of the proceeds from its sale that is received and invested.

Separate Account: An account established and maintained by an insurance company where income, gains and losses — whether or not realized — from assets allocated to the account are in accordance with the applicable contract, credited to or charged against the account without regard to other income, gains, or losses of the insurance company.

Section 3(a) — Definitions of Investment Company

An investment company is defined as a company that is engaged primarily in the business of investing, reinvesting, or trading in securities; issuing face amount certificates of the installment type; has been engaged in this business and has any certificates outstanding; or is engaged or proposes to engage in the business of investing, reinvesting, owning, holding, or trading in securities and owns or proposes to acquire investments having a value exceeding 40% of the value of the issuer's total assets on an unconsolidated basis.

Section 4 — Classification of Investment Companies

Face Amount Certificate Company: An investment company that is engaged in issuing face amount certificates of the installment type or has been engaged in this business and has any of this type of certificate outstanding.

Unit Investment Trust: An investment company that is organized under a trust indenture, contract of custodianship or agency, or similar type of organization; does *not* have a board of directors; and issues only redeemable securities, each of which represents an undivided interest in a unit of specified securities (this does not include a voting trust).

A UIT functions basically as a holding company for its investors. The managers of a UIT typically purchase an investment portfolio, consisting of other investment company shares or of fixed-income securities (such as government or municipal bonds). They then sell redeemable shares (also known as *units* or *shares of beneficial interest*) in this portfolio of securities. Each share represents the ownership of an *undivided interest* in the underlying portfolio. Under the Act of 1940, the trustee of a UIT is required to maintain a secondary market in the units, thus guaranteeing a measure of liquidity and redeemability to the shareholders.

Management Company: Any investment company other than a face amount certificate company or unit investment trust company.

Section 5 — Subclassification of Investment Companies

Open-end Company: A management company that offers for sale, or has outstanding, any redeemable security of which it is the issuer.

Closed-end Company: Any management company other than an open-end company.

Diversified Company: A management company that meets the following requirements: At least 50% of the value of its total assets is represented by cash and cash items, government securities, securities of other investment companies, and other securities. At least 75% of the fund's total assets must be invested. Assets are limited to any one issuer not controlling an amount greater in total than 5% of the value of the total assets of the fund. Not more than 10% of the outstanding voting securities can be controlled by any individual issuer.

Non-diversified Company: Any management company other than a diversified company.

Section 10 — Affiliation of Directors

Section 10(a) — Composition of Board of Directors   The board of directors of a registered investment company may consist of no more than 60% who are considered "affiliated persons" of the investment company. If a "no-load" fund then only one outside director is required.

Section 12(a) — Functions and Activities of Investment Companies

It is unlawful for a registered investment company to purchase any securities *on margin* with the exception of short-term credits that are necessary for the clearance of transactions. In addition, it's unlawful for a registered investment company to participate on a *joint basis* in any trading account except in connection with an underwriting in which the registered company is a participant. Finally, it is unlawful to effect a *short sale* of any security except where the registered company is a participant.

Section 13 — Changes in Investment Policy Requiring a Majority Vote of the Shares

A registered investment company may not change its investment policy unless authorized by a vote of a *majority* of its *outstanding voting securities*. The following changes may be made *if* an authorized vote takes place:

1. Change of subclassification from open-end to closed-end or diversified to non-diversified company
2. Borrow money, issue senior securities, underwrite securities issued by other persons (including corporations); purchase or sell real estate or commodities; or make loans to other persons
3. Deviate from its policy in respect to concentration of investments in any particular industry or group of industries as provided by the investment company's registration statement
4. Change the nature of its business so as to cease being an investment company

The 1940 ACT requires registration for those "in the business of" providing investment advice. The SEC together with the North American Securities Administrators Association (NASAA), the state securities personnel, constructed Release IA-1092 to aid in interpreting "in the business of." Unless exempt, those considered to be advisers *must* register under the 1940 Act *and* in states they do business as investment advisors.

This rule emphasized that any person holding themselves out as investment adviser or receiving *any* form of compensation for giving investment advice must register. Compensation includes any receipt, directly or indirectly, of:

- Advisory fee(s)
- Service fee(s)
- Commission(s)

Presently exempt are banks and publishers of general circulation newspapers and magazines.

QUICK QUIZ 3

11. The phrase, "Any person directly or indirectly owning, controlling, or holding with power to vote, 5% or more of the outstanding voting securities of a company; any officer, director, partner, co-partner, or employee; an investment advisor or member of the advisory board of an investment company," best defines which of the following terms?

    Reference: Page 13-14

    a. Affiliated person
    b. Interested person
    c. Broker
    d. Dealer
    e. Underwriter

12. The phrase, "Any security, other than short-term paper, under the terms of which the holder, upon presentation to the issuer, is entitled to receive approximately his or her proportionate share of the issuer's current net assets or the cash equivalent," best defines which type of security?

Reference:
Page 13-16

   a. Growth security
   b. Income security
   c. Redeemable security
   d. No-load security
   e. Certificate

13. The phrase, "An investment company that is organized under a trust indenture, that does not have a Board of Directors and issues only redeemable securities representing an undivided interest in a unit of specified securities," best defines what class of investment company?

Reference:
Page 13-16

   a. Open-end
   b. Closed-end
   c. Diversified
   d. Management
   e. Unit Investment Trust

14. The phrase, "A management company that offers for sale, or has outstanding, any redeemable security of which it is the issuer," best defines:

Reference:
Page 13-16

   a. A management company
   b. A closed-end company
   c. A face-amount certificate company
   d. A diversified company
   e. An open-end company

15. With the exception of short-term credits, which are necessary for the clearance of transactions, it is illegal for a registered investment company to purchase any security:

Reference:
Page 13-17

   a. Which is unapproved
   b. On margin
   c. Short
   d. Which is not a legal list security
   e. Which is growth oriented

ANSWERS: 11-a; 12-c; 13-e; 14-e; 15-b.

Section 15 — Investment Advisory and Underwriting Contracts

No person may serve as an investment advisor with a registered investment company without a written contract. The contract must be *approved* by a vote of a majority of the outstanding voting securities and describe all compensation to be paid, continue in effect for a period of two years from the date of its execution, provide that it may be terminated at any time by the Board of Directors *or* by a vote of the majority of outstanding voting securities, and provide for automatic termination in the event of assignment.

Section 16(a) — Changes in Board of Directors Election by Shareholders

A *director* of an investment company must be *elected* to that office by the holders of the outstanding voting securities at an annual or special meeting that is called for the purpose of election.

Section 17 — Transactions of Certain Affiliated Persons and Underwriters

It is unlawful for any affiliated person, or promoter of, or principal underwriter for, a registered investment company to knowingly sell any security or other property of the investment company, or any other company that is controlled by the investment company, unless the sale involves (solely) securities of which the buyer is the issuer, securities of which the seller is the issuer, securities that are part of the general offering to the holders of a class of its securities, or securities deposited with the trustee of a unit investment trust or a periodic payment plan. It is also unlawful to knowingly purchase from a registered investment company, or from another company controlled by that investment company, any security or other property, or to borrow money or property from the investment company. Violation of these areas is considered a *conflict of interest*.

Section 18 — Capital Structure, Limitations on Borrowing

If a registered closed-end investment company wants to issue a senior security (bond), it must have an asset coverage of at least 300%. If the security is a stock, it must have an asset coverage of at least 200%, and provision must be made to prohibit the declaration of any dividend.

Section 19 — Dividends

It is unlawful for a registered investment company to pay any dividend from any source other than the company's *accumulated undistributed net income* or the company's *net income from current or a preceding fiscal year* unless the payment is accompanied by a *written* statement that adequately discloses the source or sources of the payment. It is also unlawful for a registered investment company to distribute *long-term capital gains* more often than once every *twelve months*, i.e., annually only.

Section 21 — Loans

Loans of money or property may not be made by a registered investment company to any person directly or indirectly if the investment policies of the company do not permit this type of a loan, or if the person to whom the loan is being made controls, or is under the control of, the registered investment company.

Section 22 — Distribution, Redemption, and Repurchase of Redeemable Securities

Section 22(c) — Regulation of Underwriters and Dealers by the Commission   The SEC has power to make rules and regulations applicable to registered investment companies and to principal underwriters and dealers on the redeemable securities of any registered investment company whether or not these are members of any other securities association. The rules of the commission supersede the rules of any other associations that are applicable to registered investment companies and their underwriters or dealers.

Rule 22c-1 — Pricing of Redeemable Securities for Distribution, Redemption, and Repurchase
Registered investment companies securities are sold, redeemed, or repurchased at a price based on the *current net asset value* of each security, <u>which is next computed</u> after receipt of a tender of such a security for redemption, or of an order to purchase and sell the security. For the purpose of this rule, the current net asset value of any security is computed no less frequently than once daily in which there is a sufficient degree of trading in the investment company's portfolio of securities that it might be materially affected by changes in the value of the portfolio and at such specific time during the day as determined by a majority of the Board of Directors.

Section 22(d) — Persons to and through Whom Redeemable Securities may be Sold
A registered investment company may sell securities only to or through a principal underwriter for distribution, or at a current public offering price described in the prospectus.

Rule 22d-1 — Variations in Sales Load Permitted for Certain Sales of Redeemable Securities
A registered investment company that is the issuer of redeemable securities may permit the sale of securities at prices that reflect reductions in the sales load under any of the following circumstances:

- In accordance with a scale of reducing sales load varying with a quantity of securities purchased
- In accordance with a systematic investment or dividend reinvestment plan that provides for the reinvestment of dividends from investment income in full shares or in full and fractional shares
- In accordance with a systematic investment or dividend reinvestment plan that provides for the reinvestment of capital-gains distributions in full or fractional shares at net asset value upon sale pursuant to a uniform offer described in the prospectus.

Rule 22d-2 — Sales of Redeemable Securities without a Sales Load Following Redemption
A registered investment company may permit the sale of securities at prices that reflect the elimination of the sales load pursuant to a uniform offer described in the prospectus, to any person who has redeemed shares in that company. With the proceeds of that redemption, it may purchase shares of the company or another investment company that offers share holders a no-load exchange privilege. This type of an exchange may be subject to a specified nominal administrative charge.

Section 22(e) — Suspension of Rights of Redemption   No registered investment company can suspend the right of redemption, or postpone the date of payment or satisfaction upon redemption, of any redeemable security in accordance with its terms for more than *seven days* after the tender of the security. Exceptions to this rule apply when the New York Stock Exchange is closed or when trading on the exchange is restricted.

Section 27 — Periodic Payment Plans

Section 27a — Prohibitions   It is unlawful for any registered investment company issuing periodic payment plan certificates to sell them if the sales load exceeds 9% of the total payments made, if more than one-half of any of the first twelve monthly payments is deducted for a sales load, if the amount of the sales load deducted from any one of the first payments exceeds the amount deducted from any other payment.

Section 27(c) — Prerequisites to Sale of Periodic Payment Plan Certificate   Each periodic payment plan certificate must be redeemable security and the proceeds of all the payments for the certificate must be deposited with a trustee or custodian.

Section 27(d) — Right to Refund   Each periodic payment plan certificate must provide that the holder may surrender the certificate at any time within the first *eighteen* months after issuance and receive in cash the value of his or her account. In addition, the holder should receive an amount from the underwriter or depositor equal to that part of the excess paid for sales loading that is over 15% of the gross payments made.

Section 27(e) — Notice of Right to Refund   The investment company issuing periodic payment plans must notify in writing those certificate holders who have missed three payments or more, within thirty days following the expiration of fifteen months after the issuance of the certificate. Any certificate holder who missed one payment or more after this fifteen-month period but prior to the expiration of eighteen months after issuance, must be notified of the right to surrender the certificate. This notification must inform the certificate holder of the value of the account as of the time the written notice was given and the amount to which he or she is entitled as a result of the surrender.

Section 27(f) — Right of Withdrawal   The custodian bank for a periodic payment plan must *mail* to each certificate holder within *sixty days* after the issuance of the certificate, a statement of *charges to be deducted* from the projected payments on the certificate and a notice of the holder's *right of withdrawal*. The certificate holder may within *forty-five days* of the mailing of the notice receive payment in cash of the sum of the value of his or her account, *and* an amount from the underwriter or depositor, equal to the difference between the gross payments made and the net amount invested.

Section 27(h) — Spread Load Option   The sales load on a periodic payment plan certificate must not exceed 9% for the total of all payments made. No more than 20% of *any payment* may be deducted as a sales load. An average of no more than 16% can be deducted for sales load for the first forty-eight monthly payments (four years). For example, a "20-20-20-4 plan" means 20% each year for 3 years and 4% in the 4th year.

QUICK QUIZ 4

16.   No person may serve as an investment advisor with a registered   Reference:
       investment company without: Page 13-18
       a.   Prior approval of the SEC
       b.   Prior approval of the NASD
       c.   Prior approval of the Board of Directors
       d.   A written contract
       e.   An established commission schedule

17.   A registered closed-end investment company can issue a senior   Reference:
       security if it has an asset coverage of at least: Page 13-19
       a.   300%
       b.   200%
       c.   150%
       d.   100%
       e.   90%

18.   A registered investment company may not distribute long-term   Reference:
       capital gains to its investors any more often than once: Page 13-19
       a.   Every six months
       b.   Quarterly
       c.   Annually
       d.   Bi-annually
       e.   Monthly

19.   The Securities and Exchange Commission has power to make   Reference:
       rules and regulations applicable to registered investment companies.   Page 13-20
       If the NASD were to make a rule that contradicted an SEC regulation,
       which would have precedence?
       a.   NASD
       b.   SEC
       c.   Each would have equal weight
       d.   One would cancel out the other
       e.   A court decision would determine applicability

20.   It is unlawful for any registered investment company issuing periodic Reference:
       payment plan certificates to charge sales load that exceeds _____   Page 13-21
       of the total payments made.
       a.   50%
       b.   20%
       c.   16%
       d.   15%
       e.   9%   ANSWERS: 16-d; 17-a; 18-c; 19-b; 20-e.

Section 30 — Periodic and Other Reports

Every registered investment company must *file annually* with the commission the information, documents, and reports required of investment companies having securities registered on the National Securities Exchange. These reports are required by the Securities Exchange Act of 1934.

Section 30(b) — Periodic Reports Each registered investment company is required to file with the commission information and documents required by the commission on a *semi-annual* or *quarterly* basis. Periodic or interim reports transmitted to the company's securities holders must be filed not later than *ten days* after transmission.

Section 30(d) — Shareholder Reports Each registered investment company is required to transmit to its stockholders at least *semi-annually*, reports containing information such as a financial statement, a balance sheet, a list showing the amounts and values of securities owned, a statement of income, a statement of surplus, and a statement of aggregate remuneration paid.

Section 30(e) — Certification of Independent Public Accountants Annual financial statements submitted to the commission must be accompanied by a certificate of *independent public accountants*. This certificate must be based upon an *audit,* comparable in scope and procedures to those followed by independent public accountants in presenting comprehensive and dependable financial statements.

Section 35 — Unlawful Representations and Names

It is unlawful for an investment company to represent, or imply in any manner whatsoever, that the security offered or the company itself has been guaranteed, sponsored, recommended or approved by the United States or any agency or officer of the government. In addition, a registered investment company may not adopt as part of the name or title of its company or any security of which it is the issuer, any word or words that the commission finds, and by order declares, to be deceptive or misleading.

Section 36 — Breach of Fiduciary Duty

The SEC is authorized to bring an action in the proper district court of the United States against a person who has engaged within *five years* of the commencement of the action, or is about to engage in, any act or practice constituting a breach of fiduciary duty involving personal misconduct, if that person, in respect to any registered investment company acts as an:

- Officer
- Director
- Member of any advisory board
- Investment advisor
- Depositor
- Principal underwriter — given that the registered investment company is an open-end company, unit investment trust, or face amount certificate company

Section 37 — Larceny and Embezzlement

Any person who steals, unlawfully abstracts, unlawfully and willfully converts to his or her own use or to the use of another, or embezzles any of the moneys, funds, securities, credits, property, or assets of any registered investment company is guilty of a crime.

V.   INVESTMENT ADVISORS ACT OF 1940 (Practices that require registration)

Under the following circumstances, advisors must register with the SEC as an investment advisor (no examination currently). Once so registered, you become a <u>Registered Investment Adviser (RIA)</u>:

1.   If, for more than *fifteen* clients, their advice, counsel, publications, writings, analysis, and reports are furnished and distributed, and if their contracts, subscription agreements, and other arrangements with clients are negotiated and performed by the use of the mails and means and instrumentalities of interstate commerce.

2.   If their activities relate to the purchase and sale of securities traded on national securities exchanges and in interstate over-the-counter markets, securities issued by companies engaged in business and interstate commerce, on securities issued by national banks and member banks of the Federal Reserve System.

3.   If their activities occur in such volume as to substantially effect interstate commerce, national securities exchanges, and other securities markets, the national banking system, or the national economy.

QUICK QUIZ 5

21.   With respect to a periodic payment plan certificate, an average of not more than _____ can be deducted for sales load for the first forty-eight monthly payments.

      Reference:
      Page 13-21

    a.   50%
    b.   20%
    c.   16%
    d.   15%
    e.   9%

22.   The reports that must be filed with the SEC according to the 1934 Act, include such information as documents and financial reports. These must be filed on:

      Reference:
      Page 13-23

    a.   Annual basis
    b.   Bi-annual basis
    c.   Semi-annual basis
    d.   Quarterly basis
    e.   None of the above

23. Annual financial statements that are submitted to the SEC must be accompanied by a certificate from:
    a. An independent public accountant
    b. The Board of Directors
    c. The majority of shareholders
    d. The fund manager
    e. The fund underwriter

Reference: Page 13-23

24. If an individual is suspected of a breach in a fiduciary duty, the SEC is authorized to bring action in the proper district court for up to how many years from the date of his or her engagement in a fiduciary capacity?
    a. One year
    b. Two years
    c. Three years
    d. Four years
    e. Five years

Reference: Page 13-23

25. Every registered investment company is required to transmit to its stockholders information such as a financial statement, balance sheet, statement of income, etc., at least:
    a. Quarterly
    b. Annually
    c. Semi-annually
    d. Monthly
    e. Bi-annually

Reference: Page 13-22

ANSWERS: 21-c; 22-a; 23-a; 24-e; 25-c.

VI.   INSIDER TRADING AND SECURITIES FRAUD ENFORCEMENT ACT OF 1988

An increase in the number and severity of insider violations resulted in the creation of the Insider Trading and Securities Fraud Enforcement Act of 1988. The fundamental purpose of this act is to improve the procedures and provide remedies for the prevention of insider trading, i.e., the use of material information not yet publicly disseminated which would affect the volume and price of a security.

Section 2 — Findings

Although the Securities Exchange Act of 1934 includes regulations which prohibit the use of material, non-public information when trading securities the SEC has found it necessary to provide additional methods in an attempt to prevent and prosecute such violations. Following is a summary of the methods chosen.

Section 3 — Civil Penalties

Section 15(f)-Brokers and Dealers   Written policies and procedures must be established, maintained and enforced by brokers or dealers registered with the SEC to prevent the misuse of inside information. The SEC may adopt rules to require specific documentation of such policies and procedures.   These regulations shall also apply to investment advisers registered under the Investment Advisers Act of 1940.

Section 21A(a)-Authority to Impose Civil Penalties   The SEC retains the right to bring action in U.S. district court against any person who committed the insider violation and/or against any individual directly or indirectly controlling that person.   The amount of the penalty to the person committing the violation may not exceed *three times the profit gained or loss avoided*.   The penalty to the controlling individual (supervisor, branch manager, etc.) may not exceed the greater of *$1,000,000 or three times the profit gained or loss avoided*.

Section 21A(b)-Limitations on Liability   The SEC must establish that the controlling individual was aware of or disregarded the fact that the controlled person was committing or going to commit a violation.   Action can also be brought against a controlling individual for failure to maintain proper procedures for preventing insider violations.

Section 21A(c)-Authority of Commission   The SEC has the authority to exempt any person(s) or transaction(s) from the provisions of this section.

Section 21A(d)-Procedures for Collection   Payment of the penalties is made to the U.S. Treasury. Failure to pay the fine may be referred to the Attorney General who may use whatever action may be necessary to impose the penalty.   Actions may not be brought against any persons for violations more than *5 years after the date of the transaction*.

Section 21A(e)-Authority to Award Bounties to Informants   An award not exceeding 10% of the penalty recovered may be paid to any person or persons who provided information leading to the action. An award may not be paid to any member, officer or employee of the appropriate regulatory agency, the Department of Justice or a self-regulatory organization.

Section 21A(f)-Definitions   Two important terms are used throughout this regulation: *profit gained and loss avoided*.   These are measured by the difference between the purchase or sale price of the security and the value of the security a reasonable amount of time after the distribution of the non-public information.

Section 4 — Increases in Criminal Penalties

Persons convicted of violations of this act may be fined not more than *$1,000,000* nor imprisoned more than *ten years* unless that person is a person other than a natural person, e.g., corporation, who may be fined not more than *$2,500,000*.

Section 5 — Liability to Contemporaneous Traders for Insider Trading

This is a new section of the Securities Exchange Act of 1934 which holds persons violating the Act of 1988 liable to other individuals.

Section 20A(a)-Private Rights of Action Based on Contemporaneous Trading   Any person who has been found to violate the regulations of this act is liable to any other person who had purchased securities of the same class during the same period of time.

Section 20A(b)-Limitations on Liability   The maximum damages imposed may not exceed the *profit gained or loss avoided* less any amount the guilty person is required to give up as a result of proceedings relating to the same transaction. An individual is not liable simply as a result of employing another person who is liable, but he is responsible for supervising that person. Actions may not be brought against any person for transactions that occurred more than *5 years* ago.

Section 20A(c)-Joint and Several Liability for Communicating   The individuals who passed on the inside information are liable to the same extent as the person who used the information.

Section 20A(d)-Authority Not to Restrict Other Express or Implied Rights of Action   This section does not limit the right of any individual to bring action against any person violating the Act.

Section 20A(e)-Provisions Not to Affect Public Prosecutions   This section also does not bar any action to recover penalties, either by the SEC, Attorney General or any other person.

Section 6 — Investigatory Assistance to Foreign Securities Authorities

Section 3(a) of the Securities Exchange Act has been amended to include the following specifics.

Section 3(a)(50)-Definition of Foreign Securities Authority   Any foreign government, governmental body or regulatory organization empowered by a foreign government to administer and enforce securities laws.

Section 21(a)(2)-Authority to Provide Assistance to Foreign Securities Authorities   The SEC may provide assistance to any foreign securities authority who wishes to obtain information on individuals who have, or are about to violate insider regulations. The SEC may provide this assistance even if the actions in question may not violate U.S. securities laws.

Section 7 — Securities Law Studies

This section allows the SEC to conduct a study of current conditions as they apply to insider transactions. This includes an analysis of:

- The extent of questionable trading while holding insider information
- The adequacy of surveillance methods
- How well Federal, State and foreign enforcement authorities cooperate when dealing with potential insider violations

- The fairness and orderliness of securities markets in an attempt to prevent insider violations

The study is a result of the extensive changes that have taken place in the securities industry as a whole. In conducting this study the SEC may use whatever means they feel necessary to obtain pertinent information.

Section 8 — Cooperation with Foreign Authorities and International Organizations in Enforcement

The SEC is authorized to use a limited amount of funds for official receptions, representation expenses and membership expenses of the International Organization of Securities Commissions.

QUICK QUIZ 6

1. The maximum civil penalty for a violation of the Inside Trading and   Reference:
    Securities Fraud Enforcement Act of 1988 is: Page 13-26
    a. The profit gained or loss avoided
    b. Two times the profit gained or loss avoided
    c. Three times the profit gained or loss avoided
    d. Unlimited

2. Actions may not be brought against an individual if the violation   Reference:
    occurred more than: Page 13-26
    a. Two years ago
    b. Three years ago
    c. Five years ago
    d. Ten years ago

3. An individual who violated this act may not be imprisoned for more   Reference:
    than: Page 13-26
    a. Unlimited
    b. 10 years
    c. 5 years
    d. 3 years   ANSWERS: 1-c; 2-c; 3-b.

REAL LIFE SITUATION

Ms. Grantland P. Price is a registered representative for the Confederate Government Securities Mutual Fund Company. Ms. Price runs a rather prosperous agency in Podunk, Illinois. For the past several years, she has been utilizing the sales literature distributed by the fund and has met with moderate success. She has decided to develop her own advertising brochures and launch a direct mail campaign. In her brochure she is going to depict income and growth of the fund. In the letter she's going to send out to prospective plan investors, she is going to explain that the future success of the program is insured because of the skilled management involved with the fund. She will describe how her clients can be assured of future gains that would amount to at least 25% of their investment due to this experienced management group and the fact that the fund has made some wise investments. You, as advisor, would offer the following counsel:

Directions: *For each of the numbered recommendations that follow, please select A, B, or C as the evaluation you deem most correct. Place your selection on the line preceding each number:*

A. As a result of this recommendation, Ms. Price will be held captive by the SEC.

B. It is possible that this recommendation could be considered, but there are some serious short-comings.

C. Considering the cir-cumstances, this un-doubtedly is the best recommendation.

Answer

_____ 1.   Abandon all idea of launching your own advertising campaign, burn all prototype brochures prepared, and destroy your postage meter.

_____ 2.   Seek the advice and counsel of the legal department for assistance in launching an individual advertising campaign.

_____ 3.   Launch your advertising campaign immediately; it's caveat emptor all the way in the free enterprise system.

_____ 4.   Read Chapter 13 in The Complete Series 6 Study Book and follow the guidelines established.

_____ 5.   Tone down your advertising, but go ahead and use it anyway.

ANSWERS: 1-B; 2-C; 3-A; 4-B; 5-A.

CHECK YOUR UNDERSTANDING
(Circle one)

1.   If a registration is not in effect, a broker/dealer is prohibited from using any means of communication pertaining to interstate commerce, or the use of the mails as a means of conveying information about a particular security, a prospective customer.
         True/False

Reference:
Page 13-6

2.   The fact that a registration statement for security has been filed, or is in effect, and that the commission has not issued a stop order of one type or another, means that the commission has found that the registration statement is true and accurate as submitted.
         True/False

Reference:
Page 13-7

3.   A statement involving a material fact about the characteristics or attributes of an investment company could be misleading because

Reference:
Page 13-8

of exaggerated or unsubstantiated claims about management skill
or techniques.
    True/False

4. All of the following would be considered securities under the definition   Reference:
    specified in the Securities Exchange Act of 1934: any note, stock,   Page 13-11
    bond, debenture, sharing agreement, pre-organization certificate,
    and investment contract.
    True/False

5. When a customer requests of a broker/dealer information con-   Reference:
    cerning a recent transaction, this must be sent by the broker/   Page 13-11
    dealer, within fifteen days of the request.
    True/False

6. Protection provided under SIPC is on a per-account basis.ˑ   Reference:
    True/False   Page 13-12

7. For a company to be considered a diversified company, at least   Reference:
    75% of the value of its total assets must be represented by cash   Page 13-16
    and government securities.
    True/False

8. The Board of Directors of a registered investment company may   Reference:
    consist of no more than 60% of "affiliated persons" of the invest-   Page 13-16
    ment company.
    True/False

9. A registered investment company may not change its fundamental   Reference:
    investment policy unless, among other actions, authorized by a   Page 13-16
    majority vote of its Board of Directors.
    True/False

10. A custodian bank for a periodic payment plan must mail to each   Reference:
    certificate holder, within sixty days after the issuance of the   Page 13-21
    certificate, a statement of charges to be deducted from the projected
    payments.
    True/False

ANSWERS: 1-True; 2-False; 3-True; 4-True; 5-False; 6-False; 7-False; 8-True; 9-False;
10-True.

ˑ   Please note per-account basis is not correct answer, it must be *per separate account*.....the test is tough!

14

NATIONAL ASSOCIATION OF SECURITIES DEALERS' REGULATIONS

PRETEST
(Circle one)

1. Another qualification exam will be required of a registered principal if preceding the date of receipt of a new application, the registration has lapsed for:
    a. Six months
    b. One year
    c. One year and six months
    d. Two years
    e. None of the above

    Reference:
    Page 14-6

2. If a registered representative is promoted to a position that requires registration as a principal that individual may function in the new position:
    a. Thirty days
    b. Sixty days
    c. Ninety days
    d. One hundred twenty days
    e. One year

    Reference:
    Page 14-7

3. A firm applying for NASD membership must have how many officers or partners who are qualified to become registered principals?
    a. One
    b. Two
    c. Three
    d. Four
    e. Five

    Reference:
    Page 14-7

4.   All of the following are categories of principal registration *except:*   Reference:
   - a.   Limited options principal   Page 14-7
   - b.   General securities principal
   - c.   Limited principal -- direct participation programs
   - d.   Limited principal -- investment and variable contracts products
   - e.   Limited principal -- financial and operations

5.   If an individual's duties are considered limited and qualify for   Reference:
   registration in one of the limited principal's categories: Page 14-7
   - a.   They must apply for registration in that category only
   - b.   They must apply for general securities principal's registration
   - c.   They must register as a representative
   - d.   They must register as a general/limited principal
   - e.   They may still become registered as a general securities principal

6.   People associated with a member firm whose activities in the   Reference:
   investment banking or securities industry include the solicitation   Page 14-9
   and/or sales of options contracts are required to be:
   - a.   Registered representatives
   - b.   Registered principals
   - c.   Registered options representatives
   - d.   Registered solicitors
   - e.   All of the above

7.   The member firm or person against whom summary action is taken   Reference:
   may request a hearing within how many days of the date of official   Page 14-10
   notification?
   - a.   Five days
   - b.   Ten days
   - c.   Fifteen days
   - d.   Twenty days
   - e.   Thirty days

8.   If a hearing on a summary action is not requested, the notification   Reference:
   of the summary action is subject to the review of: Page 14-11
   - a.   Securities and Exchange Commission
   - b.   District Business Conduct Committee
   - c.   New York Stock Exchange
   - d.   Board of Governors
   - e.   Commodities Futures Trading Corporation

9.   A stay of summary action taken against an NASD member firm or   Reference:
      person associated with a member firm may be applied for through   Page 14-11
      which of the following organizations?
      a.   Board of Governors
      b.   Securities and Exchange Commission
      c.   Supreme Court
      d.   The National Association of Securities Dealers
      e.   None of the above

10.   If a registered representative is terminated by an NASD member   Reference:
      firm, that firm is required: Page 14-11
      a.   To notify the SEC in writing
      b.   To notify the employer of the registered representative
      c.   To notify the Board of Governors within twenty days of termination
      d.   To notify the NASD within twenty days of termination
      e.   To notify the NASD within thirty days of termination

11.   The bodies having the power to hear and pass upon all complaints   Reference:
      in regard to violations of the NASD rules are: Page 14-13
      a.   District Business Conduct Committees and the Board
            of Governors
      b.   District Business Conduct Committees only
      c.   Board of Governors only
      d.   Board of Governors and the SEC
      e.   District Business Conduct Committee and the SEC

12.   Which of the following may offer to the respondent a waiver of a   Reference:
      hearing and the opportunity to accept the summary complaint   Page 14-13
      procedure?
      a.   Board of Governors
      b.   District Business Conduct Committee
      c.   NASD
      d.   SEC
      e.   The Supreme Court

13.   If the summary complaint procedure is accepted by the respondent   Reference:
      the penalty can not exceed: Page 14-13
      a.   Suspension and/or a fine of $5,000
      b.   Expulsion and/or a fine of $5,000
      c.   Censure and/or a fine of $5,000
      d.   Censure and/or a fine of $2,500
      e.   Censure and/or a fine of $2,000

14. Acceptance of the summary complaint procedure by the respondent indicates:

Reference:
Page 14-14

    a. Nothing more than the compliance with the rules and regulations established by the NASD
    b. An automatic request for a hearing with the District Business Conduct Committee
    c. An admission of the violations and concludes the proceedings
    d. All of the above
    e. None of the above

15. A respondent may propose to the secretary of the DBCC a document that indicates the nature of the charges, a proposed penalty to be imposed, and a waiver of all rights of appeal. This document is known as:

Reference:
Page 14-14

    a. An admission of guilt
    b. A declaration of guilt
    c. An offer of penalty
    d. A statement of settlement
    e. An offer of settlement

16. If a person or a member firm making a complaint — or the respondent to a complaint — feels that disciplinary action taken by the Board of Governors is unsatisfactory, a review may be requested of the:

Reference:
Page 14-15

    a. Board of Governors
    b. Securities and Exchange Commission
    c. District Business Conduct Committee
    d. National Association of Securities Dealers
    e. All of the above

17. The simplified arbitration procedure may be used in a dispute between a public customer and an associated member if the dollar amount involved does not exceed:

Reference:
Page 14-16

    a. $10,000
    b. $7,500
    c. $5,000
    d. $2,500
    e. $1,000

18. The filing fee required for the simplified arbitration procedure must accompany the submission agreement. This fee amounts to:

Reference:
Page 14-17

    a. $100
    b. $50
    c. $25
    d. From $15 to $100
    e. $10

19. An arbitration panel may be made up of:
    a. Securities industry personnel
    b. Three arbitrators
    c. One arbitrator
    d. All of the above
    e. None of the above

Reference:
Page 14-17

20. All rewards rendered in proceedings under the simplified arbitration procedure must be made within:
    a. Ten days
    b. Twenty days
    c. Thirty days
    d. Twenty business days
    e. Thirty business days

Reference:
Page 14-17

ANSWERS: 1-d; 2-c; 3-b; 4-a; 5-e; 6-c; 7-b; 8-d; 9-b; 10-e; 11-a; 12-b; 13-d; 14-c; 15-e; 16-b; 17-a; 18-d; 19-d; 20-e.

OVERVIEW

The passing of the Maloney Act in June of 1938 provided for a self-regulatory body for the over-the-counter market. On July 20, 1939, the initial registration statement of the National Association of Securities Dealers, Inc. (NASD) as the self-regulatory body was filed with the SEC.

The NASD's growth in importance has been a steady influence on not only the OTC market, but the entire securities industry. This chapter discusses that influence.

Author's Note to Candidates

It is imperative that the rules and regulations discussed in this and other chapters are studied in detail and strictly adhered to in your practice. Many of the rules and regulations in this and subsequent chapters are complicated and may cause some confusion during the initial "run-through." Careful study of this material is recommended and will be tested thoroughly on the exam.

BACKGROUND

The *Board of Governors* is the controlling body of the NASD and determines policy on a national scale. This board is composed of twenty-seven members. Represented on the board are eleven administrative districts across the country. Each of these eleven districts has a *district committee* that functions as an agent of the board, in executing NASD policy.

The enforcement of the NASD rules and regulations and subsequent interpretation is the responsibility of the *District Business Conduct Committee* (DBCC). The members of this committee are composed of the same individuals as comprise the membership of the district committees, the only distinction being that the title "District Business Conduct Committee" is used when there are *disciplinary* proceedings.

I.   CERTIFICATE OF INCORPORATION

Objects and Purposes

The objects and purposes of the NASD rest in *standardizing the principles and practices* of the investment banking and securities business and *promoting high standards* among its members in observance of federal and state securities laws. The NASD is the medium through which its membership confers, consults, and cooperates with government and other public agencies in solving problems that affect the investment business. It administers and enforces rules and regulations to prevent fraudulent and manipulative acts and promotes *equitable principles of trade* for the protection of investors. The objectives include *self-discipline* among members and the *investigation* and *adjustment of grievances* between investors and NASD members.

By-Laws

Article III — Membership   A *principal* is a person associated with a member who is actively engaged in the *management* of the member's investment banking or securities business. This includes supervision, solicitation, conduct of business or the training of persons associated with the member for any investment functions. Examples of principles include sole proprietors, officers, partners, office managers, training personnel, and directors of corporations.

All principals must be *registered* with the NASD and are required to pass a *qualification examination* designed for principals. (That's right, a separate exam!) The exam is appropriate to the category for which the principal is engaged; for example, financial principal, back office principal. If a principal's registration has lapsed for a period of more than *two years,* this person is required to pass another qualification exam. This two-year rule is applicable to registered representatives, too.

Who's the registered principal around here?

If a registered representative is promoted or changes duties to that of a principal, he or she must, within *ninety days*, pass the appropriate qualification examination. Any individual who is not currently a registered representative, and seeks to be associated with a member firm as a principal, must first pass the registered representative's exam.

Any firm that seeks membership in the NASD (with the exception of a sole proprietorship) must have at least *two* officers or partners who are qualified to become registered principals. There are various categories of principal registration including:

- General securities principal
- Limited principal — financial and operations
- Limited principal — investment and variable contracts/products
- Limited principal — direct participation programs
- Registered options principals

A *General Securities Principal* (Exam Series 24) is a person whose overall duties are such that they have *general operating responsibilities* and do not deal only in one of the limited categories listed below. Every firm must have at least two general securities principals (except sole proprietor). Often a principal is *both* a general securities principals *and* a principal for the special category over which he or she has supervisory responsibility.

Now which kind of principal do you want?

The *General Securities Principal — Financial and Operations* (Exam Series 27) is applied to a person associated with a member firm, who has responsibility for the *accuracy of financial reports* that are submitted to regulatory bodies. An individual who *supervises* individuals who maintain the member firm's books and records for such reports must be registered under this category.

I'm the financial principal who "accounts" to the NASD.

The *Limited Principal — Investment and Variable Contracts Products* (Exam Series 26) is the category for those whose duties are limited solely to the transactions involving securities of companies registered pursuant to the Investment Company Act of 1940 and variable contract products (insurance premiums) registered pursuant to the Securities Act of 1933. Examples of variable contracts are variable annuities, investment annuities, and variable life insurance (sometimes called investment life insurance).

I only wear two hats around here.

The *Limited Principal — Direct Participation Programs* (Exam Series 39) category is for programs that provide for *flow-through* tax consequences (regardless of the legal structure) including, but not limited to, oil and gas programs, real estate programs, agricultural programs, cattle programs, condominium securities, S-corporation offerings and all other programs. Persons falling within this category are required to be registered as limited principals in this area.

The *Registered Options Principals* (Exam Series 4) applies to every NASD member firm that is engaged in transactions involving *put* or *call options* with the public *or* for its own account. Each must have at least one registered options principal.

QUICK QUIZ 1

1.   Another qualification exam will be required of a registered principal   Reference:
      if preceding the date of receipt of a new application, the registration   Page 14-6
      has lapsed for:
      a.   Six months
      b.   One year
      c.   One year and six months
      d.   Two years
      e.   None of the above

2.   If a registered representative is promoted to a position that requires   Reference:
      registration as a principal that individual must pass a qualifying   Page: 14-7
      exam within:
      a.   Thirty days
      b.   Sixty days
      c.   Ninety days
      d.   One hundred twenty days
      e.   One year

3.   A firm, other than a sole proprietorship, applying for NASD member-   Reference:
      ship must have how many officers or partners who are qualified to   Page 14-7
      become registered principals?
      a.   One
      b.   Two
      c.   Three
      d.   Four
      e.   Five

4.   All of the following are categories of principal registration *except*:   Reference:
      a.   Limited options principal   Page 14-7
      b.   General securities principal
      c.   Limited principal — Direct participation programs
      d.   Limited principal — investment and variable contracts products
      e.   Limited principal — financial and operations

5.   If an individual's duties are considered limited and qualify for registra-   Reference:
      tion in one of the limited principal's categories: Page 14-7
      a.   They must apply for registration in that category only
      b.   They must apply for general securities principal's registration
      c.   They must register as a representative
      d.   They must register as a general/limited principal
      e.   They may still become registered as a general securities principal

ANSWERS: 1-d; 2-c; 3-b; 4-a; 5-e.

REGISTRATION OF REPRESENTATIVES

Representatives are employees, including assistant officers other than principals, who are engaged in the investment banking or securities business for the member firm. Their functions include supervision, solicitation, conduct of business and securities, or the training of persons associated with a member firm for any of these functions.

All persons associated with a member firm who are designated as representatives must be registered and pass the appropriate examination. Any representative whose registration has been terminated for two or more years is required to pass a qualification exam.

People associated with a member firm whose activities include the solicitation and/or sales of *option contracts* shall be required to be certified as registered options representatives and pass the appropriate exam. They may choose between the registered *representative* exam and a registered *options principal* exam.

People associated with a member firm whose functions are solely and exclusively *clerical* or "ministerial" are *exempt* from NASD registration. Also *exempt* are individuals associated with a member firm whose functions relate to transactions on *national exchanges* (and who are registered with these exchanges; e.g., NYSE); transactions in exempted securities, municipal bonds and U.S. bonds; or transactions in commodities. *Foreign associates* are normally *exempt*, also.

SUMMARY SUSPENSION

The NASD may *suspend* a member firm or person associated with a member firm for violation of the rules of fair practice. The NASD may also suspend a member who is in financial or operating difficulty and notifies the SEC that the member cannot do business with safety to investors, creditors, other members or the NASD itself.

Any member firm or person associated with a member firm against whom the NASD takes some action must be notified promptly in writing. However, the summary action itself is not conditioned upon written notification but rather is effective *immediately*. The member firm or person against whom summary action is taken may request a hearing within *ten days* of date of notification. The hearing will be held within *five days* from the date requested. A written decision of the result of the hearing must be issued within *five days* of the date of the hearing, and a copy is sent to the member firm or person against whom action was taken. Notification of the summary action is subject to review by the *Board of Governors* on its own motion or as requested by a member firm or other person against whom action was taken. The decision of the Board of Governors reviewing the hearing action will be made within *thirty days* after the issuance of the decision.

Any member firm or person associated with a member firm against whom action is taken by the NASD may apply to the SEC for a *stay* of the summary action. A request may also be made to the SEC for a *review* of the decision made by the NASD.

USE OF NAME OF CORPORATION (NASD) BY MEMBERS

The Board of Governors generally allows an NASD member to use the name of the corporation on letterheads, circulars, or other advertising matter of literature, but only to a limited extent. A member's association with the NASD may be publicized but there may be no additional significance to this membership. Any other intent is strictly prohibited.

REGISTRATION OF REGISTERED REPRESENTATIVES

The term *registered representative* means any person associated with a member firm who has demonstrated qualifications to engage in the investment banking or securities business. *Schedule C* of the NASD by-laws requires registration of all appropriate personnel. The *failure* of any member firm to *register* an employee who should be registered as a registered representative may be considered as "conduct inconsistent with just and equitable principals of trade" and may be sufficient cause for *disciplinary action.*

Application for registration made to the NASD must be signed by the applicant and contain an indication of the applicant's acceptance and agreement to abide by the provisions and conditions of the certificate of incorporation and other rules and regulations of the NASD. No officer or employee of the NASD may be held liable for any action except *willful malfeasance.*

If a registered representative is *terminated* by a member firm, the member firm is required to notify the NASD of the termination within *thirty days* of the action. A member firm that does not submit the required notification is subject to a late filing fee as specified by the Board of Governors.

The termination is not effective if any complaint or action against the representative is pending. A representative remains subject to the filing of a complaint under the Code of Procedure if the complaint is filed within two years after the effective date of the termination.

QUICK QUIZ 2

6. People associated with a member firm whose activities in the investment banking or securities industry include the solicitation and/or sales of options contracts are required to be certified as:

    Reference:
    Page 14-9

    a. Registered representatives
    b. Registered principals
    c. Registered options representatives
    d. Registered solicitors
    e. All of the above

7. The member firm or person against whom summary action is taken may request a hearing within how many days of the date of official notification?

    Reference:
    Page 14-10

    a. Five days
    b. Ten days
    c. Fifteen days
    d. Twenty days
    e. Thirty days

8. If a hearing on a summary action is not requested, the notification of the summary action is subject to the review of:

    Reference:
    Page 14-11

    a. Securities Exchange Commission
    b. District Business Conduct Committee
    c. New York Stock Exchange
    d. Board of Governors
    e. Commodities Future Trading Corporation

9. A stay of summary action taken against an NASD member firm or person associated with a member firm may be applied for through which of the following organizations?

    Reference:
    Page 14-11

    a. Board of Governors
    b. Securities and Exchange Commission
    c. Supreme Court
    d. The National Association of Securities Dealers
    e. None of the above

10.   If a registered representative is terminated by an NASD member   Reference:
       firm that firm is required to notify the: Page 14-11
       a.   SEC in writing.
       b.   Employer of the registered representative
       c.   Board of Governors within twenty days of termination
       d.   NASD within twenty days of termination
       e.   NASD within thirty days of termination

ANSWERS: 6-c; 7-b; 8-d; 9-b; 10-e.

CODE OF PROCEDURE FOR HANDLING TRADE PRACTICE COMPLAINTS

The purpose of the *code of procedure* is to handle trade practice complaints regarding *violations* of the NASD Rules of Fair Practice and any other supplemental rules of the NASD. All complaints are heard by the *District Business Conduct Committees* of the NASD and the *Board of Governors*. The DBCC has "original jurisdiction" in handling such complaints and the Board of Governors acts as an appellate and review body. (NOTE: The Code of Procedure and the Rules of Fair Practice are different, and it is easy to confuse the two. The Code of Procedures *enforces* the Rules of Fair Practice; i.e., it applies to *violations*. Think of the first letter of each of the words — COP — that's right, the Code of Procedures is like the COP who enforces rules.)

   After a hearing request has been made, both the person making the complaint and the person responding are notified by the committee. The committee itself may request a hearing. both parties in a hearing are entitled to be represented by counsel and are given the opportunity to be heard.

The Code of Procedure (COP) enforces and handles trade practice complaints for violators of the rules.

   The DBCC may offer the respondent an opportunity to waive a hearing and accept *summary complaint procedure* if the violation is not a major one. This procedure, when offered by the DBCC, is on a form that specifies the charges and the rules violated. This form also specifies the appropriate penalties to be imposed based on the circumstances. This penalty cannot *exceed censure* and/or a fine of *$2,500*. An offer made by the DBCC to the respondent can include the following:

- The respondent may reject the summary complaint procedure and the regular complaint procedure will be followed (i.e., respondent wants to clear him/herself entirely).
- If acceptance is not received within ten days after the offer has been received, it is considered rejected and the regular complaint procedure will be followed.
- The respondent may accept the offer by executing the agreement and other documents specified, together with the fine that is imposed.

Acceptance of the summary complaint procedure by the respondent indicates an *admission* of the violations and concludes the proceedings. If there is more than one respondent involved in a situation and any of these respondents reject an offer, the DBCC may continue with the regular complaint procedure against some or all. The *Board of Governors* may review the proceedings within *forty-five days* after the receipt of a respondent's acceptance of the offer for summary complaint procedure. This review acts as a *stay* of any action. The board may then dismiss one or more of the charges and/or reduce the penalty imposed, or possibly remand the matter to the DBCC with instructions to institute regular complaint procedures. The position of the respondent cannot be prejudiced in any way by either a rejection of the offer of summary complaint procedure or a determination that regular complaint procedure should be followed.

OK, I admit I was a bad boy ..... can I have censure and a fine of $2,500 under "summary complaint procedure"?

The respondent to a proceeding that is before the DBCC may at any time propose in writing to the *Director of the District an offer of settlement*. The offer of settlement may be made at any time during the course of the proceeding but must be made in conformance with the provisions of the rules and must not be made frivolously or propose a penalty that is inconsistent with the seriousness of the violations involved. Each offer of settlement must be made in writing and must contain the following provisions:

- Nature of the charges
- The rule or rules alleged to have been violated
- A statement of proposed findings of fact
- A proposed penalty to be imposed that must be reasonable under the circumstances and consistent with the seriousness of the violations found
- A waiver of all rights of appeal to the Board of Governors, the SEC, and the U.S. Court of Appeals

If the offer of settlement is accepted by the DBCC, the *National Business Conduct Committee* has the final approval of any acceptance of an offer of settlement. If an offer of settlement is *rejected* by the DBCC or by the National Committee, the offer of settlement is considered *withdrawn*. The DBCC then proceeds with *regular* disciplinary procedures. If more than one respondent is involved and one or more of the respondents submits an offer of settlement, the DBCC may *accept or reject* any or all of the offers. Those that are *accepted* will *terminate* the proceedings against those respondents only. If an offer of settlement is not accepted and regular disciplinary procedures are followed, this rejection will *not* prejudice the respondent involved.

If the DBCC takes any disciplinary action or decides to dismiss any complaint, their action will be subject to review by the Board of Governors within *forty-five days*. In any case where the person or firm making the complaint, or the respondent to a complaint, feels that the disciplinary action taken by the Board of Governors is unsatisfactory, an application for review by the SEC may be made.

QUICK QUIZ 3

11. The bodies having power to hear and pass upon all complaints in regard to violations of the NASD rules are:
    Reference: Page 14-13
    a. District Business Conduct Committees and the Board of Governors
    b. District Business Conduct Committees only
    c. Board of Governors only
    d. Board of Governors and the SEC
    e. District Business Conduct Committees and the SEC

12. Which of the following may offer to the respondent a waiver of a hearing and the opportunity to accept the summary complaint procedure?
    Reference: Page 14-13
    a. Board of Governors
    b. District Business Conduct Committee
    c. National Association of Securities Dealers
    d. Securities and Exchange Commission
    e. The Supreme Court

13. If the summary complaint procedure is accepted by the respondent the penalty cannot exceed:
    Reference: Page 14-13
    a. Suspension and/or a fine of $5,000
    b. Expulsion and/or a fine of $5,000
    c. Censure and/or a fine of $5,000
    d. Censure and/or a fine of $2,500
    e. Censure and/or a fine of $2,000

14.   Acceptance of the summary complaint procedure by the respondent indicates:

Reference: Page 14-14

    a.   Nothing more than the compliance with the rules and regulations established by the NASD

    b.   An automatic request for a hearing with the District Business Conduct Committee

    c.   An admission of the violations and concludes the proceedings

    d.   All of the above

    e.   None of the above

15.   A respondent may propose to the secretary of the DBCC a document that indicates the nature of the changes, a proposed penalty to be imposed, and a waiver of all rights of appeal. This document is known as:

Reference: Page 14-14

    a.   An admission of guilt

    b.   A declaration of guilt

    c.   An offer of penalty

    d.   A statement of settlement

    e.   An offer of settlement

ANSWERS: 11-a; 12-b; 13-d; 14-c; 15-e.

CODE OF ARBITRATION PROCEDURE

The *code of arbitration procedure* is provided for the arbitration of controversies and any other securities related disputes arising out of, or in connection with, the business of any member of the NASD. The various controversies involved include those:

- Between members
- Between members and public customers (if they agree) or others
- Between members, declaring corporations, clearing banks or associated banks

Any dispute, claim, or controversy arising between a public customer and an associated person, or a member subject to arbitration involving a dollar amount that does not exceed $10,000, is arbitrated under the *simplified arbitration procedure*. The claimant is required to file with the director of arbitration:

(1)   A submission agreement

(2)   A statement of claim

    The *statement of claim* must specify the relevant facts, the remedies sought, and whether or not a hearing is demanded. The claimant pays a fee for filing. It can vary from $15 to $100 depending on the amount in controversy. The director of arbitration then serves the respondent promptly by mail a copy of both documents. The respondent, within *twenty calendar days* from receipt of the material, files with the director of arbitration a submission agreement and a copy of the respondent's answer together with the supporting documents required. If a third party is involved, the director of arbitration serves promptly by mail, or otherwise, a copy of the third part claim submitted by the respondent together with a submission agreement.

The dispute, claim, or controversy is then submitted to a single arbitrator who is knowledgeable in the securities industry and is selected by the director of arbitration. Unless the public customer demands or consents to a hearing, or the arbitrator calls for a hearing, the arbitrator decides the dispute. Any extensions may be granted by the director of arbitration if good cause is shown. If requested by the arbitrator, the director of arbitration may appoint two additional arbitrators to the panel who decide the matter in controversy.

Any dispute, claim, or controversy arising *between* members or associated persons, submitted to arbitration involving a dollar amount not exceeding $10,000, is resolved by an *arbitration panel*, unless one of the parties files within *ten business days* a request for a hearing of the matter. Any arbitration panel established for a dispute between members or an associated person consists of one but no more than three arbitrators, all of whom are from within this securities industry. Simplified arbitration of disputes of amounts up to $10,000 is the limit for members or between a member and a public customer.

All awards, rendered in proceedings under the simplified arbitration procedure must be made within *thirty business days* from the date the arbitrators review all the written statements, documents, and evidence and declare the matter *closed*; that is, the decision of the arbitrator is *final*.

It may be considered "conduct inconsistent with just and equitable principles of trade" and a violation of Article III, Section I of the Rules of Fair Practice, for a member or a person associated with a member to fail to submit a dispute for arbitration or fail to honor an award of arbitrators.

QUICK QUIZ 4

16.   If a person, or member firm making a complaint — or who is the   Reference:
respondent to a complaint — feels that disciplinary action taken by   Page 14-15
the Board of Governors is unsatisfactory, a review may be requested
from the:
   a.   Board of Governors
   b.   Securities and Exchange Commission
   c.   District Business Conduct Committee
   d.   National Association of Securities Dealers
   e.   All of the above

17.   The simplified arbitration procedure may be used in a dispute   Reference:
between a public customer and an associated member if the dollar   Page 14-16
amount involved does not exceed:
   a. $10,000
   b. $7,500
   c. $5,000
   d. $2,500
   e. $1,000

18.   The filing fee required for the simplified arbitration procedure must   Reference:
accompany the submission agreement. This fee amounts to: Page 14-17
   a. $100
   b. $50
   c. $25
   d.   From $15 to $100
   e.   Nothing

19.   An arbitration panel may be made up of: Reference:
   a.   Securities industry personnel   Page 14-17
   b.   Three arbitrators
   c.   One arbitrator
   d.   All of the above
   e.   None of the above

20.   All awards rendered in proceedings under the simplified arbitration   Reference:
        procedure must be made within: Page 14-17

        a.   Ten days
        b.   Twenty days
        c.   Thirty days
        d.   Twenty business days
        e.   Thirty business days

                                            ANSWERS: 16-b; 17-a; 18-d; 19-d; 20-e.

INVESTMENT COMPANY SECURITIES

Contractual plan withdrawal and *reinstatement privileges* permit plan holders to withdraw up to 90% of the current value of their accounts in cash and later return the money to the account *without* sales charges imposed. This program is designed to preserve the plan holder's investment, eliminating the need for borrowing on certificates or liquidating his or her account in an emergency period. When first established the withdrawal and replacement privilege was designed for *emergency* situations only. Then, a rapid increase in the utilization of this privilege resulted in its *abuse* as far as the SEC was concerned. A plan holder can undoubtedly use this privilege to his or her advantage. For example, if he or she believes — or a broker/dealer leads him or her to believe — that the market is due to turn downward, the plan holder may withdraw up to 90% of the account in cash. If the market does in fact go down, the investor will, at a point he or she considers to be the bottom of the downward trend, replace the withdrawn cash with the underwriter of the fund, thus acquiring more shares than redeemed, with no sales charge. This practice would have an adverse effect on the plan itself and other plan holders who did not take advantage of this practice.

As a result of the type of activity described above, the Board of Governors considers this type of activity a *violation*. Practices that are considered detrimental to the interest of other shareholders include:

- The suggestion, encouragement, or assistance to a plan holder in making repeated or excessive use of the withdrawal and reinstatement privilege
- Reinstating the investment within ninety days after withdrawing
- Making use of the withdrawal privilege within six months after the most recent investment in the plan
- Using the privilege to provide funds for temporary investment in other securities
- Using the privilege for the purpose of their advantage of fluctuations in the net asset value per share of the investment company

I don't know of any rule prohibiting this, do you?

Guidelines were established by the NASD to assist its members in complying with the Board of Governors interpretation on *special deals*. These guidelines apply to items or expenditures that have a material value, and are given or reimbursed directly or indirectly, to a dealer or a registered representative, or any other associated person of a broker/dealer. The following are examples of violations:

- Gifts amounting to more than $100 per person per year
- Gifts of management company stock or other securities
- Loans
- Discounts from the offering price of a security
- Wholesale commissions or overrides
- Gifts or payments of any kind by a wholesale representative to a dealer or a salesman of a dealer firm
- Payment or reimbursement of travel expenses including overnight lodging regardless of destination or purpose unless such payment or reimbursement falls within the $100 per person per year limit
  Note: If this payment is in connection with a business meeting, conference, or seminar held by the underwriter *for informational purposes* relative to the fund or its sponsorship, the payment of these items *is* permitted.

In their interpretation of special deals, the Board of Governors also lists items that are *not* considered to constitute material value. These items include:

- An occasional dinner, ticket to a sporting event or a theater or comparable entertainment
- A dinner, reception, or cocktail party given for a group of registered representatives
- Advertising items where the dollar amount of the gift is not more than $100 per person per year (pens, calendars, etc., with company advertising on them)

Are you bound by the "special deals limitation?"

An NASD member is prohibited from *selling dividends*. The broker/dealer, or registered representative, may not imply that any advantage accrues to the buyer of the shares of an investment company in anticipation of a distribution that is about to be paid. The amount of this distribution is *included* in the price he or she pays for these shares and the shares *decline* in price on the ex-distribution (ex-dividend) date by the *amount* of the distribution. To imply any advantage for buying shares prior to the ex-distribution date is considered a violation of the Rules of Fair Practice.

For many years, Regulation T of the Board of Governors of the Federal Reserve System did *not* permit the extension of *credit* on open-end investment company shares by brokers and dealers. Since January 28, 1985 the SEC has treated mutual funds as marginable securities. However, investors are required to hold their shares for 31 days before they may margin the shares.

The Securities Exchange Act of 1934 authorized the Federal Reserve Board to regulate extension of credit by brokers for the purchase of securities (margin accounts). A margin is the amount a customer must deposit to cover purchases or short sales. Only listed securities or approved OTC stocks can be purchased on margin. Under Regulation T, if a customer does not settle an account for a new purchase within five business days, the broker must sell the stock being held for collateral to liquidate the indebtedness (including commissions) unless an extension has been filed. The customer is entitled to the remainder, if any, but the account is frozen.

The NASD Board of Governors has determined that the payment of continuing commissions in connection with securities is *not* improper as long as the person receiving the commissions *remains* a registered representative of the NASD member firm and a member of the National Association of Securities Dealers. If a *bona fide contract* exists that calls for a continuing payment following the termination of the registered representative, e.g., retirement, it is also considered *permissible* by the Board of Governors.

A broker/dealer is required to *maintain* the *public offering price* of an issue. In transactions with a non-member broker or dealer, the member firm must trade, at the same prices, for the same commissions or fees, and the same general terms and conditions as the member firm trades with the *general public*.

QUICK QUIZ 5

21. The contractual plan withdrawal and reinstatement privileges permit a plan holder to withdraw up to 90% of the current value of accounts in cash and later return the money to the account:

    Reference: Page 14-19

    a. With a reduced sales charge imposed
    b. With a redemption fee charged
    c. Without a sales charge being imposed
    d. With a management fee imposed
    e. None of the above

22. As a result of the contractual plan withdrawal and reinstatement privileges being abused, the Board of Governors has placed various requirements on this practice, which include all of the following *except*:

    Reference: Page 14-19

    a. Making use of the withdrawal privilege within three months of the most recent investment in the plan
    b. Reinstating the investment within ninety days after withdrawing the shares
    c. Using the privilege to provide funds for temporary investment in other securities
    d. Using the privilege for the purpose of taking advantage of fluctuations in the net asset value per share
    e. Excess use of withdrawal privilege

23. The Board of Governors interpretation on *special deals* provides various definitions of what constitutes something of material value. All of the following are considered to have material value *except*:

    Reference: Page 14-20

    a. Loans
    b. Wholesale commissions
    c. Gifts which amounts to less than $100 per person
    d. Discounts from the offering price of a security
    e. Gifts of management company stock

24. When a registered representative implies that an advantage would accrue to the buyer of shares of an investment company due to the anticipation of a dividend distribution, this registered representative is guilty of:

    Reference: Page 14-21

    a. Selling distributions
    b. Free-riding
    c. Withholding
    d. Selling dividends
    e. Selling shares distributions

25.   The sale of investment company shares in dollar amounts that fall   Reference:
       just below the point at which a sales charge is reduced is known   Page 14-21
       as the practice of:
       a.   Ex-distribution sales
       b.   Break-even sales
       c.   Regulation T sales
       d.   Commission sales
       e.   Break-point sales

ANSWERS: 21-c; 22-a; 23-c; 24-d; 25-e.

REAL LIFE SITUATION

A neighbor of yours, Mr. F. Lester Sylvester (this one's real), took a position as a registered representative with the Munificent Mutual Fund. After being subjected to an intense training program where the dividend distributions of this fund were stressed heavily, Lester went out into the marketplace and started "selling dividends." To Lester's amazement, the NASD tracked him down in no time and made an offer for a Summary Complaint Procedure through the District Business Conduct Committee. You have guided Lester throughout his career and now is no exception. Your advice to Lester would be:

Directions: *For each of the numbered recommendations that follow, please select A, B, or C as the evaluation you deem most correct. Please your selection in the line preceding each number:*

A. This selection for Les-   B. It is possible that this   C. Considering the cir-
ter would act to short-   recommendation could be   cumstances involved, this
sheet his already floun-   considered but probably a   is the most solid recom-
dering career.   better alternative exists.   mendation.

Answer

_____ 1.   Present an offer of settlement to the district secretary stating that Lester was
              unaware of the prohibition against selling dividends due to his company's
              training program.
_____ 2.   Totally disregard the notice sent by the District Business Conduct Committee
              and file a countersuit against the NASD.
_____ 3.   Disregard the notice or call a local politician for help with the matter.
_____ 4.   Lester should recognize the error of his ways and accept summary complaint
              procedure.
_____ 5.   Lester should reject the summary complaint procedure and request that the
              regular complaint procedure be followed.

ANSWERS: 1-B; 2-A; 3-A; 4-C; 5-B.

CHECK YOUR UNDERSTANDING
(Circle one)

1. If a representative's registration is lapsed for a period of two or more   Reference:
    years this person will be required to pass another qualification   Page 14-6
    examination.
        True/False

2. If a registered representative is promoted or changes duties, he or   Reference:
    she may function in the new position for a period of time during   Page 14-7
    which they must pass the appropriate qualification exam.
        True/False

3. If an individual's duties are considered limited and qualify for a   Reference:
    principals registration in one of the limited categories, he or she   Page 14-7
    cannot become registered as a general securities principal.
        True/False

4. A person who performs solely clerical or ministerial duties does not   Reference:
    have to register, take home, etc.   Page 14-10
        True/False

5. Persons associated with an NASD member firm whose functions are   Reference:
    solely clerical or ministerial are exempt from NASD registration.   Page 14-10
        True/False

6. Any member firm or person associated with a member firm against   Reference:
    whom action was taken by the NASD may apply to the Securities   Page 14-11
    and Exchange Commission for a stay of the summary complaint action.
        True/False

7. If a registered representative is terminated by an NASD member   Reference:
    firm, the member firm is required to notify the Board of Governors   Page 14-11
    of the termination within ninety days of the action.
        True/False

8. The purpose of the Code of Procedure is to handle trade practice   Reference:
    complaints in regard to violations of the NASD Rules of Fair Practice.   Page 14-13
        True/False

9.   Any dispute, claim or controversy arising between or among members   Reference:
      or an associated person, which is submitted to arbitration involving   Page 14-16
      a dollar amount not exceeding $10,000, is resolved by an arbitration
      panel solely upon the evidence filed by the disputants.
          True/False

10.   The contractual plan withdrawal and reinstatement privileges have   Reference:
      been abused by registered representative and plan holders in the   Page 14-19
      past and have promoted the Board of Governors to issue an interpre-
      tation indicating that excessive activity of this type will be considered
      a violation of the Rules of Fair Practice.
          True/False

   ANSWERS: 1-True; 2-True; 3-False; 4-True; 5-True; 6-True; 7-False; 8-True; 9-True;
10-True.

STUDY NOTES

STUDY NOTES

15

NASD RULES OF FAIR PRACTICE

PRETEST
(Circle one)

1. An NASD member is prohibited from executing a sell order for any customer on a security unless the member has the security in his or her possession, the customer is long in the security, or the member has the reasonable assurance from the customer that the security will be received by the member in good deliverable form within:
   a. Ten business days of the execution of the order
   b. Three business days of the execution of the order
   c. Fifteen days of the execution of the order
   d. Ten days of the execution of the order
   e. Five days of the execution of the order

   Reference:
   Page 15-7

2. Securities that, immediately after distribution, trade at a premium in the secondary market well above the public offering price are commonly termed:
   a. Blue chippers
   b. High-grade corporate securities
   c. Hot items
   d. Hot issues
   e. Marketable securities

   Reference:
   Page 15-7

3. The failure on the part of a member to make a bona fide public distribution where there is a demand for a hot issue can be a factor in:
   a. Artificially raising the price
   b. Artificially depressing the price
   c. Artificially creating the price
   d. Artificially limiting distribution
   e. Artificially enhancing distribution

   Reference:
   Page 15-7

4. It is a violation of the Rules of Fair Practice in connection with a
    hot issue for a member to do all of the following *except*:
    a. Sell any of the securities to a person associated with the
        distributing member
    b. Hold any of the securities for the member's account
    c. Sell any of the securities above public offering price
    d. Sell any of the securities to a senior bank officer
    e. Sell these securities to a regular customer (small quantity)

    Reference:
    Page 15-8

5. Distribution of securities in connection with a hot issue to persons
    in the immediate family of a general partner of an NASD member is:
    a. Permissible if the amount is not disproportionate
    b. Not permissible if the amount is excessive
    c. Permissible if the family members do not reside with a
        principal of the NASD member firm
    d. A violation regardless of the circumstances
    e. None of the above

    Reference:
    Page 15-8

6. Accounts that are established to execute transactions that other-
    wise would be prohibited, such as purchasing a hot issue or dis-
    guising transactions that are against firm policy, are best defined as:
    a. Fictitious accounts
    b. Discretionary accounts
    c. Unauthorized accounts
    d. Illegal accounts
    e. Fraudulent accounts

    Reference:
    Page 15-9

7. Trading mutual fund shares on a short-term basis may raise the
    question of a rule violation because:
    a. The shares are not negotiable
    b. They are not considered proper trading vehicles
    c. They are not traded in the marketplace
    d. All of the above
    e. None of the above

    Reference:
    Page 15-9

8. Gifts or gratuities provided to any person, principal, proprietor,
    employee, agent, or representative of another person are prohibited
    if the amount exceeds:
    a. $1,000 per person per year
    b. $250 per person per year
    c. $175 per person per year
    d. $100 per person per year
    e. $25 per person per year

    Reference:
    Page 15-10

9.   What is required for an NASD member firm to exercise discretionary   Reference:
      power on behalf of the customer?   Page 15-10
      a.   Sufficient cash and/or securities in the account
      b.   A stock power
      c.   Prior written authorization from the customer
      d.   Prior written authorization from a principal of the member firm
      e.   All of the above

10.   It is not permissible for a member to lend securities carried for   Reference:
      the account of any customer unless the written authorization of   Page 15-11
      the customer is received. If an agreement exists, the member is
      still prohibited from lending or pledging more of such securities than:
      a.   An amount up to 50% of the indebtedness of the customer
      b.   An amount up to 75% of the indebtedness of the customer
      c.   An amount up to 80% of the indebtedness of the customer
      d.   An amount that is considered reasonable and fair in view of
            the indebtedness of the customer
      e.   An amount not to exceed 10% of the indebtedness of the customer

11.   An NASD member is required to conform with the laws applicable   Reference:
      to preserving all of the following except: Page 15-12
      a.   Books
      b.   Competitor's advertising material
      c.   Accounts
      d.   Memoranda
      e.   Correspondence

12.   Selling concessions, discounts, or other allowances are permissible   Reference:
      by an NASD member firm: Page 15-13
      a.   As a consideration for services rendered
      b.   As an incentive to solicit sales
      c.   To anyone other than a broker or dealer
      d.   As an inducement for customers to purchase securities
      e.   Under no circumstances

13.   The public offering price is defined as the price set forth: Reference:
      a.   In a tombstone advertisement   Page 15-14
      b.   As determined on the exchanges
      c.   As determined by the over-the-counter market
      d.   By the NYSE
      e.   In the prospectus of the issuing company

14.   The maximum sales charge for mutual fund transactions that may   Reference:
       be imposed by a member broker/dealer shall not exceed: Page 15-14
       a.   7.5%
       b.   8%
       c.   8.5%
       d.   9%
       e.   9.5%

15.   If rights of accumulation are not made available to the customer,   Reference:
       which of the following maximum sales charges are imposed on any   Page 15-15
       transaction that includes the dividend reinvestment?
       a.   6.5%
       b.   7%
       c.   7.5%
       d.   8%
       e.   8.5%

16.   If an NASD member firm provides salesmen, managers, or other   Reference:
       sales personnel with an incentive of additional compensation for   Page 15-16
       the sales of shares of a particular investment company based on
       the amount of portfolio brokerage commissions expected, this is
       considered:
       a.   An acceptable sales practice
       b.   A violation of the Rules of Fair Practice
       c.   A violation of the Code of Procedure
       d.   A violation of the Investment Company Amendments Act of 1970
       e.   A violation of the registration requirements imposed by the
             Securities Act of 1933

17.   Private securities transactions affected outside the usual or normal Reference:
       scope of employment, which are nowhere reflected on the members'   Page 15-17
       books and records, may expose the participants to:
       a.   Serious violations
       b.   Immediate expulsion from the NASD
       c.   A fine of $5,000
       d.   A fine of $15,000
       e.   Expulsion and a fine of $10,000

18. It is the responsibility of an NASD member when executing a
     transaction for the purchase or sale of a security for the account
     of an employee of another member to:
     a.   Use reasonable diligence to determine that the execution
          of such an order will not adversely affect the interest of
          the employing member
     b.   Follow the instructions from an employing member
     c.   Possibly provide notice of the transaction
     d.   Notify the person requesting the order of the member's
          intent to give notice to the employer
     e.   All of the above

Reference:
Page 15-17

19. When a variable contract provides for future voluntary payments
     (open account), the sales charge percentage may not exceed:
     a.   7%
     b.   7.5%
     c.   8%
     d.   8.25%
     e.   8.5%

Reference:
Page 15-18

20. Under variable contracts, where the value of the account exceeds
     $50,000, the sales charge of new payments may not exceed:
     a.   6%
     b.   6.5%
     c.   7%
     d.   7.5%
     e.   8%

Reference:
Page 15-18

ANSWERS: 1-b; 2-d; 3-a; 4-e; 5-d; 6-a; 7-b; 8-d; 9-c; 10-d; 11-b; 12-a; 13-e; 14-c; 15-d; 16-b;
17-a; 18-e; 19-e; 20-b.

OVERVIEW

The NASD's Rules of Fair Practice were established to provide a guide for the ethical conduct of broker/dealers and their representatives within the securities industry. Topics such as free-riding and withholding, discretionary accounts, maintenance of books and records and such are addressed throughout the Rules of Fair Practice.

The guidelines established by the Rules of Fair Practice provide the boundaries for supervisory procedures and personnel transactions by brokers/dealers. Procedures for handling complaints, advertising material, and the general business conducted by broker/dealers within the securities industry are outlined in detail.

In this chapter, we will discuss the Rules of Fair Practice and their application to a registered representative's business transactions. The material presented in this section should serve as a guide to those within the investment industry and those who are striving for admission.

Author's Note to Candidates

In this chapter is presented a series of guidelines that are intended to govern operations of those within the industry. Your thorough study of these rules, and subsequent application of the guidelines presented, is essential for your admittance to the securities industry and your further advancement in your new career. Violations of these rules are dealt with seriously by the NASD. Move through this section slowly to ensure your thorough comprehension of each point presented.

I.   RULES OF FAIR PRACTICE

Adoption and Applicability

Concerning the applicability of the Rules of Fair Practice, all members and persons associated with a member are considered equal and have the same *obligations* and *duties* that are prescribed by the Rules of Fair Practice. When a person is suspended or has been expelled from membership in the NASD, all privileges of membership and/or registration are *revoked*.

You are suspended for violating the Rules of Fair Practice.

Business Conduct of Members

Prompt receipt and delivery of securities after executing an over-the-counter market order is required by the NASD's Rules of Fair Practice. An NASD member may *not* accept a customer's purchase order for any security unless it is first determined that the customer placing the order, or the customer's agent, agrees to receive the securities against payment. Likewise, no member may execute a *sell order* (long sale) for any customer in a security unless the member has:

1.   The security in his or her possession
2.   The customer is *long* (meaning that he or she actually owns the security) in his or her account with the member

3. Reasonable assurance is received by the member that the security will be delivered in good deliverable form within *three business days* of the execution of the order

4. The security is on deposit in good deliverable form with a member of the NASD (or other broker/dealer registered with the SEC)

I've got to make this delivery in 3 business days.

It has been determined by the Board of Governors that NASD members have an obligation to make a bona fide public distribution at the *public offering price* of the offering. This is especially true if the issue is a *hot issue*. A hot issue is defined as one which *immediately* trades at a premium (greater amount) above the original public offering price.

The failure on the part of a member to make a bona fide public distribution at the public offering price can be a factor in artificially raising the price. As you can see, a member might be tempted to keep some of these hot issues for himself or herself — this is not allowed, and the violation is called *free-riding* and *withholding*.

How can you tell this is a hot issue?

It is considered a violation in connection with a hot issue for a member to:

- Hold any of the securities so acquired in any of the members' accounts.
- Sell any of the securities to any officer, director, general partner, employee, or agent of the member or to a member of the immediate family.

- Sell any securities to a senior officer of a bank, savings and loan institution, insurance company, registered investment company, registered investment advisory firm, or to any employee or other person who is involved either *directly* or *indirectly* in the function of buying or selling securities on behalf of any of these situations.
- Sell any of the securities above the public offering price to any other broker/dealer.
- Sell any of the securities to a foreign broker/dealer or bank (with conditions).

Even if you are the recipient of a hot issue as a member of the NASD, you are guilty, too.

QUICK QUIZ 1

1. An NASD member is prohibited from executing a sell order for any customer on a security unless the member has the security in his or her possession, the customer is long in the security, or the member has the reasonable assurance from the customer that the security will be received by the member in good deliverable form within: Reference: Page 15-7
    a.   Ten business days of the execution of the order
    b.   Three business days of the execution of the order
    c.   Fifteen days of the execution of the order
    d.   Ten days of the execution of the order
    e.   Five days of the execution of the order

2. Securities that, immediately after distribution, trade at a premium in the secondary market well above the public offering price are commonly termed: Reference: Page 15-7
    a.   Blue chippers
    b.   High-grade corporate securities
    c.   Hot items
    d.   Hot issues
    e.   Marketable securities

3. The failure on the part of a member to make a bona fide public distribution where there is a demand for a hot issue can be a factor in: Reference: Page 15-7
    a.   Artificially raising the price
    b.   Artificially depressing the price
    c.   Artificially creating the price
    d.   Artificially limiting distribution
    e.   Artificially enhancing distribution

4. It is a violation of the Rules of Fair Practice in connection with a hot issue for a member to do all of the following *except*:   Reference: Page 15-8
    a.   Sell any of the securities to a person associated with the

distributing member
b.   Hold any of the securities for the member's account
c.   Sell any of the securities above public offering price
d.   Sell any of the securities to a senior bank officer
e.   Sell these securities to a regular customer (small quantity)

5.   Distribution of securities in connection with a hot issue to persons   Reference:
     in the immediate family of a general partner of an NASD member is: Page 15-8
     a.   Permissible if the amount is not disproportionate
     b.   Not permissible if the amount is excessive
     c.   Permissible if the family members do not reside with a
          principal of the NASD member firm
     d.   A violation regardless of the circumstances
     e.   None of the above

ANSWERS: 1-b; 2-d; 3-a; 4-e; 5-d.

Recommendations to Customers

In recommending to a customer the purchase, sale, or exchange of any security, members have reasonable grounds for believing that their recommendation should be based on the facts disclosed to them by the customer. The *disclosed facts* should include the security holdings, financial situation, and the needs of the customer.

It is a violation if the member recommends speculative low price securities to customers without knowledge of, or in an attempt to obtain, information concerning the customer's other securities holdings, their financial situation, and other necessary data. Mutual funds shares are *not* considered proper *trading* vehicles and trading on a *short-term* basis may raise the question of a rule *violation*. The following are considered *fraudulent conduct* and, in the past, have been considered violations by the association:

- *Fictitious accounts:* Establishing fictitious accounts to execute transactions that otherwise would be prohibited, such as purchasing a "hot issue," or disguising transactions that are against firm policy.
- *Discretionary accounts:* Transactions in "discretionary accounts," which do not need the customer's approval in advance.
- *Unauthorized transactions:* Executing transactions that are unauthorized by customers or sending confirmations to make customers accept transactions they did not actually agree upon.
- *Misuse of customer's funds or securities:* Unauthorized use or borrowing of customer's funds or securities.
- *Other* fraudulent activities, e.g., forgery, non-disclosure, or misstatement of material facts.

Don't bother me with the facts, I'm consulting my broker.

The bottom line for recommending investments is to recommend only those *suitable* (suitability) to each individual customer. What follows is a more detailed discussion of potential "fraudulent" acts by members.

Influencing or Rewarding Employees of Others

Gifts or gratuities in excess of $100 per individual per year are prohibited — including gifts to any person, principal, proprietor, employee, agent, or representative of another person for business produced or expected to be produced (i.e., bribes). This rule does not apply to contracts of employment or to compensation for services.

Why don't you send some of your clients' orders for securities my way and take this for a month.

Discretionary Accounts

A member is prohibited from making purchase or sales transactions that are *excessive in size or frequency*, in view of the financial resources and character of a customer's account. *Prior written authorization* from the customer is required for a member to exercise *discretionary power*. The *acceptance* by the member firm must be evidenced in writing. A member, or person designated by the member, must *approve* in writing *each* discretionary order when entered and is charged with the responsibility of transactions that are considered excessive.

Customer's Securities or Funds

It is not permissible for a member to lend securities carried for the account of any customer unless the *written* authorization of the customer is received. If an agreement exists, the member is still prohibited from lending or pledging *more* securities than is considered "fair and reasonable" in view of the *indebtedness* of the customer.

An NASD member firm or person associated with a member firm is prohibited from *guaranteeing* a customer against loss in any securities account.

Unless specific written authorization is received from the customer prior to the transaction, a member firm or person associated with a member firm is prohibited from *sharing* directly or indirectly in the profits or losses of any customer's account. Exempt from this restriction are accounts of the immediate family of such member or associated persons.

QUICK QUIZ 2

6. Accounts that are established to execute transactions that other-   Reference:
   wise would be prohibited, such as purchasing a hot issue or dis-   Page 15-9
   guising transactions that are against firm policy, are best defined as:
   a. Fictitious accounts
   b. Discretionary accounts
   c. Unauthorized accounts
   d. Illegal accounts
   e. Fraudulent accounts

7. Trading mutual fund shares on a short-term basis may raise the   Reference:
   question of a rule violation because: Page 15-9
   a. The shares are not negotiable
   b. They are not considered proper trading vehicles
   c. They are not traded in the marketplace
   d. All of the above
   e. None of the above

8. Gifts or gratuities provided to any person, principal, proprietor,   Reference:
   employee, agent, or representative of another person are prohibited Page 15-10
   if the amount exceeds:
   a. $1,000 per person per year
   b. $250 per person per year
   c. $175 per person per year

    d. $100 per person per year
    e. $25 per person per year

9.   What is required for an NASD member firm to exercise discretionary   Reference:
      power on behalf of the customer?   Page 15-10
      a.   Sufficient cash and/or securities in the account
      b.   A stock power
      c.   Prior written authorization from the customer
      d.   Prior written authorization from a principal of the member firm
      e.   All of the above

10.   It is not permissible for a member to lend securities carried for   Reference:
      the account of any customer unless the written authorization of   Page 15-11
      the customer is received. If an agreement exists, the member is
      still prohibited from lending or pledging more of such securities than:
      a.   An amount up to 50% of the indebtedness of the customer
      b.   An amount up to 75% of the indebtedness of the customer
      c.   An amount up to 80% of the indebtedness of the customer
      d.   An amount that is considered reasonable and fair in view of
            the indebtedness of the customer
      e.   An amount not to exceed 10% of the indebtedness of the customer

                           ANSWERS: 6-a; 7-b; 8-d; 9-c; 10-d.

Books and Records

An NASD member is required to conform to the laws for preserving books, accounts, records, memoranda, and correspondence. Customer account records must contain name, address, whether the customer is of legal age, signature of the registered representative *introducing* the account, and the signature of the principal or partner *accepting* the account for the member.

If a particular customer is associated with *another* NASD member, that fact must also be noted in the record. In discretionary accounts, the member must also record the age — or approximate age — and occupation of the customer, as well as the signature of each person authorized to exercise discretion in the account.

Each member is required to keep a separate file of all written *customer complaints* and specify any action taken by the member. This is to be inspected by the NASD and is called the "Complaint File."

Disclosure of Financial Condition

An NASD member is required to make available for customer inspection any information relative to the member's financial condition as disclosed in its most recent balance sheet. The term *customer* means any person who, in the regular course of the member's business, has cash or securities in the *possession* of the member firm. It does not mean anyone on his or her mailing list or "prospective customers," just "bona fide" customers.

OK, I've got some questions I must ask.

Selling Concessions

Selling concessions, discounts, or other allowances are permissible services in the distribution of securities but are *not* allowed for anyone who is *not* a broker or dealer actually engaged in the investment banking or securities business; that is, a member can't pay commissions or concessions to unlicensed people.

Dealing with Non-members

An NASD member is prohibited from dealing with a broker or dealer who is not a member of the NASD except at the same prices for the same commissions or fees, and on the same terms and conditions as are accorded to the *general public*.

Sorry, Joe, you have to be treated as a member of the general public because you are not a member of the NASD.

Investment Companies

The term *investment company* refers to the activities of members in connection with the securities of an *open-end management investment company*. The following terms are defined by the Rules of Fair Practice:

- *Underwriter:* Principal underwriter as defined by the Investment Company Act of 1940
- *Public offering price:* A public offering price is set forth in the prospectus of the issuing company
- *Business day:* A day in which the New York Stock Exchange is open for trading
- *Rights of accumulation:* A scale of reducing sales charges based upon the *aggregate* quantity of securities *previously* purchased plus the securities being purchased.

A member is prohibited from offering or selling the shares of an open-end investment company if a public offering price includes a sales charge that is considered excessive. Sales charges are considered excessive if they do not conform with the following provisions:

- Maximum sales charge on any transaction cannot exceed 8.5% of the offering price.
- A dividend reinvestment can be made available at the *net asset value* per share to any person who requests the reinvestment privilege at least *ten days* prior to the record date. This privilege is subject only to the right to limit the availability of dividend reinvestment to holders of securities of a stated minimum value and that value cannot be greater than *$1,200*. If the dividend reinvestment privilege is not offered the maximum sales charge on any transaction can not exceed 7.25% of the offering price.
- The rights of accumulation that offer cumulative quantity discounts should be made available to any person for a period of not less than *ten years* from the date of the first purchase. If the rights of accumulation are not made available, the following represents the maximum sales charge on any transaction:

- 8% of the offering price if the dividend reinvestment privilege is offered
- 6.75% of the offering price if the dividend reinvestment also is not made available
- Quantity discounts can be made available on single purchases. Maximum sales charges are:
  A maximum sales charge of 7.5% on purchases of $10,000 or more and a maximum sales charge of 6.25% on purchases of $25,000 or more.

QUICK QUIZ 3

11. An NASD member is required to conform with the laws applicable to preserving all of the following *except*:
     a.   Books
     b.   Competitor's advertising material
     c.   Accounts
     d.   Memoranda
     e.   Correspondence

Reference: Page 15-12

12. Selling concessions, discounts, or other allowances are permissible by an NASD member firm:
     a.   As a consideration for services rendered
     b.   As an incentive to solicit sales
     c.   To anyone other than a broker or dealer
     d.   As an inducement for customers to purchase securities
     e.   Under no circumstances

Reference: Page 15-13

13. The public offering price is defined as the price set forth:
     a.   In a tombstone advertisement
     b.   As determined on the exchanges
     c.   As determined by the over-the-counter market
     d.   As in the registration statement
     e.   In the prospectus of the issuing company

Reference: Page 15-14

14. The maximum sales charge on any transaction that may be imposed by a member broker/dealer shall not exceed:
     a.   7.5%
     b.   8%
     c.   8.5%
     d.   9%
     e.   9.5%

Reference: Page 15-14

15. If rights of accumulation are not made available to the customer, which of the following maximum sales charges are imposed on any transaction that includes the dividend reinvestment?

Reference: Page 15-15

a.   6.5%
b.   7%
c.   7.5%
d.   8%
e.   8.5%

ANSWERS: 11-b; 12-a; 13-e; 14-c; 15-d.

An NASD member is prohibited from *withholding* a customer's order for any securities that profit the member as a result of the withholding action.

An NASD member may not *purchase* the securities of any open-end investment company of which it is the underwriter except for the purpose of covering purchase orders already received. Remember, mutual funds can only be purchased for two reasons:

1.   To cover orders already received, and
2.   For one's own *personal* investment.

In addition, a member who is an underwriter is not able to accept a *conditional order* for the securities of an open-end investment company on any basis other than at a *specified definite price*, i.e., the public offering price. An NASD member may not participate as a principal underwriter in the offer or sale of any security if the issuer of the security directly or indirectly redeems or voluntarily repurchases its securities at a price higher than the *net asset value*.

An NASD member is also prohibited from encouraging the distribution of shares of an investment company from which it receives a higher than normal commission.

A member is in violation of the Rules of Fair Practice if salespeople, branch managers, or other sales personnel are provided an incentive or additional compensation for the sale of shares of *specific* investment companies based on the amount of portfolio brokerage commissions received or expected from any source. This includes recommending or establishing lists of preferred investment companies.

Gentlemen, I can't encourage you to sell this one, but .... we all make more money if you do.

Supervision

An NASD member is required to establish written procedures designed to *supervise* properly the activities of each registered representative and associated person to assure their compliance with the applicable securities laws. The *responsibility* of proper supervision rests entirely with the *member*. Each Office of Supervisory Jurisdiction (OSJ) is required to have a partner, officer, or manager designated to carry out the written procedures. A copy of the procedures established by the member must be maintained in each office. *All* transactions and correspondence of registered representatives pertaining to the solicitation or execution of any securities transaction must be *endorsed* in writing and maintained as an internal record.

Each registered representative must be assigned to a supervisor and must participate, individually or as part of a group not less than annually, in a meeting which discusses compliance matters. Attendance and topics discussed must be documented.

An NASD member is responsible and has the duty to investigate the character, reputation, qualifications, and experience of any person prior to certifying the person for registration with the NASD.

Private securities include securities transactions of a limited number of purchases that may mislead customers into believing the transactions are sponsored by the member. The NASD Board of Governors has determined that no person may be involved in any way with a private securities transaction outside the regular course or scope of his or her association or employment without prior notice to the member with whom he or she is associated. Private securities transactions outside the normal scope of employment that are not reflected on the member's books may expose the participants to serious violations.

Does this make it a "private" transaction?

Transactions for Personnel of Another Member

It is the responsibility of an NASD member, when executing a transaction for the account of an employee or associated person of *another* member, to use *reasonable diligence* to determine that the transaction will not adversely affect the interest of the employing member. This NASD member must follow the *instructions* from an *employing* member with respect to providing a notice of the transaction or the mailing of duplicate confirmations to the employing member.

Hey, Ed, do you know that Barry Bigbucks, your broker, is down here opening an account?

Variable Contracts of an Insurance Company

Variable contracts refer to contracts providing benefits or values that may vary according to the investment experience of any separate or segregated account maintained by an *insurance company*. The term *purchase payment* applies to the amount paid at the time of each purchase or installment for the variable contract.

The same maximum sales charge rules apply under the Investment Company Act of 1940 as they do to all registered open-end investment companies. Variable annuities and the funding accounts of variable life insurance companies are frequently Unit Investment Trusts and are fully regulated. Under contracts (not contractual plans) providing for single payments of a sales charge, the following schedule applies:

> First $25,000 — 8.5% of purchase payment
> Next $25,000 — 7.5% of purchase payment
> Over $50,000 — 6.5% of purchase payment

The *value* of a variable contract is determined following the *receipt* of payment for the contract. Payments need not be considered as received until the contract application has been accepted by the insurance company. Each member is required to transmit promptly to the issuer all applications.

QUICK QUIZ 4

16.   If an NASD member firm provides salesmen, managers, or other   Reference:
        sales personnel with an incentive of additional compensation for   Page 15-16
        the sales of shares of a particular investment company based on
        the amount of brokerage commissions expected, this is considered:
        a.   An acceptable sales practice
        b.   A violation of the Rules of Fair Practice
        c.   A violation of the Code of Procedure
        d.   A violation of the Investment Company Amendments Act of 1970
        e.   A violation of the registration requirements imposed by the
                Securities Act of 1933

17.   Private securities transactions affected outside the usual or normal   Reference:
        scope of employment, which are nowhere reflected on the members'   Page 15-17
        books and records, may expose the participants to:
        a.   Serious violations
        b.   Immediate expulsion from the NASD
        c.   A fine of $5,000
        d.   A fine of $15,000
        e.   Expulsion and a fine of $10,000

18.   It is the responsibility of an NASD member when executing a   Reference:
        transaction for the purchase or sale of a security for the account   Page 15-17
        of an employee of another member to:
        a.   Use reasonable diligence to determine that the execution
                of such an order will not adversely affect the interest of
                the employing member
        b.   Follow the instructions from an employing member
        c.   Possibly provide notice of the transaction
        d.   Notify the person requesting the order of the member's
                intent to give notice to the employer
        e.   All of the above

19.   Insurance company variable contracts are: Reference:
        a.   Treated the same as mutual funds   Page 15-19
        b.   Require a prospectus be delivered
        c.   Are considered securities
        d.   None of the above
        e.   a, b, and c above

20.   Registered branch offices, field offices, where local supervision   Reference:
        of NASD rules is maintained are called: Page 15-18
        a.   General agents of the NASD
        b.   Office of Supervisory Jurisdiction
        c.   General Manager of Field Office
        d.   Field Office
        e.   No specific name required

ANSWERS: 16-b; 17-a; 18-e; 19-e; 20-b.

Advertising Interpretation

The NASD Board of Governors defines advertisements as any material for use in any newspaper or magazine or other public media. In addition, the Board of Governors has also determined that sales literature is also market letters, notices, circulars, reports, newsletters, research reports, form letters, and reprints of published articles. Items that are *not* considered advertising material include communications such as *letters* addressed to an *individual* containing recommendations or advice; material addressed to branch offices; material designed for the internal organizations; and tombstone advertisements that only identify the member and the security and state its price or offer literature about the security.

Advertisements, sales literature, and market letters are required to contain the *name* of the member firm, the person or firm *preparing* the material, and the *date* on which it was first published.

In making a *recommendation*, a member firm must have reasonable basis for the recommendation and the following facts must be disclosed:

- Price at the time the recommendation is made.
- That the member usually makes a market in the issue, if this is the case.
- That the member intends to buy or sell the securities recommended for the firm's own account.

The important thing that new registered representatives should realize is you can not advertise or design sales literature without home office approval.

Predictions can come back to haunt you . . .

Testimonial material concerning the member or concerning any advice or other services rendered by the member must make clear that such experiences are not necessary indicative of future performance. Testimonials also must say whether any compensation has been paid to the maker of the testimonial directly or indirectly. Any offers of free services may not be made unless the service is provided entirely free and without condition or obligation. No claim or implication can be made for research or other facilities beyond those which the member firm actually possesses or has a reasonable capacity to provide. No cautionary statements or caveats, often called *hedge clauses*, can be used if they could mislead the reader. A hedge clause is one in which the writer disclaims responsibility for inadvertent errors or omissions.

Complaints

Every member of the NASD must keep in each of its offices, in the form supplied by the Board of Governors:

- Certificate of Incorporation
- Bylaws
- Rules of Fair Practice
- Code of Procedure of the NASD

Any person who wishes to file a complaint against an NASD member may do so on the form supplied by the Board of Governors. Any complaint filed is handled in accordance with the *code of procedure* of the NASD. The DBCC may also file a complaint against an NASD member by using the same form mentioned above. In addition to the DBCC, the Board of Governors also has the authority to file a complaint or instruct any DBCC to file in its place.

For the purpose of any investigation, District Business Conduct Committee or the Board of Governors has the right:

- To require any member of the NASD or persons associated with a member to report, orally or in writing, on any matter involved in any investigation or hearing.
- To investigate the books, records, and accounts of any member with relation to any matter involved in any investigation or hearing.

Penalties

Any DBCC or the Board of Governors in the administration and enforcement of the Rules of Fair Practice may as a penalty:

- Censure any member or person associated with a member, and/or
- Impose a fine upon any member or person associated with a member, and/or
- Suspend the membership of any member or suspend the registration of a person associated with a member for a definite period, and/or
- Expel any member or revoke the registration of any person associated with the member, and/or

- Suspend or bar a member or a person associated with a member from association with all members, and/or
- Impose any other fitting penalty deemed appropriate under the circumstance.

Censure

Fine

Expulsion

Now what combination should we pick this time?

All fines imposed can be paid to the treasurer of the NASD and can be used for the general corporate purposes. Any member who fails promptly to pay any fine imposed or any costs imposed, after the fine or costs have become finalized, may after *seven days'* notice in writing, be summarily suspended or expelled for membership in the NASD. Any NASD member or person associated with a member disciplined can bear a part of the cost of the proceedings as the DBCC or the Board of Governors deems fair and appropriate in the circumstances.

QUICK QUIZ 5

21.   In making a recommendation, a member firm must have a reason-   Reference:
able basis for the recommendation and all of the following facts   Page 15-21
must be disclosed *except:*
   a.   Price
   b.   That the member is making a market in the issue (if that is the case)
   c.   The date the recommendation statement was filed
   d.   That the member intends to buy the securities
   e.   That the member intends to sell these securities

22. In testimonial material concerning the member or concerning any
     advice or other services rendered by the member firm, it must be
     clear that such experiences are:
     a.   Relevant to the individual making the statement
     b.   Indicative of future performance
     c.   Not indicative of future performance
     d.   Not made by a member of the firm
     e.   Not made by a person associated with the NASD

     Reference:
     Page 15-22

23. Every NASD member must keep in each branch office that is main-
     tained by the member firm all of the following *except*:
     a.   The registration certificate
     b.   The NASD certificate of incorporation
     c.   NASD by-laws
     d.   Rules of Fair Practice
     e.   Code of Procedure of the NASD

     Reference:
     Page 15-22

24. In the enforcement of the Rules of Fair Practice, the District
     Business Conduct Committee or the Board of Governors may do
     the following:
     a.   Censure any member
     b.   Impose a fine not in excess of $15,000
     c.   Suspend the membership
     d.   Expel any member
     e.   All of the above

     Reference:
     Page 15-22

25. All fines imposed by the NASD must be paid to the treasurer and
     can be used for:
     a.   Enforcement of the Rules of Fair Practice
     b.   Administration functions
     c.   Christmas bonuses
     d.   General corporate purposes
     e.   Advertising

     Reference:
     Page 15-23

ANSWERS: 21-c; 22-c; 23-a; 24-e; 25-d.

REAL LIFE SITUATION

Trevor Tightwad, a registered representative for the B.J. Measley Brokerage Firm, is in charge
of the public distribution of a security issued by the Ajax Manufacturing Company, which
immediately after the distribution process started trading in the secondary market at a
considerable premium. Trevor is a member of a very tight knit family and he made a decision
that his family should share in the fortunes of this hot issue. As a result of this decision, Trevor

offered each of ten relatives a 1,000 share block of the total 10,000 share distribution. You, as Trevor's supervisor, would offer the following advice:

Directions: *For each of the numbered recommendations that follow, please select A, B, or C as the evaluation you deem most correct. Place your selection in the line preceding each number.*

| A. As a result of this recommendation, Trevor will be squeezed by the NASD. | B. It is possible that this recommendation could be considered, but there are serious shortcomings. | C. Considering the circumstances involved, this undoubtedly is the best recommendation. |

Answer

_____ 1.   Resign immediately from the brokerage firm and disclaim any association with the investment industry.

_____ 2.   Remain in the brokerage business and totally disregard the NASD rules.

_____ 3.   Remain in the brokerage business, but refrain from selling any of these securities to relatives or other prohibited people as outlined by the NASD.

_____ 4.   Follow the performance of this particular security in anticipation of its reclassification from being a *hot issue.*

_____ 5.   Prohibit the transaction from taking place.

ANSWERS: 1-B; 2-A; 3-C; 4-B; 5-C.

CHECK YOUR UNDERSTANDING
(Circle One)

1.   Concerning the applicability of the Rules of Fair Practice, all members and persons associated with a member are considered equal and have the same obligations and duties that are prescribed by the Rules of Fair Practice.
        True/False

Reference:
Page 15-6

2.   NASD members have an obligation to make a bona fide public distribution of a "hot issue."
        True/False

Reference:
Page 15-7

3. Gifts or gratuities paid by an NASD member firm to a registered representative in excess of $100 per year are prohibited.
    True/False

    Reference:
    Page 15-10

4. An NASD member must receive prior written authorization from the customer before exercising any discretionary power.
    True/False

    Reference:
    Page 15-11

5. An NASD member is required to make available to any bona fide customer information relative to the member's financial condition as disclosed in its most recent balance sheet.
    True/False

    Reference:
    Page 15-13

6. A scale of reducing sales charges in which the sales charge applicable to the securities being purchased is based upon the aggregate quantity of securities previously purchased, plus the securities being purchased, describes the *rights of accumulation*.
    True/False

    Reference:
    Page 15-14

7. The maximum sales charge on any transaction cannot exceed 8.75% of the offering price.
    True/False

    Reference:
    Page 15-14

8. A member may be in violation of the Rules of Fair Practice if sales-people are provided an incentive or additional compensation to sell the shares of a *specific* investment company.
    True/False

    Reference:
    Page 15-16

9. An NASD member is responsible for the investigation into the character, reputation, and qualifications of any person prior to making application to the NASD for registration of that person.
    True/False

    Reference:
    Page 15-17

10. The sales charge for a variable contract marketed by an NASD member may not exceed 8.5% when the contract provides for multiple payments of sales charges.
    True/False

    Reference:
    Page 15-18

ANSWERS: 1-True; 2-True; 3-True; 4-True; 5-True; 6-True; 7-False; 8-True; 9-True; 10-True.

STUDY NOTES

APPENDIX A:
YOU AND THE EXAM CENTER

OVERVIEW

The NASD offers its exams through its own centers and Sylvan Learning Centers across the country and overseas.

The NASD controlled system for your examination is known as the PROCTOR® Certification System. This is a form of "exam on demand" where you take your exam on a simplified computer with results graded and reported to you within seconds of your completion.

The best part of this system is you leave the testing center knowing *the results of your exam!* These testing centers are normally open Monday through Friday and some have Saturday hours.

The most striking feature of the this system is *simplicity*. The experience of testing on the computer is a positive one and no more difficult than reading from a television screen.

Authors' Note to Candidates

There is no need to be apprehensive about taking an examination on a computer screen. In fact, there are a number of elements that will definitely work to your advantage on your test. We will explain these in this chapter. It is fitting that this chapter should be the last in your study. The NASD *wants* you to pass the test. As long as you've studied the material — YOU WILL PASS THE NASD TEST!

I.   YOU AND THE EXAM CENTER — A MATCH MADE IN HEAVEN?

Merely by typing on the keyboard, which is very similar to that on a standard typewriter, *or* by touching the screen, a student sends information (e.g., answer to questions) to the computer to be processed. Your exact test is "downloaded" to your machine by test center personnel. Rapid response time is only one of the characteristics that make it a dynamic system.

II.   WHAT TO EXPECT

Each center is equipped with terminals that are set in comfortable and private learning carrels. A learning center administrator will have made prior technical arrangements for the exam to be available. You may call the test center in advance and make an appointment. This is advisable since there can be 2-3 weeks or more back log during busy times.   You will be asked for picture identification and to sign the log sheet and then be given a ten to fifteen minute introduction to the computer test. Learning center personnel are quite knowledgeable. They are always available to provide support while the test is being taken. In order to make you feel comfortable, as much time as you desire may be spent with the tutorial before you take the test.

The NASD has provided specific instructions to learning center personnel regarding security procedures. In addition to being asked for picture identification and to sign-in, the administrator will provide scrap paper and a calculator. No other materials are permitted in the testing area. "Discrepancy forms" have been provided by the NASD to be filed, should any candidate violate security procedures.

III.   HOW IT CAN WORK FOR YOU

The most advantageous outcome of computer-delivered exams is test results *immediately* after the exam is completed. Each candidate receives their own "unique" exam as the computer randomly selects a certain number of questions from a large question pool. But don't worry, you can answer most of these correctly because you have thoroughly studied this book and sample tests. No need to be apprehensive. This is important for you — your hard work will pay off. In short: Individualized testing, immediate results, and exam security are the greatest ways the computer exam will work for you!

Yup, I passed the NASD exam!

IV.   HELPFUL HINTS!

Some features make the computer exam easy to use:

1.   The scroll bar allows you to move the questions up or down at your convenience.
2.   The clock display can be turned on to help you keep track of the amount of time remaining during the session.
3.   A confirmation box appears each time you answer a question so you can confirm your answer.
4.   Three ways to answer questions:
   - the touch-sensitive screen (where available) allows you to answer questions by simply touching the proper area on the screen;
   - the keyboard allows you to type the letter that corresponds to your answer; and
   - the mouse allows you to point and click on your answer.

 Make sure that you ask the administrator to clarify anything that seems unclear in the introduction. If anything happens that interrupts testing, be sure to call it to the attention of the administrator. When interruptions occur, don't worry: The system will place a "bookmark" where you left off. As soon as the problem causing the interruption is solved, your test will resume where it left off, and your score will *not* be altered.

Some Insights

As with any test, make sure you read question fully two or three times before carefully choosing your response. After you indicate the response you wish to make, the screen will ask you if you want to change it. At this point, you may indicate a different response or keep the one you made. Please see the Educational Training Systems, Inc. *flashcards* for a series of twenty (20) additional helpful hints on how to use the computer exam and test center to your advantage.

A Final Note to Candidates

   - Study ahead of time.
   - Don't be intimidated by the computer.
   - Use the learning center personnel as resources.
   - Take the same care in reading questions and choosing answers as you would in any testing situations.
   - Enjoy your use of state-of-the-art technology!

Thank you for studying our course to help further your career.

Dennis M. Doyle

Dennis M. Doyle, CLU, CFP, CPCU, ChFC

FINAL NOTE TO CANDIDATES

You have now completed the study of *every* topic recommended by the NASD in their Series 6 STUDY OUTLINE. You have worked the Pre-Test Questions and Quick Quizzes covering each of these topics. Each topic has not only been covered in the readings but at least once a question has been asked on every topic to further ascertain your understanding.

The following two 100-question Sample Tests will be a final check of your mastery and also provide practice in test-taking techniques — always important to your success on an exam.

Dennis M. Doyle, CLU, CFP, CPCU, ChFC

Educational Training Systems, Inc.
116 Middle Road — P.O. Box 410
Southborough, MA 01772-0410

VOICE: (508) 481-3578
FAX: (508) 481-5809
E-mail: ets@tiac.net
Web Page: http://www.ets-inc.com

SERIES 6

SAMPLE EXAM I

NOTE TO STUDENTS

Circle the correct answer. Allow yourself no more than 135 minutes (2¼ hours) to complete this exam. Once you have finished, review the Rationale and any areas in the book in which you feel weak.

1. Bankers' acceptances are an outcome of:

   A. Corporate financial needs.
   B. Import-Export transactions.
   C. Commercial paper.
   D. All of the above.

2. Which of the following is true of the assets and portfolio of a diversified investment company?

   A. 50% of its assets must be highly liquid, no more than 5% of the total assets may invested in any one company, and that may not constitute more than 10% of the voting stock of that company.
   B. 50% of its assets must be highly liquid, no more than 10% of the total assets may be invested in any one company, and that may not constitute more than 5% of the voting stock of that company.
   C. 75% of the assets must be highly liquid, no more than 5% of the total assets may be invested in any one company and that may not constitute more than 5% of the voting stock of that company.
   D. 75% of the assets must be highly liquid, no more than 10% of the total assets may be invested in any one company, and that may not constitute more than 5% of the voting stock of that company.

3. Death benefits for a variable life policy must be calculated no less than:

   A. Annually.
   B. Semi-annually.
   C. Quarterly.
   D. Monthly.

4. All of the statements below correctly describe plan completion insurance, EXCEPT:

   A. Nontransferable insurance is written on the life of the original shareholder.
   B. The custodian purchases shares from the fund to complete the intended contract.
   C. The death benefit is included in the insured's estate.
   D. Death benefits can be paid to any beneficiary designated by the insured.

5.   Which of the following types of corporate bonds would normally carry with it the highest degree of security?

   A.   Mortgage bonds.
   B.   Equipment trust certificates.
   C.   Debenture bonds.
   D.   Corporate commercial paper.

6.   An investor pays $100 per month for 10 months on a 50% contractual plan. This investor owns 120 shares. If he/she liquidates the account after 10 months when the net asset value is $9.15 and the asking price is $10.00, what will be the total proceeds?

   A. $915.00
   B. $1,098.00
   C. $1,200.00
   D. $1,448.00

7.   In a 20% contractual plan, if an investor wishes to receive a full refund of all sales charges it must be requested within:

   A.   5 days.
   B.   7 days.
   C.   45 days.
   D.   18 months.

8.   A variable annuity contract owner who has annuitized his/her contract would probably receive the largest amount of total annuity payments under which of these options if the individual lived far beyond his/her life expectancy?

   A.   Straight life annuity.
   B.   The unit refund annuity.
   C.   Joint survivor annuity.
   D.   10-year certain and continuous annuity.

9.   A registered representative is presenting information on a new issue and fails to provide a prospectus. He/she must:

   A.   Continue the presentation.
   B.   Continue the presentation as long as he/she quotes only from what he/she knows is contained in the prospectus.
   C.   Make the customer aware of the lack of the prospectus and then continue.
   D.   Stop the presentation until a prospectus can be obtained.

10.   Which of the following is guaranteed in a variable annuity contract?

    A.   Mortality.
    B.   Interest.
    C.   Expenses.
    D.   Both A and C.

11.   The amount and time at which a 12(b)-1 fee is charged is determined by the:

    A.   NASD.
    B.   Shareholders.
    C.   Board of Directors.
    D.   Investment adviser.

12.   A 4% bond selling at 50 would have a current yield of:

    A.   4%
    B.   8%
    C.   10.25%
    D.   12.50%

13.   If, in a dollar cost averaging investment program, an investor has made the following investments:

Investment	Per Share $
$800	$20
800	25
800	17
800	15

The average cost per share would be approximately:

    A. $19.25
    B. $18.60
    C. $21.22
    D.   None of these.

14.   All of these statements describe a unit refund annuity, EXCEPT:

    A.   Payments continue for the life of the annuitant.
    B.   The dollar amount of each payment is guaranteed.
    C.   The number of payments certain is determined when payments start.
    D.   The beneficiary receives payments in the event of an annuitant's early death.

15.   Mutual fund withdrawal plans:

     A.   May be legitimately compared with an annuity.
     B.   Usually require no minimum investment.
     C.   Are taxed the same as distributions or redemptions.
     D.   Payments will never be less than the investor's cost basis.

16.   All of the following types of life insurance guarantee cash values, EXCEPT:

     A.   Variable life.
     B.   Universal life.
     C.   Whole life.
     D.   All of the above guarantee cash values.

17.   Under the Investment Company Act of 1940, closed-end investment companies may do what in addition to issuing common stock?

     A.   Borrow from a bank.
     B.   Issue non-voting common stock.
     C.   Issue senior securities (preferred stock and bonds).
     D.   Issue voting trust certificates.

18.   What is the maximum penalty to a controlling person for a violation of the insider regulations?

     A. $1,000,000.
     B.   Three times the profit gained or loss avoided.
     C.   Not to exceed $1,000,000 or three times the profit gained or loss avoided.
     D.   Unlimited.

19.   Which of the following is/are true of property registered as tenants-in-common:

     A.   This is the usual form of business ownership.
     B.   Co-owners want their portion of the ownership to go to the surviving partner.
     C.   Is the best way to avoid tie up in probate.
     D.   All of the above.

20.   In which two of the following circumstances will dollar cost averaging result in an average cost per share that is always less than the average price per share?

        I.   The price of the stock has fluctuated over a period of time.
        II.   A fixed number of shares is purchased regularly.
        III.   A fixed dollar amount is invested regularly.
        IV.   A constant dollar plan is maintained.

    A.   I and II.
    B.   II and III.
    C.   I and IV.
    D.   I and III.

21.   Actions must be brought against individuals for violations of the Insider's Act within:

    A.   1 year.
    B.   3 years.
    C.   5 years.
    D.   10 years.

22.   The Securities Exchange Act of 1934:

        I.   Created the SEC.
        II.   Provided for the regulation of credit.
        III.   Provided for the regulation of the exchanges.
        IV.   Provided for the regulation of new issues.

    A.   I, II and III.
    B.   II, III and IV.
    C.   I only.
    D.   I, III and IV.

23.   A type of security whereby investors may receive an extra dividend is:

    A.   Cumulative preferred stock.
    B.   Common stock.
    C.   Straight preferred stock.
    D.   Participating preferred stock.

24. Which of the following items must appear on a mutual fund prospectus?

        I.   Deferred sales charges.
        II.   Operating fees.
        III.   12(b)-1 fees.

    A.   I only.
    B.   I and II.
    C.   I and III.
    D.   I, II and III.

25. An investor seeking high liquidity, minimum risks, and current maximum earnings should invest in which of the following?

    A.   An aggressive growth fund.
    B.   "Penny" stocks.
    C.   A money market fund.
    D.   Variable annuities.

26. If the NAV is $14.17 and the ask price is $15.32, how would you compute the percentage that the sales charge is of the net invested amount?

    A. $1.15 divided by $14.17
    B. $1.15 divided by $15.32
    C. $14.17 divided by $1.15
    D. $15.32 divided by $1.15

27. If the total net asset value of the fund is $47,000,000 and the following occurs:

Dividend earnings	$1,500,000
Dividend distribution	1,500,000
Capital gains for fund	1,000,000
Capital gains distribution	1,000,000
Unrealized capital gains	2,500,000

What is the new total asset value of the fund?

    A. $47,000,000
    B. $49,500,000
    C. $50,000,000
    D.   Cannot be determined.

28.   The maximum sales charge on a variable annuity is:

    A.   8 1/2% of the monthly purchase payments.
    B.   8 1/2% of the first $25,000 single purchase payment.
    C.   Reduced for single payments over $25,000.
    D.   All of the above.

29.   Which of the following is illustrative of things that may be said prior to a sale?

    A.   "Assured of a good return on the investment."
    B.   "Past performance shows future probability."
    C.   "Based on past performance this plan will probably continue its growth."
    D.   "Up until now, the fund has performed well."

30.   In a closed-end investment company which of the following would take place?

    I.   Sales charges are included in the ask price.
    II.   Sales charges are normal brokerage commissions paid by the investor.
    III.   The per share price is the NAV per share plus an applicable sales charge.

    A.   I only.
    B.   II only.
    C.   I and II.
    D.   I, II and III.

31.   A member must maintain the public offering price in which of the following transactions:

    I.   Selling to another member.
    II.   Selling through a non-member.
    III.   Selling to an agent of a non-member.
    IV.   A customer sells to another customer.

    A.   I only.
    B.   I and IV.
    C.   II and III.
    D.   IV only.

32.   In a declining bond market, an investor liquidates his bond fund holdings and purchases new
       bond investments with a higher yield. This investor would accomplish which of the following?

        I.   A tax loss which can be utilized in the year of sale.
        II.   A lower cost basis in the new bond investments.
        III.   A higher cost basis in the new bond investments.

    A.   I only.
    B.   I and II only.
    C.   I and III only.
    D.   None of the above.

33.   A variable annuity contract owner who owns 3,125 accumulation units dies. The inheriting heir
       of the contract would assume the contract with what cost basis?

    A.   A stepped-up cost basis at the date of death of the original owner.
    B.   The cost basis claimed by the estate to be fair market value at date of death or 9 months
            later.
    C.   Same cost basis as the original contract owner.
    D.   No cost basis because annuities do not receive any step-up in cost basis.

34.   SIPC - a benefit to investors - provides insurance for loss of cash left with a brokerage house
       up to:

    A. $100,000.
    B. $ 10,000.
    C. $ 50,000.
    D. $500,000.

35.   Under a Section 403(b) plan, a school teacher invests $10,000 in a tax sheltered annuity over
       a 10-year period ($1,000 per year). The current value of this annuity is $16,000. How much
       is taxable after the exclusion allowance if a complete liquidation is made this year?

    A. $ 0.
    B. $ 6,000.
    C. $10,000.
    D. $16,000.

36. Which of the following is the order of liquidation of a corporation's capitalization?

      I.   Secured bondholders.
      II.   Subordinated debenture holders.
      III.   Common stockholders.
      IV.   Preferred stockholders.

    A.   II, I, IV, III.
    B.   I, II, IV, III.
    C.   I, II, III, IV.
    D.   I, IV, II, III.

37. A mutual fund is going ex-dividend. A registered representative's recommendation would best be which of the following:

    A.   Advisable to purchase because of a quick profit and return.
    B.   Advisable to purchase because of a lower cost basis after dividend is paid.
    C.   Inadvisable to purchase because price will drop by the amount of the dividend.
    D.   Inadvisable to purchase because the dividend will not be received until after the ex-date.

38. Which of the following would be a primary reason why the per share value could increase in an open-end investment company?

    A.   There were more outstanding shares at the end of the year than at the beginning.
    B.   There were net redemptions of mutual fund shares during the year making each share worth more.
    C.   Favorable capital gains treatment was paid by the fund, thus reducing its tax burden.
    D.   Realized or unrealized capital appreciation of fund investments.

39. Which of the following is correct for an investor who does not put more money in under a letter of intent and the time period lapses?

    A.   Since the investor was charged the lower sales charge, the underwriter sends a bill for the difference.
    B.   The investor was charged the higher sales charge in the beginning and would have been refunded the difference if he/she did put more in.
    C.   Shares are held in an escrow account representing the sales charge difference. This account is liquidated by the fund if more payments are not completed.
    D.   The mutual fund liquidates enough shares in the investor's account to pay for the sales charge difference.

40.   Which of these investments would have the largest immediate tax liability?

> I.   An income fund.
> II.   A variable annuity.
> III.   A growth fund.
> IV.   Municipal bond unit trust.

A.   All the above.
B.   I and II.
C.   II and III.
D.   I and III.

41.   Which of the following usually supports the debt for a general obligation municipal bond?

A.   Revenue produced by the project.
B.   Good faith and taxing power of the municipality.
C.   Mortgage on municipal real estate (school, city hall, etc.).
D.   Liquor and tobacco taxes.

42.   A "breakpoint" sale is:

A.   A payment of compensation to a registered representative after he ceases to be employed by a member.
B.   The sale of investment company shares in dollar amounts just below the point at which the sales charge is reduced on quantity transactions to incur the higher sales charges.
C.   The sale of investment company shares in anticipation of a distribution soon to be paid.
D.   All of the above.

43.   If a mutual fund order arrived by wire after the NYSE was closed for the day, what price would be used to determine the number of shares purchased?

A.   The price last computed.
B.   The lowest price computed the next day.
C.   The next computed price.
D.   The market closing price listed on the exchange.

44.   In a profit-sharing plan, the employer is entitled to a credit carryover:

A.   Credit carryovers were repealed.
B.   In order to amortize past unpaid credits over a period of 10 years.
C.   In order to deduct excess contributions in succeeding years.
D.   None of the above.

45.   Which of the following best describes a money market portfolio?

        I.   Short-term debt obligations.
        II.   High liquidity.
        III.   Income is tax-exempt.
        IV.   Total disregard for current income.

    A.   I only.
    B.   III only.
    C.   I and II.
    D.   II and III.

46.   In a period of increasing interest rates, an investor owning a bond fund that automatically re-invests dividends in new bond investments would experience which of the following?

    A.   An increase in yield.
    B.   A decrease in yield.
    C.   A yield that would remain constant.
    D.   Yield would be unaffected.

47.   During a hot issue a broker/dealer must:

    A.   Make a bona fide public offering.
    B.   Not sell any of the issue to another member who is not part of the group except at the public offering price and only for an order received from a bona fide public customer.
    C.   Distribute the securities among his customers in such a manner as to prevent withholding and free-riding.
    D.   All of the above.

48.   A self-employed artist earning $38,000 a year has investment income of $3,200. The maximum contribution permissible to a pension plan is:

    A. $ 480.
    B. $5,220.
    C. $7,600.
    D. $9,500.

49.   How many custodians and minors can there be in a Uniform Gifts/Transfers to Minors account?

    A.   1 custodian, 2 minors.
    B.   1 custodian, 1 minor.
    C.   2 custodians, 1 minor.
    D.   Any of the above.

50.   Which of the following does not qualify for a quantity discount when purchasing mutual fund shares?

   A.   A trustee for a pension plan.
   B.   A husband and wife.
   C.   An advisor for his clients.
   D.   A trust account managed by a bank.

51.   Which of the following could have conversion privileges?

   I.   Common stock.
   II.   Preferred stock.
   III.   Corporate bonds.
   IV.   Certificates of deposit.

   A.   I and IV.
   B.   I and II.
   C.   II and III.
   D.   All of the above.

52.   For a mutual fund to charge 8 1/2% all the following rights must be available to the customer, EXCEPT:

   A.   Dividend reinvestment at net asset value.
   B.   Rights of accumulation.
   C.   Quantity discounts (breakpoints).
   D.   Exchange privileges.

53.   What is the value of a variable annuity contract that is not in its payout phase?

   A.   The current value of all accumulation units.
   B.   The current value of all annuity units.
   C.   The total NAV of the fund.
   D.   The total NAV of the separate account.

54.   What is the maximum sales charge over the duration of a contractual plan?

   A.   9%.
   B.   16%.
   C.   20%.
   D.   50%.

55.   Which of the following is exempt from Federal income tax on its interest?

      A.   U.S. Bond (government bond).
      B.   Municipal bond.
      C.   Series EE bond.
      D.   Series HH bond.

56.   An investment company may suspend the right of redemption for not more than:

      A.   3 business days.
      B.   10 calendar days.
      C.   7 business days.
      D.   7 calendar days.

57.   All of the following are true regarding closed-end investment company shares, EXCEPT:

      A.   A tendency to trade at discount.
      B.   The price is dictated by supply and demand.
      C.   They can be purchased in the OTC market.
      D.   They are redeemable by the issuer.

58.   An investor owns, as a tenant-in-common, a part interest in 1,000 mutual fund shares. At the
      investor's death, what is the disposition of his interest?

      A.   Automatically reverts to the surviving tenant.
      B.   Surviving tenant becomes liquidating trustee.
      C.   Disposed of as directed in the investor's will.
      D.   The investor's interest is not transferrable.

59.   A defined benefit pension plan is one in which:

      A.   Benefits are negotiable.
      B.   Actuarial assumptions determine the amount of contribution required to support a
           given level of benefit.
      C.   Payout amounts vary with inflation.
      D.   All of the above.

60.   When mutual fund shares are redeemed:

      A.   Reinstatement is never permitted.
      B.   It constitutes a sale for federal income tax purposes.
      C.   It must be complete in 3 business days.
      D.   It is exempt from the "wash sale" rule.

61.   Which type of corporate security stipulates a specific dividend to be paid annually?

    A.   Convertible bonds.
    B.   Treasury stock.
    C.   Preferred stock.
    D.   Common stock.

62.   In the case of a severe business slump, income payments under a variable annuity contract are likely to:

    A.   Be sharply reduced in dollar amounts.
    B.   Be increased in dollar amounts.
    C.   Stay the same because of the AIR.
    D.   None of these.

63.   A registration statement must be in effect:

    A.   Before a prospectus can be delivered.
    B.   Before a broker/dealer can mail information about a security.
    C.   Both A and B.
    D.   After the security is filed with the NASD.

64.   Which annuity would pay the largest amount of immediate total payments if the contract owner died five years after payments began?

    A.   Straight life annuity.
    B.   Unit refund annuity.
    C.   Joint and survivor annuity.
    D.   5-year certain life annuity.

65.   A mutual fund's contractual plan completion insurance is paid at the death of an investor:

    A.   To the investor's beneficiary who may use funds to purchase balance of shares.
    B.   To the fund (through custodian bank) which then completes contractual plan.
    C.   For charges in excess of 15%.
    D.   To close an open account.

66.   Your client desires an investment with high liquidity. Of the following list, which would normally have the highest liquidity?

    A.   Municipal bonds.
    B.   An annuity.
    C.   Money market fund.
    D.   Growth fund.

67.   Given the following: Person in a 28% tax bracket, tax exempt yield is 6%. What is the non-tax exempt equivalent?

    A.   4.32%.
    B.   6.00%.
    C.   8.33%.
    D.   21.43%.

68.   An open-end investment company March 9th had a $20 bid and a $21.40 offering price. The prospectus shows the cost of buying the fund for quantities of $25,000 through $49,999 to be 4%. How many full shares can a customer buy for $35,000?

    A.   1,600 shares.
    B.   1,635 shares.
    C.   1,680 shares.
    D.   1,750 shares.

69.   Given three (3) different variable annuity companies with the same mortality and expense assumptions, and $50,000 is to be applied for a single premium variable annuity, which company would provide a higher amount of starting monthly income as an annuity?

    A.   A company whose Assumed Interest Rate is higher (built into the annuity rate).
    B.   A company whose Assumed Interest Rate is lower (built into the annuity rate).
    C.   A company who has no Assumed Interest Rate (built into the annuity rate).
    D.   Assumed Interest Rate of an annuity will not affect the early monthly payments because this is a variable annuity.

70.   The following person(s) is/are exempt from registration under the Investment Advisor's Act:

    A.   The investment advisor's only clients are mutual funds.
    B.   The investment advisor has had fewer than 15 clients during the preceding 12 months.
    C.   All of the investment advisor's clients are residents of the state within which the investment advisor does not furnish advice or information with regard to securities on any national securities exchange.
    D.   All of the above.

71.   Under the "special deals rule", which of the following is/are prohibited?

I.   Gifts exceeding $100.
II.   Tickets to a football game valued at $45.
III.   Dinner at a seminar.
IV.   Giving a salesman a bonus out of the management fee.

A.   All of the above.
B.   I and IV.
C.   I only.
D.   IV only.

72.   An investor has just liquidated all of his/her shares in the "Wildlife Fund". Wildlife has an 8 1/2% load. The investor could reinstate in Wildlife on a no-load basis provided:

I.   He/she did so within 90 days.
II.   He/she has used the reinstatement provision only once before.
III.   He/she reinstated an amount not to exceed his liquidation.
IV.   Such reinstatement is provided in the prospectus.

A.   I, II and III only.
B.   II, III and IV only.
C.   II and IV only.
D.   All of the above.

73.   An investor has a Growth Fund and wants to change to an Income Fund. Which of these statements is/are correct?

A.   The transaction is a sale and any gain is reportable.
B.   Any gain is not reportable.
C.   Annuity rules apply.
D.   None of the above.

74.   Which U.S. Government securities are traded on a discounted basis?

A.   Series HH bonds.
B.   Treasury bills and Series EE bonds.
C.   Treasury notes.
D.   Treasury bonds.

75.   Early withdrawal from an Individual Retirement Account will subject the participant to:

        I.   Income tax.
        II.   Capital gains tax.
        III.   A 6% surcharge.
        IV.   A 10% surcharge.

    A.   I and III.
    B.   I and IV.
    C.   II and III.
    D.   II and IV.

76.   In a contractual 50% front-end loaded plan, a <u>partial</u> refund of sales charges would be made if surrender occurs within:

    A.   45 days.
    B.   18 months.
    C.   24 months.
    D.   All of the sales charges must be refunded.

77.   A balanced portfolio is correctly described by all of the following, EXCEPT:

    A.   A combination of bonds and stocks.
    B.   Could include both common and preferred stocks.
    C.   Is generally considered conservative.
    D.   Is generally considered speculative.

78.   Under the conduit theory, what is the tax treatment of investment income?

    A.   Taxes are deferred.
    B.   Taxed to investment company only.
    C.   Taxed to shareholder and investment company.
    D.   Taxed to shareholder only.

79.   The bid price of a mutual fund is $50 and the sales charge is 8%. What price will an investor pay?

    A. $50.00.
    B. $50.00 + (8% of $50) = $54.00.
    C. $50.00 x 100/92 = $54.35.
    D. $50.00 + $8.00 = $58.00.

80.   Under the terms of the Uniform Gifts/Transfers to Minors Act:

        I.   A gift is revocable until minor attains majority.
        II.   A gift is irrevocable.
        III.   Income and profits are taxable to custodian.
        IV.   Income and profits are taxable to minor.

    A.   I, II, and IV.
    B.   II and III.
    C.   II and IV.
    D.   I and IV.

81.   The following statements are true regarding EE bonds:

        I.   Issued and redeemed by municipalities.
        II.   Rising interest in later years encourages investors to hold bonds longer.
        III.   They are freely transferable.
        IV.   Interest stops at maturity.

    A.   None of the above.
    B.   All of the above.
    C.   II and IV only.
    D.   II only.

82.   The investment advisor's contract with an investment company:

    A.   Must be approved by a majority of the Board of Directors.
    B.   May be terminated without penalty by the Board of Directors.
    C.   Will continue in effect for at least two (2) years as long as it is not specifically terminated by the Board of Directors.
    D.   All of the above.

83.   An investor whose accumulated value with an investment company is $22,000, wishes to deposit an additional $6,000. The Right of Accumulation of this investment company states that a breakpoint at $25,000 is offered. Which of the following would apply?

    A. $3,000 of the investment would be at the regular sales charge and $3,000 of the investment would be at the lower sales charge.
    B.   The entire amount of the investment would qualify for the discount.
    C.   None of this investment would qualify for the discount but all future investments would, i.e., over $25,000.
    D.   None of the above.

84.   Duties of a mutual fund's transfer agent include all of the following, EXCEPT:

    A.   Issue new shares.
    B.   Maintain records of the names of shareholders.
    C.   Issue periodic reports.
    D.   Safeguard the securities owned by the fund.

85.   In a corporate defined benefit plan, the <u>maximum</u> (payout) benefit is the lesser of 100% of average compensation or:

    A. $ 25,000 (as indexed).
    B. $ 30,000 (as indexed).
    C. $ 90,000 (as indexed).
    D. $100,000 (as indexed).

86.   Series HH bonds are correctly described by which of the following?

    A.   Issued by municipalities.
    B.   May be pledged as collateral for bank loans.
    C.   Interest is paid semi-annually.
    D.   Purchased at less than face value.

87.   The statistical unit used to determine the amount of the monthly pay-out of a variable annuity is the:

    A.   Dow-Jones Average.
    B.   Cost-of-living Index.
    C.   Accumulation unit.
    D.   Annuity unit.

88.   How can the investment policy of a fund be changed?

    A.   Majority vote of the Board of Directors.
    B.   60% majority of the Board of Directors.
    C.   Majority vote of shareowners.
    D.   Majority vote of outstanding shares.

89.   The SEC, under the Securities Act of 1933, does all the following, EXCEPT:

    A.   Reviews prospectuses.
    B.   Regulates the issuance of new securities.
    C.   Regulates securities offerings.
    D.   Approves or disapproves new issues.

90.   Plan completion insurance provided in connection with a contractual mutual fund plan would have which of the following characteristics?

    A.   Payment of a death benefit to a named beneficiary.
    B.   Payment of a death benefit to the custodian bank on behalf of the contractual plan owner.
    C.   Life insurance, which is free to insure plan completion payments in the event of early death.
    D.   None of the above.

91.   Which of the following would not be a negotiable security?

    A.   U.S. Treasury bills.
    B.   U.S. Treasury notes.
    C.   Series EE bonds.
    D.   Common stock.

92. $16,500 was invested in a mutual fund and a letter of intent filed and backdated 90 days. An investor wants to start putting in equal monthly installments to achieve a $25,000 break-point. How much should each investment be?

    A. $ 653.85.
    B. $ 850.00.
    C. $ 531.00.
    D. $8,500.00.

93.   An owner of a tax-sheltered annuity purchased while employed by a qualifying public school system or non-profit organization that later leaves this employment would have a "cost basis" in the tax-sheltered annuity of:

    A.   Zero.
    B.   The total amount actually paid into the annuity.
    C.   The current market value of the annuity.
    D.   The market value of the annuity at the time they leave the employment of the organization.

94.   Under NASD rules, continuing commissions <u>after</u> retirement are allowed if:

        I.   The individual maintains registration as a registered representative.

        II.   If a bona fide contract was signed during working years calling for continuing commissions after retirement.

        III.   If a retirement contract calls for such payment signed at the beginning of retirement.

        IV.   Continuing commissions after retirement are not allowed.

    A.   II and III only.
    B.   IV only.
    C.   I and II only.
    D.   I and III only.

95.   The federal government offers a quasi guarantee on which of the following types of securities?

    A.   Municipal bonds.
    B.   University Housing Bonds.
    C.   Railroad bonds under the ICC Department.
    D.   Fannie Mae (FNMA) bonds.

96.   Issues that are agreed to go to arbitration under the NASD's Code of Arbitration would have which of the following effects?

    A.   Decisions of the Board of Arbitration panel can be appealed directly to the SEC.
    B.   Decisions of the Board of Arbitration can be appealed to the Board of Governors of the NASD.
    C.   Decisions of the Board of Arbitration are final.
    D.   Only decisions between customers and NASD Members can be appealed.

97.   The Uniform Gifts/Transfers to Minors Act:

    A.   Permits the gift of securities to minors provided it is irrevocable.
    B.   The account may be in the form of a custodial account or conventional trust.
    C.   The custodian has the right of management until his/her death.
    D.   The donor and custodian cannot be the same person.

98.   The cost basis for open-end investment company shares to the shareholder would best be described by:

     A.   Reported on a FIFO or LIFO basis but never on an identifying basis.
     B.   Include both the cost of direct purchases and distributions reinvested.
     C.   If inherited, the heir's cost basis is the fair market value when sold.
     D.   When received as gifts, the cost basis is the same as the individual giving them.

99.   If a broker/dealer acts in an agency transaction, the law requires that certain disclosures be made to his customers, which include:

     A.   The wholesale price of the security.
     B.   The actual amount of commission charges in dollars and cents.
     C.   The name of the other party in the trade if requested.
     D.   All of these.

100.   A regulated, diversified investment company cannot own more than what percentage of the outstanding voting shares of any one company?

     A.   2%.
     B.   5%.
     C.   8%.
     D.   10%.

SERIES 6

SAMPLE FINAL EXAM I

ANSWER KEY

1. B	26. A	51. C	76. B
2. A	27. B	52. D	77. D
3. A	28. D	53. A	78. D
4. D	29. D	54. A	79. C
5. A	30. B	55. B	80. C
6. D	31. C	56. D	81. D
7. C	32. B	57. D	82. A
8. A	33. C	58. C	83. B
9. D	34. A	59. B	84. D
10. D	35. D	60. B	85. C
11. C	36. B	61. C	86. C
12. B	37. C	62. A	87. D
13. B	38. D	63. C	88. D
14. B	39. C	64. B	89. D
15. C	40. D	65. B	90. B
16. A	41. B	66. C	91. C
17. C	42. B	67. C	92. B
18. C	43. C	68. C	93. A
19. A	44. A	69. A	94. C
20. D	45. C	70. D	95. D
21. C	46. A	71. B	96. C
22. A	47. D	72. C	97. A
23. D	48. C	73. A	98. B
24. D	49. B	74. B	99. D
25. C	50. C	75. B	100. D

SERIES 6

SAMPLE EXAM I

RATIONALE

1.   B

Banker's acceptances are letters of credit from foreign banks used as a means of financing foreign trade.

2.   A

According to the Investment Company Act of 1940, if an open or closed-end company is considered diversified, at least 50% of its assets must be highly liquid; no more than 5% of the company's total assets are invested in any one specific corporation and the company may never control more than 10% of one corporation's voting stock.

3.   A

The death benefits for a variable insurance policy must be calculated no less than annually.

4.   D

Plan completion insurance is used as a means of protecting against the termination of a mutual fund contractual plan as a result of the death of the planholder. Should the planholder die the proceeds of the policy are paid to the custodian bank who, in turn, uses this to make a final lump sum purchase to complete the plan. The beneficiary of this completion insurance is, and can only be, the plan itself.

5.   A

Mortgage bonds, since they use as collateral specific real estate, either land or buildings, with limitations on the amount of debt which may be issued, are considered among the highest quality of corporate debt. Generally, the equipment supporting equipment trust certificates is not considered as high a quality of collateral as real estate. The support for debenture bonds falls in line with other general creditors of a corporation and commercial paper is simply a corporate IOU with its sole support being the good faith of the corporation.

6.   D

$100 x 10 months = $1,000 total payments

$1,000 x .50 = $500 sales charge

120 shares x $9.15 NAV = $1,098 (redeemed shares)

$500 sales charge - ($1000 x .15 cancellation fee) = $350 refund

$1,098 + $350 = $1,448 total proceeds

7.   C

An investor can receive a full refund of all sales charges paid by notifying the company of his/her intent to cancel the plan. The investor must notify the company within 45 days after receiving notice of the right to cancel.

8.   A

The sole means of deciding the amount of the monthly payment in a straight-life annuity is the individual's life expectancy. The insurance company does not have a responsibility to pay anyone other than the contract holder, which results in a higher monthly payment. Should the individual live past his/her life expectancy, this settlement option should provide the greatest total cash flow.

9.   D

The Securities Act of 1933 requires the delivery of the prospectus on a new issue to be made prior to or at the time any sales literature, advertising material or presentations are provided.

10.   D

Variable annuities guarantee that adverse mortality tables or increased expenses will not affect the distribution or payout period of the annuity. Interest or the return of the annuity is not guaranteed in the variable contract, but only found in the fixed annuity.

11.   C

The amount and time at which a 12b-1 fee is charged is determined by the Board of Directors. 12b-1 fees are charged annually as a percentage of average net assets.

12.   B

$$\text{Current Yield} = \frac{\text{Yearly Interest}}{\text{Current Market Value}}$$

$$= \frac{\$40}{\$500}$$

$$= 8\%$$

13.   B

$800 Investment x 4 Payments = $3200 Total Investments

$$\frac{\$3200 \text{ Total Investment}}{172 \text{ Total Shares}} = \$18.60 \text{ Average Cost Per Share}$$

14.   B

A unit refund guarantees the number of payments that must be made to the contract holder or beneficiary. The number of payments are determined by dividing the amount of the first monthly check into the total accumulated value of the contract holder's account. However, once the number of payments are determined, each monthly payment will vary according to the value of the account.

15.   C

A mutual fund withdrawal plan may never be compared to an annuity payment schedule. Since the shares of a mutual fund are subject to market changes, the amount an individual receives for each share will vary, and also may be less than the initial investment in the fund. Most mutual funds limit the establishment of a withdrawal plan until a minimum investment (i.e., $5,000 to $10,000) has been made. When withdrawals begin they're taxed just as any other liquidation of the fund.

16.   A

Universal and whole life insurance both guarantee minimum cash value. Variable life insurance offers no guaranteed cash value.

17.   C

Closed-end investment companies may capitalize themselves through the issuance of common stock, preferred stock and bonds. Remember, open-end companies may only issue one class of common stock, but may do so on a continual basis.

18.   C

The maximum penalty to a controlling person for a violation of the insider regulations is not to exceed the greater of $1,000,000 or three times the profit grained or loss avoided.

19.   A

Tenants-in-common ownership allows individuals to share proportionately in an account. Upon death, the deceased's proportionate interest would become part of his estate, thus passing through probate and may ultimately be distributed to a specified beneficiary. Tenants-in-common accounts are the most predominant form of business ownership.

20.   D

As long as an individual maintains fixed dollar investments on a regular basis and the value of the investment fluctuates, the individual's average cost per share will always be less then the average price per share. Note that dollar cost averaging does <u>not</u> guarantee an investor a profit.

21.   C

The statute of limitations requires that actions must be brought within 5 years of a violation of the Insider's Act.

22.   A

The Securities Exchange Act of 1934 is also known as the Broker/Dealer Act and regulates individuals selling securities after they have been issued. This Act also marked the creation of the SEC and provided a guideline for an extension of credit on securities, although this is predominantly the responsibility of the Federal Reserve Bureau. The rules by which new issues are regulated is the responsibility of the Securities Act of 1933.

23.   D

Participating preferred stocks allow individuals the ability to receive dividends in excess of their stated amount. These extra dividends would be attributable to the dividends which are being paid to the common stockholders.

24.   D

The mutual fund prospectus must disclose all fees and charges made against the investor and fund.

25.   C

Money market funds offer an investor the safety of short-term investments (less than 1 year maturities) while generally maintaining market returns without significant risk. Growth funds, penny stocks and variable annuities usually carry greater risk associated with investments in common stocks.

26.   A

When determining the sales charge as a percent of the amount actually invested in the portfolio of a mutual fund, one must divide the dollar amount of the sales charge ($15.32 - $14.16) by the net asset value. Remember, however, that sales charges are normally expressed as a percent of the offering price.

27.   B

The total asset value of a fund is calculated by taking the net asset value at the beginning of a period, (in this case $47,000,000) and adding or subtracting any changes which take place during the year. In this example, the total amount of dividend earnings and capital gains were distributed to shareholders. The only change is the growth in the portfolio, i.e., unrealized capital gains of $2,500,000. This is added to the total net asset value to determine a total asset value of $49,500,000.

28.   D

The maximum sales charge on a variable annuity is 8 1/2%, either on any one payment or over the life of the contract. There is the ability for an investor to reduce his/her sales charge by either making lump sum purchases above certain amounts or accumulating contract values in excess of the breakpoints.

29.   D

An individual would be in violation of advertising regulations if he/she was to imply a specific rate of growth or performance on any non-guaranteed type of investment. Comments may only be made pertaining to the past performance of the investment.

30.   B

He/she must understand that closed-end investment companies do not carry with them a sales charge, but instead normal brokerage commissions apply. These would be added to the market price of the closed-end shares to determine the individual's total cost.

31.   C

The public offering price of a mutual fund must always be maintained when a transaction is effected through a non-member of the NASD. Non-members are considered customers and when a sale is made from a member firm to any customer, it must be done at the applicable public offering price. If a security is privately placed between two customers, it is known as an exempt transaction and may be done at any price upon which the two customers agree.

32.   B

Since the bond market is declining, the investor will be liquidating the bond fund at a tax loss. The subsequent purchase of a new bond fund providing a higher yield would be done at decreased costs, thus resulting in a lower cost basis in the individual's portfolio. A key item to remember is that as bond yields go up, bond prices decline and vice versa, as bond yields decline, bond prices increase.

33.   C

When a variable annuity contract passes from the deceased to a beneficiary, it is done so at the same cost basis as the original contract holder. There is no stepped-up cost basis in a variable annuity contract.

34.   A

The maximum coverage for cash under SIPC is $100,000. Total coverage, which includes both cash and securities, amounts to $500,000. This is on a separate customer basis.

35.   D

TSA's are salary reduction plans with total investments consisting of before-tax dollars. As a result, any investments, plus the corresponding growth, is fully taxable upon liquidation of the plan.

36.   B

Since there is specific collateral supporting the secured bonds, they would be paid first should the corporation liquidate. Any unsecured or subordinated bondholders would be paid next with preferred stockholders and finally common stockholders being compensated, if at all, last.

37.   C

When a security goes ex-dividend a reduction is made in the market price or net asset value for the amount of the dividend. As a result, an individual purchasing a security before the ex-dividend date will merely be buying the dividend that is going to be received. The receipt of the dividend is a taxable event which results in a return of less than the investment to the individual. For this reason, the individual should wait to purchase the security until after the ex-dividend date. Should the representative sell the security based upon the upcoming dividend payment, he/she is guilty of selling dividends, an illegal practice.

38.   D

The net asset value of a mutual fund would increase or decrease based upon the performance of the portfolio. Should the fund retain any dividends, capital gains or appreciation within the portfolio, the net asset value per share would increase.

39.   C

A letter of intent offers an individual the ability to receive retroactive reductions in the sales charge. In other words, the sales charge is based upon the total amount of investments made within a 13-month period. To protect itself, the fund holds enough shares in an escrow account which would be liquidated to increase the overall sales charge should the investor fail to meet the terms of the letter of intent.

40. D

Both income and growth funds may provide distributions which are taxable in the year they are received. Distributions on the securities held in the separate account of a variable annuity are reinvested, but no immediate tax is paid by the contract holder. The taxation is deferred until a liquidation is made in the annuity. The primary distribution in a municipal bond trust would be the tax-exempt income on those bonds, thus there would be no significant immediate taxable distribution.

41. B

The security or support for payment of principle and interest on general obligation bonds is the full faith and credit of the municipality. A default in any general obligation debt of the municipality means the municipality itself has gone bankrupt.

42. B

When purchasing a mutual fund, an individual has the ability to achieve reduced sales charges if the investment is above a specific dollar amount. This is known as the breakpoint. Reducing sales just below a breakpoint offers higher total sales charges than if the purchase was made above the breakpoint. Registered representatives encouraging sales just below the breakpoint are in violation of the Investment Company Act of 1940.

43. C

Mutual fund, pricing either upon liquidation or purchase, is done on a forward pricing basis. In other words, the values received or paid are determined by the next computed net asset value.

44. A

Profit sharing plans allow employers to make tax deductible contributions at a maximum of 15% of the employee's compensation. Credit carryovers have been repealed for any amounts greater than "15% of covered payroll."

45. C

The portfolio of a money market fund consists of short-term debt obligations with a maturity of less than one year. These securities are highly liquid and provide returns through interest payments in accordance with current market yields. Banker's acceptances, Treasury bills and commercial paper are typical securities held within a money market portfolio.

46.   A

Since the reinvestment of the distribution is taking place at a time when new bonds are realizing higher yields, the over-all yield on the individual's bond fund will gradually increase.

47.   D

A hot issue is a new issue of securities whose price escalates to an immediate amount above the original public offering price. It is the responsibility of the issuing broker/dealer or any member of the syndicate to maintain a bona fide public offering. The shares of the hot issue may not be directed to any one specific person or any other member or associate of the member. If this is done, the broker/ dealer would be guilty of free-riding and withholding the securities from the public.

48.   C

Only self-employed earned income is eligible for a contribution into a self-employed pension plan. The effective contribution is 20% of the gross self-employed income which is 25% of the total self-employed taxable income after the contribution.

$38,000 Earned Income   x   .20   = $7,600 Maximum Contribution

$$\frac{\$\,7,600 \text{ Contribution}}{\$38,000 - \$7,600} = \frac{\$7,600}{\$30,400} = 25\% \text{ contribution}$$

49.   B

In a Uniform Gifts/Transfers to Minors Account, there may be only one custodian and one minor. It is the responsibility of the minor to pay any applicable taxes as it is the minor's securities which are held in the account. Depending upon the age of the minor, earnings on the account above a maximum level may be taxed at the parent's highest marginal tax bracket.

50.   C

Quantity discounts are available to "any person." Entities not falling within the definition of any person would include investment clubs, investment co-ops, or any other entity who pooled assets to make purchases at reduced commission rates or sales charges. This does not apply to trustees or pension plans, but would apply to an investment advisor acting on behalf of a pool of clients.

51.   C

The conversion privilege is the ability to convert from one security into the common stock issued by the same corporation. Both preferred stock and corporate bonds may have convertible features.

52.   D

Exchange privileges, as well as reinvesting capital gain distributions at net asset value are two of the services that are not required by the NASD for a fund to charge an 8 1/2% sales charge. Should the fund not offer dividend reinvestment at net asset value, rights of accumulation, etc., amongst their services, the NASD will scale down the maximum sales charge to lower percentages.

53.   A

Prior to the distribution or payout phase of a variable annuity contract, an individual's worth is calculated by multiplying the value of one accumulation unit times the total number of units held within the client's account.

54.   A

Contractual or periodic payment plans (50% and 20% plans) may charge a maximum lifetime sales charge of 9%. These are different than the maximum 8½% sales charges assessed to level charge plans.

55.   B

The interest on municipal bonds is exempt from taxes imposed by the U.S. Government. They are subject to taxes imposed by states or municipalities. On the other hand, U.S. Government securities are exempt from state and local taxes, but subject to taxes as assessed by the federal government.

56.   D

According to the Investment Company Act of 1940, an investment company must send the checks for redemption of a mutual fund within 7 calendar days of receiving notice of a liquidation. Remember the amount of the check sent is based upon the number of shares being redeemed and the net asset value calculated after receiving the notice.

57.   D

Closed-end investment companies, although having a net asset value, are traded at prices determined by the markets, that is, the supply and demand for those shares. Should an individual wish to sell his/her shares in a closed-end company, he/she would go through the normal brokerage procedure used in other non-investment company securities. It would be rare indeed for the issuer of the security to redeem them.

58.   C

Under tenants-in-common ownership, the percentage of securities owned by the deceased becomes the property of his/her estate and dispersed according to the directions in the will.

59.   B

A defined benefit plan establishes the benefits to be paid at retirement. The amount of funding necessary to realize these benefits are determined by actuarial tables based upon the remaining years of the employee's work life.

60.   B

When a mutual fund is liquidated, it is considered a taxable event by the IRS. Redemption must be completed and a check sent within 7 calendar days of the fund's receiving notice. It is possible for the fund to allow reinstatement of the redemption without an additional sales charge if completed within a specific period of time. Any liquidation according to the IRS is subject to the wash sale rule which states that any losses generated will be disallowed should a substantially identical security be purchased within a 30-day period, prior to or after the liquidation of the shares.

61.   C

Preferred stocks carry a stated rate of dividends which are to be paid prior to any dividends being paid common stockholders. Although bonds carry a stated rate of interest, it is interest and not dividends that are paid on bonds.

62.   A

The variable annuity's value is based upon securities held within the separate account. These securities are normally common and preferred stocks, and occasionally bonds. Should the economy decline, the value of the securities held in the separate account will follow this decline or trend. This would obviously result in a loss in value of an annuity unit and a resulting loss in the income payments from the contract.

63.   C

The registration statement begins the process of creating a new issue. The prospectus is merely a consolidation of information found in the registration statement.

64.   B

A unit refund annuity guarantees that a minimum number of payments will be made. The number of payments is established when the settlement option is chosen and payout begins. Regardless of whether the contract owner dies, these minimum payments will be made, either to the estate or beneficiary. In a straight life annuity, payments cease upon a contract holder's death. This is also true in the five-year certain life annuity, although payments are guaranteed for a minimum of five years. Under a joint and survival settlement option, it is true that payments will continue to the survivor (no lump sum) and will cease once the survivor is deceased. Therefore, payments could very well be made over a longer period of time under the unit refund annuity.

65.   B

Completion insurance guarantees the payments will be made to complete a contractual plan in the event of death of the contract holder. These payments are made to the custodian bank who uses the proceeds to complete the established plan. There are no other options for distributing the benefits of completion insurance.

66.   C

Money market funds are known for their high liquidity and relative safety of principal. The portfolio consists entirely of debt obligations with less than one year to maturity. Remember that liquidity is defined as the ability to sell a security on short notice and have returned the initial investment. Municipal bonds, annuities and growth funds may be considered marketable (the ability to sell quickly) but there may be difficulty in receiving the initial investment upon the sale.

67.   C

$$\text{Tax Equivalent Yield} = \frac{\text{Tax Exempt Yield}}{100\% - \text{Tax Bracket}}$$

$$= \frac{6\%}{100\% - 28\%} = \frac{6\%}{72\%} = 8.33\%$$

68.   C

Since the customer is investing $35,000, he/she is purchasing the fund at a reduced sales charge of 4%, therefore you must re-calculate the new offer price with a 4% sales charge in order to determine the number of shares he/she may purchase.

$$\text{New Offer Price} = \frac{\$20}{100\% - 4\%} = \frac{\$20}{96\%} = \$20.83$$

$$\text{Total Shares Purchased} \quad = \quad \frac{\$35,000}{\$20.83} = 1,680 \text{ shares}$$

69.   A

The assumed interest rate is used to determine the first payment of a variable annuity contract. The higher the assumed interest rate, the higher the initial monthly payment. However, should the fund fail to achieve the assumed return, payments will gradually begin to decrease.

70.   D

According to the Investment Advisor's Act, an individual need not register as an investment advisor if his/her only clients are mutual funds; if he/she has no more than 15 clients over a period of the last 12 months; and if all of his/her clients reside within the state in which he/she does business, and information or advice provided does not relate to any securities held on a National Securities Exchange.

71.   B

Special deals generally concern bonuses or gifts given to, or from, registered representatives. The NASD prohibits gifts in excess of $100. Tickets to a football game generally will not exceed $100, and a dinner at a seminar would be considered a business expense. It is also prohibited to provide a salesman with a bonus out of a management fee as the management fee is paid to the investment advisor or manager of the portfolio of a fund. The salesman may get compensated in the form of a percentage of the sales charge for his/her marketing of the fund.

72.   C

The NASD allows for reinstatement of mutual fund purchases on a no-load basis as long as they are done on an infrequent basis and not within 90 days of the liquidation. Although the NASD allows for this reinstatement, it also must be spelled out within the prospectus for the specific fund.

73.   A

When an individual uses the exchange privilege of a fund, he's allowed to do so with little or no sales charge applied on the exchange. However, the IRS does view this as a taxable event, and any gain would be reportable.

74.   B

Both Treasury bills and Series EE bonds are sold on a discounted basis from the U.S. Government, with the difference between the purchase price and the maturity value being considered interest income. Series HH bonds, Treasury notes and Treasury bonds are all sold at face value with interest being paid on a semi-annual basis.

75.   B

A premature distribution from an IRA results in ordinary income taxes on the amount withdrawn as well as a 10% penalty on that same amount. Please note that the full amount of withdrawal along with the penalty assessed is taxed as ordinary income.

76.   B

Front-end load contractual plans (50%) allow for a partial refund of sales charge if the plan is terminated after 45 days, but within 18 months of establishing the plan. The refund is equal to the total sales charge paid, less 15% of the total payments (including sales charge) made to the mutual fund.

77.   D

Balanced funds are considered the most conservative of all mutual fund investments. The portfolio consists of a mix of common stocks, preferred stocks and bonds in already proven corporations. These would not be considered speculative investments.

78.   D

The conduit, or pipeline theory, is defined under Subchapter M of the IRS Code. This regulation states that should the investment company qualify, any distributions made to the shareholders of the mutual fund may pass through the investment company without being taxed at that level. This means the distributions flow directly from the securities held within the portfolio to the investor, without taxation at the investment company's level.

79.   C

Given the net asset value, and sales charge for a mutual fund, we can find the offering price by dividing the net asset value by 100% minus the sales charge.

80.   C

In a Uniform Gifts/Transfers to Minors Account, the securities held within the account are the property of the minor and any earnings generated by the account are taxable to the minor. Although at the control of the custodian, any gifts made to the account are irrevocable, and at all times the taxes will be paid from the account.

81.   D

Series EE bonds are non-marketable U.S. Government bonds which are sold at a discount with all the interest being paid when they are redeemed. Redemption is made by the U.S. Government or one of its agents. Interest may continue to accrue after maturity should the investor continue to hold the security. The longer the security is held, the higher the interest paid on the security.

82.   A

An Investment Advisor's contract with a mutual fund is written by the Board of Directors of that mutual fund. Initially the contract runs for a period of two years, after which it may be renewed on an annual basis.

83.   B

When using the rights of accumulation privilege, an individual qualifies for reduced sales charges on the total amount of the investment which meets or exceeds the breakpoint. In other words, the investor would pay the reduced sales charge on the entire $6,000 investment.

84.   D

The safeguard of securities held in the separate account is the responsibility of the custodian bank. The transfer agent's responsibility would be the issuance of new shares, maintaining a record of the shareholders, and as a result, the distribution of periodic financial reporting to these individual shareholders.

85.   C

A defined benefit plan offers a maximum benefit of the lesser of 100% of average compensation for the three highest paid years, or $90,000 (as indexed). Should an individual choose early retirement, these benefits will be scaled down accordingly.

86.   C

Series HH bonds are non-marketable U.S. Government securities which are sold at face value and pay interest semi-annually.

87.   D

When a variable annuity goes from its pay-in or accumulation phase to its payout phase, the units to determine the amount of payment are known as annuity units.

88.   D

Any significant changes in the operation of a mutual fund are determined by a majority vote of the outstanding shares. A change in investment policy would be considered a significant change in the status of the mutual fund.

89.   D

At no time does the SEC approve or disapprove of a security. The SEC merely reviews the registration statement provided by the corporation to judge whether full disclosure of information has been made.

90.   B

Plan completion insurance makes payment of its proceeds to the custodian bank who, in turn, uses it to make a lump sum purchase to complete the plan. This insurance is non-transferable.

91.   C

Both Series EE and Series HH are U.S. Government non-marketable securities. This means that they may never be transferred to another owner, but instead must be redeemed by an agent of the U.S. Government when an individual wishes to liquidate his/her position.

92.   B

Letters of Intent allow for investments to be made over a period of 13 months and be considered a lump sum payment. This allows individuals to receive reduced sales charges through the use of a breakpoint, even if the total amount is not available at any one time. A letter of intent may also be backdated a maximum of 90 days, but at no point may the entire letter of intent run longer than 13 months.

93.   A

TSA's are known as salary reduction plans. The contributions to these plans actually reduce the employee's salary and as a result are provided in before-tax dollars. Technically, the investor has no cost and no cost basis in this annuity.

94.   C

Continuing commissions are allowed if a bona fide contract was signed between the member firm and the individual prior to his/her retirement. In many cases, they require the individual to maintain his/her registration as a registered representative. However, the NASD will also allow continuing commissions to be received by the representative or the immediate family if this registration no longer exists. In all cases, a bona fide contract between the member and the individual must exist.

95.   D

Although the government does not directly guarantee payment of interest or principal on U.S. agency issues, there does exist a quasi-guarantee. It is believed that should the agency be unable to make principal or interest payments, the U.S. Government will provide the support. Please note, that a requirement by the U.S. Government to step in does not exist.

96.   C

Any issue that goes to the Board of Arbitration and the subsequent decision made are considered to be final. They are subject to review by both the Board of Governors of the NASD and the SEC, however, appeals may not be made.

97.   A

In a Uniform Gifts/Transfers to Minor's Account, securities are registered in the name of the custodian, but stated held for the benefit of the minor. It is the custodian who has trading authority in the account, but it is the minor who is technically the owner. All gifts to the account are irrevocable and complete ownership of the account is the minor's upon reaching legal age.

98.   B

Any purchases made with after-tax dollars would be considered in the cost basis of a mutual fund. This would include both the initial purchase and subsequent reinvestment of any distributions from the fund. The liquidation of shares may be done on a last-in, first-out basis, or on an identified basis, as long as the individual maintains adequate records. Gifts would be acquired at fair market value.

99.   D

When effecting a transaction on an agency basis, it is the broker/dealer's responsibility to disclose the net costs to the purchaser along with the total commissions on the trade. Should the client request the identity of the individual making the sale, the broker/dealer has the responsibility to disclose this.

100.   D

According to the Investment Company Act of 1940, in order to be diversified, an investment company must maintain 50% of its assets as liquid, with no more than 5% of its total assets being invested in any one corporation, and at no time may they control more than 10% of that corporation's voting securities.

SERIES 6

SAMPLE EXAM II

NOTE TO STUDENTS

Circle the correct answer. Allow yourself no more than 135 minutes (2¼ hours) to complete this exam. Once you have finished, review the Rationale and any areas in the book in which you feel weak.

1. What is the maximum benefit payable at retirement in a defined contribution plan?

    A. The lesser of 25% of earned income, or $30,000.
    B. The lesser of the average compensation for the three highest paid years, or $90,000 (as indexed).
    C. The maximum benefits are determined by the performance of the pension's investments.
    D. They are determined according to ERISA standards.

2. Decisions made by the NASD's Board of Arbitration are/may be:

    A. Subject to review by the SEC.
    B. Appealed to the Board of Governors.
    C. Appealed through the judicial system.
    D. Any of the above.

3. Mutual funds are prohibited from including which of the following investments in their portfolio?

    I.   Options.
    II.   Commodities.
    III. Real Estate.
    IV.   Warrants.

    A. I, II, and II.
    B. II and III.
    C. I and II.
    D. All of the above.

4. All deferred annuity contracts, whether fixed or variable, utilize which of the following as the major ingredients in pricing the contract?

    I.   Mortality cost.
    II.   Interest earnings.
    III. Expense cost.

    A. II only.
    B. III only.
    C. I and III only.
    D. I, II and III.

5.   The price of open-end investment company shares, disregarding sales charges, compared to closed-end investment company shares is determined:

   A.   By supply and demand for the shares themselves.
   B.   By supply and demand for the securities held by the investment company.
   C.   Not related to supply and demand and offered at fixed prices.
   D.   The prices are determined in a similar manner.

6.   The "wash sale rule" on tax deductible losses when selling securities actually covers any repurchases within:

   A.   30 days.
   B.   60 days.
   C.   61 days.
   D.   No time limit.

7.   Variable annuities utilize a system of funding known as:

   A.   Variable annuity trust account.
   B.   Open-end investment company funding.
   C.   Segregated asset account per investor.
   D.   Separate account system.

8.   With respect to investment company's sales literature the determination whether or not a statement made in the literature could be considered material depends on an evaluation of:

   A.   The statement itself.
   B.   The context in which the statement is made.
   C.   The legal test of materiality.
   D.   All of the above.

9.   A major disadvantage of the "dollar cost averaging" investing technique is that this approach:

   A.   Will not indicate to the investor when to buy.
   B.   Will not indicate to the investor when to sell.
   C.   Will only work if the market is continually going up.
   D.   Will always result in the average price being less than the average cost.

10.   An investor with a marginal tax bracket of 28% is considering a tax exempt investment in municipal bonds that will yield 7%. What non-tax exempt equivalent would this equal?

  A. 7.28%.
  B. 9.72%.
  C. 14%.
  D. 28%.

11.   Variable contracts with multiple payments into a separate account maintained by an insurance company must have sales charges that do not exceed:

  A. 7.5%.
  B. 8.0%.
  C. 8.5%.
  D. 9% over the life of the plan.

12.   An open-end investment company that is quoted at $18.30 bid and $20.00 asked in the newspaper would have a sales charge of:

  I. 8.5%.
  II. 9.3%.
  III. $1.70.
  IV. $8.50.

  A. III only.
  B. I and III only.
  C. I and IV only.
  D. II and III only.

13.   Quantity discounts, when purchasing open-end investment company shares, would be allowed under all of the following, EXCEPT:

  A. A single fiduciary account.
  B. A letter of intent backdated 90 days.
  C. A letter of intent covering 13 months.
  D. Never allowed because this is buying at a discount.

14. It is considered unlawful for any person, either directly or indirectly, to use any deceptive or manipulative device when communicating information through the mails, using interstate commerce, or any facility of a national security exchange. This rule covers any security:

   A. Which is only registered on a national exchange.
   B. Traded over-the-counter.
   C. Whether registered on a national exchange or not.
   D. Contained on a Legal List.

15. Payments under variable annuities are considered "received" when:

   A. The registered representative accepts payment and provides a receipt.
   B. When mailed to the insurance company.
   C. When received by the insurance company.
   D. When accepted by the insurance company.

16. The most common form of organization for an open-end investment company would be:

   A. An investment trust.
   B. A partnership.
   C. A S corporation.
   D. A corporation.

17. Any person directly or indirectly owning, controlling or holding with power to vote 5% or more of the outstanding voting securities of a company; any officer, director, co-partner, or employee; an investment advisor or member of the advisory board of an investment company best defines which of the following terms?

   A. Affiliated person.
   B. Underwriter.
   C. Broker.
   D. Dealer.

18. A sole proprietor or partner who participates in a qualified retirement plan <u>does not</u> have which of these advantages enjoyed by employees?

   A. Borrowing from the plan.
   B. Tax-deferred on contributions.
   C. Tax-deferred on investment earnings.
   D. Same percentage allowances for contributions.

19.   Gifts or gratuities provided to any person, principal, proprietor, employee, agent or representative of an NASD member are prohibited if the amount exceeds:

    A. $25 per person per year.
    B. $50 per person per year.
    C. $75 per person per year.
    D. $100 per person per year.

20.   An investment that can be disposed of either at a gain or loss, at nationally quoted prices, such as listed common stocks, would provide an investor with a high degree of:

    A.   Liquidity.
    B.   Marketability.
    C.   Risk/reward ratio measurement.
    D.   A & B above.

21.   An investment company organized under a trust indenture which does not have a Board of Directors and issues only redeemable securities representing an undivided interest in a unit of specified securities best defines what class of investment company?

    A.   Open-end.
    B.   Closed-end.
    C.   Diversified.
    D.   Unit investment trust.

22.   What is required for an NASD member firm in order to exercise discretionary power on behalf of the customer?

    A.   Sufficient cash and/or securities in the account.
    B.   A stock power.
    C.   Prior written authorization from the customer.
    D.   Prior written authorization from a principal of the member firm.

23.   All of the following are acceptable means of funding a pension plan, EXCEPT:

    A.   Flexible premium annuity contracts.
    B.   Fixed premium annuity contracts.
    C.   Face amount certificate contracts.
    D.   Participating term life insurance.

24.   Rob Jetson is a salaried electrical engineer for a pharmaceutical company, working 50 hours per week and is covered under their qualified pension plan. At night he often takes small jobs electrically wiring private homes. The income he earns at night:

    A.   Would not be eligible for any qualified plan because he is already covered under one.
    B.   Would be eligible only up until he actually receives benefits from his other plan.
    C.   Is eligible for either an IRA or self-employed qualified plan.
    D.   Is eligible for a Keogh Plan only.

25.   The public offering price is defined as the price set forth:

    A.   In a tombstone advertisement.
    B.   As determined on the exchanges.
    C.   In the prospectus of the issuing company.
    D.   In the registration statement.

26.   Selling concessions, discounts, or other allowances are allowed to be made by an NASD member firm only:

    A.   As a consideration for services rendered.
    B.   As an incentive to solicit sales.
    C.   To anyone other than a broker or dealer.
    D.   Considered a prohibited practice.

27.   Contractual plan withdrawal and reinstatement privileges permit planholders to withdraw up to what percentage of the current value of their accounts in cash and later return the money to the account without sales charges being imposed?

    A.   90%.
    B.   75%.
    C.   50%.
    D.   25%.

28.   A periodic plan company, qualifying under <u>Section 27 (h)</u> of the Investment Company Amendment's Act of 1970, will have no more than a 20% sales charge taken from any payment, no more than 16% average over 4 years, and no more than 9% over the life of the plan. This type of plan is a: .

    A.   Voluntary accumulation plan.
    B.   Level charge plan.
    C.   Front-end load plan.
    D.   Spread-load option plan.

29.   In relation to the Board of Governors interpretation on special deals, all of the following items are considered to constitute something of material value, EXCEPT:

A.   Loans.
B.   An occasional dinner given for a group of registered representatives.
C.   Discounts from the offering price of a security.
D.   Wholesale commissions or overrides.

30.   If a sole proprietor has earned income of $84,000 after all business deductions and contributions for employees, what is his/her maximum contribution for him/herself?

A. $21,000.
B. $16,800.
C. $30,000.
D. $12,600.

31.   Under the Right of Withdrawal privilege provided by periodic plan companies, the right to withdraw is for 45 days from the mailing of the notice and the value of the account will be paid plus:

A.   All sales charges.
B.   All sales charges over 15%.
C.   All sales charges over 20%.
D.   No sales charge refund.

32.   A prohibited transaction in which a registered representative implies that an advantage accrues to the buyer of shares of an investment company by reason of the purchase of such shares in anticipation of a distribution of dividends which are about to be paid, refers to:

A.   Selling distributions.
B.   Dividend anticipation sale.
C.   Investment opportunity expansion.
D.   Selling dividends.

33.   The type of pension plan that allows the largest possible immediate tax deductions with the greatest benefit going to older employees would be the:

A.   Keogh Plan.
B.   Defined Benefit Plan.
C.   Defined Contribution Plan.
D.   Index-Linked Plan.

34.   "Registered investment companies" are generally not permitted to engage in which of the following:

        I.   Purchase securities on margin.
        II.   Effect short sales.
        III.   Place securities as collateral for loans.

    A.   II only.
    B.   II and III only.
    C.   I and II only.
    D.   I, II and III.

35.   The form of U.S. Government securities that carries no stated rate of interest would be which of the following?

    A.   Treasury Bonds.
    B.   Treasury Notes.
    C.   Federal Agency Obligations (FHA, VA, etc.).
    D.   Series EE bonds.

36.   All of the following would probably be eligible for a "tax-sheltered annuity" under special legislation, EXCEPT:

    A.   A school teacher under Section 403(b).
    B.   A hospital employee under Section 501(c)3.
    C.   A school janitor under Section 403(b).
    D.   A student earning wages under a fellowship.

37.   The Board of Directors of a "registered investment company" may have no more than what percentage of its Board represented by "interested persons"?

    A.   10%.
    B.   40%.
    C.   60%.
    D.   75%.

38.   Which of the following would characterize the over-the-counter market?

    A.   Negotiated market.
    B.   Auction market.
    C.   Fixed prices quoted market.
    D.   All of the above would characterize the OTC.

39. The regulation established by the Board of Governors of the Federal Reserve System which regulates the extension of credit on open-end investment company shares by brokers and dealers, is called:

    A.   Regulation A.
    B.   Regulation U.
    C.   Regulation T.
    D.   Rules of Fair Practice.

40. The "Investment Advisor's Agreement" with an open-end investment company must comply with all of the following, EXCEPT:

    A.   Have a written contract.
    B.   Approved by a majority of the outstanding shares.
    C.   Can continue for up to two years initially.
    D.   Can be assigned to another by the investment advisor.

41. Open-end investment companies may issue as securities:

    A.   Only one capital issue.
    B.   Bonds, if asset coverage is 300% or more.
    C.   Preferred stock is approved by common stockholders.
    D.   None of the above.

42. Any person engaged in the business of buying and selling securities for their own account may be best defined as:

    A.   A broker.
    B.   A dealer.
    C.   Registered representative.
    D.   Account representative.

43. Predictions of future investment performance for an open-end investment company are allowed as long as:

    A.   An effective prospectus precedes or accompanies the presentation.
    B.   The SEC has approved the security presentation.
    C.   A & B above.
    D.   None of the above.

44.   An NASD member is responsible and has the duty to ascertain by investigating the character, reputation, etc. of any person prior to making:

    A.   A job offer.
    B.   Certification on the application for registration.
    C.   That person an officer of the organization.
    D.   That person an employee.

45.   All of the following would be considered securities, EXCEPT:

    A.   Leases and royalty rights to mineral deposits.
    B.   Collateral trust certificates.
    C.   A draft or bill of exchange for currency.
    D.   Bankers acceptance of more than 9 months duration.

46.   A registered representative executes a transaction for a client and a commission is charged for the service. This transaction would probably be classified as:

    A.   A principal type transaction.
    B.   A dealer type transaction.
    C.   An agency type transaction.
    D.   A buy order.

47.   Which of the following statements is correct regarding the prices and distribution process of open-end investment company shares?

    A.   It is illegal for a fund to have both an underwriter and, in addition, a plan company that distributes shares.
    B.   It is illegal for a fund to sell directly to the public.
    C.   It is illegal to have more than one "intermediary" between the fund and the shareholder.
    D.   It is illegal to sell fund shares at a price (discount) below the net asset value.

48.   Additional service features of mutual funds could include all of the following, EXCEPT:

    A.   Withdrawal and reinstatement privileges (unlimited).
    B.   Reinvestment privilege (unlimited).
    C.   Conversion privilege (unlimited).
    D.   Right of accumulation privilege (unlimited).

49.   If a registered representative is terminated by an NASD member firm, the member firm is required to notify the NASD of the termination within:

A.   30 days.
B.   20 days.
C.   15 days.
D.   10 days.

50.   A security listed on the New York Stock Exchange has a record date for its upcoming dividend of Friday, October 15. Presuming all are business days, which of the following would be the ex-dividend date?

A.   October 13.
B.   October 14.
C.   October 15.
D.   October 19.

51.   An open-end investment, qualifying under Subchapter M of the Internal Revenue Code, which distributes 95% of its net investment income and retains the remaining 5%, would be subject to which of the following?

A.   Corporate taxes on the 5% retained.
B.   Corporate taxes on the 95% distributed.
C.   Corporate taxes on 100% because they violated Subchapter M.
D.   Not subject to corporate taxes at all because they qualified under Subchapter M.

52.   Distributions from an open-end investment company which are automatically reinvested by the investor would be taxed:

A.   Deferred, until the shares are sold.
B.   Deferred, if held more than 12 months.
C.   Currently, only to the extent of the appreciation.
D.   Currently, just as if received.

53.   The income tax cost basis of a deferred annuity contract to an estate or an heir of an estate would be which of the following?

A.   The fractional interest rule applied to deferred annuities.
B.   The fresh start addition rule applies to deferred annuities.
C.   The stepped-up cost basis rule applies to deferred annuities.
D.   The cost basis is not affected, i.e., same cost basis the decedent had.

54.   Following the termination of a registered representative by an NASD member firm, the termination action does not take effect if:

A.   The registered representative files a counter suit.
B.   Less than two years have expired.
C.   His contract provides for continuing commissions.
D.   Any action or complaint is filed within one year.

55.   A corporate bond quoted at 97 1/8 would indicate a price of:

A. $97.18.
B. $97.80.
C. $971.80
D. $971.25.

56.   The value of a right, prior to ex-rights date, would be which of the following, where it takes 9 rights to buy one share, the current market price of the stock is $30.00, and cash needed is $20.00 per share?

A. $1.00.
B. $1.10.
C. $9.00.
D. $10.00.

57.   Mutual funds can be purchased by registered representatives for which of the following reasons:

I.   Client order.
II.   For inventory account.
III.   Own personal investment (investment account).

A.   I only.
B.   I and II only.
C.   I and III only.
D.   I, II and III.

58.   The bodies empowered to hear and pass upon all complaints with regard to violations of the NASD rules are the Board of Governors and:

A.   Trade Practice Complaint Panel.
B.   Code of Procedure Board.
C.   District Business Conduct Committee.
D.   NASD Conduct Committee.

59.   The Right of Accumulation, where offered, refers to:

    A.   Right of withdrawal of accumulated value in account.
    B.   Accumulation of units under a variable annuity contract.
    C.   Reducing sales charges based upon the aggregate quantity of all securities previously purchased.
    D.   The right to withdraw more than, less than, or an amount equal to, the actual increase in net asset value of all investment company shares owned.

60.   The District Business Conduct Committee may offer, for violations of the Rules of Fair Practice, an opportunity to waive a hearing and accept <u>summary complaint procedure</u>, which provides a maximum fine of:

    A. $2,500 and/or censure.
    B. $1,000 and/or expulsion.
    C. $2,000 and/or reprimand.
    D. $10,000 and/or suspension.

61.   An NASD member, when asked to open an account for a customer who is employed by another member, must:

    A.   Refuse to open the account.
    B.   Notify the employing member, in writing, and follow instructions received.
    C.   Notify the employing member and follow instructions received.
    D.   Post a fidelity bond with the employing member.

62.   A registered investment company must redeem its shares, when tendered, no later than:

    A.   Same day as tender.
    B.   5 business days after tender.
    C.   7 business days after tender.
    D.   7 calendar days after tender.

63.   Under a periodic payment plan, for sales charges that equal 50% of the first year's payments, sales charges must average, over the life of the plan, no more than:

    A.   8.5%.
    B.   9.0%.
    C.   16%.
    D.   20%.

64.   The type of bond where no specific property is pledged as collateral for the bond would be considered a:

    A.   Bond without lien.
    B.   First Mortgage bond.
    C.   Debenture bond.
    D.   Indenture bond.

65.   The exclusion ratio, as it applies to annuity contracts, would be expressed as:

    A.   Investment in contract = Exclusion ratio.

    B. $\dfrac{\text{Expected Return}}{\text{Investment in Contract}}$ = Exclusion ratio.

    C. $\dfrac{\text{Investment in Contract}}{\text{Expected Return}}$ = Exclusion ratio.

    D. $\dfrac{\text{Life Expectancy}}{\text{Expected Return}}$ = Exclusion ratio.

66.   The <u>Right to Refund</u> under periodic payment plans, where 50% first year sales charge is deducted, is the value of the account plus all sales charges over 15%. This right to refund extends for:

    A.   45 days.
    B.   1 year.
    C.   1 1/2 years.
    D.   Life of the plan.

67.   Taxation of partial redemptions of variable annuity contracts follows which of the following principles?

    A.   Full amount taxed as income.
    B.   Full amount excluded from income.
    C.   Taxable to the extent that the amount available exceeds owner's cost basis.
    D.   No tax liability until withdrawals exceed cost basis.

68.   Face amount certificates are considered securities and provide for periodic payments. They are considered a security if the periodic payments extend for more than:

    A.   6 months.
    B.   12 months.
    C.   24 months.
    D.   10 years.

69.   A stand-by underwriting would be used:

A.   To guarantee the sale of an open-end investment company issue.
B.   Where the market for a stock was weak.
C.   When best efforts underwriting was not available.
D.   In a rights offering.

70.   Guaranteed elements of a variable annuity contract, guaranteed by the insurance company itself, would be:

I.   The mortality expense guarantee (maximum).
II.   The interest expense guarantee (maximum).
III.   Nonforfeiture provisions.

A.   I and IV only.
B.   I and III only.
C.   I and II only.
D.   III and IV only.

71.   SIPC protects customers who have cash and securities on deposit with brokerage houses up to what amounts?

I. $500,000 for cash and securities per separate account.
II. $100,000 for cash only (per separate account).
III. $500,000 per account.
IV. $100,000 per account.

A.   I and IV only.
B.   II and III only.
C.   I and II only.
D.   III and IV only.

72.   Free-riding and withholding is a violation and can take place with:

A.   Margin securities.
B.   Short sales.
C.   Hot issues.
D.   Unregistered stock.

73.   All of the following are characteristics of Unit Investment Trusts, EXCEPT:

A.   No Board of Directors exist.
B.   Includes voting trust certificates.
C.   Organized under a trust indenture.
D.   Issues only redeemable securities.

74. The advantage of automatic dividend and capital gain reinvestment of mutual fund shares allows:

    I.   Deferral of taxes.
    II.   No sales charge on reinvested amounts.
    III.   Compounding of investment.

    A. I and III only.
    B. III only.
    C. II and III only.
    D. I, II and III.

75. Private securities transactions, involving securities <u>not</u> distributed through a member broker/dealer and <u>not</u> registered with the SEC, between a registered representative and a client:

    A. Are prohibited.
    B. Must be approved by the SEC in advance.
    C. Must be reviewed by the SEC in advance.
    D. Must be disclosed, in advance, to the employing member.

76. Realized capital gains on securities transactions generally are taxed at what capital gain rate?

    A. 10%.
    B. 28%.
    C. 60%.
    D. 100%.

77. Mutual fund dividend distributions:

    A. Are subject to income taxation as ordinary income.
    B. 85% may be excluded from income by individuals.
    C. Qualify for a $100 annual exclusion.
    D. Are subject to taxation to the fund as well as to the shareholders.

78. Capital losses can be offset against ordinary income for tax purposes (after offsetting against capital gains) up to:

    A. $3,000 per joint return.
    B. $6,000 per joint return.
    C. Unlimited.
    D. Is not allowed.

79.   Which of the following statements pertaining to municipal bond funds would be correct?

        I.   The tax-exempt nature of the investment passes through to the investors.
        II.   They are exempt from both federal and, sometimes, state income taxes.
        III.   Capital gains on shares are not exempt from taxation.

    A.   I only.
    B.   I and II only.
    C.   I and III only.
    D.   I, II and III.

80.   Under ERISA Rules, if the qualified fund invests in the employer's securities, the maximum allowed is:

    A.   5% of the plan's assets.
    B.   10% of the plan's assets.
    C.   A "reasonable" amount only.
    D.   This is not allowed, called a "prohibited transaction."

81.   Unrealized appreciation in the value of a mutual fund portfolio is taxed to the shareholders in what manner?

    A.   Twice a year as dividend distributions are announced.
    B.   Once a year as capital-gains distributions are announced.
    C.   Only when realized via the sale within the portfolio or a shareholder redeeming shares.
    D.   At the end of the calendar year.

82.   A mutual fund has a NAV of $32.00 and a sales charge of 7 1/2%. What is the offering price of the fund?

    A. $34.00.
    B. $34.40.
    C. $34.59.
    D. $34.65

83.   Which of the following is an appropriate basis for comparison of two mutual funds?

    A.   Past management performance.
    B.   Investment performance for a select 21-month period.
    C.   Proximity to the New York Stock Exchange.
    D.   Prestige of the bank service as the custodian of the fund.

84. A qualified profit-sharing plan must have:

       I.   Substantial and recurring contributions.
      II.   A fixed amount of profits that will be contributed.
     III.   A fixed allocation formula.

    A.   I only.
    B.   I and II only.
    C.   I and III only.
    D.   II and III only.

85. From the variable annuity company's standpoint, variable annuity contracts under qualified plans versus non-qualified plans, would refer to:

    A.   The necessity that two separate accounts be set up; one qualified, one non-qualified.
    B.   The sales charges must be, by law, less on the qualified plans.
    C.   Different tax treatment for the variable annuity company.
    D.   All of the above.

86. If a growth fund has an investment portfolio valued at $18,000,000 and there are 1,500,000 shares outstanding, what is the NAV per share?

    A.   More information is necessary.
    B. $12.00.
    C. $1.20.
    D.   NAV is determined by auction.

87. A sales charge for mutual fund shares is paid by the investor who purchases:

    A.   Directly from the fund.
    B.   From the underwriter for the fund.
    C.   From a broker/dealer appointed by the underwriter.
    D.   All of the above.

88. A registered representative, in dealing with a long-time client, tells the client that if the stock goes down in price and the client must sell at a loss in the future, the representative will personally make up any loss. This action:

    A.   Doesn't violate any rules, but is unwise for the representative to do.
    B.   Shouldn't be taken unless the Board of Directors is in accordance.
    C.   Violates the NASD's Uniform Practice Code.
    D.   Violates the NASD's Rules of Fair Practice.

89.   Registered investment companies are required to furnish shareholders a financial statement at least:

A.   Quarterly.
B.   Annually.
C.   Monthly.
D.   Semi-annually.

90.   The broker/dealer's most recent balance sheet must be made available to:

A.   All prospective and existing customers.
B.   Anyone on the firm's mailing list.
C.   All bona fide customers.
D.   All of the above.

91.   Sales literature for open-end investment companies would exclude:

A.   Annual report and supporting data.
B.   Oral discussions of an investment company.
C.   Any communication between the underwriter and dealers directly that will be shared with the public.
D.   Interoffice memoranda.

92.   A calendar year taxpayer who has no existing IRA plan, but who wishes to establish one this year, will have until what date to establish a plan and make a contribution?

A.   April 15.
B.   March 15.
C.   January 1.
D.   December 31.

93.   What is the responsibility of a mutual fund underwriter, sponsor, or distributor?

A.   To guarantee the soundness of the investment portfolio.
B.   To sell fund shares to the public directly or through dealer arrangements.
C.   To carry out the investment policy as stated in the prospectus.
D.   To prepare and publish semi-annual reports to shareholders.

94.   Which of the following would be included in the "cost basis" of investment company shares?

        I.   Original purchase price of shares.
        II.   Original purchase price less any sales charge.
        III.   Reinvested capital gain distributions.
        IV.   Undistributed capital gains.

    A.   I only.
    B.   I, II and III.
    C.   I and III.
    D.   I, II and IV.

95.   The maintenance of the individual shareholder's records, including number of shares owned and distribution of reports, is the responsibility of the:

    A.   Custodian bank.
    B.   Transfer agent.
    C.   Underwriter.
    D.   Management company.

96.   An investor has an accumulated value of $7,000 in a mutual fund with a breakpoint at $10,000 and a corresponding sales charge of 6 1/2%. How many shares will he/she purchase if he/she invests $4,000 when the fund's maximum sales charge is 8% and the NAV is $8.50?

    A.   432 shares.
    B.   435 shares.
    C.   440 shares.
    D.   442 shares.

97.   The securities held within a Uniform Gift to Minor's Account earn $2,000. In what manner will these earnings be taxed if the minor is 10 years old?

    A. $2,000 attributable to the minor's tax bracket.
    B. $2,000 attributable to the parent's tax bracket.
    C.   A portion is tax-exempt; a portion is taxable at the minor's tax bracket; and a portion is taxable at the parent's tax bracket.
    D. $2,000 taxed at 28%.

98.   A mutual fund approved for purchase on margin may not have credit extended for the first:

   A.   15 days of ownership.
   B.   31 days of ownership.
   C.   45 days of ownership.
   D.   It is illegal to extend credit on mutual fund shares.

99.   The most common form of ownership between two individuals is:

   A.   Joint tenants-with-rights-of-survivorship.
   B.   Tenants-in-common.
   C.   Tenants-by-entirety.
   D.   Joint tenants-in-common.

100.   An individual has invested $3000 in a mutual fund and signed a letter-of-intent to $10,000. Two and a half months ago he had invested $1000 in the same fund. How much must he deposit to meet the LOI?

   A. $6,000.
   B. $7,000.
   C. $9,000.
   D. $10,000.

This page intentionally

left blank

SERIES 6

SAMPLE FINAL EXAM II

ANSWER KEY

1. C	26. A	51. A	76. B
2. A	27. A	52. D	77. A
3. B	28. D	53. D	78. A
4. D	29. B	54. D	79. C
5. B	30. B	55. D	80. B
6. C	31. A	56. A	81. C
7. D	32. D	57. C	82. C
8. B	33. B	58. C	83. A
9. B	34. D	59. C	84. C
10. B	35. D	60. A	85. C
11. C	36. D	61. C	86. B
12. B	37. C	62. D	87. D
13. A	38. A	63. B	88. D
14. C	39. C	64. C	89. D
15. C	40. D	65. C	90. C
16. D	41. A	66. C	91. D
17. A	42. B	67. C	92. A
18. A	43. D	68. C	93. B
19. D	44. B	69. D	94. C
20. B	45. C	70. B	95. B
21. D	46. C	71. C	96. C
22. C	47. D	72. C	97. C
23. D	48. A	73. B	98. B
24. C	49. A	74. C	99. A
25. C	50. A	75. D	100. A

SERIES 6

SAMPLE EXAM II

RATIONALE

1.   C

In a defined contribution plan the maximum yearly contributions are set. The benefits available upon retirement are determined by the value of the securities used to fund the plan.

2.   A

Decisions made by the Board of Arbitration are considered binding and subject only to review by the SEC and the NASD's Board of Governors.

3.   B

Real estate has generally been disallowed from being included as one of the investments which a mutual fund may purchase for its portfolio. Commodities, since they are purchased entirely on a margin account basis, are prohibited from the investment companies portfolio. Warrants and options have become increasingly popular investment vehicles for a fund's portfolio.

4.   D

Each of these items are included when pricing an annuity contract. Mortality is the cost of providing payments to an annuity holder over his life expectancy. Interest earnings are the amount of money the insurance company's investments will make. Expense cost is the cost for the insurance company's maintaining the annuity contracts.

5.   B

Although the price of an open-end investment company share is determined by the net asset value plus the appropriate sales charge, the net asset value itself is determined by the supply and demand of the securities held within the portfolio. Remember that closed-end company shares are determined solely by supply and demand for those closed-end shares.

6.   C

The wash sale rule states that losses will be disallowed if a substantially identical security to the one sold for a loss is purchased within a 30 day period. This rule covers the 30 days before the trade date, the trade date, and 30 days after the trade date for a total of 61 days.

7.   D

The securities used to fund variable annuity contracts are deposited in a separate account of the insurance company. This account is used for the benefit of the variable annuity contract holders.

8.   B

Materiality is known as the value placed on a statement in making a decision as to whether to purchase or sell the security. The determination as to whether this materiality exists is the context in which the statement is made.

9.   B

Dollar cost averaging, as an investment theory, tells investors when they should buy, which is all the time, but does not tell them when to sell.

10.   B

$$\text{Tax equivalent yield} \quad = \quad \frac{\text{Tax exempt yield}}{100\% - \text{Marginal tax bracket}}$$

$$= \quad \frac{7\%}{100\% - 28\%} \quad = \quad \frac{7\%}{72\%} \quad = \quad 9.72\%$$

11.   C

The maximum sales charge on a variable annuity contract is identical to that placed on mutual funds, 8.5%. (Front-end loaded contractual plans carry a 9% maximum.)

12.   B

$$\begin{array}{lllll} \text{Sales charge} & = & \text{Ask price} & - & \text{Bid price} \\ \$1.70 & = & \$20.00 & - & \$18.30 \end{array}$$

$$\text{Sales charge percentage} \quad = \quad \frac{\text{Sales Charge}}{\text{Ask price}} \quad = \quad \frac{\$1.70}{\$20.00} \quad = \quad 8.5\%$$

13.   A

Quantity discounts, the ability to reduce the sales charges on the purchase of mutual funds, are allowed under letters of intent. This may be backdated for 90 days and extended forward for a total of 13 months. Breakpoints are not available when individuals pull their assets to make purchases. Therefore, single fiduciary accounts which include a pool of investors would not be allowed.

14. C

It is prohibited to use any unlawful devices or schemes when selling any security whatsoever.

15. C

When an individual makes a payment for the purchase of a variable annuity it is considered received when the monies arrive at the insurance company.

16. D

An open-end investment company is a corporation which pools the assets of investors and issues one class of redeemable securities.

17. A

An affiliated person is an individual who has either an invested interest of at least 5% or control of a decision-making process within a mutual fund.

18. A

The sole proprietor or partner would not have the ability to borrow money from the pension plan which has been established. This would violate the regulations imposed by the ERISA.

19. D

Gifts or gratuities to or from an NASD member are limited to a maximum of $100 per year by the NASD.

20. B

Marketability is defined as the ability to sell a security either at a gain or loss without any difficulty. Liquidity, on the other hand, is the ability to sell a security and have returned at least the initial investment.

21. D

This would best define a unit investment trust. The primary differences between this and a management company being the existence of a Board of Trustees as opposed to a Board of Directors and organization as a trust as opposed to a corporation.

22.   C

In order to maintain a discretionary account the broker/dealer must have both written authorization from the customer in the form of a discretionary account form as well as a power of attorney naming the individual who has the ability to sign on behalf of that customer.

23.   D

Term insurance is restricted from inclusion as a funding vehicle for pension plans due to its expiration at a predetermined date in the future.

24.   C

Any individual with earned income is eligible to open an individual retirement account. The Tax Reform Act of 1986 has restricted some individuals from making deductible contributions. However, we must remember that any individual may open and contribute to an IRA, it is just that the contributions may be deductible or non-deductible. Those individuals who earn self-employed income are eligible to open a self-employed pension plan and contributing to it based upon their self-employed income only.

25.   C

The prospectus of a corporation's stock, whether it is an investment company or other type of corporation has within it the definition of the public offering price and the manner in which it is determined.

26.   A

Any allowances paid corresponding to the sales of securities are determined by and allowed only to individuals selling those securities. In all cases, these individuals must be registered as representatives with the NASD.

27.   A

There are restrictions placed on the withdrawal and subsequent reinstatement of a contractual plan with no additional sales charge. One of these restrictions is that no more than 90% of the plan's current value may be withdrawn and the reinstatement must be made normally no sooner than 90 days from the withdrawal. There is also a limitation as to the frequency of these withdrawal and reinstatement privileges.

28.   D

The 20% plan is also known as the spread load plan. Any cancellation of this plan after the initial 45 day period offers no refund of sales charge.

29.   B

The NASD limits gift amounts to $100. Anything exceeding this would be considered of material value and a prohibited practice. Regardless of their value, any loans, discounts from the offering price, or wholesale commissions and overrides, are expressly prohibited. An occasional dinner given for a group of registered representatives would fall under the title of business expenses and thus not be in violation of the NASD's By-laws.

30.   B

The maximum contribution to the self-employed plan is 25% of earned income. Earned income is income after the contribution and a means of calculating the maximum contribution would be using 20% of the gross income.

| $84,000 | x | .20 | = | $16,800 maximum contribution |
| $84,000 | - | $16,800 | = | $67,200 taxable income |

$$\frac{\$16,800}{\$67,200} = 25\% \text{ maximum contribution}$$

31.   A

Under periodic payment plans (i.e., front end load and spread load), either plan may be cancelled within 45 days of establishing them and a full refund of sales charge will be returned. Also returned would be the current value of any shares that had been purchased.

32.   D

There is really no advantage to an individual purchasing shares just prior to the ex-dividend date. In reality, they would be paying for the dividend they are about to receive which would be completely taxable.

33.   B

Under a defined benefit plan it is the ultimate benefits which are established and funding must be made to meet those benefits. These plans are more advantageous for older employees.

34.   D

Unless specifically approved by the SEC, an investment company may not purchase securities on margin, effect short sales, or use securities held within their portfolio as collateral for a loan. An example of an investment company granted the authority to effect transactions in margin accounts and utilize short sales in their portfolio would be found through a hedge fund.

35.   D

Series EE bonds are sold at a 50% discount from their face value. Treasury bonds, Treasury notes and the agency obligations carry stated rates of interest. The other type of security which carries no stated rate of interest would be a Treasury bill which is also sold at a discount and pays face value at maturity.

36.   D

Individuals eligible for the tax-sheltered annuity would include employees of charitable, religious, or educational organizations. Obviously, this would not include a student earning wages under fellowship as he/she is technically not an employee of that educational institution.

37.   C

Many investment companies have what is known as an interlocking directorate. This means that members of the Board of Directors also happen to be affiliated with the management company, custodial bank, or mutual fund in some other capacity. This is legal as long as those interested persons do not make up more than 60% of the Board of Directors. In other words, at least 40% must be unaffiliated.

38.   A

The over-the-counter market is known as a negotiated market and utilize bid and ask quotes. Buyers and sellers negotiate the various prices of securities. On the other hand, an exchange market is known as an auction market. In this situation a security is put up for auction and various buyers bid against one another for ownership. Fixed prices represented by the new issue market or open-end investment companies can only occur in the over-the-counter market, but do not represent the majority of over-the-counter trades.

39.   C

Rules governing the extension of credit are determined by the Federal Reserve Board through Regulation T. Regulation T determines the amount of money an individual must deposit to pay for securities.

40.   D

The investment advisory contract must be in writing, must have been approved by a majority of the outstanding shares as well as by the Board of Directors and may be initially written for period of two years. After that period the contract is renewed on an annual basis. At no time may the investment advisor assign the contract to another without approval of the Board of Directors and a majority vote of outstanding shares of the investment company.

41.   A

According to the Investment Company Act of 1940, open-end investment companies may issue only one class of voting common stock. The capitalization structure of an open-end company is what primarily distinguishes this from other investment companies.

42.   B

A dealer, also known as a principal, buys and sells securities for his own account. An individual in the business of putting buyers and sellers together is known as a broker or an agent.

43.   D

Predictions of future investment performance are never allowed. Individuals may make reference to the past performance of a fund or security but may never imply that this is indicative of future performance.

44.   B

It is the NASD member's responsibility to investigate the qualifications and standards of an individual they wish to certify for registration.

45.   C

Any security or certificate which is issued with at least nine months to maturity would be considered a security. Currencies would not be considered a security. Face Amount Certificates are another exception requiring 24 months to maturity to be considered securities.

46.   C

When a broker is effecting transactions for the accounts of others and charging a commission for the service it is known as an agency transaction. A principal or dealer transaction is one in which the trade is negotiated and the security is marked-up so the individual's cost includes all charges.

47.   D

There are many different means of marketing mutual funds. One would be from the fund directly to the general public. Another would be from the fund through an underwriter to the public, and a third would be from the fund to an underwriter through broker/dealers maintaining signed selling agreements to the public. It is illegal to sell mutual fund shares at prices below the public offering price. Should the fund be a no-load fund, the security would sell at its net asset value.

48.   A

The reinvestment, conversion, and rights of accumulation privileges may carry with them unlimited abilities for their use. On the other hand, withdrawal and reinstatement privileges are allowed but on a limited basis (e.g., requiring a minimum investment and limited as to the number of times per year).

49.   A

When a registered representative's employment is terminated, either at his or the firms initiative, the NASD must be notified within 30 days of the termination.

50.   A

The ex-dividend date is the first day that an individual may buy a security and not receive the dividend being paid on the underlying security. The ex-dividend date is determined by counting back two business days from the record date.

51.   A

In order to be considered regulated under Subchapter M of the IRS code, an investment company must distribute no less than 90% of its net investment income to its shareholders. As long as these distribution requirements are met, the dividends and interest pass through to the shareholders. Whatever the investment company chooses to retain will be taxed at the appropriate corporate tax level. Should the investment company distribute less than 90% of the net investment income the entire amount of investment income, (including what is distributed to the shareholders), would be taxed at the corporate rates, resulting in triple taxation to the shareholder.

52.   D

Whether or not an individual chooses to reinvest the distributions made by an investment company he will pay tax on those distributions. At year's end the individual receives a 1099 form identifying the source of the distribution as either capital gains or dividends and interest. Dividends and interest are taxed as ordinary income, whereas capital gains will be treated as a capital gain.

53.   D

There is no stepped-up cost basis with annuity contracts. This means that annuity contracts are passed on to heirs at the same cost basis at which the descendent had maintained the contracts. Therefore, if the contract is liquidated immediately upon distribution to the heir, taxable income results. On the other hand, had the investment been something other than an annuity contract the heir would be receiving it at the current values and the cost basis would have been stepped-up. There would be no immediate taxation had the security been liquidated upon receipt by the heir.

54.   D

The termination of a registered representative will not become final until one year has past from the filing of the initial termination. The representative is subject to any actions filed against him/her within one year of his termination.

55.   D

Bonds are quoted as a percentage of par value ($1,000).

97 1/8   =   97 1/8%   =   97.125%   x $1,000   = $971.25

56.   A

$$\text{Cum-rights value} = \frac{\text{Market value - subscription price}}{\text{Number of rights needed} + 1}$$

$$= \frac{\$30.00 - \$20.00}{9 + 1} = \frac{\$10.00}{10} = \$1.00$$

57.   C

Mutual funds may never be placed in inventory to be marketed and sold at later dates. Mutual funds may only be purchased to fill client orders or for an individual's own personal account. When an individual wishes to redeem his/her mutual fund he/she does so only by filing to the investment company who initially issued that security.

58.   C

The District Business Conduct Committee (DBCC) has original jurisdiction over any trade practice complaints. The actions and fines they impose would be according to the Code of Procedure. The decisions are subject to review by the NASD's Board of Governors.

59.   C

As an investor accumulates values in a mutual fund he/she may qualify for reduced sales charges upon exceeding selected breakpoints. This feature is known as the Right of Accumulation and provides the investor with subsequent reductions in sales charges.

60.   A

The maximum penalty under Summary Complaint Proceedings according to the Code of Procedure as implemented by the District Business Conduct Committee is a $2,500 fine and/or censure.

61.   C

An NASD member opening an account for an employee of another NASD member must first notify the prospective client's employer of opening the account and provide, if requested, duplicate confirmations of any trades the employee may effect.

62.   D

The investment company must send the individual liquidating the shares a check within 7 calendar days of the liquidation. Remember, this check is based upon the next computed net asset value after receiving notice of the liquidation.

63.   B

The maximum sales charge over the life of a periodic payment or contractual plan is 9%. Remember, both level charge plans and variable annuities carry a maximum sales charge of 8 1/2% over the life or on any one payment.

64.   C

The most common type of corporate debt obligation is a debenture bond which has no specific security or property pledged as collateral. The corporation's responsibility for the repayment of principal and interest falls in line with that of other general creditors.

65.   C

The exclusion ratio pertains to the amount of a payment under the annuity payout schedule which would be excluded from taxation. This is represented as a percentage of the payment and is determined by dividing the investor's cost basis in the contract by the expected return.

66.   C

Under the front-end load contractual plan (50%) an individual has the right to receive at least a partial refund if the investor chooses to cancel the plan anytime within the first 18 months. This refund amounts to the total sales charge less 15% of the entire amount of deposits made under the contractual plan. The investor would also receive the full value of any shares which he/she has purchased.

67.   C

When a variable annuity contract is redeemed during its accumulation phase the amount redeemed is first considered earned income and fully taxable. Once the amount earned has been recovered the individual will begin recovering his cost basis which would not be taxable.

68.   C

A face amount certificate is technically a debt security with a minimum 24 month maturity. Should they be issued with less than 24 months to maturity the SEC will not consider a face amount certificate a security.

69.   D

Should a rights offering not be fully subscribed for by the current stockholders an underwriter many times "stands by" to bring the remaining shares to the public as a new issue. This is known as a stand-by underwriting and is used primarily in a rights offering.

70.   B

Under a variable annuity contract an insurance company guarantees mortality expenses to a maximum and nonforfeiture provisions to a minimum. Interest expenses are guaranteed in fixed but not variable annuity contracts.

71.   C

The Securities Investors Protection Corporation provides insurance for individuals in the event the brokerage firm at which they hold securities goes bankrupt. The maximum coverage provided by the SIPC is on a separate customer basis to a maximum of $500,000 total, a $100,000 of which could be cash. If viewed as a separate account, then all accounts having the same controlling individuals will be lumped together for one single $500,000 coverage total, a $100,000 of which could be cash.

72.   C

A hot issue is a new public offering which goes immediately to a price in the market above its initial public offering price. A broker/dealer acting as an underwriter for this security must make a bona fide public offering. Should they fail to do so, they would be guilty of free-riding and withholding on the new issue.

73.   B

A unit investment trust is a type of investment company which is organized under a trust indenture, issues redeemable securities, and has a Board of Trustees as opposed to a Board of Directors. A voting trust certificate is identical to a security except that all voting rights have been relinquished and left with the issuer of the certificate itself. This is most commonly found in companies suffering financial difficulties but is not found in a unit investment trust.

74.   C

Should an individual choose to reinvest the dividends and capital gains provided by a mutual fund, the reinvestment is normally at the current net asset value thus avoiding any additional sales charges. By reinvesting these distributions the individual will be building the investment for some future time. Even if he/she chooses to reinvest he/she will still be taxed as if the distributions had been taken. The amounts and origin of the distributions will be shown on a 1099 form distributed by the investment company at year's end.

75.   D

Private securities transactions are not technically illegal as long as the registered representative's broker/dealer is aware of the transaction in advance.

76.   B

Any realized capital gains, to the extent they exceed capital losses, are taxed at a specified capital gains rate, e.g., 28%.

77.   A

Dividend distributions from a mutual fund are always considered ordinary income and taxed as such. There no longer is a dividend exclusion allowed to individuals as a result of changes made by the Tax Reform Act of 1986. As long as the mutual fund qualifies as a regulated investment company these distributions will be taxed only to the individual and not to the investment company.

78.   A

If, at years end, an individual's capital losses exceed his capital gains, a deduction may be taken against ordinary income to a maximum of $3,000. This is a dollar-for-dollar deduction (capital losses versus ordinary income) up to the $3,000 maximum. Should an individual have more than $3,000 in capital losses these would be carried over in subsequent years to offset other capital gains and ultimately ordinary income to the maximum of $3,000 each year.

79.   C

The advantages of purchasing a municipal bond fund is the tax-exempt interest that is paid on the bonds held within the portfolio. This interest would pass through to the individual shareholders and maintain its tax-exempt status. This interest is federally tax-exempt; however, depending upon the state of issuance of the bonds and the state of residence of the shareholder, individual states may assess taxes on that interest. Any capital gain realized on the shares sold is fully taxable.

80.   B

It is legal for a pension fund to invest in the securities of the employer for which the plan is created. However, according to ERISA no more than 10% of the plans assets may be used to purchase the employer's securities.

81.   C

When the values of securities held in the portfolio of a mutual fund increase, there would be a corresponding increase in the net asset value of the fund. This increase will only be realized as a gain should the fund liquidate those securities held within the portfolio or the shareholder was to redeem some of the shares, thus realizing a gain on the increased net asset value.

82.   C

$$\frac{NAV}{100\% - \text{sales charge }\%} = \text{Offering price}$$

$$\frac{\$32.00}{100\% - 7\ 1/2\%} = \frac{\$32.00}{.925} = \$34.59$$

83.   A

In comparing the advantages or disadvantages of two mutual funds, a registered representative is generally restricted to using the past management performance only. He also must be careful not to intimate that this past performance is any way indicative of the future performance of the fund. Select periods, proximity to an exchange, or the prestige of any of the associated members or entities of the fund may not be used.

84.   C

Profit sharing plans are required to have substantial and recurring contributions under a fixed allocation formula. This means that any contributions made (although not required to be a fixed amount each year) must be according to a predetermined formula. Contributions need not be made in unprofitable years. However, the Tax Reform Act of 1986 does allow for contributions to be made in these unprofitable years.

85.   C

Qualified means that contributions made to the plan are with before-tax dollars thus allowing for a deferral of taxation until the distribution period. On the other hand, non-qualified plans offer contributions in after-tax dollars. The earnings on non-qualified plans are tax-deferred. However, the individuals would have a cost basis in the plan and thus distribution would utilize the exclusion ratio in determining the amount of each distributions taxable amount.

86.   B

$$\frac{\text{Net Assets}}{\text{Total outstanding shares}} = \frac{\$18,000,000}{1,500,000} = \$12.00$$

87.   D

Unless the mutual fund is a no-load fund, sales charges are always included in the offering price of that fund regardless of the manner in which the fund is purchased. It would be a violation of NASD rules to make any deals or allowances regarding the purchase of a fund if these where not stated within the prospectus.

88.   D

According to the NASD's Rules of Fair Practice, a registered representative or member firm is prohibited from guaranteeing a client against any losses or guaranteeing any gain in an individual's account. A decrease in the value of securities is a risk which the clients themselves bear.

89.   D

According to the Investment Company Act of 1940, registered investment companies are required to provide semi-annual financial reporting to their shareholders. Once a year they will be provided with an audited financial report and six months later an unaudited.

90.   C

Broker/dealers must make current financial statements available to clients holding accounts at that members office. These clients would be considered bona fide customers.

91.   D

Any communications concerning an investment company to be distributed, or in any way related to the public, is considered sales literature. Should information be created entirely for and limited to interoffice communications it would not be subject to the sales literature or advertising rules of the NASD.

92.   A

Contributions to individual retirement accounts must be made no later than the tax filing date of April 15. In no case may this period be extended.

93.   B

The sponsor, underwriter, or distributor of a mutual fund may utilize several different methods of selling that mutual fund to the public. It may be offered directly from the sponsor or underwriter to the public, offered from the sponsor to independent broker/dealers to the public, or offered to a plan company to the public.

94.   C

Cost basis is all after-tax dollars an individual has invested in the mutual fund. This would include the original purchase price of the shares (which includes the sales charge) plus any reinvested capital gain distributions or dividend distributions. Undistributed capital gains, which are normally evidenced by appreciation in securities held in the mutual fund's portfolio, are not taxable until it is actually realized by the fund or the shareholder.

95.   B

The transfer agent is responsible for maintaining records of the shareholders, including the number of shares owned and the current addresses as well as distributing any reports to these shareholders. The custodian bank is responsible for the safekeeping of securities and assets. The underwriter is responsible for the distribution of the shares. The management company is responsible for managing the portfolio of the investment company.

96.   C

$$\frac{NAV}{100\% - S.C.\%} = \frac{\$8.50}{100\% - 6\ 1/2\%} = \frac{\$8.50}{.935} = \$9.09 \text{ (Offering Price at Break point)}$$

$$\frac{\$4,000}{\$9.09} = 440 \text{ shares purchased at reduced offering price}$$

97.   C

According to the Tax Reform Act of 1986, any earnings in a Uniform Gift to Minors Account exceeding a maximum level are taxable to the minor at the parent's highest marginal tax bracket. Part is excluded from taxation, part is taxed at the minor's marginal tax bracket and anything in excess is taxed at the parent's marginal tax bracket. In other words, a portion is attributable to the minor and the remainder at the parent's bracket.

98.   B

The SEC has allowed for an extension of credit to be made on mutual fund shares. However, the first step is to make a fully paid purchase of shares which may then be used as collateral to purchase additional shares. These mutual fund shares must be held for a minimum of 31 days before they will be accepted as collateral.

99.   A

The most common form of ownership between two individuals is a joint tenants-with-rights-of-survivorship account. Tenants-in-common is normally found as the most common type of business arrangement. Tenants-by-entirety is allowed only between legally married people and is not allowed in every state. A joint tenants-in-common account is technically just the tenants-in-common account listed in Item B.

100.   A

A letter of intent may be backdated for a period not exceeding 90 days to include any investments within the letter of intent period. In this example, the $1,000 will be added to the $3,000 allowing the individual a total deposit of $4,000. To reach the $10,000 agreement the individual must deposit an additional $6,000. Remember, the letter of intent was backdated 2 1/2 months, the individual will have approximately 10 1/2 months remaining to deposit the additional $6,000, since the letter of intent will run no longer than 13 months.